Religious Lawfare

Global Health, Human Rights and Social Justice

VOLUME 2

The titles published in this series are listed at brill.com/*ghhr*

Religious Lawfare

Conscience-Based Claims in Liberal Democracies

By

Andrés Constantin

BRILL | NIJHOFF

LEIDEN | BOSTON

Library of Congress Cataloging-in-Publication Data

Names: Constantin, Andrés, author.
Title: Religious lawfare : conscience-based claims in liberal democracies / Andrés Constantin.
Description: Leiden ; Boston : Brill/Nijhoff, 2025. | Series: Global health, human rights, and social justice, 2949-8589 ; volume 2 | Includes bibliographical references and index.
Identifiers: LCCN 2024057729 (print) | LCCN 2024057730 (ebook) | ISBN 9789004685390 (paperback) | ISBN 9789004685406 (ebook)
Subjects: LCSH: Lawfare. | Religious law and legislation. | Government liability. | Government liability (International law) | Public policy (Law) | International law and human rights.
Classification: LCC K967 .C66 2025 (print) | LCC K967 (ebook) | DDC 342.08/52–dc23/eng/20241203
LC record available at https://lccn.loc.gov/2024057729
LC ebook record available at https://lccn.loc.gov/2024057730

Typeface for the Latin, Greek, and Cyrillic scripts: "Brill". See and download: brill.com/brill-typeface.

ISSN 2949-8589
ISBN 978-90-04-68539-0 (hardback)
ISBN 978-90-04-68540-6 (e-book)
DOI 10.1163/9789004685406

This book is printed on acid-free paper and produced in a sustainable manner.

For Daniel, Cecilia, Federico, Paula and Camila

Contents

Acknowledgements

This book is an adaptation of my Doctor of Juridical Science (S.J.D.) dissertation, defended at Georgetown University Law Center in August 2022.

Over these past few years, I have had the support of more people than I can possibly acknowledge. During my doctoral journey, I have had the honor of having the best mentors I could have ever asked or hoped for. Their patience, guidance, critiques, feedback, and support enriched this project and challenged me. I am forever indebted and very grateful to Professor Emerita Robin L. West (Georgetown Law), who provided unending support and intellectual stimulation to keep going; to Professor Emerita Nan Hunter (Georgetown Law), who pushed me to think harder about the assumptions and implications of my research; and to Professor Jill C. Morrison (Georgetown Law), who believed in this project from day one and provided invaluable guidance.

Moreover, I was fortunate to complete my doctoral studies while working full-time at the O'Neill Institute for National and Global Health Law, which provided the best atmosphere for continuing to explore these issues.

Finally, no words can describe my gratitude to my wife and family for their relentless support and love, which has been crucial in sustaining me during the writing of this book. They have lifted me up and supported me in every way imaginable. Special thanks are owed to my parents, Daniel and Cecilia, who instilled a love for wisdom in me and encouraged me to follow my passions and embrace creativity. To Camila, thank you for enriching my life in the most beautiful ways and for always being supportive of me and my endeavors. I hope this book makes all of you proud.

Figures

Introduction

In the last three years of his life, the prolific and best-seller Argentine short-story writer, essayist, and poet Jorge Luis Borges engaged in a series of memorable discussions with writer Osvaldo Ferrari on the national radio. These talks were transcribed, compiled, and published in a book titled *En Diálogo* in 1985. In one of those conversations, Borges, collecting centuries into one phrase, described the relevance of deliberation and dialogue: "… about 500 years B.C., faith, certainty, dogmas, anathemas, prayers, prohibitions, orders, taboos, tyrannies, wars, and glories overwhelmed the world. [In that context] some Greeks contracted, we will never know how, the unique custom of conversation. They doubted, they persuaded, they disagreed, they changed their minds, they postponed."[1] Little did he know that, over 35 years after he passed, the world would be living in an era where dialogue and deliberation are the exceptions, and polarization, and imposition are the rule.

Contrary to the initial post-World War II hopes of fostering global unity on social, cultural, and political fronts, our world has taken a different turn. Instead of moving towards harmony, we have opened the door to a fragmented society that often perceives non-native elements, individuals, and ideas as potential threats.

One prominent dimension in which this polarization has materialized is through the expansion of the concept of "rights of conscience" to resist the dictates of the law. Surprisingly, this strategy has found widespread acceptance within legal systems of many nations, thereby solidifying the belief that a "right" embedded in belief, religion or conscience equates to an unbridled license or a shield of invulnerability.

In recent years, it has become evident that the rights of conscience have been exploited as a tool to hinder, limit, intimidate, or interfere with the life choices of others.[2] This shift has significant implications for the post-World War II vision of a more united and cooperative world, as it seems that the increased emphasis on individual rights has inadvertently led to greater division and conflict, rather than fostering the global solidarity that was once aspired to.

1 Jorge Luis Borges & Osvaldo Ferrari, En diálogo I 7 (1998).

2 Robin West, *A Tale of Two Rights*, 94 B.U. L. Rev. 893–912 (2014); Robin West, *Freedom of the Church and our Endangered Civil Rights: Exiting the Social Contract, in* The Rise Of Corporate Religious Liberty (Z. Robinson, C. Flanders & M. Schwartzman eds., 2015).

 | DOI:10.1163/9789004685406_002

For years, individuals have resisted or expressed their dissatisfaction with laws. Often under the heroic guise of civil disobedience, people have resisted unjust wars,[3] racial segregation laws,[4] imperial rule,[5] gender inequality,[6] and toxic mining,[7] to name a few. Thousands have rallied behind Greta Thunberg's teenage voice and have protested current regulations and policies that exacerbate global warming in lieu of economic profits.[8] Under the Trump administration, the United States became an epicenter of resistance to unjust laws, including blockades and nationwide protests seeking to dismantle policies that allowed the separation of children from their parents or guardians in U.S. Immigration and Customs Enforcement (ICE) custody,[9] raising awareness of the wrongful treatment of Black African American individuals and other communities by police forces,[10] and organizing walkouts to demand the adoption

---

3 *See, e.g.*, ISAAC BARNES MAY, AMERICAN QUAKER RESISTANCE TO WAR, 1917–1973: LAW, POLITICS, & CONSCIENCE (2022) (discussing the Quaker's pacifist resistance to WWI, WWII, the early Cold War, the Vietnam War, and other conflicts).

4 *See, e.g.*, Randall K. Bush, *Remembering Rosa Parks: Recognizing a Contemporary Prophetic Act*, 65 THEOLOGICAL STUD. 838, 838–49 (2004); *March on Washington for Jobs and Freedom – August 28, 1963*, THE MARTIN LUTHER KING, JR. RSCH. & EDUC. INST. AT STAN. UNIV., https://kinginstitute.stanford.edu/encyclopedia/march-washington-jobs-and-freedom (last visited Nov 11, 2023); *see also*, Francesca Polletta, *Legacies and liabilities of an insurgent past: Remembering Martin Luther King Jr., on the House and Senate Floor*, 22 SOC. SCI. HIST. 479, 479–512 (1998); Jacquelyn Dowd Hall, *The long civil rights movement and the political uses of the past*, 91 J. AM. HIST. 1233–63 (2005).

5 *See, e.g.*, DENNIS DALTON, MAHATMA GANDHI: NONVIOLENT POWER IN ACTION (1993); *see also*, Peter N. Stearns, *Salt March*, *in* THE OXFORD ENCYCLOPEDIA OF THE MODERN WORLD (2008).

6 *See, e.g.*, SPEECHES AND TRIALS OF THE MILITANT SUFFRAGETTES: THE WOMEN'S SOCIAL AND POLITICAL UNION, 1903–1918 (Cheryl R. Jorgensen-Earp, ed., 1999).

7 *See, e.g.*, *Estonians stop toxic phosphorite mining, 1987–88*, GLOB. NONVIOLENT ACTION DATABASE, https://nvdatabase.swarthmore.edu/content/estonians-stop-toxic-phosphorite-mining-1987-88 (last visited Nov 11, 2023).

8 *See* Sigal Samuel, *If our governments won't stop climate change, should we revolt? Extinction Rebellion says yes.*, VOX (Jan. 14, 2020), https://www.vox.com/future-perfect/2019/12/20/21028407/extinction-rebellion-climate-change-nonviolent-civil-disobedience (last visited Nov 11, 2023); Masha Gessen, *The Fifteen-Year-Old Climate Activist Who is Demanding a New Kind of Politics*, THE NEW YORKER (Oct. 2, 2018), https://www.newyorker.com/news/our-columnists/the-fifteen-year-old-climate-activist-who-is-demanding-a-new-kind-of-politics (last visited Nov 11, 2023).

9 *See* Anita Roman, *Police arrest 4 at Abolish ICE protest outside Arizona Jail*, FOX 10 PHX. (Aug. 23, 2018), https://www.fox10phoenix.com/news/police-arrest-4-at-abolish-ice-protest-outside-arizona-jail (last visited Nov 11, 2023).

10 *See* Steve Wyche, *Colin Kaepernick explains why he sat during national anthem*, NFL MED. (Aug. 27, 2016), https://www.nfl.com/news/colin-kaepernick-explains-why-he-sat-during-national-anthem-0ap3000000691077 (last visited Nov 11, 2023); Solby Lim, *Break*

of gun control laws in the wake of national tragedies, such as the Parkland Shooting.[11]

In numerous instances, opposition to the law has taken various forms, with conscientious objection, also referred to as conscience-based claims, emerging as a prominent manifestation.[12]

For over a century, conscience-based claims have been used as a shield to protect minority views on questions of conscience from oppression by majorities—perhaps most famously, allowing individual exemptions to mandatory military service on religious grounds.[13]

Over the past decade, however, individuals and institutions have begun to use conscience-based claims not so much to protect minorities from attacks by civil authority, but rather as a mechanism to hinder the exercise of legally protected rights by co-citizens. For example, conscience-based claims are now being extended to grant hospitals and health practitioners unrestricted exemptions from any duty to provide abortion care, rendering attempts to

---

This Down: Activism and Civil Disobedience, BARNARD COLL. (Feb. 17, 2021), https://barnard.edu/news/break-down-activism-and-civil-disobedience (featuring a discussion with Erin Pineda, author of the book *Seeing Like an Activist*, on the politics of civil disobedience and global research on resistance movements) (last visited Nov 11, 2023).

11 *See* Jason Dearen, *Civil Disobedience: Teen Shooting Survivors Shake Up Capitol*, AP NEWS (Feb. 22, 2018), https://apnews.com/article/shootings-florida-ap-top-news-fl-state-wire-us-news-899b6fc6c25046b09f0fdc3834455b71; Vivian Yee & Alan Blinder, *National School Walkout: Thousands Protest Against Gun Violence Across the U.S.*, N.Y. TIMES (Mar. 14, 2018), https://www.nytimes.com/2018/03/14/us/school-walkout.html (last visited Nov 11, 2023).

12 On the ways in which civil disobedience and conscientious objection differ and are similar, see William Smith & Kimberley Brownlee, *Civil Disobedience and Conscientious Objection*, OXFORD RESEARCH ENCYCLOPEDIA OF POLITICS (May 27, 2017), https://oxfordre.com/politics/view/10.1093/acrefore/9780190228637.001.0001/acrefore-9780190228637-e-114 ("Civil disobedience and conscientious objection are distinct but related social practices that display people's opposition to specific laws, policies, directives, or schemes. In general, these two practices arise from people's deeply held commitments. Civil disobedience is more overtly communicative and political than conscientious objection. Civil disobedience is also, almost by definition, a breach of law, which people engage in to push for changes in either governmental or nongovernmental practices. Conscientious objection, by contrast, does not always break the law: sometimes it is a legally protected form of nonconformity") (last visited Nov 11, 2023); *see also* Kimberley Brownlee, *Conscientious Objection and Civil Disobedience*, *in* THE ROUTLEDGE COMPANION TO THE PHILOSOPHY OF LAW (Andrei Marmor, ed., 2012).

13 Throughout this book, "minorities" and "minority groups" are referred to from a "power dimension," where membership to a minority group is typically based on the relative disadvantage people in the group experience as compared to members of a dominant social group.

exercise an individual right to get a legal abortion futile. These claims have similarly been extended to pharmacies and pharmacists refusing to fill prescriptions for birth control, rendering a right to contraception a nullity.[14] This use of conscience-based claims as a counter-majoritarian and anti-democratic tool to veto the exercise of rights has been met with acceptance around the world. When these claims are successful, laws or policies that recognize rights objected to by individuals or institutions based on their beliefs, such as the right to abortion or LGBTQ rights, are stripped of impact.

Then, the question arises as to whether to permit *all* forms of genuine, sincerely-felt conscientious objection to laws or obligations imposed by law. At first glance, the answer appears to be yes: genuine, sincerely-felt conscience-based claims would seem to be conducive to deliberation and, hence, to democracy. That is, decisions in a well-functioning democracy gain legitimacy and validity when they are widely discussed by all—not only those who are going to be affected by them.[15] It appears logical to conclude that, in such deliberations, no voice is more crucial than that of the critics, who may represent either the majority or minority perspective. As such, allowing resistance and disagreement with laws seems to be democratically desirable.[16]

Focusing on the expansion of conscience-based claims in recent years, this book challenges the romanticized preconception of resistance to laws in the form of conscientious objection as a praiseworthy, heroic, and virtuous act. In certain cases, explored in detail in the chapters that follow, resistance should *not* be allowed, as the claims might not be conducive to democracy. Specifically, this book demonstrates that while some uses of conscientious objection are democratic and should be permitted, new applications of conscience-based claims that seek to impose a worldview on others are *not* and should be limited. Under the republican deliberative conception of democracy, restricting these new uses of conscience-based claims is justified because they run

14 With acknowledgement that the expansion of conscience-based claims poses a threat to a broader set of issues, and not just to health care, this book focuses primarily on sexual and reproductive health as it has been the fora of the most pervasive and deleterious debates on this issue. *See* THE LAW, RIGHTS & RELIGION PROJECT, PARADING THE HORRIBLES: THE RISKS OF EXPANDING RELIGIOUS EXEMPTIONS (2021) (examining how the expansive use of conscience-based claims impacts numerous rights and liberties far beyond reproductive health).

15 *See generally* THOMAS CHRISTIANO, THE CONSTITUTION OF EQUALITY: DEMOCRATIC AUTHORITY AND ITS LIMITS (2008).

16 *See* Michael P. Lynch, *Epistemic Arrogance and the Value of Political Dissent*, *in* VOICING DISSENT: THE ETHICS AND EPISTEMOLOGY OF MAKING DISAGREEMENT PUBLIC 129, 129–39 (Casey Rebecca Johnson ed., 2018); *see also* Elisabeth Anderson, *The Epistemology of Democracy*, 3 EPISTEME 8, 8–22 (2006).

counter to the democratic ideals and principles, and their costs outweigh any hypothetical benefit the claims bring to deliberation and the democratic process altogether.

Now, if new uses of conscience-based claims are merely employed as an excuse for political subversion and for purposely altering or modifying another person's normative situation and the impact of democratic decisions, how are these claims different from civil disobedience (or other forms of resistance) and the objectives that civil disobedience pursues? And if they are not different, why should new uses of conscience-based claims be restricted while some instances of civil disobedience are allowed?

The answer lies in understanding the distinctive traits of the new uses of conscience-based claims, or, as this book refers to them, "political uses of conscience-based claims." These new uses have evolved as a means to impose views on others by thwarting the implementation of a law or policy that is contrary to the objector's beliefs. The objector still wants his or her claim to attain public status and gain acceptance within society, but the ultimate goal is to manipulate and deliberatively change another person's normative situation. In other words, political conscience-based objectors aim to coerce those who disagree with their beliefs into aligning with their sincere convictions. This is an action directly intended to materially deprive others of their ability to exercise agency and control over their own lives. This is precisely why these new uses of conscience-based claims are undemocratic. They are harmful, curtailing individuals' ability to assert autonomy and make decisions in accordance with their own values and preferences, which, ultimately, erodes the foundations of democracy.

Resistance to laws has a communicative aim of expressing disagreement and discontent that is appraised in democracies. Oftentimes, this communicative goal can be achieved through persuasion and in other cases it may take the form of coercion. The former seems compatible with the understanding of democracy adopted in this book, as it acknowledges other people's autonomy and intends to induce action through reasoning or argument.[17] The latter,

17 *Persuasion*, The Oxford English Dictionary, https://www.oed.com/view/Entry/141561 (last visited Nov 11, 2023). It is important to note that *persuasion* should not be equated to "non-violence" necessarily, as it would certainly be extremely difficult to find instances of *pure persuasive* resistance. In fact, most of the famous cases of civil disobedience that are referred to in the first paragraph of this introduction occurred with violence to a certain degree. The question is, nonetheless, where the line is drawn on how much violence should be allowed and what constitutes too much violence that it defeats the communicative aims of resistance, other than violence that is likely to result in injury or death to other people. To answer those concerns, it is important to note the distinction

however, appears to do precisely the opposite by constraining people "to compliance or obedience;"[18] thus, disrespecting their status as autonomous agents.[19]

The distinction in the means of achieving the communicative aims is what, in practice, distinguishes cases of civil disobedience or uses of conscience-based claims that are compatible with democracy from instances of political uses of conscience-based claims.

This book argues that political uses of conscience-based claims are coercive and, hence, incompatible with the deliberative element of the democratic ideal. They intend to alter the will and autonomy of others by pushing them to no alternative other than to endorse the objector's particular view, often exposing people to threats to their health or life.[20] By forcing others to support a specific worldview or oppose a particular law or policy via conscience-based claims, political conscience-based objectors coerce people into a decision against their own will, treating them as mere instruments to the objector's goal.

This book reveals the resurgence of religion's influence on politics and law, igniting a global discourse on the interplay between faith and governance, and sparking profound debates about the role of religion in shaping public policy, human rights, and the foundations of liberal democracies. In an era marked

---

between *compulsion* and *coercion*. *See* JOEL FEINBERG, HARM TO SELF: THE MORAL LIMITS OF THE CRIMINAL LAW 189 (1986) (distinguishing between compulsion and coercion). Instances of compulsion interfere with a person's ability to make free choices, but do not infringe on his or her autonomy. Rather, compulsion compels he or she into further deliberation, which arguably promotes autonomy by improving the quality of political decisions. Coercion, on the other hand, represents an outright violation of resistance's communicative aims, which renders it incompatible with democracy. In other words, infringing on people's freedom to act as they choose is not the same as forcing them to do something. The degree of violence that defeats or contravenes the communicative aims of resistance is that which violates their autonomy. *See* CHRISTINE M. KORSGAARD, KANT: GROUNDWORK OF THE METAPHYSICS OF MORALS (Mary Gregor & Jens Timmermann, trans., 2d ed. 2012) (on Kant's Formula of Humanity).

18 *Coerce*, THE OXFORD ENGLISH DICTIONARY, https://www.oed.com/view/Entry/35716 (last visited Nov 11, 2023).

19 *See generally* KIMBERLEY BROWNLEE, CONSCIENCE AND CONVICTION: THE CASE FOR CIVIL DISOBEDIENCE 28–30 (2012) (providing a list of non-communicative acts of conscientious objection, which includes "the civil registrar who swaps assignments with colleagues to avoid performing same-sex civil partnership ceremonies; the grocery store employee who avoids shelving or processing the sale of alcohol; the doctor who refuses to participate in the provision of abortions; the judge who refuses to hear gay couples' applications for adoption; and the religious person who refuses to wear or not wear legally regulated clothing in public").

20 Robert Nozick, *Coercion*, *in* PHILOSOPHY, SCIENCE, & METHOD, 440 (Sidney Morgenbesser, Patrick Suppes & Morton White, eds. 1969).

by globalization, cultural pluralism, and the relentless march of technological progress, the complex interplay between religion and politics has emerged as a defining challenge for liberal democracies worldwide. This intricate dance between the sacred and the secular has birthed a phenomenon that gives the title to this book: "religious lawfare," a term that encapsulates a diverse array of strategies employed by religious groups and individuals to shape public policy and law according to their faith-based convictions. Religious lawfare operates at the nexus of deeply held beliefs and the institutions of democracy, igniting complex debates about the boundaries of freedom conscience, religion and belief, the separation of church and state, and the preservation of individual and collective rights.

Religious lawfare is a multifaceted strategy that can take many forms, including the use of conscience-based claims to shape policy and law, litigation, lobbying, and grassroots campaigns. The focus of this book on new uses of conscience-based claims as an element of religious lawfare is driven by their pervasiveness, legal significance, legal complexity, and potential to impact the lives of individuals and the fabric of contemporary democratic societies.

By focusing on the political uses of conscience-based claims, a religious lawfare strategy mainly lead by Christian Evangelical and Roman Catholic conservative religious groups, this book uncovers the intensity of these debates and shows the ways in which these groups rely on conscience-based claims as an additional avenue of political participation that is unavailable to those who do not share their beliefs.[21] This shift in the use of conscience-based claims is

---

21 In cases of conscience-based claims, freedom of conscience has often—and wrongly—been equated to the freedom to follow the moral or religious rules approved by the relevant community. If freedom of conscience is equated to what an authority, like the official of a certain institutionalized religion, mandates, then freedom of conscience becomes equivalent to freedom to homogeneous authority-controlled conscience. This approach would, in turn, contravene the very idea of freedom of conscience as freedom to exercise the individual's moral autonomy in creating, selecting, adopting, and revising the standards that govern his or her practical life. The emergence of the idea of freedom of conscience as authority-controlled freedom of conscience is one of the reasons that lies behind the recent expansion of conscience-based claims as a way to impose religious values on increasingly secular societies. Pierluigi Chiassoni, *Protecting freedom of conscience in a constitutional state*, *in* RELIGION, LAW AND THE POLITICS OF ETHICAL DIVERSITY: CONSCIENTIOUS OBJECTION AND CONTESTATION OF CIVIL NORMS 13, 13–42 (Claude Proeschel, David Koussens & Francesco Piraino eds., 2021). The book delves into context and specifically identifies some of the groups involved in this expansion later in Chapters 1 and 2; *see also* Fiona Bloomer, et al., *Abortion discourses: religion, culture, nation*, *in* REIMAGINING GLOBAL ABORTION POLITICS: A SOCIAL JUSTICE PERSPECTIVE (2018); Fred Van Geest, *Changing Patterns of Denominational Political Activity*

especially problematic in pluralistic societies and indicates a need for a framework that adequately addresses the ways in which conscience-based claims interact with the enjoyment of other peoples' rights.[22]

Debate around this issue is overdue. The expansion of conscience-based claims is now a multi-decade phenomenon. Yet, new expansive claims of conscience have not, to date, been assessed or explored in a detailed and contextualized way. The exercise of political uses of conscience-based claims constitutes a growing phenomenon globally, and debate around it will only become more heated in years to come as liberal democracies continue to experience processes of secularization.[23] This book intends to answer questions such as: What is the impact of the shift and expansion of uses of conscience-based claims? Who is behind this expansion? What do these new uses of conscience-based claims mean for democracy and human rights? And how can we effectively deal with them?

The book addresses several gaps in the existing literature and scholarly work on conscience-based claims. Firstly, it introduces a framework to define and systematize the expansion of conscience-based claims. Secondly, it identifies the reasons and actors behind this expansion, placing it within a historical and sociological context. Thirdly, the book characterizes new uses of conscientious objection as coercive, harmful, and undemocratic. Additionally, it explores efforts to regulate the expansion of conscience-based claims. Furthermore, it delves into the issue of institutional conscience-based claims and examines the role of states in regulating and limiting their exercise. Lastly, this book offers an alternative way of thinking about conscience-based claims and their relation to democracy.

As the reader embarks on a comprehensive journey that dissects and scrutinizes the complex interplay between religion, politics, and law, with a particular focus on the proliferation of conscience-based claims and their ramifications for democracy and human rights, it is imperative to establish a clear framework and understanding of the terrain the book navigates.

---

in North America: The Case of Homosexuality, 49 REV. REL. RSCH. 199, 199–221 (2007); Michele Dillon, *Asynchrony in Attitudes Toward Abortion and Gay Rights: The Challenge to Values Alignment*, 53 J. FOR SCI. STUDY REL. 1, 1–16 (2014).

22 Robert M. Cover, *The Supreme Court 1982 Term. Foreword: Nomos and Narrative*, 97 HARV. L. REV. 4, 4–68 (1984).

23 JOCELYN MACLURE & CHARLES TAYLOR, SECULARISM AND FREEDOM OF CONSCIENCE (Jane Marie Todd trans., 2011). *See also* CÉCILE LABORDE, LIBERALISM'S RELIGION (2017).

1 The Contours

In the context of this book, the term "conservative religious groups" specifically refers to two primary categories of religious adherents: Christian Evangelicals and Roman Catholics. These two groups, with their significant socio-political influence, not only in the United States but also increasingly in Latin America and to some extent in Europe, have emerged as key protagonists in the narrative of religious lawfare. Their efforts are aimed at shaping public policy and law in a manner that reflects their religiously inspired values, often at the expense of the principles that underpin democratic societies.

With their significant presence in various facets of society, including politics, education, and media, Christian Evangelicals wield substantial influence in shaping public opinion and policy. Their activism on issues such as abortion, LGBTQ+ rights, and religious freedom has galvanized a substantial portion of the population, creating a formidable voting bloc that politicians and policymakers cannot afford to ignore. Their engagement with conscience-based claims often revolves around deeply held beliefs concerning the sanctity of life and traditional family values. Consequently, they play a pivotal role in the broader religious lawfare landscape.

Roman Catholics, one of the world's largest religious denominations, possess a rich theological tradition and a hierarchical structure that extends from local parishes to the Vatican. In the context of this book's analysis, Roman Catholics have exhibited a notable presence in the religious lawfare arena, particularly on issues related to contraception, abortion, and same-sex marriage. Roman Catholics, both as individuals and as an institution, have been actively involved in legal and political initiatives aimed at influencing public policy to align with their religious beliefs. Their efforts have manifested in various forms, from legal challenges to regulations they perceive as contrary to their faith to lobbying for legislative changes that uphold their values.

What makes the focus on these two groups particularly salient is the degree of socio-political influence they have amassed. In democratic societies, Christian Evangelicals and Roman Catholics have strategically navigated the political landscape to assert their values and preferences. Their ability to mobilize voters, secure key positions in government, and influence public discourse has reshaped the contours of the religious and political landscape.

2 Approach and Perspective

It is essential to clarify the vantage point from which this book analyzes the intricate dynamics of religious lawfare. Most of the book's examination is rooted in democratic theory and international human rights law perspectives. While some chapters may touch upon aspects of medical ethics at various points, the book's primary focus lies elsewhere. The book does not intend to delve into the ethics governing the patient-physician relationship, but rather has a central aim that seeks to provide a comprehensive understanding of the challenges liberal democracies face due to the rapid expansion of conscience-based claims. Acknowledging that medical ethics plays a vital role in discussions surrounding conscience-based claims, the book's intention is not to offer a detailed analysis of the ethical considerations governing healthcare practices. Instead, the book concentrates on the broader legal and political questions raised by the strategic use of conscience-based claims in the realm of public policy and law.

From a democratic theory perspective, the book examines the foundational principles that underpin liberal democracies. These societies are built upon a commitment to individual freedoms, equal rights, and the rule of law.

The book's analysis draws upon democratic theory to assess the implications of conscience-based claims for the democratic process. Central to this framework is the delicate balance between individual liberties and the common good, a balance that is constantly negotiated and reevaluated in democratic societies. As such, some of the chapters scrutinize the extent to which these claims, when employed as tools of religious lawfare, may disrupt this balance and challenge the fundamental tenets of liberal democracy. This perspective compels the reader to critically reflect on whether the exercise of conscience-based claims aligns with the principles of fairness, equality, and justice that democratic societies hold dear.

In tandem with the democratic theory perspective, the book employs the lens of international human rights law to evaluate the legal dimension of conscience-based claims. The international human rights framework establishes a set of universally recognized rights and freedoms that should be protected and upheld by all nations, regardless of their religious or cultural contexts. From this perspective, the book assesses the implications of conscience-based claims on human rights, particularly in areas such as access to healthcare, reproductive rights, and equality before the law. Additionally, throughout the chapters there is an exploration of the tension between religious freedom and the protection of individual rights, seeking to establish a principled framework for resolving conflicts that may arise in this context.

3 The Structure

The book is divided into six chapters. The first chapter sets the historical and political background for the book, which is crucial for the purposes of providing an analytically sound account of the use of conscience-based claims to wage religious lawfare in liberal democracies. The unrealized promises of globalization and cosmopolitanism offered an ideal climate for the rise of conservative religious groups alongside right-wing populisms. These groups challenge the secularity of the State and rely on "traditional or religious values" notions to characterize their actions against liberal ideals. They often portray gender and sexual and reproductive rights as threats to religious and presumed majority's values. These conservative religious forces have recently emerged in Latin America, Europe and in the United States with political voracity.

Chapter 2 analyses how conservative religious groups and individuals appeal to freedom of religion, conscience, or belief, a constitutionally enshrined right in most legal frameworks, and particularly to conscience-based claims, as a way to respond to a rising tide of secularism. I submit that this is occurring mainly in countries that are constitutionally bound not to be religious, or that take a neutral or weak stance when religion is enshrined in their constitutions. In these types of constitutional settings, these groups have come to use conscience-based claims as tools to reclaim power and break the "wall of separation" between Church and State. As such, conservative religious groups have managed to expand the uses of conscience-based claims to exclude and hinder enjoyment of legally protected rights that they consider to be irreligious, immoral, or wrong.

Conservative religious groups' melancholic longing to return to an otherwise unrecoverable past through the expansion of conscience-based claims call into question the potential abuses that the expansion in the uses and understandings of these claims can bring. *Chapter 3* argues that, when used to counter advancements in the recognition of rights, conscience-based claims bring about legitimacy concerns as the social consequences of its exercise are less beneficial than those decided by democratic processes. In those contexts, a conscience-based claim become an illegitimate intervention, as it essentially constitutes a form of veto that conservative religious groups and individuals use over decisions taken by democratically legitimized bodies. Initially considered a shield for the protection of minorities, *Chapter 3* presents this new generation of conscience-based claims as a real threat to the very foundations of democracy.

The expansion of conscience-based claims at the service of religious lawfare opened the door to abuses of the conscientious objector status that are dangerously undemocratic. However, the law has not been inattentive to this development; rather, it has sought ways to deal with it. *Chapter 4* provides a fresh look at how the Universal Human Rights System, as well as regional European, Inter-American, and African systems have provided insights on strategic legal responses to counter religious lawfare, although with limited success.

With a focus on the expansive invocation of conscience-based claims in healthcare contexts, *Chapter 5* explores the challenges this expansion poses to the enjoyment of rights. This exploration will reveal the need for a delicate equilibrium that respects both individual autonomy and societal obligations, while underscoring the importance of extending regulatory frameworks to encompass uses that go beyond the traditional understandings of conscience, thereby safeguarding individuals' rights.

Chapter 6 explores the main arguments available in the literature and assesses scholars and experts' alternative proposals to deal with these new uses of conscience-based claims. The analysis concludes that the main arguments available in the literature fail to cure the antidemocratic deficit and threat of religious lawfare. The chapter provides a new normative framework on how to deal with conscience-based claims in liberal democracies.

The Conclusion summarizes and offers some general remarks on the findings made throughout this book.

4 The Exploration

In sum, the book traces the historical evolution of conscience-based claims and their transformation into potent tools of religious lawfare. It also critically examines the acceptance of these claims around the world, leading to the nullification of laws and policies that conservative religious groups deem contrary to their beliefs. This inquiry is contextualized within the broader global trends of secularization, multiculturalism, and globalization.

The overarching goal is to provide a normative framework that addresses the complexities of conscience-based claims in liberal democracies. By doing so, the intention is to steer current debates on the intersection of law, religion, and politics in new and constructive directions. In this quest for clarity and insight, the chapters navigate the murky waters of religious lawfare, exposing its implications for democracy, human rights, and the delicate balance between individual conscience and the common good.

In the pages that follow, the reader will embark on a journey of exploration and analysis that seeks to shed light on new uses of conscience-based claims and to offer a compelling normative account of how liberal democracies should navigate the challenges it presents. This endeavor is not only timely but also essential, as the impact of conscience-based claims reverberates through the corridors of power and the lives of citizens in liberal democracies worldwide.

CHAPTER 1

Religious Lawfare: A Challenge to Liberal Democracies

The historical, sociological, and political context in this story is essential to provide an analytically sound account of the use of conscience-based claims as tools to wage religious lawfare in liberal democracies. The unrealized promises of globalization and cosmopolitanism offered an ideal climate for the rise of conservative religious groups alongside right-wing populism. These groups challenge the secularity of the State by relying on traditional or religious values—notions to characterize their actions against liberal ideals. For instance, they often portray sexual orientation, gender identity and sexual and reproductive rights as threats to religious and presumed majority's values. These conservative religious forces have recently emerged in Latin America, Europe and the United States with political voracity.

1 The Point of Departure

Following World War II, globalization ushered in a more interconnected, secular, and liberal world, expanding the cosmopolitan perspective that laid the foundation for global governance.[1] However, despite the growing economic interdependence worldwide, the aspiration to unite the world socially, culturally, and politically has conspicuously fallen short. Globalization has not uniformly benefited individuals, countries, and regions, resulting in widening disparities both within and between nations.[2] The unfulfilled pledges of globalization created a conducive environment for the emergence of right-wing populist nationalism.[3]

1 *See* DANIELE ARCHIBUGI, THE GLOBAL COMMONWEALTH OF CITIZENS: TOWARD COSMOPOLITAN DEMOCRACY (2008); *see also* Jack Barbalet, *Globalisation and Cosmopolitanism: Continuity and Disjuncture, Contemporary and Historical*, 50 J. SOC. 199, 199–212 (2014); Bryan S. Turner, *Cosmopolitan Virtue, Globalization and Patriotism*, 19 THEORY, CULTURE & SOC'Y. 45, 45–63 (2002).

2 *See generally* JOSEPH E. STIGLITZ, GLOBALIZATION AND ITS DISCONTENTS (2002).

3 *See* Carlos de la Torre, *Populism and Democracy: Lessons from Latin America*, 18 SETON HALL J. DIPL. & INT'L REL. 33, 34–37 (2017); *see also* William A. Galston, *The Populist Challenge to Liberal Democracy*, 29 J. DEMOCRACY 5, 5–19 (2018).

 DOI:10.1163/9789004685406_003

Cosmopolitanism furthers the idea that all humans, regardless of their social or political affiliation, are a part of the same universal community.[4] With migration as its initial catalyst, the movement of peoples has created syncretism that brought together beliefs and ideas globally.[5] Societies today have grown to be more multicultural and more diverse as a result of these globalizing forces, and this growing interconnectedness has increased concern for the welfare of all peoples.[6]

Nevertheless, the factors that fostered global unity have concurrently triggered the reaffirmation of conservative and fundamentalist identities, nationalist assertions, and populist governance. While the global community became more intertwined, supranational institutions struggled to respond in a unified and consistent manner to confront escalating global inequalities, resulting in a deficit in the social legitimacy of international law and rights-based institutions.[7] Consequently, populist nationalism has emerged as a direct reaction, challenging the established global order.

1.1 *Populism as a Challenge to Cosmopolitanism*

A common attribute to recent populist campaigns in the United States, Latin America and Europe has been the appeal to a rhetoric between the "people" and the "nefarious elite" to garner political support. This narrative is oftentimes used by those most adversely affected by the social, political, or economic disruption of that time. Both right-wing and left-wing populism appeal to this characterization. However, whereas the "nefarious elite" within left-wing populism is usually characterized as the financial elites—hence, supporting

4 *See* ANTHONY APPIAH, COSMOPOLITANISM: ETHICS IN A WORLD OF STRANGERS (2007).

5 *See* David Held et al., *Globalization*, 5 GLOB. GOV. 483, 483–96 (1999); *see also*, Jason N. Brock, *Globalization*, *in* ENCYCLOPEDIA OF MODERN POLITICAL THOUGHT 356–58 (Gregory Claeys ed., 2013).

6 Dominic McGoldrick, *Multiculturalism and its Discontents*, 5 HUM. RTS. L. REV. 27, 27–56 (2005). *See* U.N. Sub-Commission on the Promotion and Protection of Human Rights, *Globalization and its Impact on the Full Enjoyment of Human Rights, Final Report*, U.N. Doc. E/CN.4/Sub.2/2003/14 (June 25, 2003); CHARLES TAYLOR, MULTICULTURALISM AND THE POLITICS OF RECOGNITION (1992); *see also* MARJORIE MAYO, CULTURES, COMMUNITIES, IDENTITIES 1–35 (2000); Pauline Kleingeld & Eric Brown, *Cosmopolitanism*, *in* THE STANFORD ENCYCLOPEDIA OF PHILOSOPHY (Edward N. Zalta ed., 2014).

7 Alicia E. Yamin & Andrés Constantin, *A Long and Winding Road: The Evolution of Applying Human Rights Frameworks to Health*, 49 GEO. J. INT'L L. 191, 191–239 (2018).

restrictions on capital movement—right-wing populism takes the enemy as anything that threatens traditional national values.[8]

In contrast with the ideals of globalization, populism seeks to retrench nations inward, with rising nationalist movements directly threatening the cosmopolitan vision underlying global governance and spurring isolationism in international affairs.[9]

As a direct response to the increasing interconnectedness of a globalizing world, the isolationist disposition of populist nationalism stands in contrast to the international cooperation that frames cosmopolitan globalization.[10] Where nation-states serve largely as "imagined communities"—that is, socially constructed communities for the sake of a national identity—populist politicians have sought to rally these communities against global governance through right-wing cries of "nationalism."[11] This counter-cosmopolitanism, rejecting global institutions and norms, thus seeks to channel a conservative vision of an imagined past to tear down the globalized world order.[12]

Economic dislocation and political polarization have provided a political opening for right-wing populist leaders to take power.[13] To garner political

---

8 *See id.* at 297; *see also* Mark Tushnet, *Varieties of Populism*, 20 GERMAN L.J. 382, 388 (2019); David Fontana, *Unbundling Populism*, 65 UCLA L. REV. 1482, 1494–96 (2018).

9 Aristotle Kallis, *Populism, Sovereigntism, and the Unlikely Re-Emergence of the Territorial Nation-State*, 11 FUDAN J. HUM. SOC. SCI. 285, 285–302 (2018).

10 *Id. See also*, Pierre Lemieux, *Populism and Protectionism*, 40 REG. 6, 6–7 (2017).

11 *See* BENEDICT ANDERSON, IMAGINED COMMUNITIES (1983); *see also* THE EUROPEAN MAINSTREAM AND THE POPULIST RADICAL RIGHT (Pontus Odmalm & Eve Hepburn eds., 2017).

12 Fareed Zakaria, *Populism on the March: Why the West is in Trouble*, FOREIGN AFF. (2016). *See also* David Fontana, *Unbundling Populism*, 65 UCLA L. REV. 1482, 1494–96 (2018). I do not intend to describe left-wing populism as socially desirable or ignore that left-wing populism can incorporate authoritarian elements. However, the focus on right-wing populism has to do with the fact that the "Us vs. Others" rhetoric in right-wing populism is aimed at particular domestic social groups, rather than domestic or foreign financial elites, and it is in this dimension where religious movements have interfered the most. *See* Samir Gandesha, *Understanding Right and Left Populism*, *in* CRITICAL THEORY AND AUTHORITARIAN POPULISM 63 (Jeremiah Morelock ed., 2018); *see also*, Huber and Schimpf, *On the Distinct Effects of Left-wing and Right-wing Populism*, 5 POL. & GOV. 146, 148 (2017) (on left-wing populisms' inclusion of social minorities in the definition of "the people" and how it tends to favor human rights in their overall political agenda, as part of their socially egalitarian tradition).

13 *See e.g.*, Omar G. Encarnación, *The Trumpification of the Latin American Right*, FOREIGN POL'Y (Apr. 16, 2018), https://foreignpolicy.com/2018/04/16/the-trumpification-of-the-latin-american-right ("[n]ot surprisingly, "left-wing fatigue" is a key explanation behind the demise of the so-called Pink Tide that swept the region beginning in the late 1990s. That fatigue has been intensified by the economic slowdown created by the end of a

support amidst this rising anger, populist leaders have focused on simple solutions to complex problems. European economic and cultural integration has given rise to right-wing populist parties and attacks on the free movement of persons throughout Europe, and also has weakened support for international governance through the European Union.[14] Similarly, the rise of right-wing populism in Latin America has embraced a nationalistic and authoritarian rhetoric—the "people" taking back power from the "elites"—with populist leaders discarding traditional restraints on governance and threatening liberal constitutional democracies.[15] Populist nationalism has exerted its influence on policymaking in the United States, notably marked by heightened focus on international migration, the conservative shift within the Republican Party, and the election of Donald Trump in 2016. This period witnessed swift pullbacks from global trade, stringent limitations on international migration, and the adoption of simplistic slogans like "build the wall." These right-leaning policy shifts are often perceived as responses to alleged surges in global migration, embodying a nativist governance characterized by a fusion of racism, xenophobia, and nationalism. These ideologies explicitly oppose the cosmopolitan vision of a "citizens of the world" perspective.[16]

Fueling divisive rhetoric, populist leaders have relied on these dividers to construct the antagonistic view of a group of "true people" and its enemies.[17] Often defined by an exclusionist, nationalist notion of citizenship, populism purports to be the "party of the people," representing an ethnocentric majority in which non-native elements, peoples, and ideas are seen to threaten the sovereignty of nation-states.[18] That ethnocentric majority has been seen to

---

China-fueled commodities boom. The boom's end, in 2012, put the left in a jam by making if very difficult to continue to fund the anti-poverty programs that made da Silva, Fernández, and Bachelet so popular. Further complicating things for the left is a mountain of corruption scandals") (last visited Nov 11, 2023).

14 Sofia Vasilopoulou, *Continuity and Change in the Study of Euroscepticism: Plus ça change?*, 51 J. COMMON MARKET STUD. 153, 153–68 (2013).

15 Tom G. Daly, *Understanding Multi-directional Democratic Decay: Lessons from the Rise of Bolsonaro in Brazil*, 14 L. & ETHICS HUM. RTS. J. 199–226 (2019).

16 *See generally* ALISON BRYSK & MICHAEL STOHL, CONTRACTING HUMAN RIGHTS: CRISIS, ACCOUNTABILITY AND OPPORTUNITY (2018).

17 ROBERT PEKKANEN ET AL., THE GLOBAL IMPLICATIONS OF POPULISM ON DEMOCRACY 5–22 (2018); *see also*, Carlos de la Torre, *Trump's Populism: Lessons from Latin America*, 20 POSTCOLONIAL STUD. 187, 187–98 (2017).

18 *See* THE EUROPEAN MAINSTREAM AND THE POPULIST RADICAL RIGHT (Pontus Odmalm & Eve Hepburn eds., 2017); *see also*, Roger Brubaker, *The Return of Assimilation? Changing Perspectives on Immigration and its Sequels in France, Germany and the United States*, *in* TOWARD ASSIMILATION AND CITIZENSHIP: IMMIGRANTS IN LIBERAL NATION-STATES (Christian Joppke & Ewa Morawska eds., 2003). The "non-native"

reject the principle of equality and carry out an Islamophobic, Romaphobic, anti-Semitic, anti-immigrant and/or homophobic and transphobic rhetoric and discrimination.[19]

In increasingly interconnected parts of the world, the populist radical right has attacked the cosmopolitan vision of a multicultural society. Racial, ethnic, and religious minorities have often been ostracized as "others."[20] Driven by state-sanctioned violence, ethnic cleansing campaigns against Rohingya Muslims in Burma and Uyghurs and other minorities in northern China have met little international resistance, leading to the disappearance of entire communities.[21] Instigating hate crimes, prominent far-right religious groups have denounced minorities, grounding nationalistic ideas in religious convictions.[22]

1.2 *The Rise of Conservative Religious Groups*

The rise of conservative religious groups alongside right-wing populism across regions has given additional support to the discriminatory foundation of far-right political parties.[23] Some authors have characterized the conservative religious movement as the "global right wing," understood as a network of religious conservatives crossing confessional lines and united by a

---

elements are referred to in the sociological sense of *nativism*, which is the political policy of promoting or protecting the interests of native-born or established inhabitants against those of immigrants. In other words, a form of nationalism predicated on the exclusion of perceived foreign elements. *See Nativism*, The Oxford Encyclopedia of the Modern World (2008), https://www.oxfordreference.com/view/10.1093/acref/9780195176322.001.0001/acref-9780195176322-e-1091 (last visited Nov 11, 2023). *See generally* Uri Friedman, *What is a Nativist?*, The Atlantic (Apr. 11, 2017), https://www.theatlantic.com/international/archive/2017/04/what-is-nativist-trump/521355/ (last visited Nov 11, 2023).

19 *See* Natalie Alkiviadou, The Far-Right in International and European Law (2019).

20 Ran Hirschl & Ayelet Shachar, *'Religious Talk' in Narratives of Membership*, *in* Constitutional Democracy in Crisis? (Mark A. Graber et al. eds., 2018).

21 *See* Christian Shepherd, *Fear and oppression in Xinjiang: China's war on Uighur culture*, Fin. Times (Sept. 12. 2019), https://www.ft.com/content/48508182-d426-11e9-8367-807ebd53ab77 (last visited Nov 11, 2023); *see also*, Hum. Rts. Watch, Report "Eradicating Ideological Viruses" China's Campaign of Repression Against Xinjiang's Muslims (2018).

22 *See generally* Nadia Marzouki, Duncan McDonnell & Olivier Roy. Saving the People: How Populists Hijack Religion (2016).

23 *See* John L. Esposito, *Foreword: Religious Fundamentalisms & the Global Resurgence*, *in* Fundamentalism, Politics, and the Law (Marci A. Hamilton & Mark J. Rozell eds., 2011); *see also*, Alison Brysk, The Future of Human Rights (2018).

common religious–political agenda.[24] The network includes organizations of a variety of faiths who are religiously conservative and generally agree that religious-based morality should have a larger role in society than it currently does, especially on particular policy issues such as same-sex marriage, gender roles, and abortion.[25]

These groups challenge the secularity of the State and rely on notions such as the "defense of the family" and "traditional values" as a common basis for the characterization of their actions against liberal ideals.[26] They also question the feminist and gender movements as movements that defend the legitimacy of the agenda of sexual and reproductive rights and fiercely oppose legislation on same-sex marriage and sexual minorities' rights.[27] Their defense of the "natural family" corresponds to traditional gender roles and the denial of the rights of women as individuals capable to make autonomous decisions.[28] According to their political agenda, women are predominantly placed in the position of mothers and outside that role they are characterized as deviant, their word

---

24 Clifford Bob, The Global Right Wing and the Clash of World Politics 36–71 (2012).

25 Jessica Glenza, *How the Religious Right Gained Unprecedented Access to Trump*, The Guardian (Jan. 31, 2019), https://www.theguardian.com/us-news/2019/jan/30/donald-trump-administration-religious-right-access (last visited Nov 11, 2023); Press Release, U.S. Commission on International Religious Freedom, Tony Perkins Elected Chair of Bipartisan U.S. Commission on International Religious Freedom (June 17, 2019), https://www.uscirf.gov/news-room/press-releases-statements/tony-perkins-elected-chair-bipartisan-us-commission (last visited Nov 11, 2023); *Alliance Defending Freedom*, S. Poverty L. Ctr., https://www.splcenter.org/fighting-hate/extremist-files/group/alliance-defending-freedom (last visited Nov 11, 2023); Naureen Shameen, Rights at Risk: Observatory on the Universality of Rights-Trends Report 31 (2017).

26 *See generally* U.N. Office of the High Commissioner for Human Rights, *Time for world leaders to honour 25-year-old promises and renew their commitments on women's rights, say human rights experts* (Nov. 11, 2019), https://www.ohchr.org/EN/NewsEvents/Pages/DisplayNews.aspx?NewsID=25282&LangID=E (noting the push back against women's rights from conservative religious and political groups in the areas of sexual and reproductive health and rights) (last visited Nov 11, 2023); Press Release, U.N. Office of the High Commissioner for Human Rights, Joint Statement by U.N. human rights experts on the occasion of the 25th anniversary of the adoption of the Programme of Action of the International Conference on Population and Development (ICPD), https://www.ohchr.org/EN/NewsEvents/Pages/DisplayNews.aspx?NewsID=25280&LangID=E (last visited Nov 11, 2023).

27 *See, e.g.,* William C. Martin, With God on Our Side: The Rise of the Religious Right in America (2005); *see also*, Francis Fitzgerald, The Evangelicals: The Struggle to Shape America (2017).

28 *See, e.g.,* Naureen Shameen, Rights at Risk: Observatory on the Universality of Rights-Trends Report 31 (2017).

distrusted and their behavior stigmatized. Infringing sexual and reproductive health rights, right-wing populist governments have sought to frame national identity by elevating traditional roles for women and hatred toward LGBTQ groups.[29] Right-wing populist leaders have sought to portray sexual and reproductive health rights as threats to religious values and national security.[30] With populist states viewing "gender ideology" as an example of liberal institutions, leaders have denounced women's empowerment and LGBTQ rights as negatively impacting the presumed majority's values.[31] These political leaders have thus embraced violations of sexual and reproductive health rights and have defunded institutions that support LGBTQ populations, sought to limit women's roles to motherhood and child-bearing, and have blocked funding for nongovernmental organizations that focus on family planning, access to contraception, and HIV/AIDS.[32]

1.3 *Conservative Religious Groups Gaining Power*

The new wave of right-wing populism seeks to mobilize religion for its own ends.[33] In that sense, the populist interest in religion is, in most cases, not

29 *See generally* Michael Lienesch, *Right-Wing Religion: Christian Conservatism as a Political Movement*, 97 POL. SCI. QUART. 403, 403–25 (1982); *see also*, Gábor Halmai, *Populism, Authoritarianism and Constitutionalism*, 20 GERMAN L.J. 296, 296–313 (2019).

30 Kenneth Roth, *World Report: The Dangerous Rise of Populism: Global Attacks on Human Rights Values*, HUM. RTS. WATCH (2017), https://www.hrw.org/world-report/2017/country-chapters/dangerous-rise-of-populism (last visited Nov 11, 2023); *see also*, Wolfgang Palaver, *Populism and Religion: On the Politics of Fear*, 58 DIALOG 1, 22–29 (2019).

31 *See* Javier Corrales, *The Expansion of LGBT Rights in Latin America and the Backlash*, *in* THE OXFORD HANDBOOK OF GLOBAL LGBT AND SEXUAL DIVERSITY POLITICS (Michael J. Bosia et al. eds., 2020); *see e.g.*, Jeff Johnston, *Casting God's Vision for Sex and Sexuality*, THE DAILY CITIZEN (May 7, 2015), https://dailycitizen.focusonthefamily.com/casting-gods-vision-for-sex-and-sexuality ("[b]ecause homosexuality…violate[s] God's intentional design for sex and sexuality, we believe that this is a cultural and theological battle that we must engage and win.") (last visited Nov 11, 2023).

32 *See, e.g.*, Trudy Ring, *Mike Pence 'Abhors' Discrimination? His Record Shows Otherwise*, ADVOC. (Apr. 1, 2015), https://www.advocate.com/politics/politicians/2015/04/01/mike-pence-abhors-discrimination-his-record-shows-otherwise (last visited Nov 11, 2023).

33 Populist campaigns expose the different uses of Christianity to garnish support. Former President Trump's "America First" agenda provided Evangelical Christians the ability to easily insert their religious values in the overall Republican agenda. The "Christian identity" was not a main objective of the Trump campaign but was utilized as a complementary device to gain popularity. In Europe, right-wing movements are deliberately employing the preservation of the Christian identity in their national campaigns. European populist leaders resort to the preservation of the Christian identity not as a way to defend Christian ideology, but rather as a tool to aggressively campaign against immigration and "Islamisation." *See* NADIA MARZOUKI, DUNCAN MCDONNELL & OLIVIER ROY.

necessarily placed on the religious values themselves, but on the pursuit of a differentiating feature that facilitates the creation of an "enemy" community, "the others," necessary for the populist discourse. As such, right-wing populists deploy religious identities and traditions to define who can and cannot be part of "the people."

For populism in Europe, the common "enemy" is embodied in Islam[34] with, for example, many populists claiming that native Christian communities are being threatened by a creeping and highly aggressive process of Islamization, with Muslims becoming a key enemy of the people.[35] Which could explain the reasons why, within the European System of Human Rights, the Russian Federation has sought to withdraw from the European Court's jurisdiction because many of the court's decisions are seen to run counter to the country's interests and values.[36]

In Latin America, the common enemy has been personified in groups that promote causes of a progressive agenda, such as same-sex marriage and legal abortion.[37] Political changes in Latin America are no exception to the global phenomenon and rise of right-wing populist leaders. Based on a new alliance with the Roman Catholic and Christian Evangelical churches against what

---

SAVING THE PEOPLE: HOW POPULISTS HIJACK RELIGION (2016); *see also*, Olivier Roy, *A Kitsch Christianity: Populists Gather Support while Traditional Religiosity Declines*, LSE REL. & GLOB. SOC'Y BLOG (Oct. 22, 2018), https://blogs.lse.ac.uk/religionglobalsociety/2018/10/a-kitsch-christianity-populists-gather-support-while-traditional-religiosity-declines (last visited Nov 11, 2023).

34 PEW RSCH. CTR., EASTERN AND WESTERN EUROPEANS DIFFER ON IMPORTANCE OF RELIGION, VIEWS OF MINORITIES, AND KEY SOCIAL ISSUES (2018).

35 NADIA MARZOUKI, DUNCAN MCDONNELL & OLIVIER ROY. SAVING THE PEOPLE: HOW POPULISTS HIJACK RELIGION (2016).

36 Maria Tsvetkova, *Russia May End Cooperation with European Court of Human Rights: RIA*, REUTERS (Mar. 01, 2018), https://www.reuters.com/article/us-russia-court-echr-withdrawal/russia-may-end-cooperation-with-european-court-of-human-rights-ria-idUSKCN1GD47U (last visited Nov 11, 2023).

37 *See generally* A. Amuchastegui et al., *Politics, religion and gender equality in contemporary Mexico: women's sexuality and reproductive rights in a contested secular state*, 31 THIRD WORLD Q. 989, 989–1005 (2010); M. BLOFIELD, THE POLITICS OF MORAL SIN: ABORTION AND DIVORCE IN SPAIN, CHILE AND ARGENTINA (2006); Louise Chappell, *Contesting women's rights: Charting the emergence of a transnational conservative counter-network*, 20 GLOB. SOC. 491, 491–520; N. CRASKE & M. MOLYNEUX, GENDER AND THE POLITICS OF RIGHTS AND DEMOCRACY IN LATIN AMERICA (2002); K. Eaton, *New Strategies of the Latin American Right*, *in* THE RESILIENCE OF THE LATIN AMERICAN RIGHT 75–93 (J.P. Luna & C. Rovira Kaltwasser, eds., 2014); C. EWIG, SECOND-WAVE NEOLIBERALISM: GENDER, RACE, AND HEALTH SECTOR REFORM IN PERU (2010); M. HTUN , SEX AND THE STATE: ABORTION, DIVORCE, AND THE FAMILY UNDER LATIN AMERICAN DICTATORSHIPS AND DEMOCRACIES (2003).

they call "gender ideology," right-wing populist leaders have found a path to upper-middle class voters within conservative parties, thus expanding their electorate. Even the Mexican President, Andrés Manuel López Obrador, who comes from a traditionally leftist party, reached an agreement for governance with the *Partido Encuentro Social* and agreements with the Evangelical Church, both of which are fierce opposers of "progressive" policies. These policies include same-sex marriage and legal abortion as, in their view, they represent manifestations of irreligiosity and secularism promoted by the corrupt and liberal elite.[38]

The resurgence of conservative religious movements in Latin America can be seen as a response to increasing secularization and the advancement of liberal policies over the past several years in the region. Achievements for the regional liberal agenda included the legalization of same-sex marriage in Argentina in 2010 and Brazil in 2013, the decriminalization of abortion in three circumstances in Chile in 2017—a country predominantly and historically ruled by ultra-conservative elites—and the 2018 abortion debate, and ultimate legalization in 2020, in Argentina that appeared on the front pages of newspapers globally and that led thousands to submit apostasy requests in protest of the Catholic Church's influence and the key role it played in obstructing abortion legalization in 2018.

Indeed, the participation of Evangelical and Catholic churches in Latin American politics nurtures the political far-right and their conservative agenda. Both churches have infiltrated politics to impose ideals opposed to the alteration of the patriarchal order, their interpretation of the concepts of family, gender ideology, and sexual and reproductive rights. As an example, in November 2019, multiple uprisings in Bolivia against electoral fraud ended with members of the opposition party entering the government palace in La Paz—the home of the President—with a Bible and a resignation letter for former President Evo Morales to sign. During his campaign, the leader of the opposition, Luis Fernando Camacho, had invoked God to argue that his cause was just and that he was going to achieve the removal of Morales from power with divine intervention. The opposition leader celebrated Morales' resignation.[39] Morales sought political asylum, which Mexico granted. It only took

38 *See* Javier Corrales, *The Expansion of* LGBT *Rights in Latin America and the Backlash*, *in* THE OXFORD HANDBOOK OF GLOBAL LGBT AND SEXUAL DIVERSITY POLITICS (Michael J. Bosia et al. eds., 2020).

39 José Arturo Cárdenas, *Bolivia: La Biblia se vuelve una inesperada protagonista del conflicto politico*, LA NACIÓN (Nov. 11, 2019), https://www.lanacion.com.ar/el-mundo/bolivia-la-biblia-se-vuelve-una-inesperada-protagonista-del-conflicto-politico-nid2305254/ (last visited Nov 11, 2023).

two days before the former vice-president of the Senate, Jeanine Áñez—supported by the opposition party—self-proclaimed herself the interim president. After this self-proclamation, she went to the government palace, appeared on the balcony, and exhibited a copy of the Bible.[40] She later stated: "God has come back to the Palace."[41] Áñez is a member of a right-wing party and has been described as a religious conservative.[42] New presidential elections in Bolivia took place in May 2020. Both Camacho and Áñez, as well as Chi Hyun Chung—a physician and Evangelical pastor that has been characterized as the "Bolivian Bolsonaro"[43] as per his public statements against the LGBTQ community and women's rights—ran for office, along with five more candidates, but ultimately lost.

Another regional example is that of Brazil. Armed with a right-wing populist rhetoric, conservative religious movements in Brazil brought Jair Bolsonaro to power. Bolsonaro's campaign was characterized by a constant construction of "us" and "the others" in an exclusionary manner that denied the existence of class, race and gender differences. As part of the campaign's strategy, Bolsonaro joined the emerging right-wing backlash against "gender ideology."[44] Bolsonaro also made many public statements opposing LGBTQ rights, including that he was a "proud homophobe" and that gay children should be "beaten straight."[45] Shortly after becoming president, Bolsonaro

---

40 Fernanda Rojas, *"La Biblia vuelve al Palacio": Jeanine Áñez, la autoproclamada Presidenta interina de Bolivia*, La Tercera (Nov. 13, 2019), https://www.latercera.com/la-tercera-pm/noticia/la-biblia-vuelve-al-palacio-jeanine-anez-la-autoproclamada-presidenta-interina-de-bolivia/898931/ (last visited Nov 11, 2023).

41 *Id.*

42 *Id. See also*, Francisco Manetto, *La senadora Jeanine Áñez se proclama presidenta de Bolivia sin quorum en el Parlamento*, El País Internacional (Nov. 14, 2019), https://elpais.com/internacional/2019/11/12/america/1573566340_453048.html (last visited Nov 11, 2023).

43 Fernanda Rojas, *Elecciones en Bolivia, Chi Hyun Chung, el Bolsonaro boliviano que busca destronar a Evo Morales*, La Tercera (Oct. 10, 2019), https://www.latercera.com/la-tercera-pm/noticia/elecciones-en-bolivia-chi-hyun-chung-el-bolsonaro-boliviano-que-busca-destronar-a-evo-morales/855074/ (last visited Nov 11, 2023).

44 Mariana Prandini Assis & Ana Carolina Ogando, *Bolsonaro, 'Gender Ideology' and Hegemonic Masculinity in Brazil*, Al Jazeera (Oct. 31, 2018), https://www.aljazeera.com/indepth/opinion/bolsonaro-gender-ideology-hegemonic-masculinity-brazil-181031062523759.html (last visited Nov 11, 2023).

45 *See* Hannah Jane Parkinson, *As Rightwing Populism Spreads, Bigotry Against the LGBT Community is Growing*, The Guardian (May 17, 2019), https://www.theguardian.com/commentisfree/2019/may/17/rightwing-populism-bigotry-lgbt-community-rights (last visited Nov 11, 2023); *see also*, Grupo Gay da Bahia, Populacao LGBT Morta No Brasil—Relatorio GGB (2018), https://grupogaydabahia.files.wordpress.com

issued an executive order that removed LGBTQ considerations from the Ministry of Women, Family and Human Rights, leaving no other federal agency in charge of LGBTQ issues.[46] He also consolidated standalone ministries together into the Ministry of Women, Family and Human Rights and appointed an ultraconservative evangelical pastor, Damares Alves, as its minister. Alves has previously characterized LGBTQ rights as the "ideological indoctrination of children."[47]

In the Brazilian congress, evangelicals formed a highly influential group with links to ultraconservative politicians who oppose liberal or secular ideals.[48] For instance, this evangelical bloc has consistently opposed legislation that would expand LGBTQ rights, such as laws that would make attacks on LGBTQ people hate crimes.[49] The Evangelical church in Brazil has pursued a political strategy of only supporting other evangelicals in politics, which has contributed to their long-standing influence and ability to elect representatives favorable to their views.[50]

/2019/01/relat%C3%B3rio-de-crimes-contra-lgbt-brasil-2018-grupo-gay-da-bahia.pdf (revealing that more than 420 LGBTQ Brazilians died in 2017 as victims of homophobia, a 30% increase from 2016) (last visited Nov 11, 2023).

46 Morgan Gstalter, *Brazil's New President Removes LGBT Concerns from Human Rights Ministry*, THE HILL (Feb. 1, 2019), https://thehill.com/policy/international/human-rights/423594-brazils-new-president-removes-lgbt-concerns-from-human (last visited Nov 11, 2023).

47 *Id.*

48 *See, e.g.*, Chayenne Polimédio, *The Rise of the Brazilian Evangelicals*, THE ATLANTIC (Jan. 24, 2018), https://www.theatlantic.com/international/archive/2018/01/the-evangelical-takeover-of-brazilian-politics/551423/ (last visited Nov 11, 2023).

49 Anthony Faiola & Marina Lopes, *LGBT Rights Threatened in Brazil under New Far-Right President*, WASH. POST (Feb. 18, 2019), https://www.washingtonpost.com/world/the_americas/lgbt-rights-under-attack-in-brazil-under-new-far-right-president/2019/02/17/b24e1dcc-1b28-11e9-b8e6-567190c2fd08_story.html (last visited Nov 11, 2023).

50 *See* Chayenne Polimédio, *How Evangelical Conservatives Are Gaining Power in Brazil*, FOREIGN AFFS. (Mar. 7, 2019), https://www.foreignaffairs.com/articles/brazil/2019-03-07/how-evangelical-conservatives-are-gaining-power-brazil (last visited Nov 11, 2023); Michael Stott, *Brazil's Evangelical Church Preaches the Bolsonaro Revolution*, FIN. TIMES (Dec. 15, 2019), https://www.ft.com/content/e7a47196-1817-11ea-9ee4-11f260415385 (last visited Nov 11, 2023); *see also*, Anthony Boadle, *Brazil's Evangelicals Say Far-Right Presidential Candidate is Answer to Their Prayers*, REUTERS (Sept. 27, 2018), https://www.reuters.com/article/us-brazil-election-evangelicals/brazils-evangelicals-say-far-right-presidential-candidate-is-answer-to-their-prayers-idUSKCN1M70D9 (last visited Nov 11, 2023).

Each of these events are not isolated cases in Latin America. Similar forces have emerged in Argentina[51] and Chile.[52] This divisive, populist, and conservative rhetoric has also percolated to the regional level. The reinvigoration of right-wing populism in Latin America is manifesting in sentiments of nationalism.[53]

Right-wing populist leaders in Latin America recognize the opportunity to garner support through complementing their agendas with social conservatism and a divisive rhetoric.[54] As the right-wing governments in Latin America create a platform against the liberal and secular elite, the Roman Catholics and Christian Evangelicals have partnered with them to tackle progressive policies, such as those related to the recognition of sexual and reproductive rights and gender identity, as they represent "manifestations of irreligiosity and secularism".[55]

In the United States, for its part, it is common knowledge that Donald Trump won the 2016 presidential election with the support of U.S.-based conservative groups.[56] Over the course of Trump's presidency, his administration fulfilled many of the political and policy goals of these conservative groups,

---

51 *See Plataforma*, FRENTE NOS, https://www.nosargentina.com.ar (last visited Oct. 19, 2019) (calling "all the Argentinians of good to the recovery of those principles and values that made our Nation great" and emphasizing "traditional family values" and the fight against gender ideology as their main goals). And, more recently, President Elect Javier Milei's political party's electoral platform highlighting the "defense of the right to life from the moment of conception" as one of their main values. *See Base de Acción Política y Plataforma Electoral Nacional*, LA LIBERTAD AVANZA, https://www.electoral.gob.ar/nuevo/paginas/pdf/plataformas/2023/PASO/JUJUY%2079%20PARTIDO%20RENOVADOR%20FEDERAL%20-PLATAFORMA%20LA%20LIBERTAD%20AVANZA.pdf (last visited Nov 22, 2023).

52 Beatriz Romero Cruzat, *Ultra-Conservative Speech as Political Capital: Chile's "Republican Party,"* OPENGLOBALRIGHTS (Aug. 27, 2019), https://www.openglobalrights.org/ultra-conservative-speech-as-political-capital-chiles-republican-party/?lang=English (last visited Nov 11, 2023).

53 Omar G. Encarnación, *The Trumpification of the Latin American Right*, FOREIGN POL'Y (Apr. 16, 2018), https://foreignpolicy.com/2018/04/16/the-trumpification-of-the-latin-american-right/ (last visited Nov 11, 2023).

54 *Id.*

55 *See* Javier Corrales, *The Expansion of LGBT Rights in Latin America and the Backlash*, *in* THE OXFORD HANDBOOK OF GLOBAL LGBT AND SEXUAL DIVERSITY POLITICS (Michael J. Bosia, Sandra M. McEvoy and Momin Rahman eds., 2020).

56 *See, e.g.*, James Cook, *US election: Trump and the rise of the alt-right*, BBC NEWS (Nov. 7, 2016), https://www.bbc.com/news/election-us-2016-37899026 (last visited Nov 11, 2023). *See also*, Ryan Kohls, *Explained: Evangelicals, the religious right and Trump*, AL JAZEERA (Nov. 6, 2018), https://www.aljazeera.com/news/2018/11/6/explained-evangelicals-the-religious-right-and-trump (last visited Nov 11, 2023).

such as reducing environmental protections, increasing military spending, and downsizing federal government agencies, to name just a few.[57] The Trump administration also supported the right-wing anti-LGBTQ and anti-reproductive rights agendas by hiring or appointing anti-LGBTQ and anti-reproductive rights individuals to powerful positions in the administration.[58]

2 Assertive Multiculturalism: A Theory

The rise of conservative religious groups alongside right-wing populism and its attempts to theocratize secular societies can be explained as the ultimate reconfiguration of multiculturalism.

Multiculturalism has been commonly understood as the accommodation of minorities and the promotion of diversity.[59] As the figure below shows, in a pre-World War II world, there was no room for minority groups or subordinate moralities. After World War II, and with the rise of globalization and cosmopolitanism, minorities gained increasing recognition, accommodation, and protection in liberal democracies.

Over time, groups that were previously considered to be the majority noticed that multiculturalism had caused them to lose certain privileges and positions of power. Scholars began to describe that moment under the notion of new- or post-multiculturalism, where the focus of these formerly majoritarian groups—that with the increasing recognition of other groups had become minority groups in quantitative terms—was on encapsulating and protecting the status quo over concerns that accommodation had gone too far.[60] The

57 *Trump Administration Embraces Heritage Foundation Policy Recommendations*, HERITAGE FUND. (Jan. 23, 2018), https://www.heritage.org/impact/trump-administration-embraces-heritage-foundation-policy-recommendations (last visited Nov 11, 2023).

58 *See, e.g.*, Jeremy Hooper, *Heritage Foundation: The [intensely anti-LGBTQ] White House Pipeline*, GLAAD (Jan. 8, 2019), https://www.glaad.org/blog/heritage-foundation-intensely-anti-lgbtq-white-house-pipeline (last visited June 11, 2022).

59 *See* WILL KYMLICKA, MULTICULTURAL ODYSSEYS: NAVIGATING THE NEW INTERNATIONAL POLITICS OF DIVERSITY (2007); *see also*, Michael Helfand, *Religious Arbitration and the New Multiculturalism – Negotiating Conflicting Legal Orders*, 86 N.Y U. L. REV. 1231, 1268–86 (2011).

60 *See, e.g.*, Will Kymlicka, *The rise and fall of multiculturalism? New debates on inclusion and accommodation in diverse societies*, 68 INT'L SOC. SCI. J. 133, 133–48 (2018); *see also*, Dorota A. Gozdecka et al., *From Multiculturalism to Post-Multiculturalism: Trends and Paradoxes*, 50 J. SOC. 51, 51–64 (2014); Steven Vertovec, *Toward Post-Multiculturalism? Changing communities, conditions and contexts of diversity*, 61 INT'L SOC. SCI. J. 83, 83–95 (2010).

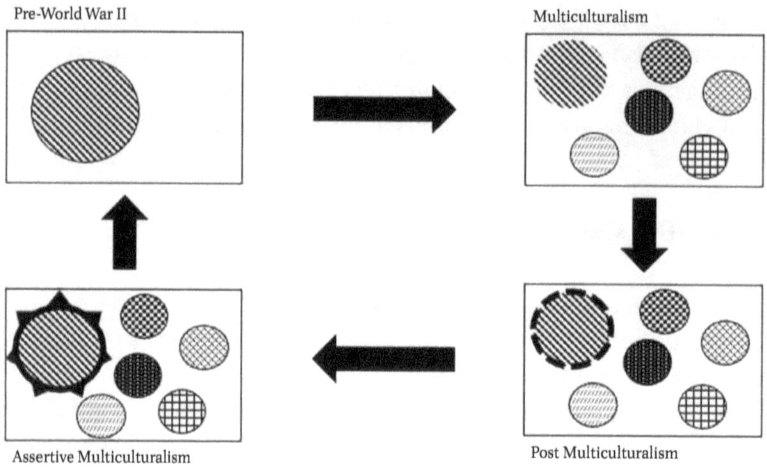

FIGURE 1 The evolution of multiculturalism and the emergence of *assertive multiculturalism*

expansion and emergence of conservative religious forces alongside right-wing populism, and their claims reflect a new dimension of the evolution of multiculturalism, which I call *assertive multiculturalism*.

Under a situation of assertive multiculturalism, these formerly majoritarian groups go beyond merely trying to maintain the status quo. They intentionally pursue an ultimate goal of imposing their views on others as well as taking an active role in efforts to return to an imagined past.

Assertive multiculturalism explains what lies beneath the recent rise of conservative religious movements alongside right-wing populist leaders and their increasing attempts to theocratize secular societies. These groups believe that they have lost their positions of power to yield to or accommodate for minorities. But now, minority groups—taken together—constitute a "new majority" with opinions that differ from that of these groups. Therefore, conservative religious groups feel a need to reclaim their place—their lost power.

The key in understanding *assertive multiculturalism* lies within the meaning of "minority." In its most literal interpretation, "minority" is a quantitative term referring to the lesser part or smaller number of a total. However, over time, the term "minority" has become increasingly complicated—and at times contested—leading to additional connotations, most of them not quantitative.[61] Some of these connotations account for the power dimension where

61 Lewis M. Killian, *What or who is a 'minority'?* 10 MICH. SOCIO. REV. 18–31 (1996).

membership to a minority group is typically based on the relative disadvantages people in the group experience as compared to members of a dominant social group.[62] In cases where subordinate groups outnumber their oppressors, or dominant group, the distinction between minority and majority groups has, nonetheless, led to confusion.[63]

To understand the contexts in which assertive multiculturalism germinates there is a need to clarify the distinction between, for the sake of the argument, what I call dominant and subordinate moralities in qualitative terms. In the past, the dominant morality corresponded with the majorities' interests from a quantitative perspective and vice versa. However, over time, subordinate moralities became the "new majorities" from a quantitative perspective. In the wake of globalization and multiculturalism, the paradigm changed and today it is common to see the majority as a heterogeneous group consisting of different minority groups that together support different subordinate moral positions.

Multiculturalism, in its traditional sense, is intended to protect quantitative minorities from majorities. Here, an accommodation of minorities is understood as the appropriate mechanism for their protection and fundamental rights are understood as trump cards against majoritarian oppression.[64] In the alternate context of assertive multiculturalism, certain groups acknowledge the potential of the rights discourse and an appeal to morality for the benefit of minoritarian interests (quantitatively speaking). Therefore, these groups benefit from a context of multiculturalism (in the traditional sense) where accommodation, and particularly religious accommodation, may be considered a tool to reverse minorities' progress towards the recognition of their rights. These conservative religious groups are using tools that had allowed minorities to gain greater recognition and protection, such as the rights discourse, to protect their own interests, which they consider to be under attack by groups that adhere to what—under their view—are or should be subordinate moralities. Assertive multiculturalism explains the situation in which these groups

62 *See* JOSEPH F. HEALEY ET AL., RACE, ETHNICITY, GENDER, & CLASS: THE SOCIOLOGY OF GROUP CONFLICT AND CHANGE (8th ed. 2018); Timothy Laurie & Rimi Khan, *The Concept of Minority for the Study of Culture*, 31 CONTINUUM: J. MEDIA & CULTURAL STUDS. 3 (2017); Kevin Johnson, *The Struggle for Civil Rights: The Need for, and Impediments to, Political Coalitions among and within Minority Groups*, 63 LA. L. REV. 759 (1995).

63 Lewis M. Killian, *What or who is a 'minority'?* 10 MICH. SOCIO. REV. 18–31 (1996). *See generally* Louis Wirth, *The Problem of Minority Groups*, *in* THE SCIENCE OF MAN IN THE WORLD CRISIS (Ralph Linton ed., 1945). For an overall critique of the term "minority," see Doris Wilkinson, *Rethinking the Concept of "Minority": A Task for Social Scientists and Practitioners*, 27 J. SOCIO. & SOC. WELFARE (2000).

64 RONALD DWORKIN, TAKING RIGHTS SERIOUSLY (1977).

resort to mechanisms that have become accepted under a multiculturalist perspective as a way to reclaim their lost power. In the context of assertive multiculturalism, the rights discourse—and particularly freedom of religion, conscience and beliefs—is used as a tool to delegitimize, hinder and/or limit the enjoyment of others' legally protected rights.

In recent times, instances of assertive multiculturalism have become evident within the context of international human rights law. In particular, assertive multiculturalism is reflected in calls to redefine human rights by referencing an original interpretation rooted in natural law and religious values.

After World War II, the doctrine of natural rights, refurbished as human rights, was one of the normative bases available to criticize a grossly immoral legal order according to international criteria.[65] The doctrine of human rights allowed for neutralizing these effects after the fall of the prior legal regime, and it fulfilled this role because whatever rights were granted to citizens of this or that State, their natural rights followed.[66]

For years, the recognition of natural law, framed under the notion of human rights, was the predominant belief in law. This idea even prompted regulatory changes at the national level and expansive interpretations of human rights at the international level. For example, in 1994, Argentina underwent a constitutional reform that incorporated a constitutional bloc to harmonize its domestic law with international human rights law, as many Latin American countries did.[67]

At the same time, supranational institutions at regional and global levels increasingly engaged in the creation and proliferation of norms and standards for countries to follow.[68] As such, international human rights law grew into expansive interpretations of rights and a recognition of new rights. Many of these interpretations were not entirely consistent with each other, as the number of procedures and institutions addressing aspects of the same issues exponentially grew.[69] Neither United Nations (U.N.) Special Procedures nor U.N. treaty monitoring bodies were aligned in their conclusions when it came to interpreting the extent and scope of specific rights and/or treaties. As such,

---

65 Horacio Spector, *La filosofía de los derechos humanos*, 15 ISONOMIA, 7–53 (2001).

66 STANLEY I. BENN & RICHARD S. PETERS, SOCIAL PRINCIPLES AND THE DEMOCRATIC STATES 88–107 (2010).

67 Roberto Gargarella, *Latin American Constitutionalism: Social Rights and the "Engine Room" of the Constitution*, 4 NOTRE DAME J. INT'L & COMP. L. 9, 9–18 (2014).

68 *See generally* David W. Kennedy, *The International Human Rights Regime: Still Part of the Problem?*, 15 HARV. HUM. RTS. J. 101 (2002).

69 Philip Alston, *Conjuring up New Human Rights: A Proposal for Quality Control*, 78 AM. J. INT'L L. 607 (1984).

the human rights regime began to show weaknesses in terms of gaps on its legitimacy and some scholars raised critical voices.[70]

In such context, conservative actors noticed that new conceptualizations of human rights did not align with their ideals of morality. This "undue" expansion or inflation of human rights resulted in strong resistance against new interpretations in recent years.[71] Conservative actors, who were considering the need to reinstate "dominant" notions of morality, adopted and adapted progressive strategies for their own objectives.[72] For instance, they turned to international forums to advance their agenda, such as the concept of the traditional family and to counter the so-called threat of gender ideology.[73]

Over time, and with the advent of right-wing populist governments that also questioned the international legal order for various reasons, conservative religious groups explored other strategies. These strategies focused on bringing back a legal view that would allow them to limit and control new understandings of fundamental rights.[74]

---

70 Alicia E. Yamin & Andrés Constantin, *A Long and Winding Road: The Evolution of Applying Human Rights Frameworks to Health*, 49 GEO. J. INT'L L. 191, 191–239 (2018). *See also* SAMUEL MOYN, NOT ENOUGH: HUMAN RIGHTS IN AN UNEQUAL WORLD (2018).

71 *See, e.g.*, Melina Girardi Fachin & Bruna Nowak, *The Joint Declaration to the Inter-American System of Human Rights: Backlash or Contestation?* INT'L J. CONST. L. BLOG (Dec. 12, 2019), http://www.iconnectblog.com/2019/12/the-joint-declaration-to-the-inter-american-system-of-human-rights-backlash-or-contestation/ (on the resistance and backlash at the Inter-American system of human rights' level) (last visited June 20, 2022).

72 *See* NAUREEN SHAMEEN, RIGHTS AT RISK: OBSERVATORY ON THE UNIVERSALITY OF RIGHTS-TRENDS REPORT 31 (2017); *see also* Jennifer Butler, *New Sheriff in Town: The Christian Right Nears Major Victory at the United Nations*, 16 PUBLIC EYE MAG. 2 (2003), http://www.publiceye.org/magazine/v16n2/PE_Butler2.html (on the George W. Bush administration's appointments of right-wing religious leaders, such as members of the Family Research Council, to join official government delegations to the U.N.) (last visited Nov 11, 2023). *See generally* JENNIFER S. BUTLER, BORN AGAIN: THE CHRISTIAN RIGHT GLOBALIZED (2006); *Mission Statement*, CTR. FOR FAM. & HUM. RTS. (C-FAM), https://c-fam.org/about-us/mission-statement/ (C-Fam's Vision: The preservation of international law by discrediting socially radical policies at the United Nations and other international institutions) (last visited Nov 11, 2023).

73 *See, e.g.*, U.N. Human Rights Council, *Promoting Human Rights and Fundamental Freedoms through a Better Understanding of Traditional Values of Humankind: Best Practices*, U.N. Doc. A/HRC/RES/21/3 (Oct. 9, 2012); U.N. Human Rights Council, *Protection of the Family: Contribution of the Family to the Realization of the Right to an Adequate Standard of Living for Its Members, particularly through Its Role in Poverty Eradication and Achieving Sustainable Development*, U.N. Doc. A/HRC/RES/29/22 (July 22, 2015).

74 Ingrid Wuerth Brunk , *International Law in the Age of Trump: A Post-Human Rights Agenda*, LAWFARE (Nov. 14, 2016), https://www.lawfareblog.com/international-law-age-trump-post-human-rights-agenda (last visited Nov 11, 2023).

As part of their efforts, right-wing populist governments alongside conservative religious groups have taken steps to reinterpret the very notion of human rights in a manner consistent with their own ideas of morality. The use of the rights discourse in a context of assertive multiculturalism gave rise to the phenomenon of "religious lawfare," which involves the use of legal and political strategies to promote a particular religious perspective or agenda. Rights are used as tools to impose belief systems and actively confront democratically sanctioned laws that recognize rights and protect interests contrary to those of conservative religious groups. Ultimately, groups who want to reinstate a previously dominant morality use these strategies to return to an imagined past where they can control and hold power.

The middle part of the 1990s witnessed several developments in international law that prompted an explosion of right-wing backlash to LGBTQ and sexual and reproductive rights in the international arena.[75] In 1994, the United Nations organized the International Conference on Population and Development in Cairo, Egypt.[76] The Cairo Conference and its main document, the Programme of Action, marked one of the first times that the "the reproductive and sexual health and rights of women became a central element" of an international agreement.[77] That same year, the U.N. Human Rights Committee decided *Toonen v. Australia*, which held that the term "sex" as a protected category in the International Covenant on Civil and Political Rights (ICCPR) included "sexual orientation."[78] Therefore, the Commission held that anti-sodomy laws violated the non-discrimination and right-to-privacy provisions of the ICCPR.[79] The next year, in 1995, the U.N. held another conference, the

75 *See, e.g.*, Scott Long, Anatomy of a Backlash: Sexuality and the "Cultural War" on Human Rights, Human Rights Watch 12–13; Naureen Shameen, Rights at Risk: Observatory on the Universality of Rights-Trends Report 16 (2017).

76 Scott Long, Anatomy of a Backlash: Sexuality and the "Cultural War" on Human Rights, Human Rights Watch 1; *International Conference on Population and Development*, United Nations Population Fund https://www.unfpa.org/icpd (last visited Nov 11, 2023); Naureen Shameen, Rights at Risk: Observatory on the Universality of Rights-Trends Report 20 (2017).

77 *International Conference on Population and Development*, U.N. Population Fund, https://www.unfpa.org/icpd (last visited Nov 11, 2023).

78 *See* Aengus Carroll & Marco Perolini, International Human Rights References to Sexual and Reproductive Health and Rights, ILGA Europe 22 (2007); Scott Long, Anatomy of a Backlash: Sexuality and the "Cultural War" on Human Rights, Human Rights Watch 12.

79 Aengus Carroll & Marco Perolini, International Human Rights References to Sexual and Reproductive Health and Rights, ILGA Europe 22

Beijing Conference on Women, which included "the first substantive discussion of sexual orientation at a U.N. forum."[80] The document drafted at that Conference, the Platform for Action, even contained express references to sexual orientation, but they were deleted when twenty states objected.[81]

In reaction to these new developments in the international sphere, the Holy See began an international lobbying effort against what it feared was a potential expansion of abortion and sexual rights.[82] For example, in direct reaction to the Cairo Conference, the Holy See's opposition effort included calling ambassadors to the Vatican, writing letters to world leaders, and instructing the Catholic Church's international network of bishops to publicly denounce the expansion of abortion rights.[83] It was this opposition strategy from the Holy See that inspired existing right-wing populist organizations, mostly ones based in the United States, to enter the international sphere to try to advance their anti-reproductive rights agenda.[84] These groups had previously focused their efforts within the United States, but quickly realized they could increase their influence if they took their fight international.[85] Some organizations were also newly created for the specific purpose of battling the expansion of sexual rights globally.[86]

During their foray into the international arena, U.S.-based conservative groups enjoyed support from the George W. Bush administration between

(2007); Scott Long, Anatomy of a Backlash: Sexuality and the "Cultural War" on Human Rights, Human Rights Watch 12.

80 Aengus Carroll & Marco Perolini, International Human Rights References to Sexual and Reproductive Health and Rights, ilga Europe 22 (2007).

81 *Id.*

82 Naureen Shameen, Rights at Risk: Observatory on the Universality of Rights-Trends Report 20 (2017).

83 *Id.*

84 *See* Naureen Shameen, Rights at Risk: Observatory on the Universality of Rights-Trends Report 20–22 (2017).; Scott Long, Anatomy of a Backlash: Sexuality and the "Cultural War" on Human Rights, Human Rights Watch 13; norad, Lobbying for Faith and Family: A Study of Religious ngos at the United Nations 13 (2013).

85 *See, e.g.*, Naureen Shameen, Rights at Risk: Observatory on the Universality of Rights-Trends Report 22 (2017); *Strange Bedfellows*, The Economist (May 4, 2013), https://www.economist.com/international/2013/05/04/strange-bedfellows/ (last visited Nov 11, 2023); Scott Long, Anatomy of a Backlash: Sexuality and the "Cultural War" on Human Rights, Human Rights Watch 14.

86 *See, e.g.*, *About C-Fam*, Ctr. Fam. & Hum. Rts., https://c-fam.org/about-us/ (last visited Nov 11, 2023) ("C-Fam was founded in the summer of 1997 in order to monitor and affect the social policy debate at the United Nations and other international institutions").

2001 and 2009.[87] As one commentator pointed out, President Bush wanted to shore up political support from the Christian far-right but did not want to lose support amongst more moderate Republicans.[88] Because mainstream media does not often report on the inner workings of the United Nations, President Bush developed a strategy of using the U.N. to "win points with Christian Right voters without losing moderate votes."[89] For example, the Bush administration appointed right-wing and religious leaders, including members of the Family Research Council, an American evangelical activist group and think tank known for its battles against LGBTQ rights, to join official government delegations to the U.N.[90] This government support gave newfound legitimacy to the views of these religious groups at the U.N., where their views were previously sidelined.[91] And, in fact, the involvement of these groups at the United Nations has had the effect of slowing down progress on other human rights issues.[92]

Now that these conservative religious groups have gained considerable influence in international policy debates, they have changed their tune on the existence of institutions like the United Nations itself.[93] U.S.-based conservative organizations have historically been critical of the very existence of the United Nations and have called for Congress to decrease U.S. involvement in the international body.[94] They have even argued that international bodies and treaties are threats to the United States.[95] Now, however, some of these

87 Daniel Crary, *U.S. Conservatives Step Up Overseas Activities*, NBC NEWS (Jan. 14, 2006), https://www.nbcnews.com/id/wbna10853178l (last visited Nov 11, 2023); Jennifer Butler, *New Sheriff in Town: The Christian Right Nears Major Victory at the United Nations*, PUBLICEYE.ORG, http://www.publiceye.org/magazine/v16n2/PE_Butler2.html (last visited Nov 11, 2023); NAUREEN SHAMEEN, RIGHTS AT RISK: OBSERVATORY ON THE UNIVERSALITY OF RIGHTS-TRENDS REPORT 30 (2017).

88 Jennifer Butler, *New Sheriff in Town: The Christian Right Nears Major Victory at the United Nations*, PUBLICEYE.ORG, http://www.publiceye.org/magazine/v16n2/PE_Butler2.html (last visited June 20, 2022).

89 *Id.*

90 *Id.*

91 *Id.*

92 *Id.*

93 *Id.*; SCOTT LONG, ANATOMY OF A BACKLASH: SEXUALITY AND THE "CULTURAL WAR" ON HUMAN RIGHTS, HUMAN RIGHTS WATCH 13.

94 Jennifer Butler, *New Sheriff in Town: The Christian Right Nears Major Victory at the United Nations*, PUBLICEYE.ORG, http://www.publiceye.org/magazine/v16n2/PE_Butler2.html (last visited June 20, 2022); SCOTT LONG, ANATOMY OF A BACKLASH: SEXUALITY AND THE "CULTURAL WAR" ON HUMAN RIGHTS, HUMAN RIGHTS WATCH 13.

95 Jennifer Butler, *New Sheriff in Town: The Christian Right Nears Major Victory at the United Nations*, PUBLICEYE.ORG, http://www.publiceye.org/magazine/v16n2/PE_Butler2.html (last visited June 20, 2022).

organizations preserve at least a veneer of supporting the U.N. in order to continue advancing their agenda at the international level.[96] Many of these groups have applied for and received consultative status at the United Nations, which allows them to attend meetings and advocate their viewpoints.[97] Because the Holy See has permanent observer status at international bodies like the United Nations and the Organization of American States, far-right and conservative religious organizations also work with the Holy See to advance their shared viewpoints on issues such as sexual and reproductive rights.[98]

An example of a U.S.-based right-wing conservative organization that has emerged in the international sphere is the Center for Family and Human Rights (C-FAM). Founded in 1997, C-FAM's self-proclaimed mission is to "defend life and family . . . [by] discrediting socially radical policies at the United Nations and other international institutions."[99] Among other things, C-FAM has called LGBTQ people "sexual fascists" who want to "take away your rights."[100] C-FAM even included a swastika over a rainbow flag in one of its fundraising emails.[101] These extremist views have led the Southern Poverty Law Center to label C-FAM as an anti-LGBTQ hate group.[102] Notwithstanding this label, C-FAM enjoys consultative status at the United Nations.[103] And, in 2017, Trump's State Department picked the Executive Vice President of C-FAM, Lisa Correnti, to

---

96 *Id.*; Scott Long, Anatomy of a Backlash: Sexuality and the "Cultural War" on Human Rights, Human Rights Watch 13.

97 Jennifer Butler, *New Sheriff in Town: The Christian Right Nears Major Victory at the United Nations*, PublicEye.Org, http://www.publiceye.org/magazine/v16n2/PE_Butler2.html (last visited June 20, 2022)

98 *Id.*; Naureen Shameen, Rights at Risk: Observatory on the Universality of Rights-Trends Report 17, 18 (2017); Scott Long, Anatomy of a Backlash: Sexuality and the "Cultural War" on Human Rights, Human Rights Watch 13.; Press Release, Organization of American States Press Department, The Vatican Opens Office Dedicated Exclusively to OAS Affairs (Sept. 16, 2019), https://www.oas.org/en/media_center/photonews.asp?sCodigo=FNE-97478 (last visited Nov 11, 2023).

99 *About C-Fam*, Ctr. Fam. & Hum. Rts., https://c-fam.org/about-us/ (last visited Nov 11, 2023); *Mission Statement*, Ctr. Fam. & Hum. Rts., https://c-fam.org/about-us/mission-statement/ (last visited Nov 11, 2023).

100 Brennan Suen, *Anti-LGBTQ hate group fundraises for its U.N. work with swastika over a rainbow flag*, MediaMatters (Dec. 8, 2017), https://www.mediamatters.org/diversity-discrimination/anti-lgbtq-hate-group-fundraises-its-un-work-swastika-over-rainbow-flag (last visited Nov 11, 2023).

101 *Id.*

102 *Blast from the Past: Anti-LGBT hate group resurrects dead "Bigotry Map" in latest fundraising attempt*, S. Poverty L. Ctr. (Feb. 15, 2018), https://www.splcenter.org/hatewatch/2018/02/15/blast-past-anti-lgbt-hate-group-resurrects-dead-bigotry-map-latest-fundraising-attempt (last visited Nov 11, 2023).

103 *Id.*

serve as one of two U.S. delegates to a session of the U.N. Commission on the Status of Women.[104]

Another example of an international anti-LGBTQ and anti-reproductive rights organization is the World Congress of Families (WCF) coalition, which is now integrated into a larger right-wing coalition, the International Organization for the Family.[105] The entire purpose of the WCF is to serve as an international network of anti-LGBTQ and anti-reproductive rights groups.[106] Indeed, one of its central tenets is the sanctity of the so-called natural family "founded on marriage between a man and a woman."[107] The WCF was founded in 1997 through the work of an ultraconservative scholar named Allan Carlson, who was a professor at a Christian college in Illinois.[108] Carlson viewed the feminist movement and the movement for sexual and reproductive rights as destructive to society.[109] Carlson teamed up with Russia-based scholars who shared his views to launch an international organization to fight against what they saw as the decline of civilization.[110] The first WCF conference was held in Prague, Czech Republic in 1997.[111] Since its founding, the WCF has stayed true to its mission as an international organization.[112] Its Board members have included

---

104 Rachel Percelay, *Reuters Foundation Exposes an Anti-LGBTQ Hate Group Representing America at U.N. Women's Rights Event*, MEDIAMATTERS (Mar. 16, 2017), https://www.mediamatters.org/donald-trump/reuters-foundation-exposes-anti-lgbtq-hate-group-representing-america-un-womens-rights (last visited Nov 11, 2023).

105 *Extremist Files: World Congress of Families*, S. POVERTY L. CTR., https://www.splcenter.org/fighting-hate/extremist-files/group/world-congress-families (last visited Nov 11, 2023) *WCF Regional and Global Conferences*, INT'L ORG. FAM., https://www.profam.org/wcf-conferences-and-events/ (last visited Nov 11, 2023).

106 NAUREEN SHAMEEN, RIGHTS AT RISK: OBSERVATORY ON THE UNIVERSALITY OF RIGHTS-TRENDS REPORT 32 (2017).; *Extremist Files: World Congress of Families*, S. POVERTY L. CTR., https://www.splcenter.org/fighting-hate/extremist-files/group/world-congress-families (last visited Nov 11, 2023).

107 NAUREEN SHAMEEN, RIGHTS AT RISK: OBSERVATORY ON THE UNIVERSALITY OF RIGHTS-TRENDS REPORT 31 (2017).

108 *Extremist Files: World Congress of Families*, S. POVERTY L. CTR., https://www.splcenter.org/fighting-hate/extremist-files/group/world-congress-families (last visited Nov 11, 2023).

109 *Id.*

110 *Id.*

111 *Id.*

112 *See, e.g.*, NAUREEN SHAMEEN, RIGHTS AT RISK: OBSERVATORY ON THE UNIVERSALITY OF RIGHTS-TRENDS REPORT 31–33 (2017); *WCF Regional and Global Conferences*, INT'L ORG. FAM., https://www.profam.org/wcf-conferences-and-events/ (last visited Nov 11, 2023).

anti-LGBTQ and anti-reproductive rights activists from Spain, Russia, Mexico, and Italy.[113]

The effect of the international work of these groups is already being felt in the form of heightened support for extreme anti-LGBTQ and anti-reproductive rights policies in countries around the world.[114] For example, during the debate in Belize over a statute that criminalized homosexual conduct with ten years in prison, the Alliance Defending Freedom (ADF) provided support to local groups who wanted to keep the law on the books.[115] Though, despite ADF's effort, in 2016, the Belize Supreme Court struck down the law as unconstitutional.[116]

As seen, these efforts have not remained confined to the domestic sphere; instead, they have extended beyond national borders. Steve Bannon—a key player in President Trump's 2016 presidential campaign—once said that the right-wing populist movement "has a certain global aspect to it."[117] The same can be said for the anti-LGBTQ and anti-reproductive rights movements behind the expansion of religious freedom in the legal and political arena.[118] Over the past several decades, right-wing and conservative religious groups have increasingly organized and networked across borders while targeting international human rights bodies, such as the United Nations, or the Organization of American States.[119] In doing so, these groups have participated in the very international systems that they often vilify and denounce, while forging unlikely political alliances between far-right religious groups.[120]

---

113 *Id.* at 32.

114 *See, e.g.*, *Dangerous Liaisons*, S. POVERTY L. CTR. (July 10, 2013), https://www.splcenter.org/20130709/dangerous-liaisons (last visited Nov 11, 2023); *Strange Bedfellows*, THE ECONOMIST (May 4, 2013), https://www.economist.com/international/2013/05/04/strange-bedfellows/ (last visited Nov 11, 2023).

115 *Dangerous Liaisons*, S. POVERTY L. CTR. (July 10, 2013), https://www.splcenter.org/20130709/dangerous-liaisons (last visited Nov 11, 2023).

116 Michael K. Lavers, *Belize's top court strikes down sodomy law*, WASH. BLADE (Aug. 10, 2016), https://www.washingtonblade.com/2016/08/10/belizes-top-court-strikes-sodomy-law/ (last visited Nov 11, 2023).

117 Ishaan Tharoor, *Trump's Victory Places U.S. at the Front of a Global Rightwing Surge*, WASH. POST (Nov. 10, 2016), https://www.washingtonpost.com/news/worldviews/wp/2016/11/09/trumps-victory-places-u-s-at-the-front-of-a-global-right-wing-surge/ (last visited Nov 11, 2023).

118 *See, e.g.*, NAUREEN SHAMEEN, RIGHTS AT RISK: OBSERVATORY ON THE UNIVERSALITY OF RIGHTS-TRENDS REPORT 16 (2017).

119 *See id.* at 16, 47; Press Release, Organization of American States Press Department, The Vatican Opens Office Dedicated Exclusively to OAS Affairs (Sept. 16, 2019), https://www.oas.org/en/media_center/photonews.asp?sCodigo=FNE-97478 (last visited Nov 11, 2023).

120 *See, e.g.*, Scott Long, *Anatomy of a Backlash: Sexuality and the "Cultural War" on Human Rights*, HUM. RTS. WATCH at 13, https://www.hrw.org/legacy/wr2k5/anatomy/anatomy

The transnational deployment of these strategies led by American conservative, anti-LGBTQ and anti-reproductive rights groups are not limited to Latin America.[121] In Africa and Eastern Europe, American right-wing religious leaders have contributed to anti-LGBTQ and anti-reproductive rights causes by going on media tours and meeting with politicians.[122] Religious groups have also provided direct financial aid to these causes.[123] One report found that U.S.-based religious groups have donated as much as $51 million dollars toward anti-LGBTQ and anti-abortion efforts in Europe alone.[124]

Right-wing populism has led to a widespread disrespect for human rights, resulting from the belief that human rights provide external constraints on government rule. Where human rights are seen as only protecting "the other," human rights are perceived as an obstacle.[125] Right-wing populists have rejected human rights standards as dispensable, unnecessary to protect individuals, and an impediment to nationalist ambitions.[126] Arguing that human rights only protect minorities while serving no purpose to the presumed majority has allowed right-wing populists to portray human rights as an obstacle to their goals of protecting the people.

More recently, in the United States, the establishment of a Commission on Unalienable Rights during President Trump's administration provided an illustrative example of efforts to engage in a process of assertive multiculturalism. The Commission, established on July 8, 2019, sought to "provide the Secretary of State advice and recommendations concerning international human rights matters … [and] provide fresh thinking about human rights discourse where such discourse has departed from our nation's founding principles of natural law and natural rights."[127] Moreover, President Trump's historic participation

.pdf (last visited Nov 11, 2023); NAUREEN SHAMEEN, RIGHTS AT RISK: OBSERVATORY ON THE UNIVERSALITY OF RIGHTS-TRENDS REPORT 16, 22 (2017).

121 *Strange Bedfellows*, THE ECONOMIST (May 4, 2013), https://www.economist.com/international/2013/05/04/strange-bedfellows/ (last visited Nov 11, 2023).

122 *Id.*

123 Sofia Lotto Persio, *US Christian groups 'donated millions to anti-LGBT causes in Europe'*, PINKNEWS (Mar. 28, 2019), https://www.pinknews.co.uk/2019/03/28/us-christian-groups-anti-lgbt-europe/ (last visited Nov 11, 2023).

124 *Id.*

125 Philip Alston, *The Populist Challenge to Human Rights*, 9 J. Hum. Rts. Prac. 1, 1–15 (2017).

126 Kenneth Roth, *World Report: The Dangerous Rise of Populism: Global Attacks on Human Rights Values*, HUM. RTS. WATCH (2017), https://www.hrw.org/world-report/2017/country-chapters/dangerous-rise-of-populism (last visited Nov 11, 2023). *See also* Alison Brysk, *Speaking Rights to Power*, AM. POL. SCI. ASS'N, 1008–10 (2017).

127 *Secretary of State Establishes Commission on Unalienable Rights*, 113 AM. J. INT'L L. 842, 842–44 (2019). *Compare* Jayne Huckerby, Sarah Knuckey & Meg Satterthwaite, *Trump's*

in the March for Life (he was the first and only U.S. President in history to attend it) and speech, where he noted that "the far-left is actively working to erase our God-given rights" and stating that he was "fighting" against them and that "[he] will win because [he] knows how to win" constitutes yet another example of an instance of assertive multiculturalism and shows how religious movements and politics interact in their efforts to return to an imagined past.[128]

3 Conservative Religious Movements and the Future of Liberal Democracies

Conservative religious movements' melancholic longing to return to an otherwise unrecoverable past can well bring risks and abuses reminiscent of the period that brought about a new world order after World War II.

The latest developments in the matter call into question the potential abuses that the expansion in the uses and understandings of freedom of religion or conscience can bring. As noted by Michael Kessler, "[t]he future instances where citizens may make demands for exemptions are not yet fully imaginable."[129] This may include the expansion of a right to conscience to new dimensions, partly distorting and denaturalizing the idea of freedom of religion and conscience itself.

"Unalienable Rights" Commission Likely to Promote Anti-Rights Agenda, JUST SEC. (July 9, 2019), https://www.justsecurity.org/64859/trumps-unalienable-rights-commission-likely-to-promote-anti-rights-agenda/ (last visited Nov 11, 2023), *with* Daniel Oliver, *The Right Way to Talk About Rights*, FIRST THINGS (Nov. 5, 2019), https://www.firstthings.com/web-exclusives/2019/11/the-right-way-to-talk-about-rights (last visited Nov 11, 2023).

128 President Donald Trump, *Remarks by President Trump at the 47th Annual March for Life*, THE WHITE HOUSE (Jan. 24, 2020), https://trumpwhitehouse.archives.gov/briefings-statements/remarks-president-trump-47th-annual-march-life/ (last visited Nov 11, 2023). Former President Trump's narrative is, arguably, the clearest example of this intention to return to an "imagined past." President Trump predicated a nationalistic narrative under the "Make America Great Again" slogan, which signified a growing desire for restoration of the national identity and values. Christian Evangelical organizations used the narrative as a platform to promote their own "Make America Christian Again" narrative and constructed national values to include the preservation of family values and religious freedom. *See* Frances Fitzgerald, *Why Evangelicals Support Donald Trump*, N.Y. TIMES (Oct. 7, 2019), https://www.nytimes.com/2019/10/07/books/review/who-is-an-evangelical-thomas-s-kidd.html (last visited Nov 11, 2023).

129 Michael Kessler, *Conflicted Ideas of Conscience*, BERKLEY CTR. (Apr. 29, 2016), https://berkleycenter.georgetown.edu/responses/conflicted-ideas-of-conscience (last visited Nov 11, 2023).

This expansion beyond the confines of conventional understandings of freedom of religion, conscience and other belief systems raises many concerns. When used as part of a religious lawfare strategy to counter advancements in the recognition of rights, these efforts bring about legitimacy concerns as the social consequences they have are less beneficial than those decisions adopted through legislative processes. In such contexts, resorting to freedom of religion, conscience or belief may be considered an illegitimate intervention over democratic decisions. In other words, it constitutes a form of veto that conservative religious actors use over decisions taken by democratically legitimized bodies.

Waging religious lawfare through the exercise of conscience-based claims has become a strategy of conservative religious groups to oppose or counteract advances that are contrary to their ideal of morality. This expansion raises questions as to the primary goal of conscience-based claims, their role in liberal democracies, and whom they intend to protect. Initially considered a shield for the protection of minorities, a new generation of conscience-based claims threatens the very foundations of democracy.

4 Conclusion

This introductory chapter conducted a comprehensive exploration of the intricate interplay between conservative religious movements and right-wing populism, as a reflection of a process assertive multiculturalism that manifest through religious lawfare. This multifaceted relationship represents a complex tapestry woven from social, political, and ideological threads that stretch across the global landscape. Understanding this intricate web and tracing the contours of this phenomenon is essential to shed light on its profound implications for the future of liberal democracies worldwide.

The book's journey began with an examination of the resurgence of right-wing populism, a powerful political force that has swept through numerous regions, challenging established norms and reshaping the political landscape. In Europe, and the Americas, right-wing populist leaders have leveraged social discontent and economic anxiety to mobilize support, often employing divisive rhetoric and identity politics to distinguish between "the people" and "the others." This populism has increasingly invoked religion as a key element of its discourse, not necessarily to champion religious values themselves, but to further this dichotomy and creating an enemy that must be defeated.

The emergence of conservative religious movements alongside right-wing populist leaders can be seen as a reaction to increasing secularization and the advancement of liberal policies.[130] The active involvement of Christian Evangelical and Roman Catholic churches in politics has given rise to a political far-right staunchly opposed to the alteration of the patriarchal order, advocating for their interpretation of the family concept, challenging gender ideology, and opposing the recognition of sexual and reproductive rights.

The culmination of these trends and developments raises critical questions about the future of liberal democracies and the role of conservative religious movements within them. It becomes essential to consider the potential risks and abuses that may arise as freedom of religion, conscience, and belief systems expand beyond conventional boundaries. The expansion beyond traditional interpretations of these freedoms poses several concerns.

First and foremost, when these expanded freedoms are employed to counter advances in the recognition of rights, they raise legitimacy concerns. The social consequences of such efforts may be perceived as less beneficial than decisions made through democratic processes, rendering the use of freedom of religion, conscience, or belief as an illegitimate intervention in democratic decisions. In essence, they can be seen as a form of veto wielded by conservative religious actors over decisions that have been validated through democratic means.

Furthermore, the consequences of expanding freedom of religion, conscience, and belief systems extend beyond our current understanding. The framing of this expansion can have far-reaching implications for the coherence and consistency of legal systems as a whole. This raises fundamental questions about the primary objectives of conscience-based claims, their role within liberal democracies, and the specific interests they aim to protect.

Initially, the concept of freedom of conscience was conceived as a shield to protect the rights of minorities, especially those who held beliefs or practices at odds with the majority. However, the evolution of conscience-based claims, particularly in the hands of conservative religious groups, has given rise to a

130 Some scholars have challenged secularism's claim of neutrality and argued that it should be considered a paganistic faith aimed at marginalizing "true" religion. *See e.g.*, Adrian Vermeule, *Liturgy of liberalism*, First Things (Jan. 1, 2017); Russell R. Reno, Resurrecting The Idea of a Christian Society (2016); Rex Ahdar, *Is Secularism Neutral?* 26 Ratio Juris 404 (2013); Steven D. Smith, Pagans and Christians in the City: Culture Wars from the Tiber to the Potomac (2018). *See generally*, Talal Asad, Formations of the Secular: Christianity, Islam, Modernity (2003) *and* David Kennedy, *Losing Faith in the Secular: Law, Religion, and the Culture of International Governance*, *in* Religion and International Law 309–319 (Mark W. Janis and Carolyn Evans eds., 2004). *But see*, Richard Schragger & Micah Schwartzman, *Religious Antiliberalism and the First Amendment*, 104 Minn. L. Rev. 1341, (2019) (aptly examining critiques on secularism).

new generation of claims that pose a direct challenge to the foundations of democracy itself.

In conclusion, this chapter introduced and illuminated a complex and evolving nexus of conservative religious movements, right-wing populism, and assertive multiculturalism through religious lawfare. The emergence of religious lawfare, fueled by conscience-based claims, threatens to reshape the landscape of human rights and democracy itself, raising profound questions about the balance between individual freedoms, societal progress, and the preservation of democratic values.

CHAPTER 2

Waging Religious Lawfare through Conscience-Based Claims

Conservative religious groups have increasingly appealed to freedom of religion, conscience, or belief, a constitutionally enshrined right in most legal frameworks, and particularly to conscience-based claims, as a way to respond to a rising tide of secularism. These groups have come to use conscience-based claims as tools to reclaim power and break the "wall of separation" between Church and State. In that way, they have managed to expand the uses of conscience-based claims to exclude and hinder enjoyment of legally protected rights that they consider to be irreligious, immoral, or wrong.

1 Religious Lawfare and Conscience-Based Claims

The rise of conservative religious groups alongside right-wing populism brought about an increasing reliance on legal claims founded on freedom of religion, conscience, or beliefs as a way to reclaim power. This phenomenon, that I call "religious lawfare," involves the use of legal and political strategies to promote a particular religious perspective or agenda.

One of the most pervasive and stealthiest religious lawfare strategies has been the resistance to laws through the appeal to conscience-based claims. For over a century, conscience-based claims had been used as a shield to protect minority views on questions of conscience from oppression by majorities—perhaps most famously, allowing individual exemptions to mandatory military service on religious grounds. However, conservative religious individuals and institutions have begun to use these claims not so much to protect minorities from attacks by civil authority, but rather as a mechanism to hinder the exercise of legally protected civil rights by co-citizens.[1] For example,

1 Although the expansion of conscience-based claims skews along denominational lines on reproductive health and gender issues, the overlap is far from exact. *See* Fiona Bloomer, et al., *Abortion discourses: religion, culture, nation, in* REIMAGINING GLOBAL ABORTION POLITICS: A SOCIAL JUSTICE PERSPECTIVE (2018); Fred Van Geest, *Changing Patterns of Denominational Political Activity in North America: The Case of Homosexuality*, 49 REV. REL. RSCH. 199, 199–221 (2007); Michele Dillon, *Asynchrony in Attitudes Toward Abortion and Gay Rights: The Challenge to Values Alignment*, 53 J. FOR SCI. STUDY REL. 1, 1–16 (2014); David Masci,

 | DOI:10.1163/9789004685406_004

conscience-based claims are now being extended to grant hospitals and health practitioners unrestricted exemptions from any duty to provide abortion services and care, rendering attempts to exercise an individual's right to get a legal abortion futile. These claims have similarly been extended to pharmacies and pharmacists refusing to fill prescriptions for birth control, rendering a right to contraception a nullity. This use of conscientious objection as a counter-majoritarian and anti-democratic tool to refuse the exercise of civil rights has been met with acceptance by legal systems around the world. When these legal challenges are successful, laws or policies recognizing the rights that

---

American religious groups vary widely in their view of abortion, PEW RSCH. CTR. (Jan. 22, 2018), https://www.pewresearch.org/fact-tank/2018/01/22/american-religious-groups-vary-widely-in-their-views-of-abortion/ (last visited Nov 11, 2023). *See generally* Robert Booth, *Conservative Christians are becoming more confident in the political arena*, THE GUARDIAN (Apr. 12, 2012), https://www.theguardian.com/world/2012/apr/12/conservative-christians-confident-political-arena (last visited Nov 11 2023); Ed Kilgore, *What's Worse Than Politics Without Religion? Politicized Religion*, NEW YORK MAG. (Apr. 4, 2021), https://nymag.com/intelligencer/2021/04/politicized-religion-is-worse-than-politics-without-religion.html (last visited Nov 11, 2023); Shadi Hamid, *America Without God*, THE ATLANTIC (Mar. 10, 2021), https://www.theatlantic.com/magazine/archive/2021/04/america-politics-religion/618072/ (last visited Nov 11, 2023); Tim Alberta, *How Politics Poisoned the Evangelical Church*, THE ATLANTIC (May 10, 2022), https://www.theatlantic.com/magazine/archive/2022/06/evangelical-church-pastors-political-radicalization/629631/ (last visited Nov. 11, 2023); David E. Campbell, *The Perils of Politicized Religion*, 149 DÆDALUS, J. AM. ACAD. ARTS & SCI. 87, 87–104 (2020); James Risen, *How America's Evangelicals Turned Themselves Into an Anti-Abortion Machine*, THE INTERCEPT (May 12, 2022), https://theintercept.com/2022/05/12/abortion-roe-v-wade-francis-schaeffer-evangelical-christians/ (last visited Nov 11, 2023). Relatedly, many denominations have become venues for some of the most intense debates over sexual and reproductive issues. Even within a specific denomination, the majority and minority positions may switch, and adherents may eventually take a position opposite to that of the official church position. *See* MARCIA PALLY, THE NEW EVANGELICALS: EXPANDING THE VISION OF THE COMMON GOOD (2011); DAVID KINNAMAN & GABE LYONS, UNCHRISTIAN: WHAT A NEW GENERATION REALLY THINKS ABOUT CHRISTIANITY … AND WHY IT MATTERS (2012); *see also* Thomas B. Edsall, *Abortion Has Never Been Just About Abortion*, N.Y. TIMES (Sept. 15, 2021), https://www.nytimes.com/2021/09/15/opinion/abortion-evangelicals-conservatives.html (last visited Nov 11, 2023); Zack Stanton, *You Need to Take the Religious Left Seriously This Time*, POLITICO (Feb. 25, 2021), https://www.politico.com/news/magazine/2021/02/25/religious-left-politics-liberal-471640 (last visited Nov 11, 2023); Julianne McShane, *Some religions support abortion rights. Their leaders are speaking up.*, NBC NEWS (May 5, 2022), https://www.nbcnews.com/news/us-news/religions-support-abortion-rights-leaders-are-speaking-rcna27194 (last visited Nov 11, 2023). *But see* Yossi Nehushtan & Stella Coyle, *The Difference Between Illegitimate Conscience and Misguided Conscience: Equality Laws, Abortion Laws and Religious Symbols*, *in* RELIGIOUS BELIEFS AND CONSCIENTIOUS EXEMPTIONS IN A LIBERAL STATE (John Adenitire ed., 2019); YOSSI NEHUSHTAN, INTOLERANT RELIGION IN A TOLERANT-LIBERAL DEMOCRACY (2015) (arguing that religion is outright inherently, uniquely, and unjustly intolerant).

these religious groups consider contrary to their beliefs—such as the right to abortion or LGBTQ rights—are stripped of impact.[2]

2 The Juridification of Conscience

Conscientious objection is the right not to perform an act, provide a service, or participate in a certain action because of a personal belief that the action is morally wrong.[3] A right to conscientious objection is the right not to be forced to fulfill legal duties through actions that contradict a person's deepest convictions. Unlike other forms of public disputation, an act of conscientious objection, at least traditionally, has been understood to be an intimate and private course of action. The objector does not publicly question the norm, he or she only claims to be exempted from it.

Traditionally, conscience-based claims have operated in contexts in which the objector does not necessarily harm other people by his or her refusal to fulfill legal duties, such as serving in the army or by displaying reverence for national symbols.

The first and most obvious duty of the inhabitants of a State is to comply with its constitutional and legal norms, respect its legitimate authorities, and obey its mandates and provisions. So, what happens when a person invokes his or her constitutionally recognized freedom of religion, conscience, or belief to refuse to fulfill a legal duty to which he or she is called by the State's law, or even by the Constitution itself, to observe? How should the conflict thus raised

---

2 Studies across various countries have shown healthcare professionals' perspectives highlighting religion as a significant factor in objecting. *See e.g.*, Rafael Toro-Flores, et al., *Opinions of nurses regarding conscientious objection*, 26 NURSING ETHICS 4, 1027–1038 (2019) (on Spain); Ryan Lawrence & Farr Curlin, *Clash of definitions: Controversies about conscience in medicine*, 7 AM. J. BIOETH. 12, 10–14 (2007) (on the U.S.); Lauren Fink, et al., *"The fetus is my patient, too": Attitudes toward abortion and referral among physician conscientious objectors in Bogota, Colombia*, 42 INT'L PERSPECTIVES ON SEXUAL AND REPRODUCTIVE HEALTH 2, 71–80 (2016) (on Colombia); Sven Nordstrand, et al., *Medical students' attitudes towards conscientious objection: A survey*, 40 J. MED. ETHICS, 9, 609–612 (2014) (on Norway); *and* Emily Freeman & Ernestina Coast, *Conscientious objection to abortion: Zambian healthcare practitioners' beliefs and practices*, 221 SOC. SCI. MED., 106–114 (2019) (on Zambia). *See generally*, Omar Ismail Darzé & Júnior Ubirajara Barroso, *Prevalence, attitudes, and factors motivating conscientious objection toward reproductive health among medical students*, 40 REV. BRAS. GINECOL. OBSTET. 10, 599–605 (2018).

3 Nancy Berlinger, *Conscience Clauses, Health Care Providers, and Parents*, *in* FROM BIRTH TO DEATH AND BENCH TO CLINIC: THE HASTINGS CENTER BIOETHICS BRIEFING BOOK FOR JOURNALISTS, POLICYMAKERS, AND CAMPAIGNS, 35–40 (Mary Crowley ed., 2008).

be resolved in a liberal-democratic state? Legal systems demand and aspire to the obedience of the rules by all people under their respective jurisdictions. In that sense, the conscientious objector status is an exceptional legal figure.[4] It is the "curious case where the State allows a person to exempt himself/herself from a legal obligation, due to his or her moral convictions."[5]

The expansive exercise of conscience-based claims examined in this book, unlike its traditional counterpart, collides not only with the rules of the legal order but also with rights and duties of third parties. Oftentimes, in cases where the public power has not transgressed the limits of its competence or ignored fundamental rights but rather legitimately imposed an obligation of obedience to promote the general welfare, it collides with democratic values and principles. The question of conscience-based claims is thus linked to the necessary and fundamental balance that must exist between freedom and power, or, in other words, between autonomy and authority, in any democratic society.

As conscience-based claims are typically raised against constitutionally valid legal mandates, it may initially appear that there should never be a right to engage in them at all. That an objection is "conscientious" does not obviously make the claim for an exemption based on it worthier of state protection than any other form of objection. Of course, the law to which the objection is lodged may infringe on fundamental rights, and when it does, the objection may be not only legitimate but constitutionally protected. But in other contexts, and indeed in most, a conscientious objector's permitted resistance to a legal mandate is simply a clear exception to the general duty to comply with rules. The objector is in a small group of people that need not comply with the otherwise general duty to obey democratically and constitutionally valid mandates.

Despite the seemingly antidemocratic nature of conscience-based claims—and hence the need to keep them cabined and restricted to only a narrow set of conflicts between public obligation and private conscience—the use of conscience-based claims in recent years has expanded significantly, putting at risk the very foundations of democracy. This chapter traces the history of conscientious objection from its roots in classical political thought to its recognition

4 Andrés Constantin & Sonia Ariza Navarrete, *Objeción de conciencia*, *in* ABORTO EN AMÉRICA LATINA: ABOGACÍA, TRABAJO EN RED Y ESTÁNDARES DE PROTECCIÓN 26–50 (Viviana Bohórquez Monsalve ed., 2021).

5 Sonia Ariza Navarrete & Agustina Ramón Michel, *Usos imprevistos y respuestas a la objeción de conciencia en el aborto legal*, 10 SERIE DOCUMENTOS REDAAS (2019).

in international law, highlighting its present incarnation as a tipping point in efforts to protect the rights of minoritarian groups and interests.

2.1 *History and Origins*

In the 8th century BC, the Greeks considered the law to reflect justice, and justice to be a mirror of the order that reigned in the cosmos. They considered justice as the foundation of a dignified human life. We can find this understanding of the law as a foundational principle in classical works, such as Homer's *Odyssey* and *Iliad*, and Virgil's *Aeneid*.[6] In his treatises *Politics* and *Nicomachean Ethics*, Aristotle articulated the value of the law for the people of his time and for the organization of the *polis*.[7] Law was considered to be the very foundation from which happiness emanated and a crucial element for the harmonic survival of the Greeks. It was impossible to consider that law could be unfair. It should be followed blindly, without further ado.

This ingrained thought is illustrated by the words of Socrates' disciple, Plato. Socrates is sentenced to death, accused of instigating the gods and corrupting the young. In Plato's *Apology*, he narrates a dialogue between Crito and Socrates while in prison. In the dialogue, Crito tries to convince Socrates to flee the country to save his own life. Socrates warns Crito that committing such an injustice—fleeing—is one of the worst things a person can do to himself as it corrupts one's soul. Socrates explains that "one must neither repay an injustice nor cause harm to any man no matter what one suffers because of him" (48d).[8] This thought is also illustrated in *Gorgias*, where Socrates concludes that it is better to suffer an injustice than commit one (473a–475e).[9]

There is only one exception—in the classical era—to this articulation of an absolute obedience to the law, and it can be found in Sophocles' tragedy, *Antigone*.[10] It happens within the framework of the ancient city of Thebes in which the conflict between the authority of the State, represented by the orders of the tyrant Creon, collides with the conscience of Antigone, who refuses to obey the unjust disposition. Antigone, violating the edict of burying his brother, responds to Creon: "… For me it was not Zeus who made that order.

6 *See* HOMER, THE ILIAD (Richmond Lattimore trans., 1951); HOMER, THE ODYSSEY (Robert Fitzgerald trans., 1990); VIRGIL, THE AENEID (Robert Fitzgerald trans., 1983).

7 ARISTOTLE, NICOMACHEAN ETHICS (Ingram Bywater ed., 1894); ARISTOTLE, POLITICS (Benjamin Jowett trans., 1905). *See also*, PLATO, THE REPUBLIC (Benjamin Jowett trans., 1943).

8 *See* PLATO, FIVE DIALOGUES: EUTHYPHRO, APOLOGY, CRITO, MENO, PHAEDO (John M. Cooper ed., George M. A. Grube trans., 2002).

9 *See* PLATO, GORGIAS (Donald J. Zeyl trans., 1987).

10 SOPHOCLES, ANTIGONE (Elizabet Wyckoff trans., 1954).

Nor did that Justice who lives with the gods below mark out such laws to hold among mankind. Nor did I think your orders were so strong that you, a mortal man, could over-run the gods' unwritten and unfailing laws. Not now, nor yesterday's, they always live, and no one knows their origin in time."[11] These are the first lines written in favor of a defense of intimate thought against a decree, in this case comparably carrying the force of law, arguing based on moral grounds to resist coercive authority.

Conflicts between adherence to the law on one hand and the need to be exempted from norms conflicting with an individual's conscience, next appeared in the early 5th century AD in *The City of God* by St. Augustine. Augustine of Hippo gave a duality to human action and described the course of history as the struggle between two cities, the *civitas caelestis* animated by the love of God and the *civitas terrena* determined by man.[12]

In its origins in both Greek thought and the Catholic natural law tradition, conflicts between conscience and law were thought of as a mechanism to protect the personal beliefs of the individual against oppression by the majority.[13] They were thought of as a "shield" against majoritarian will, as embodied by state authority. Importantly, in this classical tradition it was never understood as an absolute right, but one that should be balanced with other people's rights. Conscience-based claims, in the writings of the classical philosophers from the Greeks through St. Augustine were not meant to be used as mechanisms to impose conceptions of truth or of correctness on others.[14] This position was fully consistent with that of the Catholic Church, including its contemporary expounders. In 1991, Pope John Paul II observed that: "freedom of conscience

---

11 *Id.* at 15–16.

12 SANCTI AURELII AUGUSTINI DE CIVITATE DEI (Bernhard Dombart & Alfons Kalb eds., 1955). *See also* SAINT AUGUSTINE OF HIPPO, CITY OF GOD (CONCERNING THE CITY OF GOD AGAINST THE PAGANS) (Henry Bettenson trans., 1980); GERARD J. P. O'DALY, AUGUSTINE'S CITY OF GOD: A READER'S GUIDE (1999); AUGUSTINE'S CITY OF GOD: A CRITICAL GUIDE (James Wetzel ed., 2013).

13 *See* Martin Scheinin, *Freedom of Thought, Conscience and Religion*, 54 STUDIA THEOLOGICA—NORDIC J. THEOLOGY 5, 5–18 (2000); Matthew Chandler, *Moral Mandate or Personal Preference? Possible Avenues for Accommodation of Civil Servants Morally Opposed to Facilitating Same-Sex Marriage*, 2011 BYU L. REV. 1625, 1625–58 (2011); Claire Marblestone, *A Matter of Conscience:* United States v. Seeger *and the Supreme Court's Historical Failure to Define Conscientious Objector Status Under the First Amendment*, 38 HASTINGS CONST. L. Q. 201, 201–31 (2010); Patrick Parkinson, *Accommodating religious belief in a secular age: the issue of conscientious objection in the workplace*, 34 U. NEW SOUTH WALES L. J. 281, 281–99 (2011).

14 John Paul II, *"If you Want Peace, Respect the Conscience of Every Person,"* (Address by John Paul II at the Vatican in 1991 for the 24th World Day of Peace), ¶ 4.

does not confer a right to indiscriminate recourse to conscientious objection. When an asserted freedom turns into a license or excuse for limiting the rights of others, the State is obliged to protect, also by legal means, the inalienable rights of its citizens against such abuses."[15]

It was precisely this understanding of conscience-based claims as a shield against majoritarian will and oppression that motivated Dr. Martin Luther King Jr. to write his famous *Letter from Birmingham Jail*, where he espoused why he felt compelled to resist racial segregation using his conscience as a shield against wrong and unjust laws. Similar ideas were in the mind of Leo Tolstoy when he documented the lives of imprisoned conscientious objectors who refused to serve in the army,[16] or in Mahatma Gandhi's resistance against British rule in India.[17] Particularly, the idea that suffering that was voluntarily taken, through the exercise of conscientious objection as a shield from majoritarian will or as a way to express views against majority opinion, was laudable and a good way of combating evil.

In contrast to this romanticized view of conscience, there are scholars who argue that it is precisely King's ideas that justify the use of conscience as a sword, as a "catalyst for the struggle against injustice, […] especially injustices inflicted by or against our neighbors […] even one[s] in which we are not actively complicit."[18] Despite these scholars' efforts to depict conscience-based claims as tools to "combat" injustices perpetrated in the wider community, their interpretations and understandings of King's ideas are misleading. A closer look into the *Letter from Birmingham Jail* shows that far from arguing in favor of a violent and coercive resistance as a tool to challenge unjust laws and impose his idea on others, King advocated nonviolence to encourage dialogue and deliberation. A nonviolent resistance—a shield—that intends to "create such a crisis and establish such creative tension that … the issue can no longer be ignored."[19] As such, it is difficult to think how his ideas could be used to justify the use of conscience-based claims that we witness these days, where what is intended is to arbitrarily coerce others in order to impose a different worldview.

---

15 *Id.* ¶ 24.

16 Peter Brock, *'A Light Shining in Darkness': Tolstoi and the Imprisonment of Conscientious Objectors in Imperial Russia*, 81 SLAVONIC & EAST EUR. REV. 683, 683–97 (2003).

17 *See* RAGHAVAN IYER, THE MORAL AND POLITICAL THOUGHT OF MAHATMA GANDHI 120 (citing MAHATMA GANDHI, YOUNG INDIA (1919)).

18 *See* David Thunder, *Conscience-Based Exemptions Against Injustice*, *in* ALEKSANDER STĘPKOWKI, CONTEMPORARY CHALLENGES TO CONSCIENCE: LEGAL AND ETHICAL FRAMEWORKS FOR PROFESSIONAL CONDUCT 44 (2019).

19 MARTIN LUTHER KING, JR., LETTER FROM THE BIRMINGHAM JAIL (1994).

Therefore, in part due to deliberate misinterpretations and misconceptions around the origins of conscientious objection, this romanticized account of it as a safeguard from oppression and tyranny—as deriving positive value—has lost ground in recent years to make room for new understandings of conscience-based claims that deviate substantially from its original idea and ultimately harm democracy.

2.2 *Conscientious Objection as a Legal Right*

The conceptualization of conscientious objection as a legal right can be found foremost from the recognition of a right to freedom of religion, conscience or belief enshrined in the Universal Declaration of Human Rights (UDHR).[20] From this right enumerated in the non-binding U.N. General Assembly resolution comes the more specific form laid out in the International Covenant on Civil and Political Rights (ICCPR).

The non-binding UDHR, in Article 18, enumerated the right to freedom of religion or belief and the accompanying right to manifest such conscience.[21] It is also Article 18 of the ICCPR that provides individuals with the right to freedom of religion or conscience, stating: "Everyone shall have the right to freedom of thought, conscience and religion. This right shall include freedom to have or to adopt a religion or belief of his choice, and freedom, either individually or in community with others and in public or private, to manifest his religion or belief in worship, observance, practice and teaching."[22] However, as a legal right, it is subject to limits: while the freedom of an individual's religion or thought cannot be limited in any way by the State,[23] manifestation of such belief may be.[24] Specifically, the manifestation of one's belief may not interfere with the rights of other individuals to exercise their rights and freedoms.[25]

The U.N. Special Rapporteur on freedom of religion or belief elaborated on the right enumerated in Article 18, parsing out a fundamental distinction.[26] The right of freedom of conscience is divided in Article 18 into a *forum internum*

20 G.A. Res. 217 (III) A, Universal Declaration of Human Rights (UDHR) (Dec. 10, 1948).

21 *See id.*

22 International Covenant on Civil and Political Rights (ICCPR), art. 18, ¶ 1 (Dec. 16, 1966).

23 *See* U.N. Human Rights Committee, *CCPR General Comment No. 22*, ¶ 3, CCPR/C/21/Rev.1/Add.4 (July 30, 1993).

24 *See id.* ¶ 8.

25 *See* Pasquale Annicchino, *The Geopolitics of Transnational Law and Religion*, *in* THE CONSCIENCE WARS: RETHINKING THE BALANCE BETWEEN RELIGION, IDENTITY, AND EQUALITY 258, 264 (Susana Mancini & Michel Rosenfeld eds., 2018).

26 *See* Heiner Beilefeldt, *Report of the Special Rapporteur on Freedom of Religion or Belief* (*SR on Freedom of Religion*), ¶ 7, U.N. Doc. A/HRC/31/18 (Dec. 23, 2015).

and a *forum externum*, the former being inviolable while the latter is subject to specific limitations under certain circumstances subject to strict scrutiny.[27] The internal manifestation, or *forum internum*, of one's belief or conscience is fundamental to the individual's sense of self,[28] and may not be "subject to coercion which would impair [one's] freedom to have or adopt a religion or belief of [one's] choice."[29] In comparison, the external manifestation of one's religion or belief of choice is subject to, under Article 18, certain limited restrictions. The exact dimensions of the *forum externum* are not clear but should be interpreted broadly and on a "continuum" reflecting its interrelatedness with *forum internum*.[30]

The moral justification for a legal right to conscientious objection—the "refusal to perform a legal role or responsibility because of personal beliefs"—has been debated within human rights discourse since these first elucidations.[31] The contentious nature of conscientious objection partially stems from an unavoidable balancing inherent in its application: the exercise of conscientious objection necessarily involves prioritizing an individual's right to manifest conscience, thought, and religion against other legal rights, that may themselves be fundamental.[32] For many years, much of the debate concerned whether conscientious objection, and its exercise, was a human right in and of itself. While some scholars asserted that this "right" lacked legal pedigree, others argued that its status as a human right is unequivocal.[33] Notably, the United Nations concurs with the former view: it has contended that the exercise of conscientious objection is not a "right *per se*," as it is not "direct[ly] reference[d]" in the U.N. international instruments.[34] Rather, it is ordinarily categorized as a "derivative right," developed from an interpretation of the right to freedom of thought, conscience, and religion.[35]

---

27 *See id.*

28 *See id.* ¶ 20.

29 ICCPR, art. 18, ¶ 2.

30 Heiner Beilefeldt, *Report of the Special Rapporteur on Freedom of Religion or Belief* (*SR on Freedom of Religion*), ¶ 7, U.N. Doc. A/HRC/31/18 (Dec. 23, 2015), ¶¶ 21–22.

31 Hasan Shanawani, *The Challenges of Conscientious Objection in Health Care*, 55 J. REL. & HEALTH 384, 385 (2016).

32 *See* Luisa Cabal et al., *Striking a Balance: Conscientious Objection and Reproductive Health Care from the Colombian Perspective*, 16 HEALTH & HUM. RTS. J. 73, 74 (2014).

33 *See generally* Jeremy K. Kessler, *The Invention of a Human Right: Conscientious Objection at the United Nations, 1947–2011*, 44 COLUM. HUM. RTS. L. R. 753 (2013).

34 Office of the High Commissioner for Human Rights, *Conscientious Objection to Military Service*, at 7, U.N. Doc. HR/PUB/12/1 (2012), https://www.ohchr.org/Documents/Publications/ConscientiousObjection_en.pdf (last visited Nov 11, 2023).

35 *Id.*

Notwithstanding this classification, courts—domestic and international alike—have consistently characterized conscientious objection as a "right" that can be readily asserted in a variety of contexts. Its most conventional application has been in the context of compulsory military service. The U.N. Human Rights Committee (UNHRC) affirmed this utilization in General Comment No. 22; in defining conscientious objection as "a right to refuse to perform military service," the UNHRC noted that this "right of conscientious objection … can be derived from Article 18 [freedom of thought, conscience, and religion]."[36] In this vein, and in a nod to a metaphor first articulated by Professor Bernard Dickens, the act of conscientious objection in this context is akin to a shield: religious convictions serve as a safeguard from participation in certain activities—acts that are morally reprehensible to that individual.[37]

From originating documents, it becomes clear that, at the time of the UDHR and later the ICCPR negotiations, freedom of thought, conscience, and religion were considered absolute. However, there was a clear distinction made between the individual's internal conscience and the external expression of his or her conscience. While States agreed that an individual's inner thought or moral consciousness could not be legally restricted, the external manifestations of conscience were not granted such ironclad protection.[38] With the horrors of WWII still fresh in the collective conscience, freedom of thought, conscience, and religion appeared to prevent individuals from being coerced to abandon their religion or moral beliefs and met a desire to maintain religious diversity and harmony.[39]

One of the central debates during negotiations that led to the drafting of the UDHR and ICCPR surrounded whether to acknowledge a specific group of individuals as being conscientious objectors versus recognizing the lawfulness of conscientious objection as a concept. Many delegations expressed hesitation or explicit unwillingness to include specific details on what makes a conscientious objector. More broadly, countries, including Egypt, Chile, Uruguay

36 U.N. Human Rights Committee, *General Comment No. 22: Article 18 (Freedom of Thought, Conscience or Religion)*, ¶ 11, U.N. Doc. CCPR/C/21/Rev.1/Add.4, (July 30, 1993).

37 *See* Bernard M. Dickens, *Conscientious Objection: a Shield or a Sword?, in* FIRST DO NO HARM: LAW ETHICS, AND HEALTHCARE 337 (Sheila A.M. McClean ed., 2006).

38 *See* U.N. General Assembly, *Draft International Covenants on Human Rights (Annotation)*, U.N. Doc. A/2929 (July 1, 1955), ¶ 106.

39 Remarks from the Chairman Dr. Malik of Lebanon, wishing to "ensure a genuine respect for conscientious objectors" in countries where they were recognized "so that they would not be subjected to conditions comparable to those in concentration camps." *See* United Nations Economic and Social Council (Commission on Human Rights), U.N. Doc. E/CN.4/AC.1/SR.8 (June 20, 1947).

and Iran, thought that a mention of conscientious objectors should be entirely omitted from the ICCPR as there were countries that did not recognize this concept and thus, conscientious objection was not universally accepted or applied.

When the Philippine delegation proposed that specific language surrounding conscientious objection to military service be added to the ICCPR, they encountered significant opposition. Many delegations claimed that while they "appreciated the Philippine's sentiment" or "expressed sympathy with them," they saw the addition of a paragraph stating that "*Persons who conscientiously object to war as being contrary to their religion shall be exempt from the military service*" as beyond the article's purview. This paragraph felt either out of place, redundant, or too specific for many delegations.[40]

In general, and perhaps unsurprisingly, the development of a right to freedom of conscience was rooted in the need to protect marginalized groups or individuals from coercion of the State or from powerful and dominant religious or ideological groups. States had ambivalent attitudes toward conscientious objection and explicit protection for conscientious objectors was scant. The legal concept of a conscientious objector was relatively new and growing at the time of negotiations. Nevertheless, every time the protection of conscientious objectors was brought up, it was, once again, framed in terms of avoiding coercion and preserving dignity. At the time, conscientious objection was about protecting the objector from the coercive State, and not about enabling the objector to impart consequences on other people's lives because of his or her personal beliefs. There was a degree of nuance to protecting freedom of conscience, religion and thought—this right was not unbridled. While freedom to hold whatever beliefs people wish *internally* could not be limited, actions taken because of their beliefs were not necessarily protected.

2.3 *Juridifying Conscience*

In recent years, conservative religious groups have appealed to freedom of religion, conscience and belief, a constitutionally enshrined right in most legal frameworks, as a way to respond to a rising tide of secularism and reclaim power. This is occurring particularly in countries that are constitutionally bound not to be religious, or that take a neutral stance when religion is enshrined in their constitutions, or even in constitutional models that fall into what have been termed as "weak religious establishment," "formal separation with *de facto* pre-eminence of one denomination," or "separation alongside

40 *See* United Nations Economic and Social Council (Commission on Human Rights), U.N. Doc. E/CN.4/SR.161 (Apr. 28, 1950).

multicultural accommodation" models.[41] In these types of constitutional models, conservative religious groups have come to use conscience-based claims as tools to reclaim power and break the "wall of separation" between Church and State.[42] Often defining religion as their particular religion and disregarding other views, conservative religious movements have expanded the scope of conscience-based claims to exclude and hinder enjoyment of legally protected rights that they consider to be irreligious, immoral, or wrong.[43]

Some conservative religious groups have been able to capitalize on right-wing populist movements and have, with considerable success, recharacterized what would otherwise be straightforward religious dogma into secular arguments consistent with right-wing populist ideology.

One of the main ways in which these groups have done so is through the *juridification* of their actions.[44] These movements have begun to use and/or generate legal arguments—some of them based on international human rights law standards—to confront rights related to gender, sexuality and reproduction, among others.[45] In this sense, the opposition to the liberal agenda is channeled, with increasing intensity and success, through an appeal to a discourse of conscience rights. The intervention of rights of conscience now occurs in a range of legal institutions, including local and national legislatures, and in court proceedings in the United States and in other several countries.[46]

The process in which the law is used to entrench the status quo has long been examined.[47] However, the way in which conservative religious groups have resorted to the law as a means to perpetuate or reclaim their power over

41 Ran Hirschl, *Comparative Constitutional Law and Religion*, *in* Comparative Constitutional Law 422–40 (Tom Ginsburg & Rosalind Dixon eds., 2011).

42 Thomas Jefferson, *Letter to the Danbury Baptists*, Lib. Cong. (Jan. 1, 1802), https://www.loc.gov/loc/lcib/9806/danpre.html (last visited Nov 11, 2023).

43 *See* Bill Moyers, *9/11 and God's Sport*, 55 Cross Currents 442, 442–55 (2006). *See generally* Howard Lesnick, Religion in Legal Thought and Practice 105–41 (2010).

44 The term "juridification" here is used in the sense of a proliferation of law, an expansion of the rights discourse and the increasing appeal to law as a way to resolve conflicts in society. For more on the different dimensions of juridification, see Lars C. Blichner & Anders Molander, What is juridification? (2005).

45 Juan Marco Vaggione, *Sexualidad, derecho y religión: entramados en tensión*, *in* Sexo, delitos y pecados. Intersecciones entre religión, género, sexualidad y el derecho en América Latina (Macarena Sáez & José Manuel Morán Faúndes eds., 2016).

46 Clifford Bob, Rights as Weapons: Instruments of Conflict, Tools of Power 65–150 (2019).

47 *See, e.g.*, David Landau, *Abusive Constitutionalism*, 47 U.C. Davis L. Rev. 189, 189–260 (2013); Ozan O. Varol, *Stealth Authoritarianism*, 100 Iowa L. Rev. 1673, 1673–1742 (2015); Yvonne Tew, *Stealth Theocracy*, 58 Va. J. Int'l L. 31, 31–96 (2018).

democratic progress is still understudied. The closest account to this process of theocratization through the juridification of conscience is what Professor Yvonne Tew described as the process of "stealth theocracy." That is, the understanding that fundamental alterations of a constitution's religious or secular character often occur through informal and less transparent change by judicial and political actors.[48] According to Tew—examining the case of Malaysia—the process of stealth theocracy occurs through two mechanisms: (1) through "jurisdictional deference," understood as the civil courts' decline of jurisdiction in favor of religious Sharia courts; and (2) through judicially expansionist reinterpretations—in Malaysia the expansive reading of Article 3(1) resulting in the prioritization of Islamic norms in comparison to other constitutional norms.[49] Tew's account focuses on the role of courts in theocratizing secular societies.

By contrast, the process of theocratization through the juridification of conscience, which is part of the broader religious lawfare strategy, focuses on the role of conservative religious groups in stealthily exploiting the legal discourse and using constitutionally enshrined rights to reclaim authority. In particular, conservative religious groups have put their efforts, over the last couple of years, into expanding the scope of the understanding and uses of freedom of religion, conscience or belief through an appeal to rights discourse in cases of conscience-based claims.

As such, the process of theocratization has not been limited to countries where jurisdictional deference to a religious court is possible. It has also extended to countries with legal systems that do not establish religious courts or that do not endorse a particular religion in their constitutions. In those countries, conservative religious groups have played a key role in using legal discourse to expand conscience-based claims to obstruct lawful activities that are contrary to their beliefs where they have failed to frustrate laws adopted at a legislative level. In these cases, conservative religious groups have resorted to expansive interpretations of these claims at the judicial and political level. In most cases, they have benefited from a long-term strategy to infiltrate political spheres and strategically appoint judges in different courts.[50]

---

48 *See* Yvonne Tew, *Stealth Theocracy*, 58 VA. J. INT'L L. 31, 33 (2018).

49 *Id.* at 35.

50 The different ways in which religious conservative movements have infiltrated politics and the judiciary are examined later. For an overview of the various strategies these groups adopted, see STEVEN M. TELES, THE RISE OF THE CONSERVATIVE LEGAL MOVEMENT: THE BATTLE FOR CONTROL OF THE LAW (2008); WILLIAM C. MARTIN, WITH GOD ON OUR SIDE: THE RISE OF THE RELIGIOUS RIGHT IN AMERICA (2005); FRANCIS FITZGERALD, THE EVANGELICALS: THE STRUGGLE TO SHAPE AMERICA

The case of the United States may serve to illustrate this process of theocratization through the juridification of conscience.[51] The expansion of conscience-based claims as theocratization tools in the United States has taken

(2017). On the politicization of judicial appointments, for instance in Brazil, and its similarities with the United States, see Juliano Zaiden Benvindo, *Brazil's Increasingly Politicized Supreme Court*, INT'L J. CONST. L. BLOG (Feb. 16, 2017), http://www.iconnectblog.com/2017/02/brazils-increasingly-politicized-supreme-court/ (last visited June 20, 2022).

51 The American constitutional scheme regarding church and state may be classified as separation as state neutrality toward religion, which emphasizes the state's neutral and impartial stance toward religion rather than an assertive advancement of secularism. *See* Ran Hirschl, *Comparative Constitutional Law and Religion, in* COMPARATIVE CONSTITUTIONAL LAW 422, 424 (Tom Ginsburg & Rosalind Dixon eds., 2011). At its founding, the United States was a society of immigrants characterized by religious pluralism and a lack of strong association between religion and the ruling regime. *See generally*, Ahmet Kuru, *Passive and Assertive Secularism: Historical Conditions, Ideological Struggles, and State Policies toward Religion*, 59 WORLD POLITICS 568, 586 (July 2007). Prior to independence, the Anglican church was only formally established in six of the thirteen colonies, and even in those six colonies the establishment was largely nominal and the church's control largely ineffective. In *Passive and Assertive Secularism*, Kuru argues the lack of a colony-wide hegemonic religion made the new country's religious groups amenable to separation between church and state, while at the same time the secular elite did not see religion as an ally but also did not closely associate it with hegemonic power. In fact, evangelicals and secular rationalists found common ground in the philosophies of John Locke and several Protestant thinkers who promoted separation of church and state. Furthermore, the diversity of Protestant denominations in early America convinced many religious groups that, second to establishment of their particular denomination, separation was the best way to guarantee their own religious freedom. Therefore, the First Amendment of the United States Constitution captured this thinking and declared "Congress shall make no law respecting an establishment of religion or prohibiting the free exercise thereof." (U.S. CONST. amend. I.). The Establishment Clause forbids the state from adopting, preferring, or endorsing a religion and from preferring religion over non-religion, while the Free Exercise Clause prohibits the state from interfering with its citizens' religious freedom. *See* Ran Hirschl, *Comparative Constitutional Law and Religion, in* COMPARATIVE CONSTITUTIONAL LAW 422, 424 (Tom Ginsburg & Rosalind Dixon eds., 2011). Together, these clauses prevent the government from placing special benefits or burdens on specific religious groups unless necessary to promote a compelling state interest, thereby promoting government neutrality. However, despite the constitutional separation between church and state and popularity of separation rhetoric, religion still seems to pervade many aspects of American life. Some polls suggest Americans are some of the most likely Westerners to draw on religious morality and principles in their everyday lives and references to "God" can easily be found in the public sphere – even in the governmental sphere – such as on currency or in the Supreme Court. Thus, while the United States is constitutionally committed to separation as state neutrality toward religion, the presence of religion and its proponents is certainly still identifiable in American society.

place at the legislative, judicial and political levels.[52] This expansion can be dated, roughly, as emerging from the adoption of the Religious Freedom Restoration Act (1993) (RFRA) prompted by widespread opposition, and as a direct response to the 1990 U.S. Supreme Court decision in *Employment Division v. Smith*.[53]

In the case, which dealt with Native American religious use of peyote, the Court's majority opinion authored by Justice Scalia, essentially overturned its previous Free Exercise Clause doctrine, holding instead that the government can burden religious exercise if the law is one of general applicability, and significantly diminishing the scope of religious liberty. RFRA was conceived as a legislative remedy to the perceived erosion of religious liberties post-*Smith*. Prior to this, cases like *Sherbert v. Verner* (1963) and *Wisconsin v. Yoder* (1972) established the principle that any government action imposing a substantial burden on religious practice must be justified by a compelling government interest and be the least restrictive means of achieving that interest. The *Smith*

52 American conscience clauses originated in the context of conscientious objection to participation in war; since the Civil War, conscientious objection has been allowed on religious grounds. *See* Claire Marshall, *The Spread of Conscience Clause Legislation*, 39 HUM. RTS. 15, 15 (2013). In the 1970s, following the Supreme Court's decision in *Roe v. Wade* conscience clauses moved beyond the military context to apply to providing abortion services. Today, the United States has federal conscience clause legislation that applies to individual physicians, healthcare entities, insurance providers, and discrimination by the government against individual or institutional conscientious objectors. The 1973 Church Amendment provides that health care entities receiving certain federal funds may "refuse to provide abortion or sterilization if such services are contrary to their religious or moral beliefs." It also prohibits certain federally funded institutions from discriminating in internship and residency admission against health care professionals based on their refusal to participate in abortion and sterilization procedures that are contrary to their religious and moral beliefs. *See* Martha S. Swartz, *"Conscience Clauses" or "Unconscionable Clauses": Personal Beliefs Versus Professional Responsibilities*, 6 YALE J. OF HEALTH POL'Y, L., AND ETHICS 269, 280 (2006). The U.S. Congress passed several related pieces of legislation in the 1990s, starting with the Coats Amendment in 1991, which prohibits the government from discriminating against medical residency programs or other entities which fail to provide or require training in abortion services, followed by the 1997 Balanced Budget Act which extends conscience protections to Medicaid and Medicare managed care plans. *See* Sara Dubow, *"A Constitutional Right Rendered Utterly Meaningless": Religious Exemptions and Reproductive Politics, 1973–2014*, 27 J. OF POL'Y HIST. 1, 20–21 (2015). The 2005 Weldon Amendment to the HHS Appropriations Act prohibits federal funding to any federal agency or program or state or local government if the entity practices discrimination against an institutional or individual health care entity on the basis of refusal to provide, pay for, provide coverage of, or refer for abortions.

53 *See* Gonzales v. O Centro Espirita Beneficente Uniao do Vegetal, 546 U.S. 418, 424 (2006) (explaining the origin of RFRA and its relation to *Employment Division v. Smith*).

decision, however, replaced this strict scrutiny with a more lenient standard, prompting widespread concern among religious groups and civil liberties advocates.

Shortly after the ruling in *Smith*, people of faith and civil rights activists rallied in support of the religious minority whose rights to free exercise had been restricted.[54] About two months after *Smith*, Congress was already considering the adoption of what would come to be the Religious Freedom Restoration Act (RFRA). RFRA was Congress's attempt to restore the Court's previous Free Exercise Clause doctrine as a statutory rule. Although the Supreme Court later held that RFRA cannot be applied to the states as it exceeds Congress's enforcement powers, RFRA remains constitutional as to federal laws.[55] RFRA provides that the federal government may:

> substantially burden a person's exercise of religion only if [the government] demonstrates that application of the burden to the person (1) is in furtherance of a compelling governmental interest and (2) is the least restrictive means of furthering that compelling governmental interest.

Since its enactment, RFRA has been leveraged in various legal contexts, illustrating both its protective capacity and its potential for strategic use as a religious lawfare tool. Heralded as a significant bipartisan success for civil rights at the time, over the years RFRA turned into a controversial act, having most effectively been used by conservative Christian groups seeking exemptions from laws intended to protect sexual and reproductive rights. In the words of the ACLU, which supported the RFRA's enactment at the time under the belief that the interpretation of the Constitution at the time did not protect minority faiths sufficiently, the RFRA is now "being used as a vehicle for institutions and individuals to argue that their faith justifies a myriad of harms—to equality, to dignity, to health and to core American values".[56]

RFRA's design and judicial interpretations have provided conservative religious groups a potent tool to influence law and policy. By asserting substantial

54 *See* NOAH FELDMAN, DIVIDED BY GOD: AMERICA'S CHURCH-STATE PROBLEM AND WHAT WE SHOULD DO ABOUT IT 208 (2006).

55 City of Boerne v. Flores, 521 U.S. 507, 536 (1997); Burwell v. Hobby Lobby Stores, Inc., 573 U.S. 695–96 (2014). The U.S. Supreme Court will later elevate the status of the RFRA to the rank of a "super statute" that displaces the normal operation of other federal laws in *Bostock v. Clayton County*, holding that Title VII of the Civil Rights Act of 1964 bars employment discrimination on the basis of sexual orientation.

56 Louise Melling, *The Religious Freedom Restoration Act is Used to Discriminate. Let's Fix It*, RELIGIOUS NEWS SERVICE (May 19, 2016).

burdens on religious exercise, these groups have successfully shaped regulatory landscapes in favor of religious exemptions. Notably, cases like *Hobby Lobby* illustrate how RFRA can be used to challenge federal mandates, effectively allowing religious convictions to dictate corporate compliance with federal law.

The U.S. Supreme Court's recognition of the ability of closely-held, for-profit corporations to exercise conscientious objection in the *Hobby Lobby* case further illustrates the strategic use of religious lawfare to advance specific religious ideologies at the expense of broader public interests. In said case, the Supreme Court of the United States decided by a 5–4 vote to absolve three for-profit corporations from their obligation under the Affordable Care Act (2010) to provide contraceptive coverage to their employees on the basis of religious exemptions.[57] The Supreme Court declared that "Congress enacted RFRA in 1993 in order to provide very broad protection for religious liberty" and, consequently found that the Religious Freedom Restoration Act (1993) applied to corporations because Congress, in passing the statute, intended to provide broad protections for religious freedom and that the term "person" generally includes corporations. For the Court, the purpose of extending the right of religious freedom to corporations was to protect the people comprising the corporation, as a corporation is simply a form of organization used by individuals to achieve their desired ends. When rights, whether constitutional or statutory, are extended to companies, the purpose is to protect the rights of these people. Applied to the petitioners in the case, protecting the free exercise rights of corporations like Hobby Lobby protects the religious freedom of the individuals who own and control these companies.[58]

In short, the U.S. Supreme Court, for the first time, allowed closely held for-profit corporations to strike down generally applicable laws if they consider those laws to be contrary to their religious beliefs. This, combined with the Court's doctrine that prevented it from questioning the truth or reasonableness of the petitioner's religious claim, or for it to review that claim's accuracy and/or sincerity (to the extent that such review is relevant to determining whether the government has imposed a substantial burden on the exercise of religion by the adherent) has left the right of conscientious objection in the United States facing a rather problematic and uncertain scenario, not

57 The Affordable Care Act requires that companies with more than fifty employees guarantee health insurance to their employees that includes contraceptive coverage, or pay a fine.

58 Burwell v. Hobby Lobby Stores, Inc., 573 U.S. 682 (2014).

only from a theoretical perspective, but also from a practical one.[59] The U.S. Supreme Court partly opened the door to the religious lawfare phenomenon with its decision in the *Hobby Lobby* case, but the case reflected an already ongoing trend.

In the wake of the *Hobby Lobby* decision, the Department of Health and Human Services (HHS), under the leadership of Secretary Alex M. Azar II, issued the final version of its "Conscience Rule" in May 2019. The very same month, HHS issued another rule narrowly interpreting a nondiscrimination protection in the Affordable Care Act (ACA). The so-called "Conscience Rule" broadly defined key terms and expanded the scope of conscience protections. As the Guttmacher Institute noted with concern, under the rule:

- "Employers might be empowered to deny employees and their dependents coverage for abortion and contraceptive care, because the rule counts "plan sponsors" as health care entities with certain refusal rights;
- Health care providers might deny patients the information they need to provide informed consent about all of their medical options, because of the rule's expansive definitions of terms like "assist" and "refer" and because HHS essentially argues that providers are under no obligation to inform patients about options they do not offer;
- Hospitals and individual health care providers might delay or deny emergency care related to abortion, ectopic pregnancy and miscarriage, because the rule points to lawsuits involving such denials as potential violations of federal refusal laws;
- Pharmacists and pharmacies might refuse to fill prescriptions that they see as related to contraception or abortion, even when required by state law, because the rule explicitly adds them to its definition of health care entities."[60]

---

59 The First Amendment to the U.S. Constitution prohibits courts from questioning the truth or reasonableness of religious doctrine. *See* Employment Division v. Smith, 485 U.S. 660 (1990); Thomas v. Review Board of Indiana Employment Security Division 450 U.S. 707, 716 (1981); Boy Scouts of America v. Dale 530 U.S. 640 (2000). The Supreme Court of Canada follows the same doctrine. *See* Syndicat Northcrest v. Amselem 2 SCR 551 [50] (2004) (noting that "the State is in no position to be, nor should it become, the arbiter of religious dogma. . . courts should avoid judicially interpreting and thus determining, either explicitly or implicitly, the content of a subjective understanding of religious requirement, 'obligation', precept, 'commandment', custom or ritual").

60 Adam Sonfield, *Trump Administration Rules Prioritize Refusal of Care and Conservative Ideology Over Protecting Patients Against Discrimination*, 22 GUTTMACHER POL'Y REV. 49, 49–53 (2019).

That is, this new HHS rule expanded the list of personnel who could refuse to participate, including those who counsel, refer, train and/or make arrangements for a medical procedure. It further limited the employers' ability to inquire about employees' objections and expanded the definition of "health care entities" to include pharmacists and medical laboratories. Under the new rule, even an elevator operator or an ambulance driver could refuse on moral or religious grounds to perform certain activities. Experts criticized the rule claiming that it "widens the avenue for denying access to services, even constitutionally protected services … [and] reinforce[s] stigma or legitimize[s] discrimination against women; gay, lesbian, bisexual, or transgender individuals; persons living with HIV/AIDS; or individuals victimized by sex trafficking."[61] These HHS decisions were seen as "two major regulatory actions … to maximize social conservatives' ability … to impose their values and agenda on society at the expense of patients' health and rights."[62]

By mid-September 2019, eight cases had been filed in four federal district courts challenging the "Conscience Rule," and enforcement of the rule was delayed until November 2019.[63] Several judges blocked the new rule. The U.S. District Court for the Southern District of New York struck down the entire rule, arguing that the rule conflicted with several Congressionally enacted laws. Judge Paul A. Engelmayer also argued that the measure could be costly, burdensome, and damaging to emergency care and that the whole rationale for the rule was based on "flatly untrue" claims that there was a significant increase in complaints about workers being forced to violate their conscience.[64] Two days later, the U.S. District Court for the Eastern District of Washington

61 Lawrence Gostin, *The "Conscience" Rule: How Will It Affect Patients' Access to Health Services?* JAMA F. (May 15, 2019), https://newsatjama.jama.com/2019/05/15/jama-forum-the-conscience-rule-how-will-it-affect-patients-access-to-health-services/ (last visited Nov 11, 2023).

62 Adam Sonfield, *Trump Administration Rules Prioritize Refusal of Care and Conservative Ideology Over Protecting Patients Against Discrimination*, 22 GUTTMACHER POL'Y REV. 49, 49–53 (2019). *See also*, Emma Green, *Health and Human Services and the Religious-Liberty War*, THE ATLANTIC (May 7, 2019), https://www.theatlantic.com/politics/archive/2019/05/hhs-trump-religious-freedom/588697/ (last visited Nov 11, 2023).

63 Katie Keith, *Provider Conscience Rule Delayed Due to Lawsuits*, HEALTH AFF. BLOG (Jul. 2, 2019), https://www.healthaffairs.org/do/10.1377/hblog20190702.497856/full/ (last visited Nov 11, 2023).

64 New York et al. v. U.S. Dep't of Health and Human Services et al., 414 F. Supp. 3d 475 (S.D.N.Y. 2019). *See also*, Yasmeen Abutaleb, *Trump's 'conscience rule' for health providers blocked by federal judge*, WASH. POST (Nov. 6, 2019), https://www.washingtonpost.com/health/trumps-conscience-rule-for-health-providers-voided-by-federal-judge/2019/11/06/39aa9b74-00b1-11ea-9518-1e76abc088b6_story.html (last visited Nov 11, 2023)

held that the rule was outside of HHS's delegated authority.[65] The Trump administration's Department of Justice appealed all of the courts' decisions,[66] but the Biden administration later dismissed and dropped all the lawsuits.[67]

In April 2022, under the Biden administration, HHS's spokesperson confirmed that HHS was preparing to rescind the "Conscience Rule," as certain states moved toward limiting access to abortions and transgender care.[68] Ultimately, the final rule was partially rescinded in 2024.[69]

3 Conscience-Based Claims as Theocratization Tools

The notion of conscience-based claims has significantly evolved, increasingly being asserted as a weapon against the exercise of individuals' rights to healthcare, antidiscrimination, and sexual and reproductive liberties.[70] In this context, its exercise has been weaponized, becoming more comparable to a sword than a shield.[71] For example, conscientious objection in its contemporary form has come to limit the rights of patients to healthcare through the denial of euthanasia of the terminally ill, the denial of blood transfusions, and

---

65 Washington State, Office of the Attorney General, *Spokane Federal Judge Agrees with AG Ferguson, Strikes Down Unlawful Trump 'Conscience Rule'* (Nov. 7, 2019), https://www.atg.wa.gov/news/news-releases/spokane-federal-judge-agrees-ag-ferguson-strikes-down-unlawful-trump-conscience (last visited Nov 11, 2023).

66 Janita Kan, *Trump Administration to Appeal Decision Blocking Conscience Protections for Medical Professionals*, THE EPOCH TIMES (Jan. 6, 2020), https://www.theepochtimes.com/trump-administration-to-appeal-decision-blocking-conscience-protections-for-medical-professionals_3195415.html (last visited Nov 11, 2023).

67 Erik Larson, *Biden Administration Weighing Fate of Trump Moral Objection Rule*, BLOOMBERG (Feb. 5, 2021), https://www.bloomberg.com/news/articles/2021-02-05/biden-administration-weighing-fate-of-trump-moral-objection-rule (last visited Nov 11, 2023); Tom Strode, *Biden Administration Drops Conscience Rights Suit; ERLC Protests*, BAPTIST PRESS (Aug. 5, 2021), https://www.baptistpress.com/resource-library/news/biden-administration-drops-conscience-rights-suit-erlc-protests/ (last visited Nov 11, 2023).

68 Alice Miranda Ollstein & Adam Cancryn, *Biden Admin to rescind Trump "conscience" rule for health workers*, POLITICO (Apr. 19, 2022), https://www.politico.com/news/2022/04/19/biden-trump-conscience-rule-00026082 (last visited Nov 11, 2023).

69 Nathaniel Weixel, *Biden administration rescinds much of Trump 'conscience' rule for health workers*, THE HILL (Jan. 9, 2024), https://thehill.com/policy/healthcare/4397912-biden-administration-rescinds-much-of-trump-conscience-rule-for-health-workers/.

70 Marcelo Alegre, *Conscious Oppression: Conscientious Objection in the Sphere of Sexual and Reproductive Health, in* CONTROVERSIES IN LATIN AMERICAN BIOETHICS, 33 (Eduardo Rivera-López & Martin Hevia eds., 2019).

71 *See* Bernard M. Dickens, *Conscientious Objection: A Shield or a Sword?, in* FIRST DO NO HARM: LAW ETHICS AND HEALTHCARE 338 (Sheila A. M. McLean ed., 2006).

the denial of access to abortion as well as forms of contraception. In each arena, the personal politics and moral beliefs of physicians may be at odds with the purpose of the profession—to do no harm and put the patient's interests first. When asserted as the basis of a right to conscientious objection, those moral beliefs have consequences—patients bear the burden of a physician's refusal to provide care.[72] In the case of euthanasia or abortion, an objector may believe they are committing murder.[73]

Conscience-based claims are now consistently being used by conservative religious groups to reach an ever-expanding set of uses and rights-bearers in different areas, ranging from the military to healthcare professionals, to cake bakers, and to closely-held corporations. As seen in Figure 1, these claims have expanded *vertically* to cover different conducts and/or uses, and *horizontally* to embrace a broader set of conscience rights-bearers, including not only individuals, but also corporations. They have also expanded along what might be called the *depth axis,* to reach less and less proximate levels of complicity or degree of involvement in the objected conduct.

This threefold expansion of conscience-based claims has come to severely limit the enjoyment of other people's legally protected rights. At the same time, it poses a challenge to the cohesiveness and coherency of legal systems. This expansion has been particularly conspicuous in the context of sexual and reproductive healthcare in matters related to abortion services, the sale of contraceptives,[74] the sale of emergency contraceptive pills,[75] or the insertion of an IUD.[76] The goal of the conscientious objector in these contexts has been to

72 Udo Schuklenk, *Conscientious Objection in Medicine: Accommodation Versus Professionalism and the Public Good,* 126 BRIT. MED. BULL. 48, 48 (2018). *See generally* Julian Savulescu & Udo Schuklenk, *Doctors Have No Right To Refuse Medical Assistance in Dying, Abortion or Contraception,* 31 BIOETHICS 162–170 (2017); Udo Schuklenk, *Conscience-Based Refusal of Patient Care in Medicine: A Consequentialist Analysis* 40 THEORETICAL MED. & BIOETHICS 523–38 (2019); Udo Schuklenk & Ricardo Smalling, *Why Medical Professionals Have No Moral Claim to Conscientious Objection Accommodation in Liberal Democracies,* 43 J. MED. ETHICS 234–40 (2016).

73 *See* U.N. Human Rights Committee, *CCPR General Comment No. 36,* ¶ 10, CCPR/C/GC/36 (Sept. 3, 2019).

74 *See, e.g.,* Pichon and Sajous v. France, Case No. 49853/99, Eur. Ct. H.R. (2001).

75 *See, e.g.,* Tribunal Constitucional [Constitutional Court], June 25, 2015, Sentencia S.T.C. 145/2015, 2015–182 BOE 66654 (Spain); *see also,* High Court of England and Wales, 610 *R. (on the application of Smeaton)* v. *Secretary of State for Health* (U.K.); Brownfield v. Daniel Freeman Marina Hospital, 208 Cal. App. 3d 405 (1989).

76 *See, e.g.,* Supreme Court of Norway, Oct. 11, 2018, I. Sauherad municipality (Counsel Frode Lauareid) v. A, Norges Kristelige Legeforening (intervener) (Counsel Håkon H. Bleken), II. A, Norges Kristelige Legeforening (intervener) (Counsel Håkon H. Bleken) v. Sauherad municipality (Counsel Frode Lauareid, HR-2018-1958-A (case no. 2018/199).

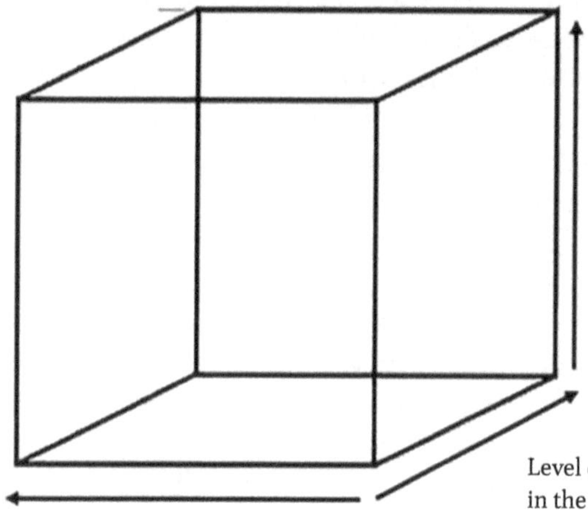

FIGURE 2 Three-dimensional expansion of conscience-based claims

hinder or even prevent women, transgender persons, and non-binary individuals from accessing sexual and reproductive health services and enjoying their rights.

Beyond the realm of sexual and reproductive healthcare, courts in France, Hungary, and the United Kingdom have dealt with challenges to same-sex marriage brought by civil servants arguing that officiating marriages of same-sex couples would compromise their freedom of conscience.[77] Conscience-based claims cases in these countries and elsewhere have now extended to refusals to lodge same-sex couples,[78] to take professional pictures for same-sex couple

77 *See* Conseil constitutionnel [CC] [Constitutional Council] Oct. 18, 2013, decision no. 2013-353 QPC, Rec. 1000, ¶ 1 (Fr.); Alkotmánybíróság [AB] [Constitutional Court] Mar. 25, 2010, No. 32/2010 (Hung.); England and Wales Court of Appeal [EWCA Civ] Dec. 15, 2009, 1357 Ladele v. London Borough of Islington (U.K.). The case ultimately reached the European Court of Human Rights (ECtHR), which upheld the Court of Appeal's decision. Eweida v. United Kingdom, 37 Eur. Ct. H.R. (2013).

78 *See, e.g.*, Supreme Court of the United Kingdom [UKSC] Nov. 27, 2013, 73 Bull v. Hall (U.K.); British Columbia Human Rights Tribunal [BCHRT] July 17, 2012, 247 Eadie v. Riverbend Bed and Breakfast (Can.).

engagement ceremonies,[79] to rent commercial facilities,[80] to host wedding receptions,[81] to allow access to adoption agencies,[82] to carry passengers with alcohol,[83] and more.

Similarly, as conscience-based claims expanded *vertically* to encompass more types of conduct, the expansion also occurred along a second axis, the *depth axis*. The *depth axis* refers to the level of engagement or involvement with the objected conduct.[84] For instance, courts have now granted exemptions to janitors from cleaning operating rooms where an abortion was performed, to police officers who wish to not be posted at an abortion clinic, and to a receptionist who refused to schedule certain medical procedures.[85] These instances are now a common occurrence. As Prof. Amy J. Sepinwall put it: "complicity claims seem to know no bounds: just so long as the objector thinks himself complicit in an act his religion opposes, the Court will conclude that the challenged legal requirement substantially burdens his religious exercise."[86]

---

79 *See, e.g.*, Elane Photography v. Willock, 309 P.3d 53 (N.M. 2013), *cert. denied,* 134 S. Ct. 1787 (2014).

80 *See, e.g.*, Victorian Civil and Administrative Tribunal [VCAT] Apr. 16, 2014, 75 Christian Youth Camps (CYC) v. Cobaw Community Health Services (Austl.).

81 *See, e.g.*, Jerusalem Magistrate Court 2012, Tal Ya'akovovich v. Yad Hashmona Guest House, CS 5901/09 (Isr.).

82 *See, e.g.*, Scottish Charity Appeals Panel 2014, St. Margaret's Children and Family Care Society v. Office of the Scottish Charity Regulator, 02/13 (Scot.).

83 *See* Sameer Ahmed, *The Religious Right to Refuse Service: Accommodating Muslims in a "Christian" America*, 7 ALB. GOV. L. REV. 379, 379–419 (2014).

84 The argument of complicity has allowed persons of faith to claim exemptions from laws concerning sex, reproduction, and marriage under the argument that the legal requirement makes them complicit in a conduct that is contrary to their beliefs. *See* Douglas NeJaime & Reva B. Siegel, *Conscience Wars: Complicity-Based Conscience Claims in Religion and Politics*, 124 YALE L. J. 2516, 2516–91 (2015); *see also*, Amy J. Sepinwall, *Conscientious Objection, Complicity, and Accommodation, in* LAW, RELIGION AND HEALTH IN THE UNITED STATES 203–14 (Holly Fernandez Lynch, I. Glenn Cohen & Elizabeth Sepper eds., 2017); Amy J. Sepinwall, *Conscience and Complicity: Assessing Pleas of Religious Exemptions in Hobby Lobby's Wake*, 82 U CHICAGO L. REV. 1897–1980 (2015).

85 *See, e.g.*, Rodriguez v. City of Chi., 156 F.3d 771 (1998).

86 Amy J. Sepinwall, *Conscientious Objection, Complicity, and Accommodation, in* LAW, RELIGION AND HEALTH IN THE UNITED STATES 203–14 (Holly Fernandez Lynch, I. Glenn Cohen & Elizabeth Sepper eds., 2017); *see also*, Joshua J. Craddock, *The Case for Complicity-Based Religious Accommodations*, 12 TENN. J.L. & POL'Y 233, 233–85 (2018). In the United Kingdom, a hospital secretary refused to write a letter referring a patient to another health care center for the purpose of undergoing an abortion. The Court rejected her argument claiming that the protection under conscientious objection did not include an action of such indirect relevance. *See* House of Lords, 1989, Janaway v. Salford Health Authority A.C. 537, 570 (U.K.); *see also*, Barr v. Matthews, 2000, 52 BMLR 217 (U.K.).

A case from 2018 illustrates this expansion in the United States. In the *Masterpiece Cakeshop* case, Mr. Jack Philips, the owner of a cakeshop, refused to bake a wedding cake for a same-sex couple on the basis of his religious convictions. Philips argued that baking the cake for a same-sex wedding would make him complicit in conduct that he considers sinful.[87] The U.S. Supreme Court ruled in his favor on narrow grounds claiming that the Colorado Civil Rights Commission—who had evaluated the case under the state's anti-discrimination law and found that the bakery discriminated against the couple, thus issuing specific orders for the bakery to follow—did not employ religious neutrality and rather expressed impermissible hostility to religion, infringing on Mr. Philips' right to free exercise.[88] With the composition of the U.S. Supreme Court as of 2024, similar cases may arise in the near future with potentially different outcomes.[89]

---

87 Masterpiece Cakeshop, Ltd. V. Colo. Civ. Rts. Comm'n, 138 S. Ct. 1719, 1724 (2018). *See also*, Mark L. Movsesian, *Masterpiece Cakeshop and the Future of Religious Freedom*, 42 HARV. J. L. & PUB. POL'Y 711, 711–49 (2019).

88 *Id.*

89 *See, e.g.*, Arlene's Flowers, Inc., dba Arlene's Flowers and Gifts, et al., v. Washington et al., No. 91615-2 (Wash. Sup. Ct. 2019) (*appeal dismissed* June 6, 2019), *petition for cert. filed*, No. 19-333 (U.S. Sept. 11, 2019) (in July 2017, the Alliance Defending Freedom petitioned the U.S. Supreme Court to take up Barronelle's case. In June 2018, the Court sent the case back to the Washington Supreme Court, after vacating that court's decision and instructing it to reconsider her lawsuit in light of the decision in *Masterpiece Cakeshop.* In June 2019, the Washington Supreme Court ruled against Barronelle a second time. Alliance Defending Freedom attorneys have once again asked the U.S. Supreme Court to take her case); Lexington-Fayette Urban County Human Rights Commission v. Hands On Originals, No. 2017-SC-000278-DG (Ky. Sup. Ct. R. Oct. 31, 2019) (a case of a business owner declining to create T-shirts for the pride festival hosted by the Gay and Lesbian Services organization. The owner argued that helping to spread a message that promotes sexual activity outside of a marriage between a man and a woman would violate his Christian beliefs. On October 31, 2019, the Kentucky Supreme Court ruled in favor of Blaine); *Telescope Media Group v. Lucero*, No. 17-3352 (8th Cir. R. Aug. 23, 2019) (a case involving the owners of a wedding video and film production company who refuse to make films celebrating same-sex marriages against the Minnesota Human Rights Act that, in their opinion, threatens to prosecute expressive business owners who decline to create speech promoting same-sex marriages); *Brush & Nib Studio v. City of Phoenix*, No. CV-18-0176-PR (Ariz. Sup. Ct. Sept. 16, 2019) (a case of two wedding invitation business owners against a Phoenix law that would require them to create invitations and other artwork for same-sex wedding ceremonies. On September 16, 2019, the Arizona Supreme Court ruled that the city of Phoenix cannot use a criminal law to force them to design and create custom wedding invitations expressing messages that conflict with their beliefs).

And finally, conscientious objector status has expanded *horizontally* to include not just individuals, but also institutions.[90] There are many arguments that groups have made to justify the institutional right to exercise conscientious objection. In most cases, similar to the *Hobby Lobby* case, the argument is that institutions can conscientiously object to a certain procedure or to the provision of certain service inasmuch as institutions can be understood as a reflection of the aggregation of the individual consciences of the people that are part of that institution. At its outset, the focus of "institutional conscientious objection" was on the institution's moral identity, social mission, or institutional conscience.[91] However, and perhaps more shockingly, Courts have misinterpreted this right and recognized a right to conscience for institutions *per se*.[92]

The constitutive elements of conscience-based claims are closely related to the holders of the right to freedom of conscience. That is, the reasons that explain the entitlement of conscience-based claims rests with its characteristics. Traditionally, conscience-based claims were solely understood as an individual right, given that it is not possible for legal persons to face a conflict between a legal duty and an individual conscience (moral duty).[93]

Indeed, over the past few years, and as part of the religious lawfare strategy of conservative religious groups, the understanding of conscience-based claims as a right that can only be exercised in its individual facet has mutated.

A first step, which has been taken mainly at the courts level, towards the expansion of conscience-based claims in a *horizontal* sense involved

90 A brief recount on how academic commentators have examined the issue of conscientious objection shows and reflects this transition. *Compare* Bernard M. Dickens, *Conscientious Objection: A Shield or a Sword?*, *in* FIRST DO NO HARM: LAW ETHICS AND HEALTHCARE 337–51 (Sheila A. M. McLean ed., 2006), Robin Alta Charo, *The Celestial Fire of Conscience—Refusing to Deliver Medical Care*, N. ENGL. J. MED. 2471, 2471–74 (2005), *and* Rebecca J. Cook & Bernard M. Dickens, *The Growing Abuse of Conscientious Objection*, 8 VIRTUAL MENTOR 337, 337–340 (2006), *with* Grattan T. Brown, *Institutional Conscience and Catholic Health Care*, 16 LIFE & LEARNING, 413–22 (2006), Elizabeth Sepper, *Taking Conscience Seriously*, 98 VA. L. REV. 1501, 1501–75 (2012), *and* Spencer L. Durland, *The Case against Institutional Conscience*, 86 NOTRE DAME L. REV. 1655, 1655–87 (2011).

91 Kevin W. Wildes, *Institutional Identity, Integrity, and Conscience*, 7 KENNEDY INST. ETHICS J. 4, 416 (1997). *See also*, MARK R. WICCLAIR, CONSCIENTIOUS OBJECTION IN HEALTH CARE: AN ETHICAL ANALYSIS 148 (2012); Melanie Di Pietro, *A Corporation's Exercise of Religion*, *in* LAW, RELIGION AND HEALTH IN THE UNITED STATES 93 (Holly Fernandez Lynch, I. Glenn Cohen & Elizabeth Sepper eds., 2017).

92 *See, e.g.*, Tribunal Constitucional de Chile [Constitutional Court] Aug. 28, 2017, decision No. 3725.

93 *See* Bernard M. Dickens, *Conscientious Objection: A Shield or a Sword?*, *in* FIRST DO NO HARM: LAW ETHICS AND HEALTHCARE 337-51 (Sheila A. M. McLean ed., 2006).

interpreting freedom of religion/conscience and freedom of association jointly. In this sense, the expansion of the right to conscientious objection from an individual dimension to institutions occurred initially under the understanding that the purpose of extending the right of freedom of conscience to institutions had to do with protecting the people associated with the institution. Thus, an institution is simply a form of organization used by human beings to achieve desired ends and the individual conscience of people manifests and is fully exercised in association with others.[94]

Shockingly, in recent years, there has been a disturbing trend toward the recognition of freedom of conscience to institutions—such as hospitals—as bearers of conscience themselves. Increasingly, conservative religious actors are invoking a right to institutional conscientious objection, wherein businesses and other organizations claim to be exempted from the application of certain laws that come into conflict with some kind of institutional belief.[95] This expansion developed primarily in the context of healthcare with claims that private hospitals, health insurance companies and laboratories can have institutional consciences that must be protected.

Recent regulatory and judicial developments show an increasing recognition of institutions as capable of claiming exemptions from generally applicable laws based on religious convictions. This has already happened in some countries, such as Chile and Ecuador. As noted, under the Trump administration there were also attempts to cement the precedent of *Hobby Lobby* with HHS's "Conscience Rule."

Future areas for expansion may include not only a refinement on the already developed standards that link freedom of conscience with freedom of association as a ground to justify a collective protection of conscience or the recognition of conscience to institutions as legal persons capable of bearing conscience, but also the use of other "legal tools," such as freedom to conduct business, which entails a freedom to decide which services or products to offer, as a way to disguise a moral judgment under a business decision or

94 *See e.g., Citizens United v. Federal Election Commission,* 558 U.S. 310 (2010); and *Burwell v. Hobby Lobby Stores, Inc.*, 134 S. Ct. 2751 (2014).

95 *See e.g.*, Private law section, decision no. 12929 (4 June 2007) (Ct. of Cass. III) (Italy) (allowing for-profit organizations to enjoy the protection of fundamental human rights, opening the door to future allowance of conscientious objection to abortion by entire institutions). *See also, Preddy v. Bull*, [2013] UKSC 73, [2014] 3 OJLR II-262 (U.K.) (recognizing that a business is capable of exercising religious freedom because it can decide business policy on the basis of religious principles, thereby warranting state protection of those rights from interference).

"professional labels."[96] This is all the more concerning in a neoliberal world order that promotes privatization of goods and services and is moving toward a shrinking role of the State.[97]

4 Religious Lawfare in Healthcare

Conceivably, healthcare has been the area in which religious lawfare in the form of conscience-based claims has been most prominent in recent years. In the context of healthcare, conscience-based claims have been invoked to shape policy and law especially in relation to the provision of sexual and reproductive health services. In particular, it has been invoked to deny the provision of services for the termination of pregnancy.[98] In some cases, not only the providers who participate directly in the service, such as doctors and nurses, invoke this objection, but also those who participate indirectly, such as administrators, directors or heads of service, who refuse to hear cases related to legal abortion.[99]

The exercise of "conscientious objection" in healthcare settings places the preferences of providers over the rights of patients and puts those rights in tension with the objectives of the profession, their civil duties as citizens, and other moral duties that require consideration for other people; especially, those who are in situations of vulnerability, such as people who are going through a pregnancy and must interrupt it.

An important, underlying issue around the question of conscientious objection in the context of sexual and reproductive health services such as abortion is that, while conscientious objection may be a permissible exercise of a recognized right, in cases where entire regions, states, or even countries are

96 Verónica Undurraga & Michelle Sadler, *The Misrepresentation of Conscientious Objection as a New Strategy of Resistance to Abortion Decriminalization*, 27 SEXUAL & REPROD. HEALTH MATTERS 17, 17–19 (2019).

97 *See* PRIVATISATION AND HUMAN RIGHTS IN THE AGE OF GLOBALISATION (Koen De Feyter & Felipe Gómez Isa eds., 2005); *see also*, Aoife Nolan, *Privatization and Economic and Social Rights*, 40 HUM. RTS. Q. 815, 815–58 (2018); Philip Alston, *Rep. of the Special Rapporteur on Extreme poverty and human rights*, U.N. Doc. A/73/396 (Sept. 26, 2018), ¶ 81.

98 D. NeJaime & R. Siegel, *Conscience Wars in Transnational Perspective: Religious Liberty, Third-Party Harm, and Pluralism*, *in* THE CONSCIENCE WARS: RETHINKING THE BALANCE BETWEEN RELIGION, IDENTITY, AND EQUALITY (S. Mancini & M. Rosenfeld eds., 2018).

99 Judith Bueno de Mesquita & Louise Finer, CONSCIENTIOUS OBJECTION: PROTECTING SEXUAL AND REPRODUCTIVE HEALTH AND RIGHTS (2008).

dominated by objectors, effective access to legal abortion services is not guaranteed. In fact, the European Committee of Social Rights condemned the fact that Italy did not supervise the exercise of conscientious objection by a growing number of professionals to the point that the majority of suppliers in the country declared themselves objectors, and access to abortion, though legal, was practically non-existent.[100]

The invocation of conscientious objection to deny the provision of services in healthcare places significant tensions on the ethical and professional obligations of healthcare providers, who must put the health and well-being of their patients first.[101] Health professionals who practice obstetrics, gynecology, midwifery, pharmacy, or other fields that include the provision of sexual and reproductive health services have professional obligations to provide abortion, contraception, and other essential services. For this reason, conscientious objection should only be used "after weighing principles, moral beliefs and legal duties, to excuse oneself from a certain practice, since carrying it out would severely damage their integrity. Somehow, [with their conscientious objection, healthcare professionals] acknowledge not having been able to resolve their moral conflict in a more beneficial way for patients, their colleagues and the healthcare system. Put like this, conscientious objection appears as an act of humility, not moral arrogance or even moral rejection."[102] However, today there is "an enormous dissonance between what is envisaged by the texts and practice: the version of conscientious objection as a reflexive act, sincere and humble of a person who is part of a minority has yielded to other uses much more problematic and much less ethical."[103] Chapter 5 will delve deeper on the tensions and implications arising from the exercise of conscience-based claims in healthcare settings.

5 Conclusion

This chapter examined the complex and multifaceted landscape of religious lawfare and its role in the theocratization of secular societies. One of the central

100 European Committee of Social Rights. *International Planned Parenthood Federation European Network (IPPF-EN) v. Italy*, No. 87/2012 (2014).

101 World Med. Ass'n, WMA Declaration of Geneva World Medical Association (1948).

102 Sonia Ariza Navarrete & Agustina Ramón Michel. Usos imprevistos y respuestas a la objeción de conciencia en el aborto legal (2019).

103 *Id.*

themes encountered is the expansion of the arsenal of conscience-based claims. Conscience, traditionally seen as a shield protecting individual beliefs and freedoms, has increasingly been wielded as a sword to restrict the rights and liberties of others. This evolution has been particularly notable in the domains of healthcare, antidiscrimination, and sexual and reproductive rights. Conscientious objection has been weaponized to limit access to healthcare services, obstruct antidiscrimination measures, and impede the exercise of sexual and reproductive liberties.

The chapter illustrated how conscience-based claims have expanded along three distinct dimensions: vertical, horizontal, and depth. Vertically, these claims have extended to cover an ever-widening array of behaviors and practices. Horizontally, they have encompassed not only individuals but also institutions, expanding the notion of collective conscience. Additionally, the depth axis of expansion refers to the level of engagement or involvement with the objected conduct, granting exemptions to individuals even in roles only tangentially related to the contested actions. This three-dimensional expansion has had significant repercussions, severely limiting the enjoyment of legally protected rights, and challenging the coherence of legal systems.

Moreover, the chapter briefly introduced the discussion around the role of *religious lawfare*, particularly in the realm of sexual and reproductive rights. It is in this arena that conservative religious groups have vigorously employed conscience-based claims to obstruct access to essential healthcare services, such as abortion and contraception. The consequences have often been borne by individuals in situations of vulnerability. The exercise of conscientious objection in healthcare settings has placed the preferences of providers over the rights of patients, creating ethical and professional dilemmas and impeding access to lawful services. Cases like that of Italy, where the widespread exercise of conscientious objection has led to the *de facto* unavailability of abortion services, underscore the profound impact of this phenomenon.

This phenomenon places tension between conscientious objection and the principles of democracy. While acknowledging the importance of protecting individual beliefs, there is a need to ensure access to essential services and respect the rights and well-being of all citizens. Conscientious objection, when taken to extremes, can challenge the fundamental tenets of democracy. Striking a balance between individual freedom of conscience and the collective rights of a democratic society remains a complex and ongoing challenge.

Concluding this chapter, it becomes clearer that religious lawfare, with its weaponization of conscience-based claims, presents significant challenges to secularism, democracy, and individual rights. However, the landscape remains dynamic, with opportunities for dialogue, legal reforms, and societal discussions.

Ultimately, the challenge lies in balancing the rights and freedoms of individuals and institutions in a pluralistic society. While religious liberty is a fundamental principle, it should not become a tool to undermine the rights and well-being of others.

CHAPTER 3

Religious Lawfare: A Threat to Democracy and Human Rights

Conservative religious groups' desires to return to an otherwise unrecoverable past through the expansion of conscience-based claims call into question the potential abuses that the expansion in the uses and understandings of these claims can bring. When utilized to resist the advancement of rights recognition, claims rooted in conscience give rise to concerns about legitimacy because their social outcomes are less advantageous than those determined through democratic processes. In these scenarios, conscience-based claims turn into an unauthorized intervention, functioning as a veto exercised by conservative religious groups and individuals over decisions made by democratically authorized bodies. Initially considered a shield for the protection of minorities, this new generation of conscience-based claims is a true threat to the foundations of democracy.

1 Political Uses of Conscience-Based Claims

Contrary to what was thought would come out of the ashes of World War II, parts of the world have left behind the ideals of bringing the world together socially, culturally, and politically. Instead, the door has been opened to a divided world where non-native elements, peoples, and ideas are seen as threats. One of the means through which this polarization has manifested has been the expansion of rights of conscience that allow adherents to do what they please regardless of its impacts on others, reinforcing the idea that certain "rights" provide a free pass or a letter of immunity. Rights of conscience are now being used as weapons to hinder, limit, intimidate, or restrict other people's life choices.[1]

Resort to religious lawfare through the use of rights of conscience as means to contest ordinary democratic politics with the goal of transforming the social order forces us to rethink how we deal with conflicts of rights in a way that

---

1 Robin West, *A Tale of Two Rights*, 94 B.U. L. Rev. 893–912 (2014); Robin West, *Freedom of the Church and our Endangered Civil Rights: Exiting the Social Contract*, *in* The Rise Of Corporate Religious Liberty (Z. Robinson, C. Flanders & M. Schwartzman eds., 2015).

 | DOI:10.1163/9789004685406_005

is both conciliatory of differing views and, at the same time, protective of democracy.[2]

There are many examples of conscience-based claims. For instance, conscientious objections to state-sanctioned same-sex marriage take two forms—the refusal of some state officials to officiate same-sex marriages and complicity-based objections to antidiscrimination laws governing the sale of goods and services to same-sex couples.[3] There also exist conscientious objectors to military service, to the servicing, providing or funding of abortions, the use of fetal tissue for medical research, and some forms of reproductive technologies, among other things.[4] The analysis in previous chapters showed that conservative religious groups have construed political power as a question of religious liberty or freedom of conscience to limit ordinary democratic politics. Thus, when conscience-based claims are exercised laws and policies recognizing the rights that these groups consider to be contrary to their "moral compass," such as the right to an abortion or LGBTQ rights, are undercut.

In recent years, conservative religious actors have resorted to conscience-based claims as a means of imposing their views on others when they disagree with democratic decisions.[5] Many of these actors have increasingly become more aggressive in their claims. Put bluntly, they do not just intend to be tolerated but rather persistently abuse the protection afforded to rights of conscience, even if that means circumventing the will of the people and inflicting harm on others. The old paradigm of religious freedom as non-interference, or the mere absence of violent persecution, has in effect given rise to a new paradigm where these groups demand to live according to their own religious beliefs without suffering, to the furthest extent possible, any disadvantageous outcome as a result of their non-abidance with laws or norms, and intend to impose their worldview on others. This represents a new challenge: religious freedom is no longer defined as a demand to live according to one's own beliefs

---

2 I rely on Brian Hutler's characterization of the use of religious exemptions to advance political goals. *See* Brian Hutler, *Against the Political Use of Religious Exemptions,* 47 PHIL. & PUB.AFFS. (2019). In his piece, Hutler argues that political uses of religious freedom are inconsistent with the justification for providing religious freedom protection, given a democratic state's commitment to political equality.

3 Chris Johnson, *Jeb Bush endorses religious discrimination legislation,* WASH. BLADE (Mar. 20, 2015), https://www.washingtonblade.com/2015/03/20/jeb-bush-endorses-religious-discrimination-legislation/ (last visited Nov 11, 2023).

4 Grégor Puppinck, *Conscientious Objection and Human Rights: A Systematic Analysis,* 1 BRILL RSCH. PERSPS. IN L. & REL. 1, 3 (2017).

5 Douglas NeJaime & Reva B. Siegel, *Conscience Wars: Complicity-Based Conscience Claims in Religion and Politics,* 124 YALE L. J. 2516, 2565–66 (2015).

but rather is used as a tool to change the social order when the progress of the democratic consensus is contrary to the objector's own beliefs.

Uses of conscience-based claims that are intended as counter-majoritarian and antidemocratic tools to refuse the exercise of rights have been met with acceptance by a substantial number of courts around the world. When ruling on conscience-based claims, courts have increasingly engaged in virtually no balancing of the opposing interests at stake. Instead, in some countries, courts have shown a clear preference for freedom of conscience over other people's rights. They have invalidated portions of legislation aimed at balancing interests, for example, by rejecting the referral requirement when it comes to the provision of abortion services. In cases where courts have engaged in balancing tests aimed at reconciling competing rights, those tests have only resulted in prioritizing one right over the other, with little to no regard to the particular subjectivities and interests involved in the case.

The question, then, is whether a democratic state should allow *all* forms of genuine, sincerely-felt conscientious objection to laws or obligations imposed by law. On initial consideration, the answer appears to be affirmative: genuine, sincerely-felt conscience-based claims would appear to enhance deliberation, thereby strengthening democracy. In a well-functioning democracy, decisions gain legitimacy and validity when widely discussed by all—not solely by those who are going to be affected by them.[6] Consequently, there is seemingly no voice more essential than that of the critics, whether they represent the majority or minority. Therefore, allowing resistance and disagreement to laws appears to be democratically desirable. Conscience-based claims would then serve as a manifestation of dissent and aim at communicating specific claims to other citizens.[7]

In this chapter, I challenge the preconception that resistance to law in the form of conscience-based claims is always a praiseworthy, heroic, and virtuous act. In certain cases, this resistance should *not* be allowed, as the claims might instead harm democracy. In what follows, I show that while some uses of conscience-based claims are democratic and should be allowed, new uses that are part of religious lawfare and aim at imposing a worldview on others are *not* and should be limited. As shown later, according to a republican deliberative

6 *See generally* THOMAS CHRISTIANO, THE CONSTITUTION OF EQUALITY: DEMOCRATIC AUTHORITY AND ITS LIMITS (2008).

7 *See* Michael P. Lynch, *Epistemic Arrogance and the Value of Political Dissent, in* VOICING DISSENT: THE ETHICS AND EPISTEMOLOGY OF MAKING DISAGREEMENT PUBLIC 129, 129–39 (Casey Rebecca Johnson ed., 2018); *see also* Elisabeth Anderson, *The Epistemology of Democracy*, 3 EPISTEME 8, 8–22 (2006).

perspective on democracy, justifying the limitation of these novel applications of conscience-based claims would be reasonable, as the potential democratic drawbacks of permitting them outweigh any hypothetical advantages they may offer to deliberation and the democratic process as a whole.

To show that while some forms of conscientious objection are healthy for a democracy, others undermine fundamental democratic values, this chapter focuses on potential conflicts arising between freedom of conscience and sexual and reproductive rights, as well as between freedom of conscience and non-discrimination claims. These are exemplary only; many of these arguments should also apply in other areas where individuals raise conscience-based objections to democratically passed legal norms.

In contexts where abortion is legal, physicians might conscientiously object to performing them based on a religious or moral belief that abortion is wrong. In the United States, while nationwide abortion was legalized nearly 50 years ago under *Roe v. Wade*—recently overturned in *Dobbs v. Jackson Women's Health*—legislators and governmental agencies have sought to codify physicians' ability to object based on their religious or moral beliefs. The primary ethical principle behind these conscience-based claims was physician autonomy and moral integrity.[8] Physicians are not mere instruments of the State or a medical institution, bound to do an entity's bidding without regard for their conscience.[9] Furthermore, the psychological and emotional strain of being forced to engage in an activity that violates one's moral or religious code can have harmful effects on an individual's identity and even humanity.[10]

Similarly, recognizing the right to same-sex marriage and other LGBTQ rights has also led, in some countries, to numerous conflicts between LGBTQ people and religious institutions or religious people. Controversies related to LGBTQ rights have also arisen in the healthcare setting with, for example, doctors at assisted reproductive fertilization clinics refusing to perform an otherwise indicated procedure when that action would support the establishment of an LGBTQ family because to do so would mean violating their conscience, given their religious perspectives on what a family is or should be.

---

8 Martha S. Swartz, *"Conscience Clauses" or "Unconscionable Clauses": Personal Beliefs Versus Professional Responsibilities*, 6 YALE J. OF HEALTH POL'Y, L. & ETHICS 269, 277 (2006). *See also*, TOM L. BEAUCHAMP & JAMES F. CHILDRESS, PRINCIPLES OF BIOMEDICAL ETHICS (6th ed. 2009); MARK R. WICCLAIR, CONSCIENTIOUS OBJECTION IN HEALTH CARE: AN ETHICAL ANALYSIS (2011); Mark R. Wicclair, *Preventing Conscientious Objection in Medicine from Running Amok: A Defense of Reasonable Accommodation*, 40 THEORETICAL MED. & BIOETHICS 539–64 (2019).

9 Stephen J. Genius & Chris Lipp, *Ethical Diversity and the Role of Conscience in Clinical Medicine*, INT'L J. OF FAM. MED. 1, 5 (2013).

10 *Id.* at 8.

The emergence of these and more complex controversies has sparked both litigation and academic debates. Legitimizing the use of conscience-based claims has been alleged to, over time, stigmatize the practice or enjoyment of the right sought to be protected by legislation.[11] On the one hand, those who profess a faith wish to have the freedom to live according to it publicly and in all areas of their life. On the other hand, LGBTQ people have a right not to be discriminated against because of their sexual orientation. In Massachusetts, for example, Catholic Charities of Boston, a Catholic institution that, through charity, founded and ran foster homes for orphans, refused to entrust children to the custody of same-sex couples. It was determined that such an institution could only continue providing this service if it also served these couples who could adopt children through other institutions in that state, contrary to its religious beliefs, which is why the institution stopped acting in the adoption field.[12] Analogous situations have occurred in the United Kingdom.[13] As illustrated in previous chapters, conflicts can also arise in the private marketplace with religious individuals who work in the provision of services related to wedding ceremonies—photographers, party house owners, confectioners, ceremonialists, decorators, etc.

Conscience-based claims typically implicate conflicting ethical principles often held by those persons for whom the law was written, and as such, almost always affect others.[14] In the healthcare field, patients' bodily autonomy and freedom of choice are at stake when a conscience-based objection to a reproductive practice is upheld.[15] Likewise, conscience-based claims are likely to inflict both material and dignitary harms on would-be buyers who find

---

11 Douglas NeJaime & Reva Siegel, *Conscience Wars in Transnational Perspective: Religious Liberty, Third-Party Harm, and Pluralism, in* THE CONSCIENCE WARS: RETHINKING THE BALANCE BETWEEN RELIGION, IDENTITY, AND EQUALITY 187, 196 (Susanna Mancini & Michel Rosenfeld eds., 2018).

12 Roger Severino, *Or for poorer? How same-sex marriage threatens religious liberty*, 30 HARV. J. L. & PUB. POL'Y 975 (2007).

13 John Finnis, *Equality and Religious Liberty: Oppressing Conscientious Diversity in England, in* RELIGIOUS FREEDOM AND GAY RIGHTS: EMERGING CONFLICTS IN NORTH AMERICA AND EUROPE 6 (Timothy Shah, Thomas Farr & Jack Friedman eds., 2016).

14 Nancy Berlinger, *"Conscience Clauses, Health Care Providers, and Parents," in* FROM BIRTH TO DEATH AND BENCH TO CLINIC: THE HASTINGS CENTER BIOETHICS BRIEFING BOOK FOR JOURNALISTS, POLICYMAKERS, AND CAMPAIGNS, 35–40 (Mary Crowley ed., 2008).

15 *See* Martha S. Swartz, *"Conscience Clauses" or "Unconscionable Clauses": Personal Beliefs Versus Professional Responsibilities*, 6 YALE J. OF HEALTH POL'Y, L. & ETHICS 269, 314 (2006); Sara Dubow, *"A Constitutional Right Rendered Utterly Meaningless": Religious Exemptions and Reproductive Politics, 1973–2014*, 27 J. OF POL'Y HIST. 1, 1, 16 (2015).

themselves unable to access a service or procure a good when a seller withholds it to assuage conscience.[16]

Thus, conscience-based claims can be a zero-sum game: as the ability to refuse to provide a service or good expands, the opportunity to access those goods or services diminishes.[17] In most cases, conscientious objection disproportionately impacts certain groups, such as women seeking to terminate pregnancies and LGTBQ people, and particularly those within lower economic groups who have reduced access to transportation or alternative sources of getting the service or good withheld.[18]

In countries, such as Poland, Brazil, or Argentina, conflicts between freedom of conscience and other rights reflect little to no balancing of conflicting interests. They have expanded beyond the protection of individuals' conscience and personal integrity to serve as a tool of a right-wing state or Church power.[19] In the healthcare context, in particular, while conscience-based claims are justified in part on the ethical principle that physicians are not mere tools of the State, even when physicians have invoked them, they have been used as a tool to carry out the State's conservative, anti-abortion or anti-LGBTQ agenda as well as to reinforce the moral authority of the Catholic and Evangelical churches.[20] In those cases, individual invocations of conscience-based claims entrench the political and moral power of both the State and the Church.

2 Coercion, Democracy and Conscience

Conventional uses of conscience-based claims were long considered as shields to protect minority views from the oppression of majorities, for instance,

16 *Compare* Douglas NeJaime & Reva B. Siegel, *Conscience Wars: Complicity-Based Conscience Claims in Religion and Politics*, 124 YALE L. J. 2516, 2566 (2015), *with* Gerald Chipeur and Robert Clarke, *The Art of Living with Ourselves: What Does the Law Have to Do with Conscience*, in RELIGIOUS BELIEFS AND CONSCIENTIOUS EXEMPTIONS IN A LIBERAL STATE 175 (John Adenitire ed., 2019) (characterizing dignitary harm as involving "feelings" and arguing that protecting LGBTQ people from dignitary harm would allow the State to enter into the dangerous territory of protecting offence and humiliation, which are daily occurrences in social life).

17 Rachel White-Domain, *Making Rules and Unmaking Choice: Federal Conscience Clauses, Provider Conscience Regulation, and the War on Reproductive Freedom*, 59 DEPAUL L. REV. 1249, 1265 (2010).

18 *See id.* at 1280–81.

19 *See* Joanna Z. Mishtal, *Matters of "Conscience": The Politics of Reproductive Healthcare in Poland*, 23 MED. ANTHROPOLOGY Q. 161, 170 (2009).

20 *Id.* at 173.

allowing exemptions to mandatory military service on religious grounds, or as atomistic "exit rights" to create "separate spheres of sovereignty,"[21] or as a means by which to insulate the right holder from the attacks of civil authority. However, society now faces new uses that have turned conscience-based claims into mechanisms to hinder legally protected rights and impose invasive beliefs on the social order.[22]

Freedom of religion or freedom of conscience are rights that ought to be recognized and duly protected by the State, particularly to protect the rights of minority religious groups. However, rights granted to conscientious objectors are now being employed as a license to discriminate and impose the objector's views on others. By allowing people to elevate their prejudices, whether religion-based or conscience-based, above fairness and equality, a broader principle—that people should not be refused goods and services solely because of who they are—is threatened.[23] Also threatened is the dignity of the people whose lifestyles are objected to, that their rights and well-being are not valued and are contingent on the goodwill of others. These new claims have started to cause tension and legal conflicts in some parts of the world. Consequently, adjusting legal and juridical structures to religious diversity remains a pressing challenge of contemporary societies.

The impact of these new uses of conscience-based claims, which I call "political uses of conscience-based claims", extends beyond the boundaries of the religious group and enters the political realm. With these uses of conscience-based claims, governmental and societal interests are prisoners of what a specific individual—or institution—says to be their sincerely held belief. If this line of argument is followed, the denial of democracy can be found on one of its extremes.

To start, conscience-based claims can be characterized as *intra-group repression*, arising as a result of granting a conscience-based accommodation to a group that in turn subordinates more vulnerable members of the accommodated group.[24] Ayelet Shachar lucidly captured this issue. Concerned by the perpetuation of existing power structures and intra-group repression, she

---

21 Robin West, *A Tale of Two Rights*, 94 B.U. L. Rev. 893–912 (2014); Robin West, *Freedom of the Church and our Endangered Civil Rights: Exiting the Social Contract*, *in* The Rise Of Corporate Religious Liberty (Z. Robinson, C. Flanders & M. Schwartzman eds., 2015).

22 Robert M. Cover, *The Supreme Court 1982 Term. Foreword: Nomos and Narrative*, 97 Harv. L. Rev. 4 (1984).

23 *Id.*

24 Ayelet Shachar, Multicultural Jurisdictions: Cultural Differences and Women's Rights 3 (2001).

asked "[H]ow do we protect group members from routine violations [of their rights] when those violations arise from the traditional practices of the group which we have already sanctioned through accommodation?."[25] This was a major problem in the famous *Yoder* case.[26] In *Yoder*, the U.S. Supreme Court decided that the state's compulsory school attendance law unduly burdened the free exercise clause of the First Amendment by forcing Amish parents to send their children to public school after the eighth grade, violating core Amish religious beliefs requiring them to remain "aloof from the world."[27] The court held that the state must not require an individual "to perform acts undeniably at odds with fundamental tenets of their religious belief."[28] With its decision, the court subordinated the interests of Amish children to the claims of their religious group.

While claims that lead to intra-group repression are defined based on the risk of or actual exploitation of group members, political uses of conscience-based claims often go beyond the group sphere. The ultimate goal of political uses of conscience-based claims is not simply to look for accommodation, but rather to impose moral values and a worldview on others—even if they are not part of the "group"—in ways that run contrary to democratic outcomes reached through constitutionally valid laws.

The closest approximation to this can be found in Brian Hutler's work where he describes political uses of religious exemptions as those occurring when the claimant uses an exemption to publicly protest or undermine the implementation of the law or policy from which the exemption is sought.[29] Hutler criticizes these uses as problematic inasmuch as the granting of such exemptions by the State creates legal inequalities between citizens on the basis of their beliefs and that the role of the State should, instead, be to ensure that the legal inequalities arising from religious exemptions do not function to privilege some citizens over others in the political process.[30] In other words, Hutler considers that political uses of religious exemptions are contrary to the equal participation

---

25 *Id.*

26 *See, e.g.*, Kent Greenawalt, *Freedom of Association and Religious Association, in* FREEDOM OF ASSOCIATION 124 (Amy Gutmann ed., 1998); Richard Arneson & Ian Shapiro, *Democratic Autonomy and Religious Freedom: A Critique of Wisconsin v. Yoder, in* NOMOS XXXVIII: POLITICAL ORDER (Ian Shapiro & Russel Hardin, eds., 1996).

27 Wisconsin v. Yoder, 406 U.S. 205 (1972).

28 *Id.* at 220.

29 Brian Hutler, *Against the Political Use of Religious Exemptions*, 47 PHIL. & PUB. AFFS. (2019).

30 *Id. See also* CHRISTOPHER L. EISGRUBER & LAWRENCE G. SAGER, RELIGIOUS FREEDOM AND THE CONSTITUTION Ch. 3 (2010).

principle, according to which "all channels of political participation, including opportunities for voting, campaigning, holding office, and public speaking, must be legally available to all citizens on equal terms, unless a deviation from this formal equality can be justified".[31] In their 2018 book, Mancini and Rosenfeld similarly described conscience-based claims being used as a "collective instrument designed to subvert existing laws and practices with the purpose of eliminating rights in the name of 'the good of society.'"[32]

Of course, all uses of conscience-based claims are arguably political "in the sense that [they are] a public expression of the claimant's politically salient religious identity."[33] I do not argue that conscientious objection "is or could be completely apolitical,"[34] but rather that there is a particular use of conscientious objection, which has increased in recent years, that attempts to thwart the implementation of a law or policy through coercion.

While some of these authors argue that these uses have a negative impact on the equal participation principle, conversely, I further argue that the impact of political uses of religious exemptions goes beyond simply running contrary to such principle. These uses affect two other essential elements of the democratic ideal: the equal influence element and the deliberative element, ultimately hindering democracy altogether. These elements are explained further below.

Interestingly, these new uses of conscience-based claims represent a substantial departure from the original purpose of conscientious objection. When individuals or groups of individuals use conscience-based claims in this manner, freedom of conscience or religious freedom disguises or turns into an excuse for political subversion. Political uses of conscience-based claims are increasingly being exerted as mechanisms to obstruct the effectiveness of democratically adopted norms.

The non-fulfillment of a legal duty on the part of the objector is, in most cases, still the result of a sincere conviction based on religious, moral, philosophical principles, or of conscience in general. Nonetheless, it manifests itself as a way of countering democratic decisions. In other words, political conscience-based objectors intend and seek that their claim take a public status, and achieve adhesion within society, but ultimately do it through coercing

31 Brian Hutler, *Against the Political Use of Religious Exemptions*, 47 PHIL. & PUB. AFFS. 332–33 (2019).

32 THE CONSCIENCE WARS: RETHINKING THE BALANCE BETWEEN RELIGION, IDENTITY, AND EQUALITY (Susanna Mancini & Michel Rosenfeld eds., 2018).

33 Brian Hutler, *Against the Political Use of Religious Exemptions*, 47 PHIL. & PUB. AFFS. 324 (2019).

34 *Id.*

those who disagree with them into their sincere convictions. A key element of political uses of conscience-based claims is that they seek legal and policy change by nullifying the effect of laws that go against the claimant's beliefs, compelling others to unconsented religious participation.

Political uses of conscience-based claims differ from conventional uses of conscience-based claims in that they seek more than just an exemption from the law. They are rather intended as a political strategy to resist a contentious policy, law, or court decision that differs from the objector's worldviews by virtually vetoing the effect of such decision. Political uses of conscience-based claims may ultimately achieve policy reform, but its effectiveness as a religious lawfare strategy does not necessarily depend on such a change.

Political uses of conscience-based claims' exercise is deliberate in nature with the goal of nullifying the effect of the contested measure. Instead of focusing on challenging the root problems of the measure—for instance, if it is just or unjust—political uses of conscience-based claims direct their efforts toward resisting the effects of the measure by rendering it ineffective or unenforceable. By doing so, they manipulate and coercively impose their worldviews on others.[35] To a certain extent, this use manifests as a way to exert pressure on others to believe what the claimant believes.

If the newfound applications of conscience-based claims serve merely as a pretext for political subversion, intentionally altering someone else's normative situation and the impact of democratic decisions, one may validly ask how do these claims diverge from acts of civil disobedience (or other forms of resistance)? If there is no distinction, why should the new uses of conscience-based claims be curtailed while certain instances of civil disobedience in democratic regimes are deemed acceptable?

Naturally, conscientious objection, as other forms of disobedience, is unavoidable and, indeed, integral to well-functioning democracies. This does not mean that all forms of conscience-based claims should be allowed, inviting to general lawlessness. Thus, it becomes important to develop a framework that allows us to identify and cabin forms of conscience-based claims that are not conducive to democracy.

As anticipated in the introduction, to answer these questions it is necessary to look into the distinct characteristics of political uses of conscience-based claims. These uses have evolved into a method of imposing perspectives on others by shaping and obstructing the enactment or implementation of a law or policy conflicting with the objector's beliefs. While the objector

35 *See* Chapter 6 (on domination).

seeks public acceptance for their claim and societal adherence, the ultimate objective is to manipulate and alter another person's normative situation. Political conscience-based objectors aim to compel those who disagree with their beliefs to align with their sincere convictions. This is precisely why these applications of conscience-based claims are undemocratic. They are coercive, harmful, undermine the autonomous agent status of others, and are not aimed at promoting deliberation.

It could be argued, though, that most conscience-based claims are at least partly deliberative in the sense that they often involve at least a minimal attempt at conveying the claim that the objectors are morally authorized to be exempted from a particular act and that the objector's demands are legitimate. Even purely conventional uses of conscience-based claims may impose costs on others since it is in many cases impossible to reach other people's ears without intruding on others' rights at least partially. All of this may suggest that conventional uses and political uses of conscience-based claims cannot be readily distinguished.

Generally, resistance to laws - in any of its forms - pursues a communicative aim of expressing disagreement and discontent that is appraised in democracies. This communicative aim may manifest as persuasion, while in other instances, it manifests as coercion. Persuasion is, on the surface, consistent with representative democracy, as it recognizes the autonomy of others and seeks to prompt action through reasoning or argument.[36] Coercion, however, accomplishes the opposite by restricting individuals "to compliance or obedience;"[37] thus, disrespecting the autonomy of others and undermining or putting at risk the communicative goals.[38] In practice, what distinguishes cases of conventional uses of conscience-based claims that are compatible with democracy from instances involving political uses of conscience-based claims is the distinction in the methods employed to attain these communicative objectives.

Political uses of conscience-based claims are coercive in nature, which makes them run counter to the deliberative element of the democratic ideal.

---

36 *Persuasion*, THE OXFORD ENGLISH DICTIONARY, https://www.oed.com/view/Entry/141561 (last visited June 20, 2022). *See also*, JOEL FEINBERG, HARM TO SELF: THE MORAL LIMITS OF THE CRIMINAL LAW 189 (1986). *See* CHRISTINE M. KORSGAARD, KANT: GROUNDWORK OF THE METAPHYSICS OF MORALS (Mary Gregor & Jens Timmermann, trans., 2d ed. 2012).

37 *Coerce*, THE OXFORD ENGLISH DICTIONARY, https://www.oed.com/view/Entry/35716 (last visited June 20, 2022).

38 *See generally* KIMBERLEY BROWNLEE, CONSCIENCE AND CONVICTION: THE CASE FOR CIVIL DISOBEDIENCE 28–30 (2012).

They aim to exert domination, and alter the will and autonomy of others by pushing them to no alternative other than to endorse the objector's specific viewpoint, often exposing individuals to a threat to their health or life.[39] By coercing individuals into supporting a particular worldview or opposing a specific law or policy through conscience-based claims, political conscience-based objectors force people into a decision contrary to their own will, treating them as mere instruments to achieve the objector's goal.

The emergence of political uses of conscience-based claims as part of a conservative religious group's religious lawfare strategy, relies on an additional avenue of political participation unavailable to those with different beliefs, which fundamentally goes against democratic ideals.[40] Moreover, this shift in the application of conscience-based claims poses particular challenges in pluralistic societies.[41]

In functionally differentiated societies,[42] democracy must create spaces for dissent to survive.[43] As such, conscience-based claims become an instance of societal constitutionalism, guaranteeing bottom-up control and political deliberation. By making possible communicative reflexive processes within social systems, conscientious objection brings to the foreground societal responsibility, and it functions as a protective shield against fundamental rights violations. In cases where the proclaimed institutional mechanisms for the protection of minorities fail, constitutional protection of conscientious objection should function as the ultimate safeguard of democratic control and public debate. Most of the times, conventional uses of conscience-based claims aim, precisely, at communicating specific claims or attitudes to other

39 Robert Nozick, *Coercion*, *in* PHILOSOPHY, SCIENCE, & METHOD, 440 (Sidney Morgenbesser, Patrick Suppes & Morton White, eds. 1969). *See generally*, Chapter 6.

40 Pierluigi Chiassoni, *Protecting freedom of conscience in a constitutional state*, *in* RELIGION, LAW AND THE POLITICS OF ETHICAL DIVERSITY: CONSCIENTIOUS OBJECTION AND CONTESTATION OF CIVIL NORMS 13, 13–42 (Claude Proeschel, David Koussens & Francesco Piraino eds., 2021).

41 Robert M. Cover, *The Supreme Court 1982 Term. Foreword: Nomos and Narrative*, 97 HARV. L. REV. 4, 4–68 (1984).

42 Niklas Luhmann, *Differentiation of Society*, 2 CAN. J. OF SOCIO. 29 (1977).

43 HANNAH ARENDT, DU MENSONGE À LA VIOLENCE 101 (1972); GUNTHER TEUBNER, CONSTITUTIONAL FRAGMENTS: SOCIETAL CONSTITUTIONALISM AND GLOBALIZATION 88–89 (2012). On the epistemic value of dissent, see Michael P. Lynch, *Epistemic Arrogance and the Value of Political Dissent*, in VOICING DISSENT: THE ETHICS AND EPISTEMOLOGY OF MAKING DISAGREEMENT PUBLIC 129–39 (Casey Rebecca Johnson ed., 2018). *See also* Elisabeth Anderson, *The Epistemology of Democracy*, 3 EPISTEME 8–22 (2006).

citizens.[44] On the other hand, however, instead of engaging in deliberation, political uses of conscience-based claims actively and intentionally try to get others to do (or prevent them from doing) something by levying the costs of them doing otherwise, leaving them no choice but to adhere or be at the mercy of the objector.

More specifically, according to the representative democracy approach and a pure proceduralist account of democratic legitimacy adopted in this book, political uses of conscience-based claims differ from conventional uses in that political uses are contrary to at least two common elements of the democratic ideal: the equal influence element and the deliberative element.[45]

Pure proceduralist theories consider political decisions to be legitimate only if they are the result of a process of democratic decision-making that embodies political equality among members of the democracy.[46]

First, a central element of the democratic ideal is that citizens should have *equal influence* over at least some critical decisions in the political process.[47] Equal influence, in this instance, means formal and informal equal opportunity for influence.[48] Equal formal opportunity for influence is the absence of unequal legal barriers for influence. An equal informal opportunity to

44 Emanuela Ceva, *Political Justification through Democratic Participation: The Case for Conscientious Objection*, 41 SOC. THEORY & PRAC. 26 (2015).

45 A proceduralist account of democratic legitimacy is consistent with a republican view of democracy, which considers democracy as a freestanding political value and stresses the procedural aspects of democracy, highlighting the connection between individual and collective self-governance in the quest for liberty. This view explains democratic authority in terms of the affective consequences of engagement with the democratic political process. *See* Daniel Markovits, *Democratic Disobedience*, 114 YALE L. J. 1897 (2005). *See also*, ROBERT POST, CONSTITUTIONAL DOMAINS: DEMOCRACY, COMMUNITY, MANAGEMENT (1995); and Robert C. Post, *Between Democracy and Community: The Legal Constitution of Social Form*, *in* NOMOS XXXV: DEMOCRATIC COMMUNITY 163 (J. W. Chapman and I. Shapiro eds., 1993).

46 In such process, participants in democratic policy-making come to identify with and take ownership of collective decisions even when they have been outvoted in the political realm. *See generally*, Robert C. Post, *Between Democracy and Community: The Legal Constitution of Social Form*, *in* NOMOS XXXV: DEMOCRATIC COMMUNITY 163 (J. W. Chapman and I. Shapiro eds., 1993), and HANS KELSEN, GENERAL THEORY OF LAW AND STATE (1945) (arguing that a subject is politically free when her individual will is in harmony with the collective will expressed in the social order).

47 THOMAS CHRISTIANO, THE CONSTITUTION OF EQUALITY: DEMOCRATIC AUTHORITY AND ITS LIMITS (2008); JEREMY WALDRON, LAW AND DISAGREEMENT (1999).

48 Niko Kolodny, *Rule Over None II: Social Equality and the Justification of Democracy*. 42 PHIL. & PUB. AFFS. 287 (2014).

influence occurs when subjects have an equal share of the necessary resources for influencing.

Second, political uses of conscience-based claims are undemocratic under the deliberative democracy element of the democratic ideal. According to the deliberative democratic element, legitimate political decisions should be the outcome of a deliberative process involving all affected or subjected individuals on an equal standing. On this view, political uses of conscience-based claims are undemocratic simply because imposing a belief on others is just the opposite of engaging in deliberation with them.

Political uses of conscience-based claims are problematic from the point of view of equal influence. As noted, these uses are part of a religious lawfare strategy led by conservative religious actors that have exploited their power and influence to capture and subvert democratic processes. According to social movement theory,[49] the ability a group has to influence political agents and decisions by employing political uses of conscience-based claims depends on the group's economic or organizational *resources*. Previous chapters have shown that the rise and expansion of political uses of conscience-based claims did not happen by chance but is rather the result of a broader strategy led by conservative and religious groups.

Moreover, regardless of the amount of power these groups have, allowing political uses of conscience-based claims essentially means that individuals who can claim these exemptions have an additional avenue of political participation that is unavailable, legally speaking, to those who do not share their beliefs.[50]

Aside from noticeable differences, political uses of conscience-based claims are democratically objectionable for the same reason that mechanisms, such as lobbying, bribery, extortion, or corporate funding of political campaigns where individuals or institutions translate financial power into political power are democratically objectionable: rather than engaging in deliberation

---

49 CHARLES TILLY & SIDNEY TARROW, CONTENTIOUS POLITICS (2015).

50 Brian Hutler, *Against the Political Use of Religious Exemptions*, 47 PHIL & PUB. AFFS. 330 (2019). Religious groups still have other avenues for political participation, such as propaganda, public advertisement, and other forms of campaigns. *See generally* Pierluigi Chiassoni, *Protecting freedom of conscience in a constitutional state*, *in* RELIGION, LAW AND THE POLITICS OF ETHICAL DIVERSITY: CONSCIENTIOUS OBJECTION AND CONTESTATION OF CIVIL NORMS 24 (Claude Proeschel, David Koussens & Francesco Piraino eds., 2021) (examining Carlo Augusto Viano, La libertà dalla religione (2007) (unpublished manuscript) (detailing what legitimate democratic participation of religious groups would look like).

and compromise political decisions end up being swayed by differences among people that are morally arbitrary or unjust.[51]

What is undemocratic is that opportunities for influence are unequal and arbitrary, not that people exercise those unequal opportunities. Those who can exert unequal influence over political processes through political uses of conscience-based claims do something morally problematic when they exert that influence.

It is important to note that conscience-based claims can sometimes be compatible with democracy understood as equal influence, and even with democracy understood as deliberative democracy. The fact that a specific type or use of conscience-based claims—referred to here as "political uses"—is not compatible with democracy does not imply that all conscience-based claims are undemocratic.[52]

Under both understandings of the democratic ideal (equal influence and deliberation), *conventional uses of conscience-based claims* are compatible with democracy, even when they may be illegal. From the point of view of the deliberative democratic ideal, conventional uses of conscience-based claims can be regarded as a crucial channel for conveying opinions and attitudes to public officials and the public, becoming part of a healthy deliberative democracy.[53] Persuading a person into doing something is not the same as imposing the idea onto that person.[54] Even though it might be true that communicating something to someone might cause that person to change his or her mind, the act of communicating a weighty reason is not *per se* an act of pressure, imposition, or force.

---

51 *See generally* Thomas Christiano, *Money in Politics*, *in* THE OXFORD HANDBOOK OF POLITICAL PHILOSOPHY (David Estlund ed., 2012) (identifying several mechanisms through which individuals turn financial power into political power). The same can be applied to the role of religious groups with great economic resources. For instance, those groups can financially support political parties and individuals; they can also use their platforms to set the agenda and/or influence public opinion; and they can wield their economic prowess as a threat against or in favor of certain agendas, such as threatening to tell their congregation to vote for another candidate if disfavored agendas are enacted. *See also*, Daniel Markovits, *Democratic Disobedience*, 114 YALE L. J. 1897 (2005).

52 DELIBERATIVE SYSTEMS: DELIBERATIVE DEMOCRACY AT THE LARGE SCALE, (John Parkinson & Jane Mansbridge eds., 2012).

53 JOHN RAWLS, A THEORY OF JUSTICE (1971). *See also* Emanuela Ceva, *Political Justification through Democratic Participation: The Case for Conscientious Objection*, 41 SOC. THEORY & PRAC. 26, 26–50 (2015). *See generally* Ronald Dworkin, *Civil Disobedience and Nuclear Protest*, *in* A Matter of Principle (1985) (in particular, the discussion around persuasive and non-persuasive strategies).

54 Ronald Dworkin, *Civil Disobedience and Nuclear Protest*, *in* A MATTER OF PRINCIPLE (1985).

Conventional uses of conscience-based claims can thus be compatible with democracy understood as equal influence in two ways. First, in political systems where equal influence is not safeguarded, conscience-based claims can be necessary to equalize such influence. Conscience-based claims may be required to equalize influence indirectly or directly in the following ways: on the one hand, conscience-based claims may be needed to reform formal and informal social norms that enable unequal influence; on the other hand, conscience-based claims may be themselves a form of influence that equalizes and/or counters the influence of wealth or privilege on the political process.

The second way in which conscience-based claims might be compatible with equal influence is when such an appeal aims to prevent *future* unequal influence. Some processes where everyone has equal influence can result in decisions that will cause formal or informal unequal influence in the future. A clear example of this is judicial review, which has often been protected under the argument that it is a means to prevent undemocratic outcomes. If a democratic decision takes away the equal right to vote, a court is entitled to render the decision legally invalid.[55] Similarly, we can rely on the same rationale to justify the use of conscience-based claims. If current democratic processes that preserve the status quo would cause millions of people to suffer from infringements to their deeply held sincere beliefs in the future, these victims will lack equal informal opportunities for influence in future political decisions. Thus, political uses of conscience-based claims might be justified to preserve the preconditions for future equal influence. This rationale, however, is problematic. The main reason for engaging in conscience-based claims is to prevent actual infringements on the objector's sincere beliefs, not to secure future equal influence. It would likely even be *offensive* to potential objectors if people who engage in political uses of conscience-based claims justified their actions on the fact that they will preserve future equal influence for those potentially affected.[56] The primary justification for conscience-based claims is that not granting them can, at times, lead to serious rights violations. As such, it would be offensive to the potential victims of infringements on their sincerely held beliefs to argue that the use of conscience-based claims is justified to preserve their equal political influence instead of their beliefs.

55 Ronald Dworkin, *Equality, Democracy, and Constitution: We The People in Court*, XXVIII ALTA. L. R. 324 (1990); JOHN HART ELY, DEMOCRACY AND DISTRUST: A THEORY OF JUDICIAL REVIEW (1980).

56 *See* Aleksander Stępkowki, *Contemporary Conscience-Related Controversies Against Philosophical Background*, *in* ALEKSANDER STĘPKOWKI, CONTEMPORARY CHALLENGES TO CONSCIENCE: LEGAL AND ETHICAL FRAMEWORKS FOR PROFESSIONAL CONDUCT (2019).

Conscience-based claims can also be compatible with democracy understood as deliberation. When deliberative spaces to foster a reengagement with an issue that a citizen or group perceives as a deficit in democracy are closed, conscience-based claims may be justified to open up those spaces to deliberation, insofar as its use is intended to correct substantial democratic deficits resulting from a substantial failure of democratic engagement in the processes that produced the objected outcome, instead of just opposing mere political defeats.[57]

It may be argued, however, that relying on a pure proceduralist account of democratic legitimacy substantially limits the space for disobedience as, essentially, when rules abide by the process and are democratically adopted, no one could claim to have a good reason for disobedience. This is wrong or, at the very least, an inaccurate depiction of the proceduralist account based on a common claim that democracy entails legitimacy. Acknowledging that laws were adopted within the democratic process and in accord with its procedures, it follows that the government has the right to enact and enforce its laws and policies. Therefore, resistance to law is still allowed, but assuming one chooses to oppose these laws, the only requirement is that it is done within the system.[58]

Opposing a law or decision within the system would involve utilizing ways to challenge it in courts, political forums, the media, or through public demonstrations. In extreme cases, this opposition may even manifest as civil disobedience, which remains within the system as long as the individual accepts the government's right to penalize them for their actions.[59] By accepting such penalty, one underscores the intensity of their conviction, draws attention to the perceived injustices, and strengthens their claim for a democratic hearing.[60]

In turn, opposing a decision outside the system could still be permissible, so long as the opposition aims at correcting substantial democracy deficits

57 Archong Fung, *Deliberation before the Revolution: Toward an Ethics of Deliberative Democracy in an Unjust World*, 33 POL. THEORY 397 (2005); William Smith, *Democracy, Deliberation and Disobedience*, 10 RES PUBLICA 353 (2004). *See also*, Daniel Markovits, *Democratic Disobedience*, 114 YALE L. J. 1897 (2005).

58 *See* Philip Pettit, *The Democratic Riddle*, 1 ARGUMENTS 2, 147–160 (2016).

59 Civil disobedients are typically expected to acknowledge their actions and accept the legal consequences for breaking the law. *See* Carl Cohen, *Civil Disobedience and the Law*, RUTGERS L. REV., 21 (1): 1–17, 6 (1966); *see also* KIMBERLEY BROWNLEE. CONSCIENCE AND CONVICTION: THE CASE FOR CIVIL DISOBEDIENCE (2012), chapter 1; Candice Delmas, *Civil Disobedience, Punishment, and Injustice*, *in* K. K. FERZAN AND L. ALEXANDER (EDS.), THE PALGRAVE HANDBOOK OF APPLIED ETHICS AND THE CRIMINAL LAW (2019), pp. 167–188.

60 *See* Philip Pettit, *Legitimacy and Justice in Republican Perspective*, 65 CURRENT LEGAL PROBLEMS, 59–82 (2012).

(for instance, in political systems where equal influence is not safeguarded, or where there has been a substantial failure of democratic engagement in the process), as explained above.[61] Naturally, these instances, would be difficult to diagnose and often imprecise, but at a minimum, they would involve situations where a policy option enjoys significant public support but is entirely excluded from the political agenda by democratic institutions or relevant stakeholders. As Prof. Markovits notes, this would occur in cases where despite the significant public support "no major political party adopts the policy, the mainstream press ignores it, and this state of affairs does not respond to the legal forms of protest [within the system]".[62]

For the purposes of the themes addressed in this book, such situations would rarely be found in contemporary debates around issues like the tension between legal abortion or LGBTQ rights and conscience rights. These topics are undeniably part of regular public discourse, present in the streets, academia, mainstream media, and central to political agendas. Therefore, for instance, if a government adopts a policy liberalizing abortion, groups opposing this policy cannot simply resort to political uses of conscience-based claims as a way to virtually veto its effect. Such tactics would not address, nor would aim at resolving, a democratic deficit.

3 Political Uses of Conscience-Based Claims Are Harmful

In addition to being undemocratic, political uses of conscience-based claims are harmful. Rather than promoting or protecting civil rights, political uses of conscience-based claims have come at the cost of other people's rights. As mentioned, one area where this has been particularly clear is in the healthcare realm, where political uses of conscience-based claims have impaired access to sexual and reproductive health services.

The refusal of health professionals to provide sexual and reproductive services on the basis of conscientious objection harms people who are denied the care they want and need, in violation of the ethical principle of doing no harm. Because denial of care forces patients to seek services elsewhere, face delays, or even forgo care, this is particularly damaging to those already in vulnerable situations, such as low-income women or women in rural areas. In most cases, finding another provider who is willing to provide, for instance, an abortion can be costly both in terms of time and resources, and in some situations it

61 Daniel Markovits, *Democratic Disobedience*, 114 YALE L. J. 1897 (2005).
62 *Id.*

may not even be possible. A woman who is denied services may have no choice but to resort to an unsafe and clandestine abortion, with serious consequences for her health and life. Furthermore, a woman faced with the denial of a service to which she is entitled to receive may feel that she has nowhere to go, which in turn can contribute to stigmatization, isolation, and shame. All these scenarios can cause mental anguish, trauma, and economic difficulties and, therefore, an impairment of the rights to health, personal integrity, and of every person not to be subjected to cruel, inhuman or degrading treatment.[63]

Healthcare providers who refuse to provide care and services exacerbate existing inequalities.[64] The status and authority of healthcare professionals, especially physicians, make it difficult for patients to challenge their decisions or even ask questions.[65] In addition, health professionals often have a monopoly on the provision of services. The claim that their "right" to deny care, based on their personal beliefs, takes precedence over patients' rights and health gives them even more power in an already unequal relationship.[66] The more marginalized the person seeking services, the more likely they will face difficulties in overcoming this imbalance of power to demand the services to which they are entitled.[67]

---

63 Rana E. Barar, *Best Practice for Abortion Policies: Listen to Women's Stories*, THE COSTA RICA STAR, (Sept. 8, 2015), https://news.co.cr/best-practice-abortion-policies-listen-womens-stories/54415/ (last visited Nov 11, 2023); Diana Greene Foster, *Introduction to the Turnaway Study*, *in* ADVANCING NEW STANDARDS IN REPRODUCTIVE HEALTH (Feb. 2018), https://www.ansirh.org/research/ongoing/turnaway-study (last visited Nov 11, 2023); Jane Harries et al., *An Exploratory Study of What Happens to Women Who Are Denied Abortions in Cape Town, South Africa*, 12 REPRO. HEALTH 1–6 (2015); H. Shanawani, *The Challenges of Conscientious Objection in Health Care*, 55 J RELIG. HEALTH 384–93 (2016); Wendy Chavkin et al., *Conscientious objection to the provision of reproductive healthcare*, 123 INT'L J. GYNECOLOGY & OBSTETRICS (2013).

64 Martin Hevia & Andrés Constantin, *Gendered Power Relations and Informed Consent: The I.V.v. Bolivia Case*, 20 HEALTH & HUM. RTS. J. 197–204 (2018).

65 *See* T. L. BEAUCHAMP & J. F. CHILDRESS, PRINCIPLES OF BIOMEDICAL ETHICS 176 (2001); *see also* R. Kaba & P. Sooriakumaran, *The evolution of the doctor-patient relationship*, INT'L J. SURGERY 57–65 (2007).

66 T. Murphy, *Health confidentiality in the age of talk*, *in* FEMINIST PERSPECTIVES ON HEALTH CARE LAW 155–71 (S. Sheldon ed., 1998). MARCELO ALEGRE & ROBERTO GARGARELLA, EL DERECHO A LA IGUALDAD. APORTES PARA UN CONSTITUCIONALISMO IGUALITARIO 166–67 (2007); U.N. General Assembly, *Report of the U.N. Special Rapporteur on the Right to the Highest Attainable Standard of Physical and Mental Health, Anand Grover*, U.N. Doc. A/64/272 (Aug. 10, 2009), ¶ 17.

67 *C.f.*, R. J. Cook, *International human rights to improve women's health*, *in* WOMEN'S HEALTH AND HUMAN RIGHTS: THE PROMOTION AND PROTECTION OF WOMEN'S HEALTH THROUGH INTERNATIONAL HUMAN RIGHTS LAW 26 (1994) (clarifying, in contrast, that "the role of health professionals [should be] to give the individual decision-maker

From a public health perspective, conscientious objection to healthcare services has several ramifications derived from the obvious consequence of having fewer providers offering services. First, the decrease in the number of providers available to provide a health service generates a decrease and/or delay in access to these services, which, in turn, increases the risks of mortality and morbidity. Conscientious objection may impose an undue burden on those seeking health care by forcing them to incur additional costs, such as travel costs, or they may need more time off work to find another professional, hospital, or facility for medical care.[68] Furthermore, delays in access to health services derived from the exercise of conscientious objection can result in a significant increase in morbidity.

In many cases, conscientious objection prevents patients from receiving adequate, accurate, and unbiased information about their treatment options, which can undermine the standard of care.[69] In this sense, extending the exercise of conscientious objection beyond the people directly involved in carrying out the procedure or providing the service may have a disproportionate impact on access to health services. Meanwhile, access barriers may be exacerbated by the extensive use of conscientious objection by administrative or support personnel who refuse to provide care—including even a referral to another health center—prior to or after the intervention. Such exercise of conscientious

medical and other health-related information that contributes to the individual's power of choice and does not distort or unbalance that power.")

68 Christian Fiala & Joice Arthur, *"Dishonourable disobedience"—Why refusal to treat in reproductive health care is not conscientious objection*, 1 PSYCHOSOMATIC GYNECOLOGY & OBSTETRICS 12–23 (2014).

69 T.A. Weitz & S. Berke Fogel, *The denial of abortion care information, referrals, and services undermines quality care for U.S. women*, 20 WOMEN'S HEALTH ISSUES 7–11 (2010). This has been clear in cases of ectopic pregnancies, where the only alternative to treat such condition requires the termination of pregnancy with medication or surgery. In some cases, doctors have withheld information about what an ectopic pregnancy entails, its risks and treatment alternatives under the belief that doing so would make them complicit to an abortion. *See* Jennifer Dalven, *Kansas to Pregnant Women: "A Little Lie from Your Doctor Won't Hurt You,"* ACLU SPEAK FREELY (Mar. 12, 2012), https://www.aclu.org/news/reproductive-freedom/kansas-pregnant-women-little-lie-your-doctor-wont-hurt-you (last visited Nov 11, 2023). Some U.S. states have passed laws to prevent medical care for ectopic pregnancies. *See* Anna North, *This life-threatening pregnancy complication is the next frontier in the abortion debate*, VOX (Sept. 11, 2019), https://www.vox.com/2019/9/11/20859034/ectopic-pregnancy-abortion-federalist-intrauterine-ohio-surgery (last visited Nov 11, 2023); Charlotte Huff, *In Texas, abortion laws inhibit care for miscarriages*, NPR (May 10, 2022), https://www.npr.org/sections/health-shots/2022/05/10/1097734167/in-texas-abortion-laws-inhibit-care-for-miscarriages (last visited Nov 11, 2023).

objection by personnel not directly involved with health care would imply an unacceptable violation of the right to health.[70]

Likewise, health personnel who refuse to provide medical care exacerbate existing inequalities, and in this way, go against the principle of beneficence in ethics, which requires them to act beneficially in favor of others and make a balance or judgment of proportionality between the benefits and the disadvantages of their decisions. In this sense, the health system barriers faced by its users, especially those who are in vulnerable conditions, imply that the decision to deny the provision of a health service has drawbacks consisting of the imposition of additional burdens to seek care elsewhere and the possible complete denial of access to these services putting the life, personal integrity, and health of the user at risk.

In Italy, for example, when it comes to access to sexual and reproductive health services, 69% of all gynecologists refuse to carry out legal terminations of pregnancy, and the figure rises to more than 80% in some regions.[71] According to government figures, seven out of ten doctors in Italy are conscientious objectors.[72] This figure is even higher in Sicily where 87.6% of doctors are

---

70 *See, e.g.*, Constitutional Court of Colombia, Oct. 17, 2018, Judgment SU096/18; *see also*, Constitutional Court of Colombia, May 28, 2009, Judgment T-388/09 (noting that "[i]n effect, it bears no relation with the nature of conscientious objection that the personnel in charge of opening the medical history, the institution's archive, receiving patients, cleaning the facilities, etc. refrain from carrying out their work, since it will be difficult to find a real connection with moral, philosophical or religious reasons; in the same way, this possibility will not exist with respect to the personnel that performs the preparatory medical tasks, such as conducting the necessary preparatory exams, the orientation regarding the consequences of the procedure, the psychological assistance prior to the intervention, etc. Finally, it does not make sense that the medical personnel who must help the patient in her recovery stage after the intervention intends to exercise conscientious objection, since the connection between the possible moral, religious or philosophical reasons and the non-compliance with the work that is being carried out at that precise moment lacks any foundation, being, on the contrary, a sign of a simple disapproval of the conduct already carried out, a situation that is completely unrelated to conscientious objection").

71 Italy Ministry of Health, *Report of the Ministry of Health on the Performance of the Law Containing Rules for the Social Care of Maternity and Voluntary Interruption of Pregnancy* (2007–2008). *See also* Christian Fiala & Joice Arthur, *Refusal to Treat Patients Does Not Work in Any Country—Even If Misleadingly Labeled "Conscientious Objection,"* 19 HEALTH & HUM. RTS. J. 299 (2017).

72 Ilaria Maria Sala, *Abortion in Italy, a Right Wronged*, N.Y. TIMES (Nov. 13, 2017), https://www.nytimes.com/2017/11/13/opinion/abortion-italy-conscientious-objectors.html (last visited Nov 11, 2023).

objectors.[73] In Molise (in central Italy), 93% of gynecologists are conscientious objectors.[74] Similarly, in Austria, providers of abortion services have to travel from Vienna to Salzburg once a week to practice in a public hospital, because gynecologists in this region invoked conscientious objection after suffering intense pressure and stigmatization within their communities.[75] This situation is not unique to Europe. It is also happening in Latin America. In Uruguay, studies indicate that there are entire localities where 100% of sexual and reproductive healthcare professionals are objectors.[76] After the adoption of the law that decriminalized abortion in 2020 in Argentina, data from the capital of the province of Salta, the seventh most populous city in Argentina, indicated that there are only 19 health professionals willing to guarantee the right to legal abortion in public hospitals. Moreover, in the city's Maternal and Child Hospital, a staggering 90% of the 70 gynecology specialists refuse to provide abortion services on conscientious grounds.[77]

---

73 *Id. See also* Gaia Pianigiani, *On Paper, Italy Allows Abortions, but Few Doctors Will Perform Them,* N.Y. Times (Jan. 16, 2016), https://www.nytimes.com/2016/01/17/world/europe/on-paper-italy-allows-abortions-but-few-doctors-will-perform-them.html?module=inline (last visited Nov 11, 2023).

74 Claudia Torrisi, *Abortion in Italy: how widespread 'conscientious objection' threatens women's health and right,* Open Democracy (Jun. 15, 2017), https://www.opendemocracy.net/5050/claudia-torrisi/abortion-italy-conscientious-objection (last visited Nov 11, 2023).

75 Christian Fiala & Joice Arthur, *"Dishonourable disobedience"—Why refusal to treat in reproductive health care is not conscientious objection,* 1 Psychosomatic Gynecology & Obstetrics 12–23 (2014).

76 For instance, in the localities of Mercedes, Young and Castillos. In other cases, such as in the department of Rivera, 67% of health care professionals are conscientious objectors. *See* MySU, Servicios Legales De Aborto En Uruguay: Logros y desafíos de su funcionamiento (2017); MySU, Estado de situación de los servicios de salud sexual y reproductiva y aborto en los departamentos de Florida, Maldonado y Rivera (2016); MySU, "Objeción de conciencia" en cifras (2021).

77 La Izquierda Diario, *En hospital de Salta el 95% de los médicos se declaran objetores de conciencia,* La Izquierda Diario (Dec. 25, 2020), https://www.laizquierdadiario.com/En-hospital-de-Salta-el-95-de-los-medicos-se-declaran-objetores-de-conciencia (last visited Nov 11, 2023). *See generally* A. Constantin and K. Zamanian, *How New Uses of Conscience-Based Claims Hinder Progress on Abortion Rights,* OpenGlobalRights (Dec. 6, 2021), https://www.openglobalrights.org/how-new-uses-of-conscience-based-claims-hinder-progress-on-abortion-rights/ (last visited Nov 11, 2023); Daniel Politi, *Argentina legalizó el aborto, pero los opositores dificultan el acceso,* N.Y. Times (Mar. 7, 2021—updated Sept. 13, 2021), https://www.nytimes.com/es/2021/03/07/espanol/ley-aborto-argentina.html (noting that 29 out of 30 obstetricians in a Jujuy Province hospital have declared themselves as "conscientious objectors" to the provision of abortion services) (last visited Nov 11, 2023); Página 12, *Faltan médicos para garantizar la IVE en clínicas y*

Moreover, the decline in the number of providers available to provide legal health services has a double impact on those that do provide these services.[78] On the one hand, the providers available to provide this service may experience work overloads and burnouts that affect their productivity and have a negative impact on the health system. On the other hand, available providers may suffer a greater risk of stigmatization from the communities where they live, which can have an impact on their mental and, in some cases, physical health when this stigmatization translates into physical violence. In other words, even physicians who may be willing to provide health care may be forced to refuse provision or be unable to provide service for fear of stigmatization or discrimination.

The effects of conscientious objection may extend beyond objectors who have religious beliefs. Conscientious objection can promote opportunistic behaviors: health personnel who are indecisive may choose to adopt conscientious objection when given that option, thus distorting the purpose of conscientious objection, which is precisely to protect conscience against acts that are considered contrary to it.[79]

In the same sense, health professionals can benefit from the invocation of conscientious objection since by doing so they can dedicate more time to more "reputable" or "profitable" treatments. Consequently, they escape stigma and improve their careers, reputations, and salaries while health personnel who fully comply with the provision of health services, are subjected to burdens and stigmas.

Additionally, political uses of conscience-based claims that intend to extend these claims from the individual to the institutional realm can harm the very healthcare professionals that work at institutions that claim an institutional conscientious objection. Healthcare professionals are people dedicated to such a profession due to their conscience, formed by different personal convictions and, often, by a strong vocation of service to others. Therefore, it would not be proper to ask them to abandon their conscience when the institution in which they work declares itself to be a conscientious objector. Respecting the conscience as well as the personal and professional autonomy of healthcare professionals in institutions that declare themselves to be objectors requires

---

hospitales de Salta, PÁGINA 12 (Mar. 31, 2021), https://www.pagina12.com.ar/332850-faltan-medicos-para-garantizar-la-ive-en-clinicas-y-hospital (last visited Nov 11, 2023).

78 Wendy Chavkin et al., *Conscientious objection and refusal to provide reproductive healthcare*, 123 INT'L J. GYNECOLOGY & OBSTETRICS 41–56 (2013).

79 Megan Millward, *Should pregnant doctors work in termination of pregnancy clinics?*, BMJ 340 (2010).

understanding that conscience based on secular convictions—such as philosophical, social, political, professional, or other convictions—is not less worthy of respect than conscience guided by religion.[80] The exercise of conscience-based claims as a way to restrict access to health services for reasons of conscience may violate the rights and autonomy not only of patients but also of healthcare providers.

Healthcare professionals' independence constitutes one of the main guarantees in the exercise of the medical profession. These professionals should be able to enjoy professional freedom allowing them to care for their patients without interference. In turn, they must have professional independence to represent and defend the needs of their patients in health matters against all those who would deny or limit the care they need.[81]

The concept of healthcare professionals' independence protects professionals whose conscience motivates them to provide sexual and reproductive health services and who give priority to patient care over adherence to religious doctrines or to their own religious interest.[82] The full respect of conscience and professional autonomy requires that both the objection to participate and the commitment to the provision of services be such that this last group of providers is not subject to discrimination based on their convictions.[83] Respect for ideological freedom is intimately related to respect for the dignity and privacy of the worker. These rights are central elements of democracy. The employment contract cannot deprive workers of their rights, dignity, and freedom. Freedom of enterprise and the employment contract do not function as a "legitimizing title" to restrict fundamental rights, since workers do not lose their basic entitlements when becoming part of a company or institution. Undergoing an employment relationship cannot imply losing one's rights.

It is true that institutions may, in some circumstances, limit the exercise of certain rights of their workers when necessary for the proper functioning of

80 Bernard M. Dickens & Rebecca J. Cook, *Conscientious commitment to women's health*, 113 INT'L J. GYNECOLOGY & OBSTETRICS 163–66 (2011). *See also* L. Harris, *Recognizing Conscience in Abortion Provision*, 367 NEW ENG. J. MED., 981–83 (2012).

81 Asociación Médica Mundial, *Declaración de la Asociación Médica Mundial sobre la independencia y libertad profesional del médico.* [Adopted by the 38th World Medical Assembly, Rancho Mirage, Cal., U.S.] Oct. 1986.

82 B.M. Dickens & R.J. Cook, *Conscientious commitment to women's health*, 113 INT'L J. GYNECOLOGY & OBSTETRICS 163–66 (2011). *See also* L. Harris, *Recognizing Conscience in Abortion Provision*, 367 NEW ENG. J. MED., 981–83.

83 FIGO COMMITTEE FOR THE ETHICAL ASPECTS OF HUMAN REPRODUCTION AND WOMEN'S HEALTH: INTERNATIONAL FEDERATION OF GYNECOLOGY AND OBSTETRICS, ETHICAL GUIDELINES ON CONSCIENTIOUS OBJECTION (2006).

the organization. However, the right to institutional conscientious objection cannot be used as an element to legitimize the imposition of beliefs, ideas, or religions, since this would be hard to argue that it is necessary for the normal functioning of an organization and, therefore, it would constitute an unwarranted interference in the private sphere and personal autonomy of healthcare providers that, for instance, may be willing and consciously committed to provide legal interruption of pregnancy services.[84] Not to mention that institutions that impose sanctions against those exercising their right to freedom of conscience and decide to perform, for instance, an abortion, would weaken the justification for the protection that they themselves demand.

4 Conclusion

The landscape of political uses of conscience-based claims presents a complex and multifaceted set of challenges and considerations. This chapter explored various dimensions of these conscience-based claims, examining the implications they carry for democracy, rights, and health. This analysis made it clear that the issues surrounding conscience-based claims are far from straightforward and necessitate a nuanced understanding to navigate effectively in contemporary society.

The historical foundations of conscience-based claims, which have roots deeply embedded in the principles of freedom of religion and conscience, initially served as shields to protect minority views from the oppression of majorities, aiming to ensure that individuals and groups could live according to their deeply held beliefs without fear of persecution or discrimination. Over time, they evolved to encompass a wider range of applications, giving rise to political uses of conscience-based claims. The evolving landscape of

84 It is important to note that an institution that wants to exercise a claim for institutional conscientious objection would have a hard time defending such decision from a labor law perspective. Even if the institution circumvents the challenges already mentioned, the institution would have a very limited range of action in any efforts that would require potential hires to disclose their beliefs at the time of hiring, as such attempt would essentially violate their privacy and establishing the "conscientious objector status" as an exclusive condition for hiring would further constitute a form of discrimination. This would potentially contravene multiple legal frameworks at the domestic and the international level. *See* The General Conference of the International Labor Organization, Convention No. 111 concerning Discrimination in Respect of Employment and Occupation art. 1 (1958).

conscience-based claims now extends beyond their original purpose and presents new challenges.

The undemocratic aspects of political uses of conscience-based claims emphasize the potential for these claims to be weaponized, leading to discrimination and erosion of other essential democratic principles. Political uses of conscience-based claims are a particularly contentious issue, as they have the potential to undermine democratic processes and hinder equal participation, equal influence, and deliberative elements of democracy.

The harmful consequences of conscience-based claims, in turn, have pervasively been present in the healthcare sector, specifically in the context of sexual and reproductive health services. The refusal of healthcare professionals to provide these services, despite its legality, on the grounds of conscientious objection can result in serious harm to patients, particularly those in vulnerable situations. Denial of care under the guise of a conscience-based claim can lead to delays, increased costs, and even force individuals to seek unsafe alternatives, jeopardizing their health and well-being. Furthermore, this practice exacerbates existing inequalities and reinforces the power imbalance between healthcare providers and patients.

Additionally, political uses of conscience-based claims can spillover and extend beyond religious believers and serve as a means for healthcare professionals to prioritize certain treatments or avoid others for personal gain or reputation. This opportunistic behavior distorts the intended purpose of conscientious objection and can further compromise overall patient care. Moreover, when entire regions or countries are dominated by objectors, as observed in some European and Latin American contexts, access to essential healthcare services becomes severely limited, affecting thousands of individuals.[85]

In summary, the issues surrounding conscience-based claims are multifaceted and require careful consideration of the balance between individual freedom of conscience and the broader societal interests in democracy, rights, and public health. Finding a path forward that respects the rights of all individuals, while safeguarding the principles of democracy, remains a pressing challenge for liberal democracies.

85 European Committee of Social Rights, 2014, International Planned Parenthood Federation European Network (IPPF-EN) v. Italy, No. 87/2012.

CHAPTER 4

Legal Efforts to Counter Religious Lawfare

The expansion of conscience-based claims to wage religious lawfare opened the door to abuses of the conscientious objector status that are dangerously undemocratic. However, the law has not remained inattentive to this development, but rather has sought ways to deal with it. A fresh look into how the Universal Human Rights System, as well as regional European, Inter-American and African systems have dealt with this issue in the context of sexual and reproductive health provides insights on strategic legal responses to counter religious lawfare.

1 Countering Religious Lawfare: Universal Human Rights System

In the global landscape, religious lawfare—where religious beliefs are strategically used to challenge or obstruct legal norms—has become increasingly prevalent, particularly in the realm of reproductive rights. International human rights law mechanisms have strived to navigate the complex interplay between such claims and the imperative to protect sexual and reproductive rights. The Universal Human Rights System, through key instruments like the International Covenant on Economic, Social, and Cultural Rights (ICESCR), plays a pivotal role in countering these conscience-based claims when they are employed as tools of political or religious influence.

The International Covenant on Economic, Social and Cultural Rights (ICESCR) enshrines the right to health in Article 12: "The States Parties to the present Covenant recognize the right of everyone to the enjoyment of the highest attainable standard of physical and mental health."[1] Over the years, the Committee on Economic, Social and Cultural Rights (CESCR) has published General Comments No. 14 (establishing that sexual and reproductive health is included in the right to health[2]) and No. 22 to elaborate on this right, describing how "[t]he right to sexual and reproductive health is … indivisible from and interdependent with other human rights … such as the rights to life; liberty and

1 International Covenant on Economic, Social and Cultural Rights (ICESCR), art. 12, ¶ 1, Dec. 16, 1966.

2 *See* U.N. Committee on Economic, Social and Cultural Rights, General Comment No. 14, U.N. Doc. E/C.12/2000/4 (Aug. 11, 2000).

 | DOI:10.1163/9789004685406_006

security of person; freedom from torture and other cruel, inhuman, or degrading treatment; privacy and respect for family life; and non-discrimination and equality."[3]

The CESCR described specific obligations of states under the respect, protect, and fulfill framework, including states' obligation "to ensure that medical practitioners and other health professionals meet appropriate standards of education, skill, and ethical codes of conduct."[4] It also enumerated as a "core obligation" that States "ensure reproductive, maternal (pre-natal as well as post-natal), and child healthcare."[5] An example of an appropriate ethical code of conduct in the reproductive health sphere comes from the International Federation of Gynecology and Obstetrics (FIGO), whose 2015 Study of Ethical Aspects of Human Reproduction and Women's Health described guidelines in conscientious objection surrounding abortion services.[6]

The guidelines emphasize that a practitioner's first priority and duty is to serve the healthcare needs of the patient, but when issues of conscience arise and the practitioner "feel[s] obliged to place their conscientious interests before their patient's interests, they have a conflict of interest."[7] Practitioners also have a duty to inform patients of "all medically indicated options for their care, including options in which the practitioners decline to participate."[8] According to FIGO's ethical framework, if the patient chooses such an option, the practitioner "should make every effort to achieve [an] appropriate referral."[9] The importance of a referral mechanism is emphasized by the medical association just as it is in treaty monitoring bodies' recommendations.[10]

Further, FIGO outlines its expectations of practitioners who, despite having a right to conscientiously object, "as medically trained and licensed practitioners [...] are bound to apply the profession's understanding of medical and reproductive science, and not to superimpose different characterizations of

3 U.N. Committee on Economic, Social and Cultural Rights, *General Comment No. 22*, ¶ 10, U.N. Doc. E/C.12/GC/22 (May 2, 2016).
4 U.N. Committee on Economic, Social and Cultural Rights, *General Comment No. 14*, ¶ 35, U.N. Doc E/C.12/2000/4.
5 *Id.* ¶ 44(a).
6 *See* INTERNATIONAL FEDERATION OF GYNECOLOGY AND OBSTETRICS, ETHICAL ISSUES IN OBSTETRICS AND GYNECOLOGY 38 (2015).
7 *Id.* at 37.
8 *Id.*
9 *Id.* at 37–38.
10 *Id.* at 38; U.N. Committee on Economic, Social and Cultural Rights, *General Comment No. 22*, ¶ 10, U.N. Doc. E/C.12/GC/22 (May 2, 2016).

procedures based on their personal beliefs."[11] This echoes the priority of the patient's needs over the practitioner's conscience, as does the requirement in the ethical framework that "in an emergency [...] [when] practitioners cannot refer such patients to non-objecting practitioners [in a timely manner] [...] [they] must give priority to their patients' lives, health and well-being by performing ... the indicated procedures."[12] The World Health Organization (WHO) also issued guidelines, though also non-binding, requiring an objecting physician to refer to another willing, able, and accessible physician, and if unavailable or in an emergency, the physician is "obligated to provide a safe abortion to preserve the woman's life and to prevent risks to her health."[13] In March 2022, the WHO issued new guidelines on abortion to help countries deliver lifesaving care.[14] In them, it recommended that access to and continuity of comprehensive abortion care be protected against barriers created by the exercise of conscientious objection, as it recognized that the exercise of conscience-based claims continues to operate as a barrier to access abortion care in contradiction with human rights obligations and previous WHO recommendations.[15] The WHO also acknowledged that conscientious objection may become "indefensible" if its exercise becomes incompatible with abortion rights.[16]

The Committee on Economic, Social and Cultural Rights (CESCR) expressed further concern that conscience-based refusal of services in the context of abortion services increases rates of maternal mortality.[17] In its General Comment No. 22, it specifically outlined the obligations of States to respect, protect, and fulfill the right to sexual and reproductive health as they relate to

---

11 *See* INTERNATIONAL FEDERATION OF GYNECOLOGY AND OBSTETRICS, ETHICAL ISSUES IN OBSTETRICS AND GYNECOLOGY 38 (2015).

12 *Id.*

13 Michelle Truong & Susan Y. Wood, UNCONSCIONABLE: WHEN PROVIDERS DENY ABORTION CARE 9 (2018).

14 World Health Organization, *WHO issues new guidelines on abortion to help countries deliver lifesaving care*, WHO NEWS (Mar. 9, 2022), https://www.who.int/news/item/09-03-2022-access-to-safe-abortion-critical-for-health-of-women-and-girls (last visited Nov 18, 2023). *See generally* WORLD HEALTH ORGANIZATION, ABORTION CARE GUIDELINE (2022).

15 WORLD HEALTH ORGANIZATION, ABORTION CARE GUIDELINE 60 (2022).

16 *Id.* This particular assertion drew strong criticism from religious groups. *See e.g.*, Kevin J. Jones, *WHO guidelines on abortion imply conscience objections are 'indefensible'*, CATH. NEWS AGENCY (Mar. 21, 2022), https://www.catholicnewsagency.com/news/250748/who-guidelines-on-abortion-imply-conscience-objections-are-indefensible (last visited Nov 18, 2023).

17 *See* U.N. Committee on Economic, Social and Cultural Rights, *General Comment No. 22*, ¶ 10, U.N. Doc. E/C.12/GC/22 (May 2, 2016).

conscientious objection.[18] First, in relation to conscientious objection under the obligation to respect, "States must reform laws that impede the exercise of the right to sexual and reproductive health ... includ[ing] laws criminalizing abortion."[19] Additionally, it clarified that the International Covenant on Economic, Social and Cultural Rights "requires States to repeal, and refrain from enacting, laws and policies that create barriers in access to sexual and reproductive health services."[20]

The CESCR specifically addressed concerns of conscientious objection regarding refusal to provide abortion services in the context of States' obligation to protect.[21] It noted that "[w]here health-care providers are allowed to invoke conscientious objection, States must appropriately regulate this practice to ensure that it does not inhibit anyone's access to sexual and reproductive health care."[22] Additionally, it recommended regulations in this sphere that include "requiring referrals to an accessible provider capable of and willing to provide the services being sought," and not allowing the invocation of conscience-based refusals in the event of an obstetric emergency requiring a termination of the pregnancy.[23] This obligation to protect places the burden on States to defend the right to sexual and reproductive health from third-parties that may "directly or indirectly interfere" with it.[24] Further, the CESCR explained that any third-party conduct that causes harm to the "physical or mental integrity" of the rights-bearer, or "undermines the full enjoyment of the right," must be prohibited by law of the State party.[25] Such third parties may include private healthcare providers or even religious groups whose manifestation of freedom of religion or belief goes beyond the imagined limits of the International Covenant on Civil and Political Rights (ICCPR). For instance, in *L.M.R. v. Argentina*, a Catholic group demonized a hospital for authorizing abortion services, leading to the services never being provided.[26] This would seem to be harmful third-party conduct, though the court did not rule on the merits of a violation of Article 18 of the ICCPR—on the right to freedom of

18 *See id.* ¶ 39.

19 *Id.* ¶ 40.

20 *Id.* ¶ 41.

21 *See id.* ¶ 43.

22 *Id.*

23 *Id.*

24 *Id.* ¶ 42.

25 *Id.*

26 *See* U.N. Human Rights Committee, *Communication No. 1608/2007* (L.M.R. v. Argentina), ¶ 3.1, U.N. Doc. CCPR/C/101/D/1608/2007 (Apr. 28, 2011).

thought, conscience and religion-, concluding that the claim was not substantiated sufficiently for admissibility purposes.[27]

Finally, the obligation to fulfill the right to sexual and reproductive healthcare "requires States to take measures to eradicate practical barriers to the full realization of the right [...] such as disproportionate costs and lack of physical or geographical access to [services]."[28] As briefly noted in the previous chapter, the exercise of conscientious objection by healthcare professionals may often result in *de facto* physical barriers due to high costs of alternatives, delays, mental stress and anguish, or geographic distance from willing and capable physicians. Fulfilling the right to sexual and reproductive healthcare also requires States to "take affirmative measures to eradicate social barriers in terms of norms or beliefs that inhibit individuals ... from autonomously exercising their right to sexual and reproductive health."[29] States violate the obligation to respect when "banning or denying access in practice to sexual and reproductive health services and medicines."[30] Additionally, States are obligated to "effectively monitor and regulate ... private health-care providers [and] health insurance companies ... to ensure that they do not undermine or violate enjoyment by individuals of the right to sexual and reproductive health."[31]

Poland offers a crucial example, and cautionary tale, of how conservative religious forces have effectively employed religious lawfare to institutionalize conscience-based refusals and impose religious morality on healthcare.[32]

Just a few weeks before the Law and Justice Party (PiS, for its acronym in Polish) took power in the 2015 parliamentary election,[33] the Polish Constitutional

---

27 *See* U.N. Human Rights Committee, *Communication No. 1608/2007* (L.M.R. v. Argentina), ¶ 3.1, U.N. Doc. CCPR/C/101/D/1608/2007 (Apr. 28, 2011).

28 *Id.* ¶ 46.

29 *Id.* ¶ 48.

30 *Id.* ¶ 57.

31 *Id.* ¶ 60.

32 In Poland there is a formal separation of church and state, with a *de facto* preeminence of one denomination: Catholicism. Indeed, despite the formal separation, the state cooperates closely with the Catholic Church, which continues to hold significant weight in legal and political debates. *See* Ran Hirschl, *Comparative Constitutional Law and Religion*, *in* COMPARATIVE CONSTITUTIONAL LAW 422, 430 (Tom Ginsburg & Rosalind Dixon eds., 2011). *See also*, Kyriaki Topidi, *Religious Freedom, National Identity, and the Polish Catholic Church: Converging Visions of Nation and God*, 10 RELIGIONS 5, 1 (2019); and Joanna Z. Mishtal, *Matters of "Conscience": The Politics of Reproductive Healthcare in Poland*, 23 MED. ANTHROPOLOGY Q. 161, 179 (2009).

33 In 2015, the Law and Justice Party (PiS, for its acronym in Polish), which has the backing of the Catholic Church and supports many of the church's policies, won a parliamentary majority, kicking off an era of increasing nationalism, authoritarianism, and Catholic morality. *See* Julia Hussein, et al., *Abortion in Poland: Politics, Progression and Regression*,

Tribunal ruled that Article 39 of the 1996 Medical Profession Act's requirement that physicians who conscientiously object to performing abortion services must refer patients to an alternative doctor or medical facility violates the Polish Constitution by interfering too greatly with physicians' freedom of conscience protected under Article 53.1.[34] The Tribunal also held that Article 39 was unconstitutional insofar as it required physicians to perform medical procedures that conflicted with their conscience in urgent cases requiring immediate treatment, finding immediacy to be an imprecise standard that does not allow unambiguous determinations as to when the law applies.[35]

In its Concluding Observations on Poland in 2016, the CESCR expressed its concern that "neither medical practitioners invoking conscientious objection grounds to perform an abortion, nor the institution concerned, are under a duty to refer the woman seeking an abortion to another service."[36] This lack of a referral mechanism, which resulted from the 2015 decision of the Constitutional Court of Poland, "further limit[s] access to safe and legal abortion" in violation of the rights to health and life under the ICESCR.[37] The Committee recommended that Poland "immediately establish and regulate an effective referral mechanism in cases where conscientious objection by medical

---

26 REPROD. HEALTH MATTERS 52 (2018); Kornelia Zaręba, et al., *Moral Dilemmas of Women Undergoing Pregnancy Termination for Medical Reasons in Poland*, 22 EUR. J. OF CONTRACEPTION & REPROD. HEALTH CARE 4 (2017). Through court packing and legislation that lead to a court's paralysis, the PiS effectively disabled the Constitutional Tribunal and transformed it into an active tool at the service of its political agenda. *See* WOJCIECH SADURSKI, POLAND'S CONSTITUTIONAL BREAKDOWN 62–79 (2019).

34 Polish Constitutional Tribunal Ref. Act K 12/14 Journal of Laws 2015, item 1633, 7 October 2015. Prior to this decision, Polish prosecutors and courts had already demonstrated a disinclination to prioritize patients' rights and freedoms in conscience clause cases. The *P. and S. v. Poland* case, examined below, came before the European Court of Human Rights in 2012 after a fourteen-year-old girl with a legal right to an abortion under Polish law was refused by three doctors who conscientiously objected to performing it and did not refer her to an alternative provider, in violation of Article 39 of the Medical Profession Act, which was still in effect at the time. *See* P. and S. v. Poland, App. No. 57375/08, Eur. Ct. H.R. (2013).

35 *See* FIDH, ALL DOWNHILL FROM HERE: THE RAPID DEGRADATION OF THE RULE OF LAW IN POLAND: WHAT IT MEANS FOR WOMEN'S SEXUAL AND REPRODUCTIVE RIGHTS, AND LGBT+ PERSONS' RIGHTS (November 2018).

36 U.N. Committee on Economic, Social and Cultural Rights, *Concluding Observations on the Sixth Periodic Report of Poland*, ¶ 46, U.N. Doc. E/C.12/POL/CO/6 (Oct. 26, 2016).

37 *Id.* The CEDAW Committee also expressed concerns about how the conscientious objection clause, which was further strengthened by the 2015 decision, constitutes a *de facto* barrier to access abortion in Poland. Committee for the Elimination of All Forms of Discrimination Against Women, *Inquiry concerning Poland conducted under article 8 of the Optional Protocol to the Convention*, ¶ 18, U.N. Doc. CEDAW/C/POL/IR/1 (Aug. 21, 2024).

practitioners is exercised."[38] The Committee has also addressed similar concerns about the growing practice of conscientious objection in Romania and Canada as creating a barrier to women's access to legal abortion services.[39] This concern demonstrates the importance of a referral mechanism as a tool to counter religious lawfare and mitigate the impact of the exercise of conscience-based claims, ensuring the full enjoyment of the right to sexual and reproductive health.

In 2016, the U.N. Human Rights Committee expressed similar concerns regarding Poland's practices, emphasizing, beyond the lack of a reliable referral mechanism, issues created by the "conscience clause" codified in Poland's "Act on Medical and Dental Profession."[40] The effect of the clause has been to allow healthcare professionals to "inappropriately invoke[]" a conscience-based objection, thus resulting in "legal abortion [being] unavailable in entire institutions and in one region of the country."[41] Additionally, Poland's Constitutional Tribunal rendered a judgment essentially eliminating any "reliable referral mechanism" that would provide women with access to a legal abortion from a non-objecting physician.[42] Finally, the increasingly widespread invocation of conscientious objection has created an environment in which wide swaths of the country have few to no willing providers of abortion services.[43] Regarding this development, the U.N. Human Rights Committee expressed its concern that Poland was creating an environment in which women would be forced to seek out clandestine abortions, putting the woman's life at risk.[44]

In response to these concerns, the U.N. Human Rights Committee concluded that Poland "should … [e]nsure that its legislation does not prompt women to resort to clandestine abortions that put their lives and health at risk."[45] The Committee directly linked the exercise of conscientious objection to its ultimate impact: women "resort[ing] to clandestine abortion", and provided

38 *Id.* ¶ 47.

39 *See* U.N. Committee on Economic, Social and Cultural Rights, *Concluding Observations on the Combined Third to Fifth Periodic Reports on Romania,* ¶ 22, U.N. Doc. E/C.12/ROU/CO/3–5 (Dec. 9, 2014); U.N. Committee on Economic, Social and Cultural Rights, *Concluding Observations on the Sixth Periodic Report on Canada,* ¶ 52, U.N. Doc. E/C.12/CAN/CO/6 (Mar. 23, 2016).

40 U.N. Human Rights Committee, *Concluding Observations on the Seventh Periodic Report of Poland,* ¶ 23, U.N. Doc. CCPR/C/POL/CO/7 (Nov. 23, 2016).

41 *Id.*

42 *Id.*

43 *See id.*

44 *See id.* at ¶ 24.

45 *Id.*

specific recommendations for steps to reduce this occurrence.[46] These steps include "establishing and regulating standardized guidelines in public health for the provision of legal abortion services throughout the country [and] enhancing the effectiveness of the referral mechanism to ensure access to legal abortion in cases of conscientious objection by medical practitioners."[47]

The U.N. Human Rights Committee has also issued numerous observations to other national governments warning them of the need to adopt measures to ensure that providers do not impede women's access to abortion services through the exercise of conscientious objection. For example, after reviewing Italy's compliance with the rights guaranteed in the ICCPR in 2017, the U.N. Human Rights Committee received "with concern the information referring to difficulties in accessing legal abortion, given the high number of doctors who refuse to perform abortions for reasons of conscience and the distribution of these doctors throughout the country. It is also concerned that, with this, the number of clandestine abortions is considerable."[48] In this regard, it demanded in its Concluding Observation that Italy adopt "the necessary measures to guarantee unrestricted and timely access to legal abortion services in its territory, among other means by creating an effective referral system for women interested in accessing such services."[49] This Concluding Observation is significant for its articulation of the use of conscientious objection as a barrier to accessing the services that women and other pregnant people are entitled to receive and the corresponding obligations of the State to ensure that access to legal abortions is effective in practice.

In its concluding observations drafted in response to country reports filed pursuant to the Optional Protocol of the ICCPR, the U.N. Human Rights Committee has elaborated further on these concerns. Specifically, it expressed that the exercise of conscientious objection in reproductive healthcare violates the fundamental right to health of individuals seeking care. The Committee's 2016 Concluding Observations on Colombia expressed its concern over the barriers to access abortion services women faced resulting from conscientious objection by "health-care personnel without appropriate referrals."[50] It recommended that the State "step up its efforts" to break down these barriers to access, calling upon the State to "establish an effective referral mechanism to ensure the

---

46 *Id.*

47 *Id.*

48 U.N. Human Rights Committee, *Concluding Observations on the Sixth Periodic Report of Italy*, ¶ 16, U.N. Doc. CCPR/C/ITA/CO/6 (May 1, 2017).

49 *Id.* ¶ 17.

50 U.N. Human Rights Committee, *Concluding Observations on the Seventh Periodic Report of Colombia*, ¶ 20, U.N. Doc. CCPR/C/COL/CO/7 (Nov. 17, 2016).

availability of safe abortion services" when women are confronted with a physician who objects to performing the procedure on conscience-based grounds.[51]

These recommendations build upon the analysis contained in the U.N. Human Rights Committee's General Comment No. 22 and shed some light upon what fundamental rights are not to be infringed upon in the manifestation of freedom of belief. The right to life and the right to health are both implicated by a medical professional's choice to refuse treatment to an individual seeking a legal abortion. By this refusal, and the often lacking referral to a willing physician, the pregnant person's health and life are put at risk as they must find an alternative, either by resorting to clandestine abortion or by carrying the pregnancy to term due to insurmountable costs in the effort to obtain proper medical care. Additionally, unreasonable delays often result from a refusal to provide care when a patient seeks to challenge the refusal through the State's courts, frequently resulting in the woman reaching a gestation point at which abortion becomes illegal within the state's framework.

The effect of unregulated or under-regulated invocations of conscientious objection by medical professionals is to allow the manifestation of one's freedom of religion to reach beyond the limits intended in its traditional understandings and origins.[52] Thus, a state may be justified in incorporating into its laws limitations upon this manifestation because of its impact on the "fundamental rights and freedoms of others."[53] While it would be difficult to completely abolish the exercise of conscientious objection by the medical profession, arguments are certainly available for limiting it and mitigating its impact on the enjoyment of rights. A large hurdle exists in the form of conservative religious groups co-opting the term "conscientious objection" to serve their own interests in a field in which it does not naturally apply.[54]

The U.N. Special Rapporteur on the right of everyone to the enjoyment of the highest attainable standard of physical and mental health, Anand Grover, released a report back in 2011 discussing his concerns over "ancillary personnel" exercising conscientious objection, thus creating "barriers to access" that "serve to reinforce the stigma that abortion is an objectionable practice."[55] The

---

51 *Id.* ¶ 21.

52 *See* ICCPR, art. 18; *see also U.N. Human Rights Committee, General Comment No. 22*, ¶ 8 CCPR/C/21/Rev.1/Add.4.

53 ICCPR, art. 18, ¶ 3.

54 *See* Michelle Truong & Susan Y. Wood, UNCONSCIONABLE: WHEN PROVIDERS DENY ABORTION CARE (2018).

55 U.N. General Assembly, *Report of the U.N. Special Rapporteur on the right of everyone to the enjoyment of the highest attainable standard of physical and mental health, Anand Grover*, ¶ 24, U.N. Doc. A/66/254 (Aug. 3, 2011).

expansion across the *depth* axis described in Chapter 2, has brought about significant concerns about conscience-based refusals spreading beyond the medical professionals taking direct part in the procedure, such as nurses and administrative staff. As the practice spreads, women's access to safe and legal abortion services necessarily decreases, leading to an increase in maternal deaths attributable to abortion,[56] a concern that becomes all the more important when considering the desire across U.N. treaty-monitoring bodies to work positively toward decreasing maternal mortality.[57] The U.N. and other international organizations, like the WHO, could—and should—emphasize the argument that the abusive exercise of conscientious objection not only to abortion, but to sexual and reproductive healthcare generally, is linked to maternal mortality.[58] This may be one of the stronger arguments for limiting conscientious objection in the universal human rights system, which has decreasing maternal mortality as one of its core goals.[59]

The interplay between the right to health and freedom of conscience then becomes dire, and these concerns are echoed by U.N. Special Rapporteur Anand Grover's statement that "States must take measures to ensure that legal and safe abortion services are available, accessible, and of good quality."[60] The exercise of conscientious objection even when women are seeking post-abortion care after undergoing a clandestine abortion leads to a further violation of the right to health.[61] However, U.N. Special Rapporteur Grover did not seek to outlaw conscientious objection on these grounds. Instead, he recommended that states "[e]nsure that conscientious objection exemptions are well-defined in scope and well-regulated in use and that referrals and alternative services are available in cases where objection is raised by a service provider."[62]

---

56 *See id.* ¶ 25.

57 *See* U.N. Economic and Social Council, *General Comment No. 14*, ¶ 21, U.N. Doc E/C.12/2000/4; United Nations Human Rights Council, *Report of the U.N. Special Rapporteur on torture and other cruel, inhuman or degrading treatment or punishment*, Juan E. Méndez, ¶ 43, U.N. Doc. A/HRC/31/57 (Jan 5, 2016).

58 *See* Michelle Truong & Susan Y. Wood, UNCONSCIONABLE: WHEN PROVIDERS DENY ABORTION CARE 15 (2018).

59 *See* U.N. General Assembly, *Report of the U.N. Special Rapporteur on the right of everyone to the enjoyment of the highest attainable standard of physical and mental health, Anand Grover*, ¶ 6, U.N. Doc. A/66/254 (Aug. 3, 2011).

60 U.N. General Assembly, *Report of the U.N. Special Rapporteur on the right of everyone to the enjoyment of the highest attainable standard of physical and mental health, Anand Grover*, ¶ 25, U.N. Doc. A/66/254 (Aug. 3, 2011).

61 *See id.* ¶ 33.

62 *Id.* ¶ 65(m).

The Universal Declaration of Human Rights (UDHR) and the International Covenant on Civil and Political Rights (ICCPR) also enshrine the right to non-discrimination.[63] As this right is one of the fundamental freedoms against which manifestations of freedom of conscience must be weighed, it is useful to better understand the arguments surrounding the exercise of conscientious objection to the provision of abortion services and how it may amount to discrimination.[64] First and foremost, the expansion of conscience-based claims, and its use as a tool of religious lawfare, will disproportionately affect women and pregnant people, who are the ones seeking abortion services. For a closer look at this issue, the Convention on the Elimination of All Forms of Discrimination Against Women (CEDAW) provides a useful starting point.

Discrimination under the CEDAW follows a broad definition described in Article 1 as "any distinction, exclusion or restriction made on the basis of sex which has the effect or purpose of impairing or nullifying the recognition, enjoyment or exercise by women ... of human rights and fundamental freedoms."[65] Article 12 of the Convention describes the obligations of State Parties to "take all appropriate measures to eliminate discrimination against women in the field of health care ... [and] ensure to women appropriate services in connection with pregnancy."[66] Further, Article 16 obliges States to "ensure, on the basis of equality of men and women ... the same rights to decide freely and responsibly on the number and spacing of their children and to have access to the information, education and means to enable them to exercise these rights."[67] To elaborate on the obligations enumerated in Article 12, the CEDAW Committee -the body of experts that monitors the implementation of the CEDAW- published its General Recommendation No. 24 on Women and Health.[68]

The CEDAW Committee has directly addressed the concern of refusals to provide abortion services, proclaiming that "it is discriminatory for a State party to refuse to provide legally for the performance of certain reproductive health services for women."[69] Going on to require that "if health service providers refuse to perform such services based on conscientious objection,

63 *See* ICCPR, art. 26; UDHR, art. 7.

64 *See* ICCPR, art. 18.

65 Convention on the Elimination of All Forms of Discrimination Against Women (CEDAW), art. 1 (Dec. 18, 1979).

66 *Id.* art. 12.

67 *Id.* art. 16.

68 *See* Committee on the Elimination of All Forms of Discrimination Against Women, *General Recommendation No. 24*, U.N. Doc. A/54/38/Rev.1, chap. I (1999).

69 *Id.* ¶ 11.

measures should be introduced to ensure that women are referred to alternative health providers."[70]

The CEDAW Committee has applied these recommendations in its Concluding Observations on the compliance of State Parties to the Convention. Unsurprisingly, Poland provides a good example of this, as it sits among the list of countries needing to reform their systems to conform with international standards.

Responding to concerns over the high rate of illegal abortions in the country and the increasing "use, or abuse,"[71] by service providers of the State's conscientious objection clause, the CEDAW Committee recommended that Poland "[e]stablish clear standards for a uniform and non-restrictive interpretation of the conditions for legal abortion so that women may access it without limitations owing to the excessive use of the so-called conscientious objection clause by doctors and health institutions and ensure effective remedies for contesting refusals of abortion."[72] It is worth noting that the CEDAW Committee acknowledged that institutions are using the conscientious objection clause, not just doctors.

In its Concluding Observations on Hungary in 2013, the CEDAW Committee expressed concerns over the State's efforts to "stigmatize abortion and seek to negatively influence the public view on abortion and contraception" and the "increasing resort to conscientious objection by health professionals in the absence of an adequate regulatory framework."[73] In response, the CEDAW Committee "urge[d] [Hungary] to cease all negative interference with women's sexual and reproductive rights," and to "[e]stablish an adequate regulatory framework and a mechanism for monitoring of the practice of conscientious objection by health professionals and ensure conscientious objection is accompanied by information to women about existing alternatives and that it remains a personalized decision rather than an institutionalized practice."[74]

70 *Id.*

71 Committee for the Elimination of All Forms of Discrimination Against Women, *Concluding Observations on the Combined Seventh and Eighth Periodic Reports of Poland,* ¶ 36, U.N. Doc. CEDAW/C/POL/7-8 (Nov. 7, 2014). *See also,* Committee for the Elimination of All Forms of Discrimination Against Women, *Inquiry concerning Poland conducted under article 8 of the Optional Protocol to the Convention,* ¶ 18, U.N. Doc. CEDAW/C/POL/IR/1 (Aug. 21, 2024).

72 *Id.* ¶ 37.

73 Committee for the Elimination of All Forms of Discrimination Against Women, *Concluding Observations on the Combined Seventh and Eighth Periodic Reports of Hungary,* ¶ 30, U.N. Doc. CEDAW/C/HUN/CO/7-8 (Mar. 26, 2013).

74 *Id.* ¶ 31(d).

Here, the CEDAW Committee took a harsher line, choosing to define parameters for the exercise of conscientious objection as being a manifestation of an individual's right to freedom of conscience—not a mechanism to be practiced by institutions.

Similarly, with regards to Italy, the CEDAW Committee expressed concern over "the limited availability and accessibility of abortion services owing to the significant number of health personnel conscientiously objecting to carrying out such operations and the lack of health centers providing these services, leading pregnant women to undergo unsafe abortions."[75] It specifically referred to its General Recommendation No. 24 in recommending that Italy "identify [...] existing hindrances and adopt [...] a procedure common to all provinces in order to guarantee access to abortion services and appropriate referral services, and ensure that the exercise of conscientious objection by health-care personnel does not pose an obstacle for women who wish to terminate a pregnancy."[76]

The CEDAW Committee's concerns with regards to Romania focused not only on "the refusal of health professionals and entire hospitals to perform medical abortions, thus causing women to seek unsafe abortion," but also on "the use of abortion as a means of contraception, the discontinuation of funding for the provision of free contraceptives in 2013 and the lack of awareness among adults of modern means of contraception."[77] These aggravating social circumstances arguably led to even more unsafe abortions in Romania. The CEDAW Committee thus recommended that Romania "ensure unimpeded and adequate access to legal abortion and post-abortion services for all women in the State party, including by ensuring that institutions are precluded by law from raising conscientious objections."[78] Once again, the CEDAW Committee, in an attempt to ameliorate the expansion of conscience-based claims, focused on the issue of institutional conscientious objection, stating that it must be outlawed, while recommending further that Romania "defin[e] the grounds on which it is permissible for health

75 Committee for the Elimination of All Forms of Discrimination Against Women, *Concluding Observations on the Seventh Periodic Report of Italy*, ¶ 41(d), U.N. Doc. CEDAW/C/ITA/CO/7 (July 21, 2017).

76 *Id.* ¶ 42(d).

77 Committee on the Elimination of All Forms of Discrimination Against Women, *Concluding Observations on the Combined Seventh and Eighth Periodic Reports of Romania*, ¶ 32(c), U.N. Doc. CEDAW/C/ROU/7-8 (July 21, 2017).

78 *Id.* ¶ 33(c).

professionals to raise such objections and guarantee mandatory referrals in cases of conscientious objections."[79]

Finally, in its Concluding Observations to Canada in 2016, the CEDAW Committee had a less condemning tone, noting "the measures taken to facilitate access to legal abortion services."[80] However, it recommended that Canada "ensure that the invocation of conscientious objection by physicians does not impede women's access to legal abortion services."[81] The focus of the CEDAW Committee on referral mechanisms and its opposition to institutional invocation of conscience-based claims is iterative of the wider debate surrounding the practice in other U.N. bodies.

One additional area within the framework of the universal human rights law system where arguments to counter religious lawfare efforts regarding the exercise of conscientious objection to sexual and reproductive health services can be found relates to the Convention on the Rights of the Child (CRC). The CRC includes each of the above enumerated rights and the States' obligations with respect to the child.[82] Article 3 states that "In all actions concerning children, whether undertaken by public or private social welfare institutions, courts of law, administrative authorities or legislative bodies, the best interests of the child shall be a primary consideration."[83]

The CRC Committee—the body of experts in charge of monitoring the implementation of the CRC—also issues concluding observations. In its report on Slovakia in 2016, it described concerns over adolescent health.[84] And specifically expressed concern over "the lack of a comprehensive national policy on adolescent sexual and reproductive health and rights … [and] the inadequate regulation of conscience-based refusals of reproductive health care leading to lack of access for adolescent girls."[85] The CRC Committee recommended that Slovakia "[a]mend legislation to explicitly prohibit institutions from adopting institutional conscience-based refusal policies or practices."[86] It also recommended that the State "establish effective monitoring systems

79 *Id.*

80 Committee on the Elimination of All Forms of Discrimination Against Women, *Concluding Observations on the Combined Eighth and Ninth Periodic Reports of Canada*, ¶ 40, U.N. Doc. CEDAW/C/CAN/CO/8-9 (Nov. 18, 2016).

81 *Id.* ¶ 41(b).

82 *See* Convention on the Rights of the Child, arts. 14, 24, 36 (Nov. 20, 1989).

83 *Id.*, art. 3.

84 Committee on the Rights of the Child, *Concluding Observations on the Combined Third to Fifth Periodic Reports of Slovakia*, ¶ 40, U.N. Doc. CRC/C/SVKCO/3-5 (July 20, 2016).

85 *Id.*

86 *Id.* ¶ 41.

and mechanisms to enable the collection of comprehensive data on the extent of conscience-based refusals of care and the impact of the practice on girls' access to legal reproductive health services."[87]

The CRC Committee is not just considering abortion here, but also sexual and reproductive health services generally, including access to contraceptives for adolescents, and the impact of conscience-based refusals on children.[88] Arguments under the CRC involve all of those discussed above, from the freedom of conscience to the right to health and nondiscrimination. Therefore, if it is found that those seeking abortion care are more often under the age of 18, arguments under the CRC may be especially useful and comprehensive to push back against the expansive and abusive exercise of conscientious objection.

The Universal Human Rights System's approach to balancing conscience-based claims with the right to health and nondiscrimination is a crucial element in the broader efforts to counter religious lawfare. International bodies have issued guidance aimed at preventing the misuse of conscientious objection as a political tool that undermines access to essential healthcare. The legal principles discussed in this section underscore the need for vigilance in protecting individual rights against the encroachment of religious lawfare.

2 Countering Religious Lawfare: Regional Human Rights Systems

2.1 *European Human Rights System*

In Europe, religious lawfare through the resort to political uses of conscience-based claims has created significant legal challenges, particularly in the context of reproductive healthcare. Although explicit guidance on conscientious objection to sexual and reproductive health services under the European Human Rights System is presently limited, language from case law in other contexts is instructive and can likely be utilized in a broader healthcare framework. The most fundamental argument to be made in this context is that conscientious objection is not an inherent "right"—or positive entitlement—that practitioners have an absolute ability to exercise.

One such argument can be made by relying on the language of the European Social Charter (the "Charter")—a Council of Europe treaty that guarantees fundamental social and economic rights.[89] Often seen as the "social constitution

87 *Id.*

88 *See id.*

89 *The European Social Charter*, COUNCIL OF EUR., https://www.coe.int/en/web/european-social-charter (last visited Nov. 18, 2023).

of Europe," the Charter serves as a counterpart to the European Convention on Human Rights (ECHR), protecting a broad range of rights, including those related to education, employment, and health.[90] Implementation of—and compliance with—the Charter is overseen by the European Committee on Social Rights (ECSR).[91] Frequently thought of as a complementary body to the European Court of Human Rights (ECtHR), the ECSR issues decisions and conclusions that "must be respected by the states concerned."[92]

Conscientious objection, and its status as an inherent "right" under auspices of the Charter, has been addressed in the context of an assessment of Article 11, which guarantees the "right to the protection of health."[93] Notably, the language of Article 11 has been interpreted as "not impos[ing] on states a positive obligation to provide a right to conscientious objection for healthcare workers."[94] In *FAFCE v. Sweden*, the Federation of Catholic Families in Europe (FAFCE) alleged that Sweden had violated Article 11 through its failure "to enact a comprehensive and clear legal and policy framework governing the practice of conscientious objection by healthcare providers."[95] In its categorical rejection of this argument, the ECSR noted that "Article 11 of the Charter does not as such confer a right to conscientious objection on the staff of the health system of a State Party."[96] The ECSR similarly dismissed FAFCE's assertion that practitioners, who are unable to refuse on grounds of conscience, suffer discrimination on the basis of religion under Article E of the Charter—a non-discrimination provision.[97]

This ECSR's decision suggests that a "right" to conscientious objection is not inherent in the Charter. Thus, states have no positive obligation to provide for such a right in their healthcare systems. This language can be particularly useful in States where no affirmative right to conscientious objection presently exists within its domestic legal system. It also suggests that the Council of Europe is of the view that conscientious objection is not—in and of itself—a positive, unequivocal right that must be guaranteed to all individuals, which is

90 *Id.*

91 *The European Committee of Social Rights*, COUNCIL OF EUR., https://www.coe.int/en/web/european-social-charter/european-committee-of-social-rights (last visited Nov. 18, 2023).

92 *Id.*

93 European Social Charter, art. 11, May 3, 1996, E.T.S. No. 163.

94 European Committee of Social Rights [ECSR], Complaint No. 99/2013, Federation of Catholic Families of Europe (FAFCE) v. Sweden, ¶ 70.

95 *Id.* ¶ 2.

96 *Id.* ¶ 70.

97 *Id.* ¶ 72.

a crucial contention from a legal standpoint, particularly as it relates to efforts to counter religious lawfare.

It is essential, however, to note the relative weaknesses of the preceding contention. While those favoring a weak notion of conscientious objection can capitalize on the Charter's language, those promoting vitality in religious freedoms also have a variety of tools at their disposal within the European system that can be used to advance their religious agenda. One of the most essential elements would be an assertion of Article 9 of the European Convention on Human Rights (European Convention) before the ECtHR: a seemingly more advantageous forum. Article 9 of the European Convention provides the framework for manifesting one's religion or belief, and accordingly, the exercise of conscientious objection.[98]

In contrast to the progressive Charter language and interpretation, the ECtHR relies on a definition of conscientious objection that reflects inclinations of conservativism. In its *Guide on Article 9*, the ECtHR conflates conscientious objection with the "negative aspect" of Article 9, defining it as "the *right not* to act contrary to one's conscience and convictions"[99] (emphasis added). In this vein, rather than framing conscientious objection as an individualistic and positive entitlement, conservative religious actors could advocate for a "negative" or "non-interventionist" conception of a "right" to conscientious objection.[100] A negative right—as opposed to a positive right—is typified by state inaction: it requires a state to "refrain from interfering" with an individual's right to exercise, for example, his or her freedom of religion under Article 9.[101] This is a beneficial framing mechanism for conservative religious groups, as judicial interpretation of negative rights is "inclined to be much more generous."[102]

This "generosity" exhibited through judicial promulgation is evident in the context of conscientious objection to compulsory military service. In using conscience-based claims as a religious lawfare tool, conservative religious groups will likely assert a violation of Article 9, referencing jurisprudence that

98 European Convention on Human Rights, art. 9, Nov. 4, 1950, E.T.S. No. 5.

99 Council of Eur., Guide on Article 9 of the European Convention on Human Rights: Freedom of thought, conscience and religion 22–23, https://www.echr.coe.int/Documents/Guide_Art_9_ENG.pdf (last updated Aug. 31, 2022) (last visited Nov 18, 2023).

100 Ran Hirschl, *"Negative" Rights vs. "Positive" Entitlements: A Comparative Study of Judicial Interpretations of Rights in an Emerging Neo-Liberal Economic Order*, 22 Hum. Rts. Q. 1060, 1063 (2000).

101 *Id.* at 1098.

102 *Id.*

lengthens the bounds of Article 9 safeguards. While the ECtHR has not explicitly designated conscientious objection as a positive "right," it has, rather, conferred a positive obligation of non-interference.[103]

For example, in *Bayatyan v. Armenia*, the court addressed an applicant's conviction for evading military conscription under the Armenian Criminal Code.[104] The applicant—who was a Jehovah's Witness—refused compulsory military service on conscientious objection grounds.[105] Essential to the applicant's argument was Armenia's deficiency in civilian alternatives, as the court noted the state enjoys a "limited margin of appreciation" where it is not equipped with substitute modes of service.[106] The court further provided that if no accommodations for conscientious objectors are provided, the state "must present convincing and compelling reasons for *any interference whatsoever*" (emphasis added). In particular, it must demonstrate that the interference corresponds to a "pressing social need."[107] Ultimately, the court held that Armenia had violated Article 9 by issuing a conviction for draft evasion where alternative civilian service methods were unavailable.[108]

This view was reiterated a year later in *Savda v. Turkey*.[109] In interpreting the "convincing and compelling" standard put forth in *Bayatyan*, the court conferred a positive obligation on states to offer "an effective and accessible procedure ... that allows [the petitioner] to learn whether or not he has a right to be a conscientious objector."[110] Here, the applicant's argument turned on the state's "failure to have enacted a law implementing the right to conscientious

---

103 *See generally*, Bayatyan v. Armenia, App. No. 23459/03, Eur. Ct. H.R. (2011).

104 *Id.* ¶¶ 14–22.

105 *Id.* ¶¶ 10–13.

106 *Id.* ¶123. The margin of appreciation is a doctrine of the European Court of Human Rights that permits a member state a certain degree of discretion when taking legislative, administrative, or judicial actions. The doctrine allows the Court to consider divergent legal and cultural traditions among member states. Member states are given a narrow or limited margin of appreciation in cases where: a particularly important facet of an individual's identity or existence is at stake; the justification for a restriction is the protection of the authority of the judiciary; the rights protected by Art. 2 and 3 of the Convention are absolute rights, generating obligations for member states which cannot be balanced against other rights or against the pursuit of any legitimate interest; racial or ethnic discrimination is implicated; or an intimate aspect of private life is at stake under Art. 8. Respectively, see Evans v. U.K, (2007); Sunday Times v. U.K. (1979); Pretty v. U.K. (2002); D.H. v. Czech Republic (2007); Dudgeon v. U.K. (1981).

107 *Id.*

108 *Id.* ¶ 128.

109 *See* Savda v. Turkey, App. No. 42730/05, Eur. Ct. H.R. (2012).

110 *Id.* ¶ 99.

objection."[111] Ultimately, the court found a violation of Article 9, citing Turkey's lack of procedural mechanisms guaranteeing an evaluation of one's ability to assert conscientious objection.[112]

This jurisprudence is indicative of a judicial disposition favoring strong Article 9 protections: it necessitates a high standard of proof—"convincing and compelling" evidence—to justify even a miniscule interference on behalf of the State. Moreover, finding violations of Article 9 on this procedural basis effectively mandates state recognition of conscientious objection. Thus, this language could be used by conservative religious groups to frame regulation of conscientious objection in healthcare as an unjustified interference—particularly in the case of state actors, such as state-run hospitals. Ultimately, it could be framed to confer a positive obligation on states to guarantee the "negative aspects" of Article 9 by mandating states to provide avenues for asserting conscientious objection in healthcare.

Balancing these seemingly contrary positions—Charter language indicating conscientious objection's nonexistence as a right, and the strength of Article 9 protections elicited from the ECtHR—is a difficult but necessary task for proponents of conscientious objection regulation. Given that the ECSR and the ECtHR are different forums, and advocates of conscientious objection will likely bring petitions to the most advantageous forum, countering the robust Article 9 argument in the ECtHR is essential. This defense is particularly useful when petitioners bring complaints before the ECtHR asking for recognition of strong Article 9 protections utilizing case law in the compulsory military service context. There are likely two primary ways to respond to conservative religious groups in this context: (1) distinguishing healthcare from military service; and (2) analogizing other rights characterized by state noninterference, such as the freedom of association.

First, petitions brought before the ECtHR involving conscientious objection to compulsory military service have been characterized by strong Article 9 positions. In other words, the court has often found Article 9 violations in this context. However, preventing the exercise of conscientious objection is associated with limitations on Article 9 freedoms. One way to justify such interference is to distinguish providing healthcare services from the compulsory military service context, suggesting that the strength of Article 9 freedoms is not universally applicable in dissimilar circumstances.

---

111 Press Release, Eur. Ct. of Hum. Rts., Refusal to Grant Conscientious Objector Status is not Necessary in a Democratic Society, at 3 (Dec. 6, 2012).

112 Savda v. Turkey, App. No. 42730/05, ¶ 100, Eur. Ct. H.R. (2012).

For one thing, unlike compulsory military service—which necessitates obligatory compliance with civil service regulations—providing elective procedures in the healthcare setting does not imply any such obligation of forced labor.[113] A mandatory requirement of civil service is not comparable to one's conscious decision to become a health practitioner.[114] This idea is encompassed in the "incompatibility thesis," which asserts that professional obligations take precedence to personal manifestations of conscience and belief.[115] Essentially, "[i]f people are not prepared to offer legally permitted, efficient, and beneficial care to a patient because it conflicts with their values, they should not be doctors."[116] This language reflects the idea that entering the medical profession is an optional and conscious choice, unlike that of mandatory civil service, which is a significant distinguishing factor.[117] In fact, this was the position that the European Court of Human Rights ultimately adopted in February 2020, when deciding the inadmissibility of two cases involving two nurses who decided to start their studies to work as midwives, but were not considered for employment as midwives because they indicated that they would not participate in performing abortions. The European Court of Human Rights argued that the requirement for those who occupy the position of midwives in the health system, which includes providing all the services inherent to that position, including abortions, was not an unjustified or disproportionate restriction on the freedom of conscience for nurses. Likewise, it indicated that in both cases, the nurses had voluntarily decided to become midwives and when applying for vacancies in this position, they knew that this would imply participating in the provision of abortions.[118]

Additionally, the exercise of conscientious objection in the healthcare context is distinct in that it has the potential to affect the rights of third-party,

113 International Planned Parenthood Federation, imap Statement on conscientious objection: refusal of care and professional conduct of reproductive health services in the context of legal restrictions 2 (2016).

114 *See id.*

115 Gustavo Ortiz-Millán, *Abortion and Conscientious Objection: Rethinking Conflicting Rights in the Mexican Context,* 29 Glob. Bioethics 1–15 (2017).

116 *Id.*

117 One counterargument to this is a specific scenario in which certain practices—such as abortion—are decriminalized after one makes the choice to enter the medical profession. This was exactly the case in Mexico City in 2007, where abortion was decriminalized in the first trimester.

118 European Court of Human Rights – Third Section. *Application no. 62309/17 Linda* STEEN *against Sweden,* ¶ 21 (Feb. 11, 2020); European Court of Human Rights, *Application no. 43726/17 Ellinor* GRIMMARK *against Sweden,* ¶ 26 (Feb. 11, 2020).

private individuals.[119] When an individual objects to mandatory military service, the risk of third-party repercussions is low. Although conscientious objection in this context is often conflated with national security implications, the nexus is weak: only extremely high numbers of conscientious objectors would necessarily affect national security.[120]

On the other hand, when a healthcare professional conscientiously objects to providing legally available health services, there are numerous human rights implications: it implicates third parties' right to health and autonomy, as well as in some cases, their right to life.[121] Because a variety of rights are affected—coupled with the fact that conscientious objection in healthcare cannot be equated to forced labor—Article 9 protections should not be extended proportionately in the healthcare context. These two distinctions are likely sufficient to justify greater limitations on the exercise of conscience-based claims in healthcare settings.

An additional way to respond to the strong Article 9 positions is to push back on the negative dimension of the right: this can be accomplished by analogizing case law where state interference was justified, notwithstanding the freedom from intrusion inherent in the right itself. A prime example of this is Article 11 of the ECHR, which guarantees the freedom of assembly and association.[122] Like Article 9, Article 11 carries a negative dimension; this includes the right *not* to join an association, or alternatively, freedom from unjustified state interference—which is often seen through an association's dissolution or state refusal of registration.[123] Essential to this argument is the contention that the negative scope of the right is not absolute: state interference is justified in certain circumstances.[124] For instance, in *Herri Batasuna and Batasuna v. Spain*, the ECtHR upheld the state-sponsored dissolution of political parties with ties to terrorist organizations.[125] Dissolution was also

---

119 Marcelo Alegre, *Conscious Oppression: Conscientious Objection in the Sphere of Sexual and Reproductive Health, in* CONTROVERSIES IN LATIN AM. BIOETHICS 2 (E. Rivera-López & M. Hevia eds., 2019).

120 Matthew Lippman, *The Recognition of Conscientious Objection to Military Service as an International Human Right*, 21 CALIF. W. INT'L L. J. 31, 32 (1990).

121 *See* INTERNATIONAL PLANNED PARENTHOOD FEDERATION, IMAP STATEMENT ON CONSCIENTIOUS OBJECTION: REFUSAL OF CARE AND PROFESSIONAL CONDUCT OF REPRODUCTIVE HEALTH SERVICES IN THE CONTEXT OF LEGAL RESTRICTIONS (2016).

122 European Convention on Human Rights, art. 11, Nov. 4, 1950, E.T.S. No. 5.

123 COUNCIL OF EUR., GUIDE ON ARTICLE 11 OF THE EUROPEAN CONVENTION ON HUMAN RIGHTS 25 (2019).

124 *Id.*

125 *Id.* at 28.

upheld in *Les Authentiks and Supras Auteuil 91 v. France,* where the group at issue was involved in repeated acts of violence.[126] These cases represent the ECtHR's willingness to justify state interference in the negative dimension of human rights. Due to the court's willingness to limit the negative aspects of Article 11, it is likely that the same willingness would be present with respect to the strong Article 9 arguments put forth by conservative religious groups. Thus, this argument would be instructive to counter religious lawfare's assertions of absolutism in the negative dimension of Article 9.

The aforementioned argument and its corresponding counterarguments, however, have a particularly limited scope: they are not necessarily pragmatic in states that presently guarantee a right to conscientious objection in their domestic legal frameworks. In Europe, for example, the European Parliamentary Assembly has allowed Member States the competence to "guarantee the right to conscientious objection in relation to … medical procedure[s]."[127] For states that have exercised this capability, the strategy will necessarily require a shift from preventing its exercise to effectively mitigating its ultimate ramifications.

Conscientious objection at the level of general healthcare has sparingly been addressed at the ECtHR. Where it is mentioned, it is done only tangentially, as seen in *Jehovah's Witnesses of Moscow and Others v. Russia* regarding the right of Jehovah's Witness individuals to refuse blood transfusions.[128] In its conclusion, the court noted that the prohibition of receiving blood transfusions embedded in the Jehovah's Witness tradition could not serve as a justification for dissolving the organization. Specifically, it stated that "[t]he freedom to accept or refuse specific medical treatment, or to select an alternative form of treatment, is vital to the principles of self-determination and personal autonomy."[129] Although the case references the *patient's* ability to conscientiously object to his or her own medical treatment, it is possible that the language could be equally applicable to a *physician* asserting conscientious objection, suggesting that refusing to perform blood transfusions may be acceptable and protected under the freedom of conscience and religion. However, the ECtHR has not explicitly addressed this question. Moreover, it is essential to note that healthcare professionals, as opposed to patients, have

126 *Id.*

127 *Eur. Par. Ass. Res. 1763: The Right to Conscientious Objection in Lawful Medical Care* (2010), http://assembly.coe.int/nw/xml/XRef/Xref-XML2HTML-en.asp?fileid=17909 (last visited Nov 18, 2023).

128 *See generally* Jehovah's Witnesses of Moscow and Others v. Russia, App. No. 302/02, Eur. Ct. H.R. (2010).

129 *Id.* ¶ 136.

distinct rights and obligations. While patients always have the right to undergo a procedure legally guaranteed in domestic law, physicians do not *always* have the ability to invoke conscientious objection. For example, a physician's assertion of conscientious objection is often inapplicable in emergency scenarios.[130]

The ECtHR has also held in *R.R. v. Poland* that "States are obliged to organize the health services system in such a way as to ensure that an effective exercise of the freedom of conscience of health professionals in the professional context does not prevent patients from obtaining access to services to which they are entitled under the applicable legislation."[131] Although this case arose in the reproductive health context, its language is highly generalized. If, for example, a practitioner asserted his or her right to conscientiously object to a medical procedure the *R.R. v. Poland* precedent would effectively be a strong argument to advocate for the establishment of, at the very minimum, certain referral mechanisms. In this vein, States are under a positive obligation to ensure patients have access to any medical procedure that is legal under domestic law. If access is not guaranteed—through referral procedures or otherwise—or if the policies in place are ineffective in making these medical procedures readily accessible, the state could be in violation of human rights law. Ultimately, this can serve as a vehicle to hold States accountable when they allow abusive use of conscience-based claims in the healthcare context.

In the reproductive health space, the exercise of conscientious objection often involves balancing an individual's positive freedom to manifest one's religion or beliefs—as guaranteed by Article 9 of the European Convention—against the "protection of the rights and freedoms of others."[132] This balancing mechanism is inherent in Article 9(2), and has been used by the ECtHR on multiple occasions.[133]

In *Pichon and Sajous v. France*, the ECtHR consciously differentiated between the two sub-parts of Article 9.[134] *Pichon* involved an application submitted by

130 *See Eur. Par. Ass. Res. 1763: The Right to Conscientious Objection in Lawful Medical Care* (2010), https://assembly.coe.int/nw/xml/XRef/Xref-XML2HTML-en.asp?fileid=17909&lang=en ("[s]tates should develop "clear regulations that define and regulate conscientious objection with regard to health and medical services, and which: … ensure that patients receive appropriate treatment, *in particular in cases of emergency*.") (emphasis added) (last visited Nov 18, 2023).

131 R.R. v. Poland, App. No. 27617/04, Eur. Ct. H.R., ¶ 206 (2011).

132 European Convention on Human Rights, art. 9, Nov. 4, 1950, E.T.S. No. 5.

133 *Id.* at art. 9(2). ("[f]reedom to manifest one's religion or beliefs shall be subject only to such limitations as are prescribed by law and are necessary in a democratic society in the interests of public safety, for the protection of public order, *health* or morals, or *for the protection of the rights and freedoms of others*.") (emphasis added).

134 Pichon and Sajous v. France, App. No. 49853/99, Eur. Ct. H.R. (2001).

two co-owners of a pharmacy who refused to provide contraception pills to their customers, on the basis of a conscientious refusal.[135] In its reasoning, the court noted that "Article 9 of the Convention does not always guarantee the right to behave in public in a manner governed by that belief;" and given this interpretation, the court thereby declared the pharmacists' application inadmissible on grounds that their rights under Article 9 had not been implicated.[136]

This idea was reiterated nearly a decade later in *R.R. v. Poland*. In citing *Pichon*, the Court stated that "the word 'practice' used in Article 9 (1) does not denote *each and every act* or form of behavior motivated or inspired by a religion or belief."[137] Notably, in *R.R v. Poland* the court held that a woman's right to access reproductive health treatment outweighed the practitioner's right to manifest religion.[138] These decisions suggest that there are limits as to the extent to which one can manifest his or her religion or beliefs if it interferes with the fundamental rights of others. To this end, experts have suggested that medical professionals cannot unequivocally "prioritize belief over professional obligations."[139]

Limitations on a practitioner's ability to exercise conscientious objection in the healthcare professional setting could also be imposed by a variety of additional arguments. One of the most prevalent concerns is that a practitioner's assertion of conscientious objection infringes on an individual's right to respect in the context of both family and private life, as guaranteed under Article 8 of the European Convention.

Many components of reproductive and sexual health are shielded by virtue of Article 8. For example, the ECtHR has held that the right to become, or not become parents falls within the purview of Article 8.[140] Moreover, although the court has held that Article 8 cannot be interpreted as conferring a positive right to terminate a pregnancy, it has found that the prohibition of abortion—when sought for reasons of health and/or well-being—falls within the scope of the right to respect for one's private and family life, and accordingly, Article 8.[141] Notably, the court has also used Article 8 as a vehicle to prohibit policies that substantially limit a woman's right to access legal healthcare services. Along

135 *Id.*

136 *Id.*

137 R.R. v. Poland, App. No. 27617/04, Eur. Ct. H.R., ¶ 206 (2011).

138 *See* Pichon and Sajous v. France, App. No. 49853/99, Eur. Ct. H.R. (2001); *see also* R.R. v. Poland, App. No. 27617/04, Eur. Ct. H.R. (2011).

139 Ctr. for Repro. Rts., Conscientious Objection and Reproductive Rights: International Human Rights Standards 4 (2013).

140 *See* Evans v. United Kingdom, App. No. 6339/05, Eur. Ct. H.R. (2007).

141 *See* A. B. and C. v. Ireland, App. No. 25579/05, Eur. Ct. H.R. (2010)

these lines, a state party to the ECHR violates Article 8 when it "arbitrar[ily] interfere[s]" with a woman's right to access legal family planning or abortion services.[142] This is a significant observation as a basis for regulating conscientious objection. In certain contexts, and if largely unregulated, conscientious objection can effectively serve as a barrier to accessing legal abortion and reproductive health services, potentially violating Article 8. In fact, this consideration has been explicitly acknowledged by the European Parliamentary Assembly. In a 2008 resolution, the legislative body recognized that "the lack of doctors willing to carry out abortions ... ha[s] the potential to make access to safe, affordable, acceptable, and appropriate abortion services more difficult."[143]

In recognizing this correlation between conscientious objection and barriers to accessing sexual and reproductive healthcare, ECtHR jurisprudence attempts to mitigate the effect of conscience-based claims through mandated procedural mechanisms ensuring the removal of barriers to access.[144]

In *R.R. v. Poland*, R.R. submitted an application to the ECtHR claiming that her Article 8 rights were violated "by the authorities' failure to provide her with access to genetic tests."[145] The violation was alleged to have occurred in two contexts; for present purposes, the relevant context involves a violation by way of "the absence of a comprehensive legal framework to guarantee her rights."[146] In analyzing R.R.'s application, the ECtHR addressed conscientious objection directly, stating:

> ... [w]here a State allowed providers to conscientiously object to providing health services, **it *must* ensure that it had other adequate procedures** in place to safeguard women's ability to effectively exercise their rights under Article 8 of the Convention, including the right to an abortion where legal and the right to information regarding their health status (emphasis added).[147]

Significant in the court's articulation of this standard is its use of the word "must," as opposed to a permissive norm, such as "may." This language suggests that states are under a mandatory—rather than permissive—obligation

142 R.R. v. Poland, App. No. 27617/04, Eur. Ct. H.R., ¶ 183 (2011).

143 *Eur. Par. Ass. Res. 1607: Access to Safe and Legal Abortion in Europe* (2008), http://assembly.coe.int/nw/xml/XRef/Xref-XML2HTML-en.asp?fileid=17638 (last visited Nov 18, 2023).

144 *See* R.R. v. Poland, App. No. 27617/04, Eur. Ct. H.R. (2011), *see also* P. and S. v. Poland, App. No. 57375/08, Eur. Ct. H.R. (2013).

145 R.R. v. Poland, App. No. 27617/04, Eur. Ct. H.R., ¶ 91 (2011).

146 *Id.*

147 *Id.* ¶ 127.

to implement "adequate procedures" for a woman to exercise her rights under Article 8. Here, R.R. experienced a complete denial of access to information regarding her condition, in violation of Article 8.[148] This breach of Article 8 occurred because of Poland's outright failure to have *any* procedural mechanisms in place to eliminate barriers of access erected through the exercise of conscientious objection. Thus, it can be readily inferred from this decision that completely unregulated conscientious objection cannot constitute an "adequate procedure."

Given that *R.R.* merely signals the inadequacy of a complete lack of procedural framework, effective legal strategies will grapple with what is considered an "adequate procedure" under Article 8. This issue was expressly addressed in *P. and S. v. Poland*, where the first applicant submitted that her Article 8 rights "had been violated by the absence of a comprehensive legal framework guaranteeing her timely and unhindered access to abortion."[149] In interpreting Poland's obligations under Article 8, the court reiterated that "the State is under a positive obligation to create a procedural framework enabling a pregnant woman to effectively exercise her right of access to lawful abortion."[150] The court then proceeded to decipher certain appropriate components of an effective procedural structure. While it left the design of the procedural mechanisms to State Parties, the court did note that "effective access to reliable information on the conditions for the availability of lawful abortion, and the relevant procedures to be followed, is directly relevant" for the exercise of human rights.[151] Essentially, the ECtHR suggests that an integral component of an "adequate" procedural system includes access to information . This could be a particularly useful argument in states where (1) conscientious objectors do not render information on legal reproductive services to their patients; or (2) an implemented procedural system is largely inadequate, effectively resulting in barriers to access and information. Thus, the ECtHR has effectively negated proponents of unregulated conscientious objection: unless conscientious objection allows for "timely and unhindered access to [legal] abortion," its exercise results in a violation of Article 8.[152]

Moreover, the European Committee of Social Rights has highlighted the correlation between high volumes of objecting practitioners and a corresponding violation of Article 11. For example, in *IPPF-EN v. Italy*, a collective

148 *Id.* ¶ 214.

149 P. and S. v. Poland, App. No. 57375/08, Eur. Ct. H.R. (2013), ¶ 78.

150 *Id.* ¶ 99.

151 *Id.* ¶ 11.

152 *Id.* ¶ 78.

complaint was filed alleging a relationship between large amounts of conscientious objections to abortion and violations of Article 11.[153] To establish this alleged link, the complainants had to carry the initial burden of framing their complaint within the scope of Article 11. Because domestic legislation had "classified [abortion] as a form of medical treatment that relates to the protection of health," the ECSR considered it as falling within the purview of the Article's reach.[154]

The ECSR went on to assert that Italy's "primary obligation" under Article 11 is to "make health care available as it is needed, which applies with particular force to time-sensitive procedures such as abortion."[155] The Committee's decision further emphasized that "adequate measures must be taken to ensure the availability of non-objecting medical practitioners," suggesting that Article 11 issues arise when the number of available non-objecting professionals is insufficient.[156] Although the ECSR qualified this assumption by stating that a "high number of objecting health personnel" does not constitute "*per se* evidence" of an ineffective procedural framework at the domestic level, the ECSR explained how this phenomenon could possibly have potent adverse ramifications, which include the following: excessive wait times to access abortion services, a decrease in the number of medical facilities offering abortion services nationwide, etc.[157] Ultimately, the ECSR held that the present situation in Italy violated Article 11 of the Charter.[158]

IPPF-EN stands for the premise that high numbers of objecting professionals can have the effect of rendering access to a legal service inadequate, thereby necessitating action on behalf of the state to ensure the availability of non-objecting practitioners to not violate Article 11. This argument can be especially useful in countries where statistics reveal an exceedingly high number of conscientious objectors, even in areas where referral procedures—or other procedural safeguards—are currently in place.

An additional argument that has been utilized in limiting medical professionals' ability to exercise conscientious objection is framing a lack of access as an issue of discrimination. Given that "unregulated use of conscientious objection may disproportionately affect women"—notably from marginalized populations—it is often a useful supplementary discussion in complaints

153 European Committee of Social Rights [ECSR], Complaint No. 87/2012, *Int'l Planned Parenthood Federation European Network* (*IPPF-EN*) *v. Italy*, ¶ 76.

154 *Id.* ¶ 161.

155 *Id.* ¶ 164.

156 *Id.* ¶ 163.

157 *Id.* ¶ 169.

158 *Id.* ¶ 177.

brought to the European Committee of Social Rights.[159] As mentioned previously, the proper vehicle for asserting this contention is Article E of the Charter, which ensures that "[t]he enjoyment of the rights set forth in th[e] Charter shall be secured without discrimination on any ground."[160]

Although scholarship relating to this argument is rather limited, complainants have included this discussion in *IPPF-EN v. Italy* and *CGIL v. Italy*. In *IPPF-EN*, the complainant organization alleged that "the shortcomings indicated with respect to the alleged violation of Article 11 of the Charter also constitute[d] a breach of the principle of nondiscrimination guaranteed by Article E."[161] The organization asserted discrimination on two separate grounds: (1) socioeconomic status; and (2) gender and/or health status.[162] In the end, the ECSR agreed with the organization's contention, noting that "as a result of the lack of non-objecting medical practitioners ... the Committee holds that the women concerned are treated differently than other persons in the same situation with respect to access to healthcare."[163] An integral factor in the ECSR's decision was the fact that in many cases, women were forced "to move from one hospital to another ... or to travel abroad."[164] This assertion was reiterated three years later in *CGIL v. Italy*.[165]

These decisions indicate the European Committee of Social Rights' willingness to find an additional violation, by way of Article E, when conscientious objection leads to increased financial and geographic barriers to access—especially in cases where the ultimate effect and burden falls on the most vulnerable populations.

Another argument that could be advanced in efforts to counter religious lawfare relates to the rights of non-objecting medical professionals. The essential premise of this argument is that excessive, unregulated assertion of conscientious objection violates the economic and social rights of non-objecting practitioners. The relevant provision of the Charter in this context is Article 1

159 *Eur. Par. Ass. Res. 1763: The Right to Conscientious Objection in Lawful Medical Care* (2010), https://assembly.coe.int/nw/xml/XRef/Xref-XML2HTML-en.asp?fileid=17909&lang=en (last visited Nov 18, 2023).

160 European Social Charter, art. E, May 3, 1996, E.T.S. No. 163.

161 European Committee of Social Rights [ECSR], Complaint No. 87/2012, *Int'l Planned Parenthood Federation European Network* (*IPPF-EN*) *v. Italy*, ¶ 179.

162 *Id.* ¶ 190.

163 *Id.* ¶ 191.

164 *Id.*

165 European Committee of Social Rights [ECSR], Complaint No. 140/2016, *Confederazione Generale Italiana del Lavoro* (*CGIL*) *v. Italy*, ¶ 210.

(the right to work). Importantly, this argument's formulation expands the possibilities for filing complaints with the ECSR.

The ECSR explicitly addressed this argument in *CGIL v. Italy*, and it proved successful for the complainant. First, the Committee noted that "non-objecting medical practitioners face several types of cumulative disadvantages at work both direct and indirect."[166] These disadvantages ranged from workload allocation and task distribution to career development opportunities.[167] To this end, the Committee found that this "difference in treatment ... arises simply on the basis that certain medical practitioners provide abortion services in accordance with the law."[168] Consequently, the Committee held that this "difference in treatment ... amount[ed] to discrimination in violation of Article 1."[169]

The European Human Rights System's approach to conscientious objection highlights the delicate balance between protecting religious freedom and preventing its misuse. The jurisprudence of the ECtHR and ECSR reflects a recognition that while conscience-based claims must be respected, they cannot be allowed to serve as political tools that obstruct access to healthcare. The cases discussed in this section demonstrate how European legal standards are evolving to counter the strategic use of religious lawfare, ensuring that individual rights are not sacrificed to political or religious agendas.

2.2 *Inter-American Human Rights System*

The Inter-American Human Rights system has yet to develop jurisprudence regarding a healthcare professional's right to conscientiously object to providing reproductive health services.[170] It is important, however, to note the degree of influence the ECtHR's jurisprudence has on its Inter-American counterpart: "from the early stages ... to the most recent cases decided by the Inter-American Court, the impact of the European Court of Human Rights Jurisprudence has been significant."[171] To this end, "the [Inter-American] Court often cites decisions of the European Court of Human Rights on comparable issues."[172] Thus,

166 *Id.* ¶ 243.

167 *Id.*

168 *Id.* ¶ 245.

169 *Id.* ¶ 246.

170 CTR. FOR REPRO. RTS., CONSCIENTIOUS OBJECTION AND REPRODUCTIVE RIGHTS: INTERNATIONAL HUMAN RIGHTS STANDARDS 4 (2013).

171 Eduardo Andrés Bertoni, *The Inter-American Court of Human Rights and the European Court of Human Rights: A Dialogue on Freedom of Expression Standards*, 3 EUR. HUM. RTS. L. R. 332, 348 (2009).

172 Gerald L. Neuman, *Import, Export, and Regional Consent in the Inter-American Court of Human Rights*, 19 EUR. J. INT'L L. 101, 109 (2008).

notwithstanding the fact that the following strategies are largely theoretical, they are primarily elicited from the European Court's jurisprudence, which would likely be instructive if the Inter-American Court ever took up a case on the issue of conscientious objection in healthcare.

Like in the European system, a physician's ability to assert conscientious objection could be based on the freedom of conscience and religion. In the Inter-American system, this right is enshrined in Article 12 of the American Convention on Human Rights.[173] Just as Article 9(1) of the ECHR provides for the freedom to manifest one's religion and beliefs, Article 12(1) of the American Convention maintains that "[e]veryone has the right to freedom of conscience and religion."[174] Moreover, the balancing mechanism inherent in Article 9(2) of the ECHR is also embodied in Article 12(3) of the American Convention, which states that the "freedom to manifest one's religion and beliefs" is subject to certain "limitations," such as "the rights of freedoms of others."[175] This comparison signifies that the Inter-American Court has the ability—by way of language in the American Convention—to impose similar restrictions on an individual's ability to exercise conscientious objection in the professional setting.

As mentioned, within the Inter-American Human Rights System, beyond the general standards of freedom of conscience and religion in other contexts, the Inter-American Court of Human Rights has not had the opportunity to rule on conscientious objection. For its part, the Inter-American Commission on Human Rights ("the Commission") addressed the matter in some of its Annual Reports, inviting Member States to consider conscientious objection to compulsory military service, providing for "either the exemption from military service or the provision of a service alternative in cases of conscientious objection."[176] Subsequently, the Commission had the opportunity to learn about the subject in two individual cases.[177]

---

173 Organization of Am. States, American Convention on Human Rights, Art. 12, Nov. 22, 1969, O.A.S.T.S. No. 36, 1144 U.N.T.S. 123.

174 *Id.*, art. 12(1).

175 *Id.*, art. 12(3).

176 Inter-Am. Comm'n on Human Rights, *1997 Annual Report of the Inter-Am. Commission on Human Rights*, OEA/Ser.L/V/II.98, Doc.6, Feb. 17, 1998; Inter-Am. Commission on Human Rights, 1998 Annual Report of the Inter-Am. Comm'n on Human Rights, OEA/Ser.L/V/II.102 Doc 6. Rev, Apr. 16, 1999.

177 Inter-Am. Comm'n on Human Rights, Report No. 43/05, Case 12.219, Merits, Cristián Daniel Sahli Vera et al. v. Chile, Mar. 10, 2005. *See also*, Inter-Am. Comm'n on Human Rights, Report No. 97/05, Petition 14/04, Friendly Settlement, Alfredo Díaz Bustos v. Bolivia, Oct. 27, 2005.

Moreover, the Inter-American Commission has expressly recognized a correlation between conscientious objection and the erection of barriers to accessing reproductive health services.[178] In a report titled *Access to Information on Reproductive Health from a Human Rights Perspective*, the Commission offered authoritative guidance on how to address conscientious objection within its jurisdiction. It first recognized "that health professionals have the right to have their freedom of conscience respected,"[179] but made an explicit reference to the balancing mechanism and stated that in exercising conscientious objection professionals must "show equal respect for their patients' rights to conscience."[180]

Significantly, the report went beyond the language articulated by the ECtHR in *P. and S. v. Poland* and *R.R. v. Poland*—rather, it specifically noted how this balance can be achieved: "the balance between the rights of healthcare professionals and the rights of patients is maintained through referrals."[181] Instead of vaguely referencing a state's positive obligation to implement procedural mechanisms, the report offered a specific proposition in the form of a referral mechanism. Furthermore, in stating its reasoning for preferring this proposal, the report cited *R.R. v. Poland*, specifying that the reasoning behind the approach was such as to "not create barriers in access to services."[182] Moreover, similar to the language in ECtHR jurisprudence, the Commission stressed:

> States *must* guarantee that women are not prevented from accessing information and reproductive health services, and that in situations involving conscientious objectors in the health arena, the States should establish referral procedures, as well as appropriate sanctions for failure to comply with their obligation.[183] (emphasis added).

This language signals the Commission's willingness to compel State Parties to adopt procedural mechanisms to ensure the removal of barriers to accessing reproductive health services. Given that this report was authored by the Inter-American Commission itself, it could be particularly influential if an

---

178 *See Access to Information on Reproductive Health from a Human Rights Perspective*, Inter-Am. Comm'n H.R., OEA/Ser.L/V/II. doc. 61 (2011), https://www.oas.org/en/iachr/docs/annual/2012/women_access_information.pdf (last visited Nov 18, 2023).

179 *Id.* at 27.

180 *Id.*

181 *Id.* at 28.

182 *Id.*

183 *Id.*

application moved beyond treatment at the Commission's level and was ultimately heard by the Inter-American Court of Human Rights.

An application utilizing this language would necessarily include other key components. Most importantly, an applicant would have to assert the violation of a right guaranteed under the American Convention. Two possible avenues for this assertion could be based on Article 11 (right to private life) or Article 5 (right to have physical, mental, and moral integrity respected).[184]

Considering the correlation between mandated procedural mechanisms and the right to private life established in the European system, an application citing shortcomings in relation to Article 11 of the American Convention may be viable. Article 11(2) of the American Convention provides that "[n]o one may be the object of arbitrary or abusive interference with his private life … ,"[185] and it has been interpreted by the Inter-American Court in the reproductive health space. In *Artavia Murillo v. Costa Rica*, the Inter-American Court held that Costa Rica's blanket ban on in-vitro fertilization violated infertile couples' rights to private life under Article 11.[186] In its reasoning, the court explicitly recognized a relationship between "the right to private life" and "access to reproductive health services."[187] And although *Artavia Murillo* is not a case pointedly referencing conscientious objection, its language mimics cases like *R.R.* and *P. and S*, making an evident linkage between Article 11 and access to reproductive health services. Thus, if conscientious objection renders a patient's access to certain reproductive health services unattainable, it is likely that patients could assert a violation of their Article 11 rights.

An additional vehicle for asserting violations in the Inter-American Human Rights system is Article 5 of the American Convention. Article 5(1) provides for every person's "right to have their physical, mental, and moral integrity respected."[188] Notably, the Inter-American Court—through its jurisprudence—has gradually developed an integral link between Article 5 and a woman's right to health. Essentially, "the provision of ***adequate*** and ***timely*** maternal health services is one of the principal ways to ensure a woman's right to personal

184 American Convention, arts. 5 and 11.

185 American Convention, art. 11(2).

186 *Artavia Murillo v. Costa Rica*, Preliminary Objections, Merits, Reparations, and Costs, Inter-Am. Ct. H.R. (Ser. C) No. 85/10 (Nov. 28, 2012); *see also* Barbara Fraser, *Tide Begins to Turn on Abortion Access in South Africa*, 383 LANCET 2113, 2114 (2014), https://www.thelancet.com/journals/lancet/article/PIIS0140-6736%2814%2961017-5/fulltext?rss=yes(lastvisited Nov 18, 2023).

187 *Artavia Murillo v. Costa Rica*, Preliminary Objections, Merits, Reparations, and Costs, Inter-Am. Ct. H.R. (Ser. C) No. 85/10 (Nov. 28, 2012) ¶ 146.

188 American Convention, Art. 5.

integrity" (emphasis added).[189] If the exercise of conscientious objection affects the timeliness or adequacy of reproductive health services—as is customary in the creation of barriers to access—it is likely that a petitioner could successfully assert violations of her Article 5 rights.

Although this issue has not been explicitly undertaken by the Inter-American bodies, it has been discussed in a friendly settlement negotiation. In its Report No. 21/07, the Inter-American Commission addressed the petition of Paulina Del Carmen Ramírez Jacinto, a minor who became pregnant as the result of sexual violence.[190] Although her circumstances fell within the legally provided exceptions for abortion under Mexican law, Paulina faced a variety of barriers in exercising her legal right to abortion: these included delayed scheduling of appointments, unavailability of practitioners, and having to seek approval from a review board.[191] She asserted violations of Article 5 on this basis.

In its report, the Commission emphasized the nexus between one's full enjoyment of human rights and "having a timely access to comprehensive health care services."[192] This language stands for the proposition that Article 5, like the right to private life, is closely interrelated with limiting barriers to accessing legally available reproductive health services. Additionally, the delays and intimidation tactics that Paulina endured are synonymous to those likely to occur in scenarios where medical practitioners exercise conscientious objection. Thus, Article 5, coupled with Article 12 could be a successful strategy in the Inter-American system to tackle barriers to access sexual and reproductive health services.

An additional method to counter the use of conscience-based claims in healthcare within the Inter-American system could rely on the economic and social rights framework as embedded in Article 26 of the American Convention.[193] Article 26 of the American Convention provides for the "progressive

189 *Access to Maternal Health Services from a Human Rights Perspective*, Inter-Am. Comm'n H.R., OEA/Ser.L/V/II. Doc. 69, ¶ 22–23 (2010), https://www.oas.org/en/iachr/women/docs/pdf/saludmaternaeng.pdf (last visited Nov 18, 2023).; *see also Albán Cornejo et al v. Ecuador*, Merits, Reparations and Costs, Inter-Am. Ct. H.R. (Ser. C) No. 171 (Nov. 22, 2007) ¶ 177.

190 Inter.-Am. Comm'n. H.R., Report No. 21/07, *Petition 161–02: Friendly Settlement,* Paulina del Carmen Ramírez Jacinto v. Mexico (Mar. 9, 2007), https://www.cidh.org/annualrep/2007eng/Mexico161.02eng.htm (last visited Nov 18, 2023).

191 *Id.* ¶ 11.

192 *Id.* ¶ 19.

193 *See* American Convention, art. 26; *see also* Organization of Am. States, Additional Protocol to the American Convention on Human Rights in the Area of Economic, Social, and Cultural Rights, "Protocol of San Salvador," Nov. 16, 1999, O.A.S.T.S. No. A-52.

development" of economic, social, and cultural rights.[194] Moreover, economic, social, and cultural rights are also ensured through the additional protocol to the American Convention on Human Rights in the area of Economic, Social, and Cultural Rights, more commonly known as the Protocol of San Salvador ("the Protocol").[195] The Protocol entered into force in 1999, and has subsequently been ratified by nineteen members of the Organization of American States ("OAS").[196] Relevant provisions of the Protocol—for present purposes—include the obligation of nondiscrimination (Article 3), the right to work (Article 6), and the right to health (Article 10) .

The viability of the economic and social rights framework in the Inter-American system has notably increased in recent years. Prior to 2017, the Inter-American Court had never found a violation of Article 26. This changed in *Lagos del Campo v. Peru* where the Inter-American Court found that Peru had violated Article 26 when a trade union representative was wrongfully terminated.[197]

Ultimately, *Lagos Del Campo* paved the way for the direct justiciability of economic and social rights in the Inter-American system. After the right to work was addressed in *Lagos del Campo*, the Inter-American Court expressly examined the justiciability of the right to health in *Poblete Vilches and others v. Chile*.[198] In the landmark decision, the court indicated that the right to health—derived from Article 26—was "directly justiciable," or alternatively, "capable of being directly invoked in complaints filed before the main bodies of the Inter-American Human Rights System."[199] This notion was reiterated by the court a mere few months later in *Cuscul Pivaral and Others vs. Guatemala*.[200]

---

194 American Convention, art. 26

195 Organization of Am. States, *Protocol of San Salvador*, SEDI (2015), http://www.oas.org/en/sedi/dsi/protocol-ssv/ (last visited Nov 18, 2023).

196 *Id.* The ratifying states are: Argentina, Bolivia, Brazil, Colombia, Costa Rica, Ecuador, El Salvador, Guatemala, Honduras, Mexico, Nicaragua, Panama, Paraguay, Peru, Suriname and Uruguay.

197 Lagos del Campos v. Peru, Preliminary Objections, Merits, Reparations, and Costs, Inter-Am. Ct. H.R. (ser. C) No. 340, ¶ 166 (Aug. 31, 2017). *See* Pamela Huynh, *Lagos del Campos v. Peru*, 42 LOY. L.A. INT'L & COMP. L. REV 1083 (2015); *see also* Lagos del Campo v. Peru, Preliminary Objections, Merits, Reparations, and Costs, Concurring Vote of Judge Eduardo Ferrer Mac-Gregor Poisot, Inter-Am. Ct. H.R. (ser. C) No. 340, ¶ 47 (Aug. 31, 2017).

198 Quotes included here are from the following summary, *see* Nicolás Carrillo-Santarelli, *The Autonomous Justiciability of the Right to Health and Supervision of Immediate Obligations of States in the Inter-American Human Rights System*, 4 DPCE ONLINE 1207 (2018), https://www.dpceonline.it/index.php/dpceonline/article/view/602 (last visited Nov 18, 2023).

199 *Id.* at 1207.

200 Cuscul Pivaral and Others v. Guatemala, Preliminary Objections, Merits, Reparations and Costs, Inter-Am. Ct. H.R. (ser. C) No. 359 (Aug. 23, 2018), https://www.escr-net.org/sites/default/files/caselaw/seriec_359_esp.pdf (last visited Nov 18, 2023).

After reaffirming the right to health as an "autonomous right" that could be enforced in litigation, the court found violations of the right to health regarding the treatment of HIV positive individuals.[201] In determining its violation of the right to health—and in turn, Article 26—the Inter-American Court explicitly referenced a lack of access to certain healthcare mechanisms.[202] Specifically, in its "final decision," the court asserted that "[t]he state must ... improve accessibility, availability, and quality of health benefits for people living with HIV."[203]

These decisions signal the Inter-American Court's willingness to rule on the right to health under the auspices of Article 26. As the justiciability of economic and social rights becomes increasingly refined, asserting violations of these rights may become feasible in the context of conscientious objection, especially when it comes to access to sexual and reproductive health services where the language referring to "access" in *Cuscul Pivaral* would be particularly instructive. Moreover, in 2021, the Inter-American Court for the first time considered the obstacles women face in accessing reproductive healthcare and established standards throughout the region to protect women seeking abortion.[204] Given that the abusive exercise of conscientious objection has the tendency to lead to increasing barriers to access to health services, an applicant could assert a violation of her right to health on this basis. In this sense, conscientious objection could be readily connected with state accountability and the right to health.

The Inter-American Human Rights System, while still developing its approach to conscience-based claims, offers a promising framework for countering religious lawfare. As the region continues to grapple with the misuse of conscience-based claims, the Inter-American system will play a critical role in ensuring that the rights to health and autonomy are protected against the encroachment of religiously motivated legal strategies.

2.3 *African Human Rights System*

The African Human Rights System—the youngest of the regional human rights systems—faces a unique set of challenges as religious lawfare, often fueled by external conservative influences, increasingly intersects with conscience-based claims in the realm of reproductive health. Especially considering that the system does not have significant jurisprudence around

201 *Cuscul Pivaral and Others vs. Guatemala*, ESCR-NET, https://www.escr-net.org/caselaw/2019/cuscul-pivaral-and-others-vs-guatemala (last visited Nov. 18, 2023).

202 *Id.*

203 *See* Cuscul Pivaral and Others v. Guatemala, ¶ 225.

204 Manuela et al. v. El Salvador, Preliminary Objections, Merits, Reparations and Costs, Inter-Am. Ct. H.R. (ser. C) No. 441 (Nov. 2, 2021), https://www.corteidh.or.cr/docs/casos/articulos/seriec_441_ing.pdf (last visited Sept. 10, 2024).

conscientious objection and protections for reproductive freedoms across the continent vary significantly.

However, pulling language from the optional protocol to the African Charter of Human and People's Rights, and reading it in conjunction with strategies implemented in the European system, may be instructive. Formulating strategies to be implemented in this region may be crucial in the near future, as conservative movements are becoming increasingly influential in African countries.[205] For example, in 2019, a U.S-led conservative group—World Congress of Families ("WCF")—held a two-day conference in the Ghanaian capital city of Accra.[206] During the conference, WCF's president touted "pro-family" and anti-abortion ideals.[207] The following month, religious and conservative groups held a "counter-summit" in Nairobi, in an attempt to protest the International Conference on Population and Development.[208] As more conservative religious groups move into the continent to promote ideals contrary to sexual and reproductive health and rights it is likely that religious lawfare through political uses of conscience-based claims will become prevalent across the region.

The primary legal instrument that could be referenced in this context is the Protocol to the African Charter on the Rights of Women in Africa, colloquially known as the "Maputo Protocol."[209] The Maputo Protocol has been ratified by forty-four countries of the African Union and refers explicitly to sexual and reproductive health and rights in Article 14.[210] Moreover, the African Commission on Human and Peoples' Rights ("African Commission") issued General

---

205 *See* Chapter 1.

206 *See American-led 'pro-family' summit in Ghana condemned for 'shocking' white supremacist, Islamophobic links*, OPENDEMOCRACY (Oct. 31, 2019), https://www.opendemocracy.net/en/5050/american-led-pro-family-summit-in-ghana-condemned-for-shocking-white-supremacist-islamophobic-links/ (last visited Nov 18, 2023).

207 *Id.*

208 Nandini Archer, Mary Fitzgerald & Claire Provost, *US isolated at 'failed' anti-abortion summit in Nairobi*, OPENDEMOCRACY (Nov. 15, 2019), https://www.opendemocracy.net/en/5050/us-isolated-at-failed-anti-abortion-summit-in-nairobi/ (last visited Nov 18, 2023).

209 Protocol to the African Charter on Human and Peoples Rights on the Rights of Women in Africa, July 11, 2003, https://www.ohchr.org/sites/default/files/Documents/Issues/Women/WG/ProtocolontheRightsofWomen.pdf (last visited Nov 18, 2023).

210 Protocol to the African Charter on Human and Peoples Rights on the Rights of Women in Africa, July 11, 200, art. 14; African Union, *List of Countries Which Have Signed, Ratified/Acceded to the Protocol to the African Charter on Human and Peoples' Rights on the Rights of Women in Africa* (last updated 2023), https://au.int/sites/default/files/treaties/37077-sl-PROTOCOL_TO_THE_AFRICAN_CHARTER_ON_HUMAN_AND_PEOPLES_RIGHTS_ON_THE_RIGHTS_OF_WOMEN_IN_AFRICA.pdf (last visited Nov 18, 2023).

Comment No. 2, which interprets Article 14, expressly referring to conscientious objection, while also alluding to a variety of previously proposed strategies:

> The right to freedom from being subjected to discrimination prohibits any deprivation concerning access to family planning/contraception services by health care providers for reasons of conscientious objection. While it is true that they may invoke conscientious objection to the direct provision of the required services, State parties must ensure that the necessary infrastructure is set up to enable women to be knowledgeable and referred to other health care providers on time. In addition, State parties must ensure that only the health personnel directly involved in the provision of contraception/family planning services enjoys the right to conscientious objection and that it is not so for the institutions. However, the right to conscientious objection cannot be invoked in the case of a woman whose health is in a serious risk, and whose condition requires emergency care or treatment.[211]

The first sentence, which refers to the "freedom from being subjected to discrimination," makes apparent the correlation between conscientious objection and discrimination, signaling the substantiality of a non-discrimination argument in this context. This argument could find additional support in Article 18(3) of the African Charter, which provides that "[t]he State shall ensure the elimination of every discrimination against women ... ."[212] Thus, when conscientious objection inevitably results in discriminatory practices, this language would give an applicant a vehicle for challenging that discrimination.

The language of General Comment No. 2 also refers to a duty to "ensure that the necessary infrastructure is set up" when conscientious objection is exercised. This language is comparable to that issued by the ECtHR in *R.R. v. Poland* and *P. and S. v. Poland*, associating the assertion of conscientious objection with mandatory infrastructure adjustments.[213] Arguments based on barriers to access, such as this, are routinely rooted in the right to private life, which is notably absent from the African Charter. However, unlike the ECHR or the American Convention, the African Charter does include explicit references to

---

211 African Commission on Human and Peoples' Rights, *General Comment No. 2 on Article 14.1 (a), (b), (c) and (f) and Article 14. 2 (a) and (c) of the Protocol to the African Charter on Human and Peoples' Rights on the Rights of Women in Africa*, ¶ 26.

212 African Charter on Human and Peoples' Rights, art.18(3), June 27, 1891.

213 *See* discussion in Chapter 2 on the exercise of conscientious objection and barriers to accessing reproductive health care.

a right to work (Article 15) and a right to health (Article 16), both of which may provide alternate mechanisms for setting forth this argument.

Finally, the African Commission's General Comment No. 2's language could also be used in formulating an argument justifying limitations on conscientious objection based on complicity. Complicity—a prevalent ethical principle—refers to the idea that "[o]ne becomes complicit in the wrongdoing of someone else by performing actions that contribute to that wrongdoing."[214] Examples of these arguments include a janitor's refusal to clean areas where an abortion was performed, receptionists refusing to schedule certain elective procedures, or police officers declining to guard an abortion facility.

In a response to these commonplace "complicity claims," General Comment No. 2's language obligates states to limit the ability to assert conscientious objection only to those "***directly*** involved" (emphasis added) with the provision of contraception or abortion services. Successful strategies utilizing this language will grapple with who is "directly" engaged in providing these purportedly objectionable healthcare services, attempting to limit the scope of the term. It is clear from the language of General Comment No. 2 that conscientious objection is not available "for the institutions," but there is inherent ambiguity in the parameters of those categorized as "healthcare personnel."[215] Surely, there must be a line drawn somewhere between licensed medical doctors and ancillary personnel, such as administrative and janitorial staff. In this sense, it may be instructive to advocate for—given that no jurisprudence has been developed in this area—a standard similar to the "but for" causation test in U.S. tort law. While the "but for" test of actual causation has been criticized for its "weakness" in comparison to other causation standards, it could be particularly useful for limiting the scope of the phrase "directly engaged."[216] Under this standard, an individual could only assert conscientious objection if the abortion, for example, would not have been performed "but for" his or her actions. This standard would necessarily reach licensed medical doctors. It would also extend to those individuals who are legally authorized to perform abortion, such as nurses and midwives in South Africa.[217] It would not

214 Joshua J. Craddock, *The Case for Complicity-Based Religious Accommodations*, 12 TENN. J.L. & POL'Y, 233, 234 (2018).

215 Afr. Commission on Human and Peoples' Rights, *General Comment No. 2 on Article 14.1 (a), (b), (c) and (f) and Article 14. 2 (a) and (c) of the Protocol to the African Charter on Human and Peoples' Rights on the Rights of Women in Africa*, ¶ 26.

216 *But-For Test*, LEGAL INFO. INST., https://www.law.cornell.edu/wex/but-for_test (last visited Nov. 18, 2023).

217 Jane Harries et al., *Conscientious Objection and its Impact on Abortion Service Provision in South Africa: a Qualitative Study*, 11 REPRO. HEALTH J. 16 (2014).

include, however, administrative staff, janitorial staff, and nurses not "directly engaged" in the procedure. Although the standard does leave a significant gray area—nurses tangentially involved in the procedures and pharmacists providing medications, for example—it is a small, yet significant step in regulating conscientious objection in areas where it is most egregiously exercised. This argument could prove useful in the African system, as there is currently no jurisprudence defining standards on this basis. Additionally, this strategy could be used to cabin expansive assertions of conscientious objection and counter religious lawfare, providing an incremental step in the path forward to broader and bolder regulation.

It is crucial, however, to note the hypothetical nature of these arguments, as there are multiple limitations to their ultimate viability. First, although the language contained in the African Commission's General Comment No. 2 is largely progressive, there has yet to be jurisprudence suggesting it would be enforced. Moreover, successful strategies implemented in the European system were based on an underlying legality of the reproductive health services at issue. This is not the case in Africa, where approximately 93% of women of reproductive age live in areas with extremely restrictive abortion laws.[218] Resorting to human rights mechanisms at the regional level may be largely ineffective without structural change at the domestic level.

Finally, the freedom of conscience provision (Article 8) of the African Charter—unlike its Inter-American and European parallels, does not have a strong balancing mechanism inherent in its language. The only restrictions that can be placed on one's freedom of conscience are those prescribed by "law and order."[219] Notwithstanding the language in General Comment No. 2 stating that "conscientious objection cannot be invoked in the case of a woman whose health is in a serious risk, and whose condition requires emergency care or treatment," there are no explicit components of the balancing test under Article 8.[220] Considering the weakness of the balancing mechanism, conscientious objectors may have more of a basis to exercise their freedom of conscience.

In the African context, the use of conscientious objection as a form of religious lawfare presents a significant threat to reproductive rights. The Maputo

218 Guttmacher Inst., Abortion in Africa Fact Sheet (2018), https://www.guttmacher.org/sites/default/files/factsheet/ib_aww-africa.pdf (last visited Nov 18, 2023).

219 African Charter on Human and Peoples' Rights, art.18(3), June 27, 1891, art. 8.

220 African Commission on Human and Peoples' Rights, *General Comment No. 2 on Article 14.1 (a), (b), (c) and (f) and Article 14. 2 (a) and (c) of the Protocol to the African Charter on Human and Peoples' Rights on the Rights of Women in Africa*, ¶ 26.

Protocol and related legal instruments provide a critical foundation for countering these tactics, though much work remains to be done in building a robust legal response. As conservative religious groups continue to exert influence across the continent, it becomes imperative to develop legal strategies to prevent the political uses of conscience-based claims.

3 Conclusion

The intricate terrain of conscientious objection within the context of reproductive and sexual healthcare demands an exhaustive examination of its multifaceted dimensions across diverse human rights domains. The comprehensive analysis in this chapter traversed the European, Inter-American, African, and Universal human rights systems. Conscientious objection has surfaced as an increasingly formidable challenge to the full realization of sexual and reproductive rights on a global scale. This chapter unpacked the legal standards and nuanced considerations that need to be considered in any endeavor to harmonize the rights of healthcare providers with the rights of patients seeking access to essential healthcare services.

The European human rights landscape seems to have meticulously sculpted an approach that accommodates conscientious objection. Central to this approach is the concept of a delicate equilibrium, whereby healthcare providers' freedom of religion and conscience, enshrined in Article 9 of the ECHR, is considered a fundamental right but not an absolute one. Rather, it must be subject to prescribed limitations when its exercise encroaches upon the rights and freedoms of others. The nuanced jurisprudence of the European Court of Human Rights underscores that the right to conscientious objection can legitimately be limited, particularly when it serves as an impediment to the right to access reproductive and sexual healthcare services. Two landmark cases, *R.R. v. Poland* and *P. and S. v. Poland*, epitomize this trajectory by elucidating that states bear a positive obligation to implement procedural mechanisms, such as referral systems, to ensure that conscientious objection does not become an insurmountable barrier to access.

Though the Inter-American human rights system has yet to forge a jurisprudential path concerning conscientious objection in reproductive healthcare, it derives substantial inspiration from the European paradigm. By transplanting strategies reminiscent of the European framework, such as invoking violations of the right to private life or the right to physical, mental, and moral integrity under the American Convention, compelling arguments could be designed to counter religious lawfare. Furthermore, the nascent acceptance of the direct justiciability of economic and social rights within the Inter-American system ushers in novel avenues for contesting conscientious objection in healthcare. The recognition of the right to health as directly justiciable could allow for persuasive arguments contending that barriers to healthcare services arising from conscientious objection contravene this right.

Within the African human rights framework, addressing conscientious objection in reproductive healthcare is a crucial endeavor, exacerbated by the limited protection afforded to reproductive freedoms in the African Charter on Human and Peoples' Rights. Nonetheless, the Maputo Protocol emerges as a potential panacea by explicitly acknowledging sexual and reproductive rights. General Comment No. 2, though yet untested in practical application, furnishes a blueprint for tackling conscientious objection within the African context.

The expansion of conscience-based claims transcends geographical boundaries, affecting individuals irrespective of their global coordinates. The International Bill of Rights encapsulates principles that resonate with the issue of conscientious objection. While these international instruments may not expressly proffer guidance on how to deal with conscience-based claims, they serve as bulwarks for the overarching principles of nondiscrimination, equality, and the safeguarding of individual rights.

Ultimately, the resolution of conscience-based claims in liberal democracies necessitates a nuanced, inclusive, and rights-oriented approach—one that respects sincere convictions of objectors while upholding the rights and dignity of others by capturing the full spectrum of subtler forms of coercion and domination. In this collective endeavor, states, international human rights bodies, and advocates bear shared responsibility for navigating this intricate terrain. Ensuring that individuals can exercise their rights unencumbered by undue impediments is not only a legal imperative but a moral one—a testament to the paramount importance of safeguarding the autonomy and dignity of all individuals on a global canvas.

CHAPTER 5

Religious Lawfare at Play: Conscientious Objection in Healthcare

As anticipated in Chapters 2 and 3, in the healthcare context, conscience-based claims have been invoked especially in relation to the provision of sexual and reproductive health services, particularly as a way to deny the provision of legal services for the termination of pregnancy.[1] In some cases, and according to the *depth* categorization described before,[2] not only the providers who participate directly in the service, such as doctors and nurses, invoke this objection, but also those who participate indirectly in it, such as hospital administrators, directors or heads of service, who refuse to deal with legal abortion cases.[3]

The exercise of conscience-based claims in healthcare settings places the preferences of providers over the rights of patients and puts providers in tension with the objectives of the profession, their civil duties as citizens, and other moral duties that demand consideration for other people, especially for those who are in situations of vulnerability. A troubling consequence of conscience-based objections to sexual and reproductive health services is that while individuals may be exercising their recognized rights, such objections can severely limit access to legal abortion services. This issue becomes particularly problematic in regions, states, or even entire countries where objectors are predominant.

As discussed in Chapter 4, current international human rights standards do not require states to guarantee a right to "conscientious objection" in the provision of healthcare services. On the contrary, the human rights treaty-monitoring bodies have consistently stated that the exercise of conscientious objection must be limited when the states allow it, in order to guarantee that health care providers do not obstruct access to sexual and reproductive health services and, therefore, do not infringe upon the rights of patients. These treaty-monitoring bodies have drawn attention to insufficient regulation on

1 Douglas NeJaime & Reva Siegel, *Conscience Wars in Transnational Perspective: Religious Liberty, Third-Party Harm, and Pluralism*, *in* The Conscience Wars: Rethinking the Balance Between Religion, Identity, and Equality (Susanna Mancini & Michel Rosenfeld eds., 2018).

2 *See* Chapter 2.

3 Judith Bueno de Mesquita & Louise Finer, Conscientious Objection: Protecting Sexual and Reproductive Health and Rights (2008).

 | DOI:10.1163/9789004685406_007

the exercise of conscientious objection and have demanded that States take measures to guarantee access to these services. They have also asserted that institutions cannot invoke conscientious objection to exempt themselves from providing services.[4] It is essential to understand what these standards mean regarding practical limits to expansions of conscience-based claims in the healthcare space and suggest a path forward in terms of what adequate regulation of conscience-based claims might look like.

1 Conscience-Based Claims to the Provision of Healthcare Services

The invocation of conscientious objection to refuse the provision of services in healthcare places significant tensions on the ethical and professional obligations of healthcare providers, who are called to put the health and well-being of their patients first.[5] Health professionals practicing obstetrics, gynecology, midwifery, pharmacy, or other fields that include the provision of sexual and reproductive health services have professional obligations to provide abortion, contraception, and other essential sexual and reproductive health services. For this reason, conscience-based claims should only be used "after weighing principles, moral beliefs, and legal duties, to excuse oneself from a certain practice, since carrying it out would severely damage their integrity. Somehow, [with their conscientious objection, healthcare professionals] acknowledge not having been able to resolve their moral conflict in a more beneficial way for patients, their colleagues and the healthcare system. Put like this, conscientious objection appears as an act of humility, not moral arrogance or even moral rejection."[6]

However, as Ariza Navarrete and Ramón Michel explain, today there is "an enormous dissonance between what is envisaged by the texts and practice: the version of conscientious objection as a reflexive act, sincere and humble of a person who is part of a minority has yielded to other uses much more problematic and much less ethical,"[7] as demonstrated in preceding chapters.[8]

4 Ipas, "Human Rights Standards": The Storehouse for Abortion Law and Policy, http://www.ipas.org/en/The-Storehouse-for-Abortion-Law-and-Policy/Conscientious objection/Human-rights- (last visited Nov 18, 2023).

5 World Med. Ass'n, wma Declaration of Geneva World Medical Association (1948).

6 Sonia Ariza Navarrete & Agustina Ramón Michel. Usos imprevistos y respuestas a la objeción de conciencia en el aborto legal (2019).

7 *Id.*

8 *See* Chapters 2, 3 and 4.

This dissonance and expansion of conscience-based claims to new frontiers highlights the need for mitigating the risks of the exercise of conscientious objection in order to guarantee that healthcare providers do not violate the rights of third parties by limiting access to services. Insufficient or inadequate regulation of the exercise of conscientious objection demands that states adopt measures to guarantee effective access to health services.[9]

Protecting and respecting women's right to health, according to the CEDAW Committee, requires States to remove barriers that limit women's access to health services.[10] The Committee on Economic, Social and Cultural Rights (CESCR), for its part, has recognized that "[t]he unavailability of goods and services due to ideology-based policies or practices, such as conscientious objection to providing services, should not be an obstacle to access to services."[11] In other words, at all times, a sufficient number of healthcare service providers must be "willing to provide those services and able to do so in public and private establishments within a reasonable geographical distance."[12] The

---

9 *See, e.g.*, U.N. Committee on the Elimination of Discrimination against Women, *Concluding Observations on Croatia*, U.N. Doc. A/53/38 (1998), ¶ 109, 117; U.N. Committee on the Elimination of Discrimination against Women, *Concluding Observations on Italy*, U.N. Doc. A/52/38 Rev.1, Part II (1997), ¶ 353, 360; U.N. Committee on the Elimination of Discrimination against Women, *Concluding Observations on South Africa*, U.N. Doc. A/53/38/Rev.1 (1998), ¶ 113; U.N. Committee on the Elimination of Discrimination against Women, *Concluding Observations on Romania*, CEDAW/C/ROU/CO/7-8, ¶ 33 c); *Argentina*, CEDAW/C/ARG/CO/7, ¶ 33 c); *Report of the Special Rapporteur on the right of everyone to the enjoyment of the highest attainable standard of physical and mental health, Anand Grover – Mission to Poland*, May 20, 2010, U.N. Doc. A/HRC/14/20/Add.3; *Memorandum to the Polish Government, Assessment of the progress made in implementing the 2002 recommendations of the Council of Europe Commissioner for Human Rights*, ¶ 92 to 98 and Recommendation 15, https://rm.coe.int/16806db77d; U.N. Committee on the Elimination of Discrimination against Women, *General Recommendation* N° 24: *Article 12 of the Convention on the Elimination of all Forms of Discrimination Against Women – Women and Health* (1999), ¶ 11; U.N. Human Rights Committee, *Concluding observations on the sixth periodic report of Mexico*, CCPT/C/MEX/CO/6, ¶ 17.c), Dec. 4, 2019 ("[t]he State Party should:… Regulate conscientious objection so that it does not in effect constitute a barrier to voluntary termination of pregnancy in safe, legal conditions"); U.N. Human Rights Committee, *Concluding observations on the third periodic report of Lebanon*, CCPR/C/LBN/CO/3, ¶ 26, May 9, 2018; and U.N. Human Rights Committee, *Concluding observations on the fifth periodic report of Romania*, CCPR/C/ROU/CO/5, ¶ 26, Dec. 11, 2017; U.N. Committee on Economic, Social and Cultural Rights, General Comment 22, E/C.12/GC/22, May 2, 2016, ¶ 14, 43.

10 U.N. Committee on the Elimination of Discrimination against Women, *General Recommendation* N° 24: *Article 12 of the Convention on the Elimination of all Forms of Discrimination Against Women – Women and Health* (1999), ¶ 31 (b).

11 U.N. Committee on Economic, Social and Cultural Rights, *General Comment 22*, E/C.12/GC/22, May 2, 2016, ¶ 14.

12 *Id.* ¶ 14.

CESCR has recommended that States adopt limits on the exercise of conscientious objection, such as requiring that objecting providers "refer cases to an accessible provider with the capacity and willingness to provide the required service" and not prevent "the provision of services in urgent or emergency situations."[13] Along the same lines, the European Court of Human Rights, in the *Pichon* decision, declared the conscience-based claim of two pharmacists inadmissible and held that "applicants cannot prioritize their religious beliefs and impose them on others […] since they can manifest those beliefs in many ways outside of the professional sphere."[14]

It is worth noting that, in his report of February 27, 2020, the U.N. Special Rapporteur on freedom of religion or belief, Ahmed Shaheed, recommended that States reaffirm that appeals to traditional, historical, religious or cultural notions should not be used as a mechanism to justify the violation of human rights.[15] In particular, with regard to healthcare, the U.N. Special Rapporteur recommended that all States "ensure that legal protections for people to express their religion or belief, such as those that are manifested in the sphere of medical care, do not have the effect of denying women, girls or sexual or gender minorities the right to non-discrimination or other rights. In all cases, States must guarantee the right to physical and mental integrity, as well as the right to health, including reproductive health, for women, adolescents and LGBTQ people, and effective access to reproductive health services and comprehensive sexuality education, in accordance with international standards."[16]

Moreover, the former U.N. Special Rapporteur on the right of everyone to the enjoyment of the highest possible level of physical and mental health, Dr. Dainius Püras, in an effort to provide guidance on how to deal with these claims in the healthcare context, declared that "any provision that allows conscientious objection should: a) be accompanied by clear guarantees regarding a sufficient number of and adequate geographic coverage of public and

---

13 *Id.* ¶ 43 (citing U.N. CESCR, *Concluding Observations: Poland*, ¶ 28, U.N. Doc. E/C.12/POL/CO/5 (2009)); U.N. General Assembly, *Provisional Report of the United Nations Special Rapporteur on the Right to the Highest Attainable Standard of Physical and Mental Health, Anand Grover*, U.N. Doc. A/66/254 (2011), ¶ 24, 65 m; and U.N. Committee on the Elimination of Discrimination against Women, *General Recommendation* N° 24: *Article 12 of the Convention on the Elimination of all Forms of Discrimination Against Women—Women and Health* (1999), ¶ 11.

14 Pichon and Sajous v. France, 2001-X Eur. Ct. H.R. 375, 388.

15 U.N. Report of the Special Rapporteur on freedom of religion or belief, Ahmed Shaheed, Feb. 27, 2020, U.N. Doc. A/HRC/43/48 (Advance Unedited Version), Recommendation (a)(i).

16 U.N. Report of the Special Rapporteur on freedom of religion or belief, Ahmed Shaheed, 27 Feb. 2020, U.N. Doc. A/HRC/43/48 (Advance Unedited Version), Recommendation (a)(vi).

private providers that are willing to provide the services in question; b) limit its exercise to individuals and prohibit institutions from denying care; c) establish an effective referral system that allows access to a medical professional who is willing and able to provide the health products and services that have been denied; d) impose clear restrictions on the legality of refusals, for example ensuring that they are prohibited in urgent or emergency situations; and e) establish adequate monitoring, supervision and enforcement mechanisms to monitor compliance in practice."[17]

2 Dealing with "Vertical Expansions" of Conscience-Based Claims

Sexual and reproductive rights are a conquest achieved as a result of important historical struggles, particularly by women in recent decades. In light of the longstanding opposition against these rights, defending them and protecting access to the benefits that make them effective must be a priority within the public policy of all States. The *vertical* expansion of conscience-based claims in healthcare, especially regarding the provision of sexual and reproductive health services, has established itself as a central barrier to access to legal health services.[18] Consequently, and due to the characteristics of the unequal relationship between doctors and patients, it is necessary to regulate the exercise of conscience-based claims so that its exercise does not result in a harmful practice.

Conscientious objection should not constitute an additional barrier to sexual and reproductive health services. Yet the invocation of conscience-based claims has become one of the most significant stumbling blocks to the realization of these fundamental rights. Governments must stop pretending that conservative religious groups' abusive use of conscience-based claims to limit enjoyment of other people's rights is merely a reflection of the rules of the democratic game. Rather, States must recognize the undemocratic nature of

---

17 U.N. Human Rights Committee, *Report of the U.N. Special Rapporteur on the Right to the Highest Attainable Standard of Physical and Mental Health, Visit to Ecuador*, May 6, 2020, U.N. Doc. A/HRC/44/48/Add. 1, ¶ 23.

18 *See* Wendy Chavkin, et al., *Regulation of conscientious objection to abortion: An international comparative multiple-case study*, 19 Health & Hum. Rts. J. 1, 55–68 (2017). *See also*, Fiona de Londras, et al., *The impact of 'conscientious objection' on abortion-related outcomes: A synthesis of legal and health evidence*, 129 Health Pol'y (2023); *and* Jasmine Meredith Davis, et al., *A narrative literature review of the impact of conscientious objection by health professionals on women's access to abortion worldwide 2013–2021*, 17 Glob. Public Health 9, 2190–2205 (2022).

protecting the right to conscientious objection when its intended use is to veto the enjoyment of other people's rights. Making sexual and reproductive health services accessible in practice, and not solely in theory, requires an intensive exploration into the necessary limits of invoking conscientious objection in healthcare.[19]

2.1 *The Need to Limit Conscientious Objection in Healthcare*

According to current standards under universal and regional human rights law, the exercise of conscientious objection in healthcare must be reconciled with the rights of third parties that may be affected by it.[20] There must be an adequate balance that allows for the full enjoyment and respect for the rights of objecting providers and affected women. Conscientious objection cannot be a barrier that interferes with access to health, education, and information services.[21] This includes the area of sexual and reproductive health. Denial of these rights can have devastating health consequences; in many cases, endangering people's lives.[22]

In this vein, the Constitutional Court of Colombia has recognized that "[the adequate balance between conscientious objection and individuals' rights] is not about making the interest of one or a few prevail over many or the great majority. It is a problem of democratic quality and respect for basic individual rights: when the State admits the conscientious objection of a private individual, it is promoting that fundamental value for the benefit of the whole of society."[23]

Health centers and health services, as previously elucidated by various international and regional bodies, must be accessible to all individuals and groups without discrimination or obstacles.[24] Even if one recognizes the

---

19 *See* Andrés Constantin & Kayla Zamanian, *How New Uses of Conscience-Based Claims Hinder Progress on Abortion Rights*, OpenGlobalRights (Dec. 6, 2021), https://www.openglobalrights.org/how-new-uses-of-conscience-based-claims-hinder-progress-on-abortion-rights/ (last visited Nov 18, 2023).

20 *See* Chapter 4.

21 U.N. Committee on Economic, Social and Cultural Rights, *General Comment No. 14*, U.N. Doc. E/C.12/2000/4 (Aug. 11, 2000), ¶ 21.

22 United Nations Economic and Social Council, *Report of the Special Rapporteur on violence against women, its causes and consequences, Ms. Radhika Coomaraswamy, in accordance with Commission on Human Rights resolution 1997/44, policies and practices that impact women's reproductive rights and contribute to, cause or constitute violence against women*, January 21, 1999, U.N. Doc. E/CN.4/1999/68/Add.4, ¶ 1.

23 Constitutional Court of Colombia, Decision SU108-16, Mar. 3, 2016.

24 U.N. Committee on Economic, Social and Cultural Rights, *General Comment No. 14*, U.N. Doc. E/C.12/2000/4 (Aug. 11, 2000), ¶ 55; U.N. Committee on the Elimination of

possibility of refusing to provide these services based on conscience, such a right should not be absolute, but rather be subject to restrictions to guarantee the exercise of other rights, including the right to health and the principle of non-discrimination.[25]

Objection to the provision of health services under conscience grounds should not be an obstacle to the effective enjoyment of access to health services. The lack of availability of goods and services due to policies or practices based on moral or religious beliefs precisely represents an obstacle to exercising the right to health.[26] Health services must be always available, and a sufficient number of health service providers must ensure that there are those who are willing to provide such services and who can do so in public and private facilities within a reasonable geographical distance to prospective patients.[27]

Recent legal developments have tried to shed light on the intersection of conscientious objection to healthcare services and international human rights law. For instance, in September 2021, the Mexican Supreme Court of Justice issued a decision that effectively harmonized comparative law principles with international human rights standards. In this context, the court astutely

---

Discrimination against Women, *General Recommendation* Nº 24: *Article 12 of the Convention on the Elimination of all Forms of Discrimination Against Women—Women and Health* (1999), ¶ 31.b.

25 U.N. Committee on Economic, Social and Cultural Rights, *General Comment No. 14*, U.N. Doc. E/C.12/2000/4 (Aug. 11, 2000), ¶ 30 (noting the obligation to guarantee that the right to health without discrimination and to adopt measures aimed at its full realization are obligations of immediate effect).

26 *See* Tomasso Autorino, et al., *The impact of gynecologists' conscientious objection on abortion access*, 87 Social Science Research 102403 (2020); Mary Favier, et al., *Safe abortion in South Africa: "We have wonderful laws but we don't have people to implement those laws"*, 143 Int'l J. of Gynecology & Obstetrics S4, 38–44 (2018); Chelsey E. Brack, et al., *"It's a race against the clock": A qualitative analysis of barriers to legal abortion in Bogotá, Colombia*, 43 Int'l Perspectives on Sexual and Reprod. Health 4, 173–182 (2017); Emily Freeman & Ernestina Coast, *Conscientious objection to abortion: Zambian healthcare practitioners' beliefs and practices*, 221 Soc. Sci. Med., 106–114 (2019) (arguing that there is a link between insufficient providers due to high numbers of objecting providers and inadequate access to abortion services). *See also*, John Koku Awoonor-Williams, et al., *Exploring conscientious objection to abortion among health providers in Ghana*, 46 Int'l Perspectives on Sexual and Reprod. Health 1, 51–59 (2020); and Jane Harries, et al., *Conscientious objection and its impact on abortion service provision in South Africa: A qualitative study*, 11 Reprod. Health 1 (2014).

27 U.N. Committee on Economic, Social and Cultural Rights, *General Comment No. 14*, U.N. Doc. E/C.12/2000/4 (Aug. 11, 2000). U.N. Committee on Economic, Social and Cultural Rights, General Comment No. 22, ¶ 14, U.N. Doc. E/C.12/GC/22 (May 2, 2016). *See also*, European Commission of Social Rights, *International Planned Parenthood Federation European Network (IPPF-EN) v. Italy*, No. 87/2012 (2014).

recognized that freedom of conscience encompasses three dimensions, establishing a crucial precedent in addressing the challenges posed by conscience-based claims to health services:

> "a) implies the right to the free formation of conscience, that is, to have one or another conviction and, consequently, one or another worldview (these phenomena are legally irrelevant and not controllable by law); b) includes the freedom to express and manifest or not those convictions and to share or transmit them to other people; and c) entails a freedom to behave in accordance with those convictions (beliefs and ideas), as well as not being forced to behave in contradiction with them."[28]

This last aspect of freedom of conscience is what "takes on legal relevance and gives rise to conscientious objection,"[29] which occurs "when a legal norm or an act entails a legal obligation or duty that opposes the convictions of a person, and he refuses to comply with that duty … it is a confrontation between the legal duty and the personal convictions of the objector."[30]

The Mexican Supreme Court considered that conscientious objection is not only "a form of concretization or materialization of the human right to religious, ideological, and conscientious freedom," but that "it forms part of its essential nucleus and shares the direct binding force of all rights recognized by the [Mexican] Constitution."[31]

In the opinion of the Court, to be considered a conscientious objection, it must be "linked to a *strong religious, ideological or belief conviction*" (emphasis added).[32] The reasons for a collision with the legal norm can be "religious, ethical or moral, ideological and any other of a similar nature, as long as that contradiction affects beliefs, ideas or values that are an inseparable part of personal identity".[33] The contradiction of the norm with conscience or personal convictions must "compromise the dignity of the person."[34]

Conscientious objection, as understood by the Court, is "an individual position contrary to a legal duty, acts of the authority, and even labor authorities"[35]

28 Mexican Supreme Court of Justice, acción de inconstitucionalidad 54/2018, Sept. 21, 2021 (Mex.), M.P., Luis María Aguilar Morales, ¶ 267.

29 *Id.* ¶ 268.

30 *Id.* ¶ 270.

31 *Id.* ¶ 283, 387.

32 *Id.* ¶ 272.

33 *Id.* ¶ 273.

34 *Id.* ¶ 273.

35 *Id.* ¶ 274, 386.

whose purpose is "the non-application of the law or act in question or its sanction."[36] The Court considered that conscientious objection "does not constitute an absolute or unlimited right that can be invoked in any case and under any modality."[37] Thus, in the opinion of the Court, the right to conscientious objection:

> "can be limited by the concurrence of legal rights worthy of special protection, such as the respect for the fundamental rights of other people, general health, the prohibition of discrimination, constitutional order, the democratic principle and, in general, all principles and values that [the Mexican] Constitution proclaims."[38]

Faced with a possible conflict between the right to conscientious objection and other legally relevant rights, such as the right to health, the Court recalled the general theory of fundamental rights,[39] and noted that conscientious objection is not about "a general right to disobey the law,"[40] nor is it a mechanism "to defend ideas contrary to the Constitution."[41] The Court stressed that conscientious objection cannot be valid either when it is "intended to disregard the fundamental principles of the Mexican State, as would be, for example, a hypothetical case in which medical and health personnel denied medical attention for discriminatory reasons or hate."[42]

As such, the Court stated that conscientious objection should not become an obstacle to access to sexual and reproductive health services.[43] Recalling its doctrine on the right of access to health and reiterating that Mexico has a positive obligation to adopt, without discrimination, all necessary measures, using the maximum available resources, to progressively achieve the full realization of the right to health,[44] the Court noted that it is the State's responsibility to adequately regulate the exercise of conscientious objection by medical, nursing, and other healthcare personnel, while protecting the health of people.[45]

---

36 *Id.*
37 *Id.* ¶ 289, 388.
38 *Id.* ¶ 291.
39 *Id.* ¶ 287.
40 *Id.* ¶ 289.
41 *Id.*
42 *Id.* ¶ 292.
43 *Id.* ¶ 336.
44 *Id.* ¶ 344.
45 *Id.* ¶ 346.

Consequently, States must put mechanisms in place through which they guarantee that the exercise of conscientious objection does not become a *de facto* barrier to the effective enjoyment of rights. States should supervise and monitor the number of clinics where most of the healthcare staff are objectors and individual providers seeking objector status, as well as ensuring that a reasonable proportion of willing and able providers are available.

2.2 *Dealing with Conscientious Objection in Healthcare beyond Human Rights Standards*

Most of the analysis calling for the need to regulate the exercise of conscience-based claims in healthcare settings in this chapter has focused on international and regional human rights standards. However, while recognizing that health is not a commodity to be allocated by the market,[46] to underscore the imperative for comprehensive regulation of conscientious objection in healthcare, we can explore the need for regulation not only from the standpoint of international human rights law but also from the vantage point of legal obligations theory, which would provide a different perspective in terms of the course of action to be pursued when a healthcare provider invokes conscientious objection.

When a doctor exercises conscientious objection as a means of refusing to provide a health service it could be argued that the nature of the obligation of conduct changes. Thus, by exempting him- or herself from the obligation to provide care, treatment, and service to these patients, the nature of these obligations turn into obligations to facilitate access to health services for these patients. In this sense, the obligations that derive from the exercise of conscientious objection in a healthcare settings include: the duty to properly and in a timely manner diagnose the person who requested the health service, the duty to refer this person to alternative providers that are non-objectors in an adequate and timely manner, and the duty to inform the person about the objector's status, their diagnosis, their treatment, and the different alternatives available.

From a general theory of obligations' perspective, under Contract Law, the exercise of conscientious objection generates a modifying novation in the professional obligations of the objector physician. The modifying novation takes place when the alteration of any of the elements of the original obligation to

46 Alicia Ely Yamin, *Will we take suffering seriously? Reflections on what applying a human rights framework to health means and why we should care*, 10(1) HEALTH & HUM. RTS., 45–63 (2008). *See generally*, MARTHA NUSSBAUM & AMARTYA SEN, THE QUALITY OF LIFE (1993).

provide a health service through the exercise of conscientious objection does not extinguish the obligation, but rather it subsists (since in emergency cases the service must be provided, regardless of conscientious objector status) in a modified form (a change is generated to the object of the obligation, which goes from being that of providing the service to that of diagnosing, reporting and referring in an adequate and timely manner).[47] In other words, a modification in the expected behavior is generated from the conversion or metamorphosis of the original obligation by a separate obligation.[48] Even if it were considered that the exercise of conscientious objection extinguished the original obligation, there would still be a case of novation. In such case, the situation would be framed as an "extinctive novation," through which the extinction of the original obligation (to provide the health service) takes place and is replaced by a new obligation (the obligation to diagnose, to inform, and to refer).[49]

In the case of the exercise of conscientious objection to providing health services, all the necessary requirements for the configuration of the novation are met: (1) the preexistence of a valid obligation whose fulfillment is still pending and whose fulfillment is possible;[50] (2) the birth of a new obligation that replaces the previous one, which implies that the creditor (the patient)

---

47 Federico Arnau Moya, Lecciones de Derecho Civil II: Obligaciones y Contratos (2009); Curso de Derecho Civil (II), Derecho de obligaciones 39–62 (Martínez De Aguirre coord.., 2000); J. Orduña Moreno, *Cumplimiento de las obligaciones*, *in* Derecho de obligaciones y contratos 125–60 (Valpuesta Fernández coord., 1994). Jacques Dupichot, Derecho de las Obligaciones 119 (1984). Philippe Malaurie & Laurent Aynes, Cours de Droit Civil. Les Obligations 594 (3d ed. 1992); Emilio Betti, Teoría General de las Obligaciones, Tomo II 316 (José Luis de los Mozos trans., 1969).

48 Philippe Malaurie & Laurent Aynes, Cours de Droit Civil. Les Obligations 594 (3d ed. 1992); Jorge Eugenio Castañeda, Instituciones de Derecho Civil, Tomo III 193 (1957); Antonio José de Souza Levenhagen. Código Civil: Comentários Didáticos 148 (1978); Jorge Joaquín Llambias, Tratado de Derecho Civil, Obligaciones, Tomo III 24–25 (4th ed. 1983). Raymundo M. Salvat, Tratado de Derecho Civil Argentino, Obligaciones en General, Tomo III 1 (1952).

49 Robert Joseph Pothier, Tratado de las Obligaciones, Segunda Parte 241 (3d ed.); Francesco Messineo, Manual de Derecho Civil y Comercial, Tomo IV 401 (1979); Andreas Von Thur, Tratado de las Obligaciones, Tomo II 147 (1934); Guillermo Suarez Suarez, La Novación, En: Serie Tesis presentadas por los alumnos con ocasión de su Grado, Volumen II 294 (1943); C. Demolombe, Cours de Code Napoléon, Tomo XXVIII 156 (1870).

50 Pedro N. Cazeaux & Félix A. Trigo Represas, Compendio de Derecho de las Obligaciones, Tomo II 248 (1986); Manuel Borja Soriano, Teoría de las Obligaciones 614 (1994); Luis María Boffi Boggero, Tratado de las Obligaciones, Tomo IV 313 (1979).

has not renounced the exercise of a right, but rather faces the termination (as an extinctive novation) or modification (as a modifying novation) of the original credit (receiving the health service), subordinated to the creation of a new debt (to receive pre- and post-care information, be diagnosed, and be timely and appropriately referred to another service provider);[51] and (3) the existence of the will to novate or *animus novandi*, which implies a willingness of the parties to introduce modifications in the existing legal relationship.[52]

The third necessary requirement—the will to novate—exists in the medical professional whenever a professional exercises his or her right to conscientious objection. The health professional knows that, although by exception he or she may object to the provision of a service, his or her profession requires the fulfillment of the duties associated with being a medical professional. In this case, the will to novate is manifested as a necessary corollary to achieve a balance between respect for the exercise of conscientious objection by the health professional and respect for the right of the person requesting medical attention to access health services. For their part, patients agree not to be treated by certain medical professionals, insofar as health services are guaranteed, as they are organized in such a way that the effective exercise of freedom of conscience does not prevent the patient from gaining access to services to which they are legally entitled.

Thus, in a healthcare context, the exercise of conscientious objection implies a novation that generates two primary obligations: (1) the duty to properly diagnose, in a timely manner, those who requested the service and inform them about the objector status, their diagnosis, their treatment, and the different alternatives available; and (2) the duty to refer those people to alternative providers—not objectors—in an adequate and timely manner.

This analysis shows that the exercise of conscientious objection leads to -at least- two derivative obligations, which, in turn, are consistent with and align with current international human rights law standards and the views of treaty-monitoring bodies and U.N. special procedures on the matter.[53]

---

51 Marcel Planiol & Georges Ripert, Tratado Práctico de Derecho Civil Francés, Las Obligaciones, Tomo iv 346 (Mario Díaz Cruz trans., 1945); Manuel Borja Soriano, Teoría de las Obligaciones 617 (1994). Raymundo M. Salvat, Tratado de Derecho Civil Argentino, Obligaciones en General, Tomo iii 1 (1952).

52 Philippe Malaurie & Laurent Aynes, Cours de Droit Civil. Les Obligations 597 (3d ed. 1992); Henri Mazeaud et al., Lecciones de Derecho Civil, Volumen ii 461–62 (1974).

53 *See* Chapter 4. *See also*, Heiner Bielefeldt, *Conscientious objection in the medical sector: towards a holistic human rights approach, in* Healthcare as a Human Rights Issue:

2.2.1 Duty to Diagnose and Inform

The exercise of conscience-based claims does not exclude the duty that all doctors and institutions have to inform their patients of all available health alternatives, to diagnose, and to report their objector status. Once the patient has been informed of all the alternatives, and if the physician or institution opposes the chosen practice, then the patient must be referred to an alternative provider of services.

The duty of healthcare providers and institutions to diagnose and report the nature and scope of their objections is part of the duty to ensure informed consent. Failure to do so can harm patients. Therefore, failure to comply with this duty could give rise to subjective civil liability derived from medical negligence for not reporting adequately. The reasoning behind this is that, at minimum, an objecting provider is expected to demonstrate such professionalism as to inform their patients of all available healthcare alternatives so that patients can make the most informed decision. Of course, objectors will argue that providing this information makes them complicit in what they object. However, this is a necessary sacrifice that physicians accept when they agree to enter the profession.[54] In other words, the obligation to inform exists regardless of whether it is foreseen in the law insofar as it derives from the professional standards of care required of medical professionals and their duty not to cause harm to patients. Access to information is a vital component of the right to health and when conscientious objection is used to deny women information about the availability of essential services, it violates women's right to information and privacy in health.[55] Legally, patients must be provided with information regarding available treatment options to ensure their informed decision-making in selecting appropriate methods of care, a process that may entail physicians dutifully referring patients to alternative providers if necessary. Deliberate withholding of information by physicians regarding medically recommended treatment options, to which they hold conscientious objections, not only infringes upon patients' freedom of choice but also exacerbates

---

Normative Profile, Conflicts and Implementation 201–226 (Sabine Klotz, et al., eds., 2017); *and* Dan W. Brock, *Conscientious refusal by physicians and pharmacists: Who is obligated to do what, and why?* 29 Theoretical Med. & Bioeth. 3, 187–200 (2008).

54 Nadia N. Sawicki, *A Common Law Duty to Disclose Conscience-Based Limitations on Medical Practice, in* Law, Religion and Health in the United States (Holly Fernandez Lynch, I. Glenn Cohen & Elizabeth Sepper, eds., 2017).

55 Sandra Coliver, The Right to Know: Human Rights and Access to Reproductive Health Information 61 (1995).

the infringement of patients' fundamental human rights to autonomously and knowledgeably make decisions pertaining to bodily interventions.

The duty to inform a pregnant person of their right to abortion is essential to protect their rights in countries that allow healthcare providers to refuse to provide such services on the basis of their beliefs. Timely access to information about a health condition is particularly important "when there are rapid developments in the condition of the person and thus reduces their ability to make relevant decisions."[56] This is precisely the case in the abortion context, where the pregnancy can quickly become dangerous or "irreversible" if timely access to information is not made available. The Inter-American Commission on Human Rights and the wider international community have stated the critical importance of raising awareness in women, families, and communities about health services and the ability to know when to seek medical care.[57] In the UK,[58] Brazil,[59] and South Africa,[60] despite allowing the exercise of healthcare providers' right to conscientious objection, those providers still have a duty to inform pregnant persons of their right to abortion. In particular, in the UK, this implies a duty to inform the pregnant person of their right to see another doctor and to provide information so that they can effectively exercise such right. In South Africa, the pregnant person must be informed of their right to abortion and the location of the medical care centers where they can receive the service. France, Portugal, and the Netherlands have similar laws.[61]

56 European Court of Human Rights. R.R. v. Poland, Nro. 27617/04. 2011. ¶ 197.

57 Inter-American Commission on Human Rights, *Access to Maternal Health Services from a Human Rights* Perspective, June 7, 2010, OEA/Ser.L/V/II. Doc. 69, ¶ 33; United Nations ECLAC, *The Millennium Development Goals: A Latin American and Caribbean Perspective* Ch. V, 154, https://repositorio.cepal.org/server/api/core/bitstreams/567a2ac3-09e7-4a23-82c7-308d1825bf9c/content (last visited Nov 18, 2023); U.N. Committee on the Elimination of Discrimination against Women, *General Recommendation* Nº 24*: Article 12 of the Convention on the Elimination of all Forms of Discrimination Against Women—Women and Health* (1999), ¶ 20.

58 General Medical Council, 2013, *Personal beliefs and medical practice London* (U.K.).

59 Ministério da Saúde, Secretaria de Atenção à Saúde, Departamento de Ações Programáticas Estratégicas. *Prevenção e tratamento dos agravos resultantes da violência sexual contra mulheres e adolescentes.* Norma técnica. Série A. Normas e Manuais Técnicos. Série Direitos Sexuais e Direitos Reprodutivos—Caderno nº 6. 3ª edição atualizada e ampliada. Editora MS: Brasília, 2012, p. 75. (Braz.)

60 South African Regulations on the Choice on Termination of Pregnancy (S. Afr.).

61 Code de la Sante Publique (France); Código Deontologico da Ordem dos Medicos (Port.), art. 37(2); Law of 1 May 1981 (Stb. 257) (Neth.). *See also* Act of 5 December 1996 on the Medical Profession [Dz. U. z 2002 r. Nr 21 poz. 204 z po'n. zm.], Art. 39 (Pol.); Croatia Law of Doctoring, Art. 20; Croatia Code of Medical Ethics, Art. 2, párr. 15; Croatia Act No. 154, *§§* 125–37 (Croat.); Hungary Ministry of Health Decree No. 30/2007, § 11.9 (Hung.).

2.2.2 Duty to Refer

Similarly, the duty to refer becomes crucial given the time-sensitive nature of a pregnant person seeking information about an abortion procedure.[62] One method of preserving the balance between the rights of health professionals and the rights of patients is by ensuring compliance with the duty to refer.[63]

Patients, except in life-threatening or health-endangering cases, cannot legally compel providers or institutions to provide services to which providers or institutions have exercised conscientious objection under any jurisdiction. To strike a balance between the rights of patients and the rights of professionals and institutions not to participate in the care of patients who object based on conscience, it is generally adopted as the duty of professionals and institutions to refer the patient to another health center or treating professional. In other words, the duty imposed on conscientious objectors is not necessarily to refer patients to specific providers but rather to professional individuals or agencies capable of appropriately directing patients, thereby facilitating the discharge of individuals' legal duties of care owed to their patients through professional networks.

62 In the 2014 case of *Greater Glasgow and Clyde Health Board v. Doogan*, the UK Supreme Court analyzed legislation pertaining to conscientious objection and emphasized the importance of a conscientious objector's duty to refer cases to a professional who does not share the objection. Greater Glasgow Health Board v. Doogan and another [2014] UKSC 68 (appeal taken from CSIH). The court asserted that such referral obligations are intrinsic to a healthcare professional's duty of care toward the patient (*Doogan*, ¶ 40). This legal duty of care, encompassing the duty of due referral, may find expression in codes of medical professional practice, which are subject to enforcement by professional disciplinary tribunals. For instance, in 2015, the Ontario College of Physicians and Surgeons issued Policy Statement #2-15, titled "Professional Obligations and Human Rights," mandating conscientious objectors to provide patients, for whom they object to indicated care on conscientious grounds, with what it terms an "effective referral." The College defines this as a referral made in good faith to "a non-objecting, available, and accessible physician, other health-care professional, or agency." Following an extensive human rights challenge launched by the Christian Medical and Dental Society of Canada, alleging a violation of freedom of religion rights, the Ontario Court of Appeal upheld the constitutionality of the College's policy in a landmark decision (see *Ontario Court of Appeal*, 2019 ONCA 393). For a comprehensive summary of the case, please refer to Bernard Dickens, *Conscientious Objection and the Duty to Refer*, 155 INT'L J. GYNECOLOGY & OBSTETRICS 556, 556–560 (2021).

63 Inter-American Commission on Human Rights, *Access to Maternal Health Services from a Human Rights* Perspective, June 7, 2010, OEA/Ser.L/V/II. Doc. 69, ¶ 41. *See also*, Bernard Dickens, *Conscientious Objection and the Duty to Refer*, 155 INT'L J. GYNECOLOGY & OBSTETRICS 556, 556–560 (2021).

In cases where there is no possibility of referral due to urgency or a lack of available providers within a reasonable distance, the healthcare provider or the institution cannot object to the provision of the service. The European Court of Human Rights took this position in the *Pichon* case in which two French pharmacists who operated the only pharmacy in a remote area refused, based on their religious beliefs, to sell contraceptives to women with valid prescriptions. The Court declared the pharmacists' claim inadmissible and held that "applicants cannot prioritize their religious beliefs and impose them on others … since they can manifest those beliefs in many ways outside of the professional sphere."[64]

The objecting health professional or institution has the obligation to refer the pregnant woman to another non-objecting health professional or center in an appropriate, timely, and prompt manner. This obligation to refer also extends to institutions in cases where institutional conscientious objection is accepted.[65]

To be sure, conscientious objectors could argue that the duty to refer their patients in and of itself violates their freedom of conscience, religion, and belief, as it would force them to be complicit in others' wrongdoing, even in cases where the referral is not to a specific provider, but to a network of providers willing to perform the health services that they claim to be objectionable.[66] The complicity claim, however, is weak since the referring practitioner has no hand in any procedure that might be conducted by the provider to whom a referral is made.[67]

---

64 Pichon and Sajous v. France, 2001-X Eur. Ct. H.R. 375, 388.

65 *See, e.g.*, Decreto No. 375/012, art 27 (Uru.): "When the user requests the interruption of pregnancy before one of the institutions covered by the second paragraph of article 10 of Law 18,987, the institution must carry out all the procedures prior to the medical service that are required for the interruption of pregnancy. In this case, the institution must refer the user to another institution that provides the service for the purpose of the interruption" (unofficial translation).

66 *See* Christian Med. & Dental Soc'y of Canada v. Coll. of Physicians and Surgeons of Ontario (2019), 147 O.R. 3d 398 (Can. Ont. C.A.). For a deeper discussion on this issue, *see generally* Mark R. Wicclair, Conscientious Objection in Health Care: An Ethical Analysis (2012). *See also*, Christopher Cowley, *Conscientious objection in healthcare and the duty to refer*, 43 J. Med. Ethics 4, 207–212 (2017); Thomas Finegan, *Conscientious objection to referrals*, 45 J. Med. Ethics 4, 277–279 (2019); and Frank A. Chervenak & Laurence B. McCullough, *The ethics of direct and indirect referral for termination of pregnancy*, 199 Am. J. Obstetrics & Gynecology 3, 232.E1-232.E3 (2008).

67 *See Doogan* [2014] UKSC 68. *See also*, Corte Constitucional [C.C.] [Constitutional Court], Sentencia T-209/08, Gaceta de la Corte Constitucional [G.C.C.] (Colom.). *See generally*, Bernard Dickens, *Conscientious Objection and the Duty to Refer*, 155 Int'l J. Gynecology & Obstetrics 556, 556–60 (2021).

Things get trickier, however, when the complicity claim is wielded against the health system of which they are part. Access to an adequate health system, including a transportation and referral system, is considered a basic obligation that States must guarantee. States must design health systems in ways that ensure patients' access to health services—even to those that objectors oppose. This State obligation extends even when the provision of the health service is in the hands of private institutions.[68] In many constitutions, this obligation is not subject to progressive realization and rather must be fulfilled immediately.[69] Adequate care in a health system is not only limited to all the care necessary to preserve health, but it also includes the establishment of a referral system for instances of insufficient facilities or providers, or a denial to provide service based on personal beliefs.[70]

In such cases, conscientious objectors confront the dilemma of whether to continue to participate in such systems without compromising their conscience, which is a contested issue—with some scholars arguing that healthcare providers that find themselves in such a situation should not be allowed to practice, and most medical law regimes siding with the patients' interests and agreeing that physicians that give priority to their own interests over those of their patients could be performing professional misconduct.[71]

Despite the ongoing debate, the majority of legal frameworks that have aimed to strike a balance between conscience-based claims and access to health services through establishing a duty to refer have not addressed this specific concern.

For instance, in Argentina, the 2020 abortion law remained silent and simply stipulated that:

> "The healthcare professional who must intervene directly in the interruption of pregnancy has the right to exercise conscientious objection. For the purposes of exercising the same, they must:

68 *See* Alyne da Silva Pimentel v. Brazil (CEDAW Committee) (2011), *Communication No. 17/2008*, CEDAW/C/49/D/17/2008, ¶ 7.4, 7.5 and 7.6.

69 *See, e.g.*, NATIONAL CONSTITUTION (2010) (Kenya); NATIONAL CONSTITUTION (1996) (S. Afr.).

70 *See* Soobramoney v. Minister of Health, (1) SA 765 (CC) (S Afr.) (1998). In Chile, for instance, there are national norms regulating the State's obligation to provide healthcare and the obligation not to refuse healthcare; Law No. 18.469 (Chile), art.2; Law No. 20.584 (Chile); Decree 161/82 (Chile).

71 *See* Bernard Dickens, *Conscientious Objection and the Duty to Refer*, 155 INT'L J. GYNECOLOGY & OBSTETRICS 556–560 (2021).

> a. Maintain their decision in all areas, public, private or social security, in which they exercise their profession;
> b. Refer the patient in good faith to be treated by another professional in an adequate and timely manner, without delay;
> c. Comply with the rest of their professional duties and legal obligations.
>
> Healthcare personnel cannot refuse to perform the interruption of pregnancy in cases where the life or health of the pregnant person is in danger and requires immediate and urgent attention.
>
> Conscientious objection may not be invoked to refuse to provide post-abortion health care.[72]

Additionally, the law sets out a series of obligations for healthcare institutions. It stated:

> Those health care providers of the private or social security subsector that do not have professionals to carry out the interruption of pregnancy due to the exercise of the right of conscientious objection ... must anticipate and arrange the referral to an institution or healthcare professional that effectively performs the service and that is of similar characteristics to the one that the person requesting the benefit consulted. In all cases, the performance of the healthcare service must be guaranteed in accordance with the provisions of [the] law. The procedures and costs associated with the referral and transfer of the patient will be borne by the institution who makes the referral. All the referrals ... must be invoiced in accordance with the coverage in favor of the institution/professional who performs the service.[73]

72 *See* Law 27610, Dec. 30, 2020 (Arg.), art. 10, https://www.boletinoficial.gob.ar/detalleAviso/primera/239807/20210115 (last visited Nov 18, 2023); Law 17132, art. 40 (Arg.); Law 26529, art. 21 (Arg.). *See generally* Ministerio de Salud—Dirección Nacional de Salud Sexual y Reproductiva, *Protocolo para la atención integral de las personas con derecho a la interrupción voluntaria y legal del embarazo, Actualización 2021*, Ministerial Resolution 1531/2021), 35–38 (Arg.).

73 *See* Law 27610, Dec. 30, 2020, art. 11 (Arg.), https://www.boletinoficial.gob.ar/detalleAviso/primera/239807/20210115 (last visited Nov 18, 2023).

This is consistent with the practice in other countries and regions. Brazil;[74] Portugal;[75] Victoria, Australia;[76] Madagascar;[77] Northern Ireland;[78] Uruguay;[79] France;[80] and Mexico City have similar laws and policies.[81]

Echoing these views, the Declaration on Therapeutic Abortion of the World Medical Association establishes that "if the doctor's convictions do not allow him or her to perform an abortion, he or she may choose not to do it, as long as he or she guarantees the continuity of medical care for a qualified colleague."[82]

In the same vein, the Delhi Court in India ordered a review of the healthcare administration system to ensure that maternal operations are carried out in rooms suitable for the number of children to be cared for and ordered an improvement in the referral system to private health institutions to ensure fast and safe transport of pregnant women from their places of residence to public health institutions or private hospitals and vice versa.[83] In 2011, the European Court of Human Rights held that "states are obliged to organize the health services system in such a way as to ensure that an effective exercise of the freedom of conscience of health professionals in the professional context does not prevent patients from obtaining access to services to which they are entitled."[84] Similarly, in *Poblete Vilches v. Chile*, although not dealing with sexual and reproductive rights, the Inter-American Court of Human Rights considered the omission of dispensing the patient to another medical center that

74 Ministério da Saúde, Secretaria de Atenção à Saúde, Departamento de Ações Programáticas Estratégicas. *Prevenção e tratamento dos agravos resultantes da violência sexual contra mulheres e adolescentes.* Norma técnica. Série A. Normas e Manuais Técnicos. Série Direitos Sexuais e Direitos Reprodutivos—Caderno nº 6. 3ª edição atualizada e ampliada. Editora MS: Brasília, 2012, p. 75 (Braz.).

75 Portaria No. 741-A/2007 do Ministério da Saúde, art. 12 (Port.).

76 Abortion Law Reform Act 2008 (Victoria, Austl.).

77 Decree No. 98–945, Dec. 4, 1998 (Madag.).

78 Guidance on the Termination of Pregnancy: The Law and Clinical Practice in Northern Ireland, (Department of Health, Social Services and Public Safety, 2008) (N. Ir.).

79 Decree No. 375/012, art. 29 (Uru.).

80 World Med. Ass'n, Declaration on Therapeutic Abortion (1970).

81 Manual de Procedimientos para la Interrupción Legal del Embarazo en las Unidades Médicas, 2008 (Mex.), procedimiento 5.8, 2, https://clacaidigital.info/handle/123456789/777 (last visited Nov 18, 2023).

82 World Med. Ass'n, Declaration on Therapeutic Abortion (1970).

83 Laxmi Mandal v. Deen Dayal Harinagar Hospital, WP(C) No. 8853/2008 (Del. H.C.) (India) (2010).

84 R.R. v. Poland, 2011-III Eur. Ct. H.R. 215, 253.

had the necessary facilities when condemning the Chilean State for not having guaranteed the right to health without discrimination to Mr. Poblete Vilches.[85]

2.3 *A Model Regulation of Conscientious Objection in Healthcare*

Based on international and comparative law standards, a model regulation for conscientious objection in healthcare could be delineated. In any case, it must be noted that although the challenges that conscience-based claims pose can be similar in different contexts, regulatory responses that are viable, adequate, and effective should be designed according to each context, taking into account indicators including the organizational and social culture of the provider facility, the quantity and training of health personnel, the type of practices and available technology, and the regulatory context, giving priority to access to services and the guarantee of the rights of the users of the services above all.

When it comes to the use of foreign law as a justification for the regulation of conscientious objection there must be a consideration of the validity and efficacy of said "normative transplants" depending, at least in part, on the characteristics of the receiving legal system, the norms previously in force in the recipient legal system, and the culture and tradition of the recipient country. Even in situations in which the use of foreign law as an argument used to justify decision-making is undoubtedly persuasive, it may happen that the transplantation of these norms to the local order is not effective[86] or has a negative impact.[87]

To avoid the abusive, political uses of conscience-based claims, States that allow its exercise in the context of the provision of healthcare services must strictly limit its expansion along the three axis described in Chapter 2 and regulate it, as well as ensure effective compliance with those regulations, in a way that protects the rights of third parties.

A model regulation of the exercise of conscientious objection in healthcare settings should require, at a minimum, that health professionals who are considered objectors to certain health services provide prior and comprehensive care, which includes the obligation to diagnose and provide accurate

---

85 Inter-American Court of Human Rights, Poblete Vilches et al. v. Chile, Mar. 8, 2018, ¶ 138–143.

86 Horacio Spector, *Constitutional Transplants and the Mutation Effect*, 83 CHICAGO-KENT L. REV. 144, 144–45 (2017).

87 *See* S. Vogenauer, *Sources of Law and Legal Method in Comparative Law*, in THE OXFORD HANDBOOK OF COMPARATIVE LAW 875 (M. Reimann & R. Zimmermann eds., 2006); *see also* M. Andenas, D. Fairgrieve, *Intent on making mischief: seven ways of using comparative law, in* METHODS OF COMPARATIVE LAW 26–50 (P.G. Monateri ed., 2012).

information and impartial advice to their patients about their objector status and available alternatives. In the case of a referral to an alternative medical provider chosen by the service recipient, the regulations should require that medical personnel refer patients in a timely manner to other non-objector providers who are within a reasonable distance. In the event of a medical emergency or if another provider is not accessible, the regulation should require the objecting provider to provide the necessary care, which should be understood as a permissible restriction on freedom of conscience, considering the rights at stake.

The exercise of conscientious objection should ideally be limited to those directly involved in the performance of the procedure at issue or the provision of the service.[88] Therefore, administrative and support personnel who provide care before or after the intervention cannot make use of conscientious objection, as this would imply an unacceptable violation of the right to health. Governments must closely monitor and strictly enforce these regulations to ensure that all people can exercise their right to affordable, accessible, acceptable and quality comprehensive care, without discrimination.

In summary, the foregoing indicates areas of agreement based on efforts to regulate the exercise of conscientious objection in healthcare settings across different jurisdictions, as well as a desire to find an adequate solution that respects both the health professionals' freedom of conscience and the patients' right to health. Such regulation must, at least:

- Ensure the adequate availability and dispersion of willing providers, both in public and private health establishments and within a reasonable geographic scope.
- Establish effective and accessible referral systems for medical professionals who refuse to provide healthcare for reasons of conscience. Ensure a record of these refusals and refer patients to other available, accessible, willing, and capable providers or health centers, without delays.
- Disseminate accurate information on the rights of patients and the obligations of providers in health care, including the obligation to provide information to patients based on scientific evidence and not on their beliefs.
- Limit conscientious objection to those who directly intervene in the requested or indicated health procedure and not allow conscientious objection to be exercised on the pre- or post-service care that was objected to.
- Demand compliance with the obligation to diagnose and inform the patient. In turn, demand provision of healthcare in urgent or emergency situations

88 Constitutional Court of Colombia, Decision T-388/09, May 28, 2009 (Col.).

or in the absence of alternative providers within a reasonable distance that could guarantee adequate care.
- Implement adequate supervision, monitoring, and compliance mechanisms to guarantee compliance with the pertinent regulations, both in public and private institutions.
- Ensure that patients affected by conscientious objection have legal and procedural resources available that guarantee them an adequate, effective, and immediate recourse to access the requested health service.

While regulatory frameworks in many countries have increasingly sought to address and manage the exercise of conscientious objection in healthcare settings, a significant gap remains in the scope of these regulations. Typically, these regulations have primarily focused on cases of individual conscientious objection by healthcare practitioners while disregarding the broader social and cultural contexts within which these conscience-based claims take place. This issue, along with the need for a more robust normative basis for laws and guidelines established to strike a balance between respecting these beliefs and ensuring that patients receive the care to which they are entitled is analyzed in more detail in Chapter 6.

3 Dealing with "Horizontal Expansions" of Conscience-Based Claims

Upon an in-depth analysis into the intricacies of religious lawfare within liberal democracies in the preceding chapters, it has become evident that a new dimension of conscience-based claims has emerged: the institutional exercise of conscientious objection. This *horizontal* expansion of conscience-based claims, as described in Chapter 2, represents a rising challenge that poses additional risks to the provision of healthcare services and individuals' access to their legal rights.

In contrast to individual conscientious objection, where a healthcare practitioner personally objects to providing a particular medical service, institutional conscientious objection occurs when healthcare institutions themselves assert a collective moral or religious stance that influences the care they offer. These institutions may include hospitals, clinics, pharmacies, or healthcare systems as a whole. Such entities claim conscientious objection as a basis for limiting or restricting certain medical procedures, treatments, or services within their facilities. In doing so, they create an environment where access to these services is obstructed or denied, often leaving patients without options for care.

One of the prominent examples of institutional conscientious objection lies in the realm of reproductive healthcare. Hospitals or healthcare systems, often with religious affiliations, assert their conscientious objection to procedures like abortion or contraception, refusing to provide these services on their premises. While this stance aligns with the institution's religious or moral principles, it can have severe consequences for individuals seeking these healthcare services. Patients may face delays, increased costs, or even complete unavailability of essential medical procedures due to the institution's objection.

The rise of institutional conscientious objection raises complex ethical and legal questions that challenge the existing regulatory paradigms. It underscores the need to expand the scope of conscientious objection regulations to encompass not only individual practitioners but also healthcare institutions altogether.

The uncharted territory of institutional conscientious objection demands a robust examination of its multifaceted manifestations and implications for patients, healthcare providers, and the broader healthcare system. Delving into the complexities of regulating institutions' conscientious objection allows for an articulation of normative frameworks that effectively address this evolving aspect of religious lawfare.

Understanding the dimensions of institutional conscientious objection is essential to safeguarding the principles of equality and non-discrimination, and access to healthcare services within liberal democracies. While recognizing the rights of institutions to operate in alignment with their values, it is equally imperative to ensure that these rights do not infringe upon individuals' rights to receive healthcare services that are legally available to them. Striking this balance is a formidable challenge, but it is one that liberal democracies must confront to preserve the integrity of their healthcare systems and the rights of their citizens. In essence, the emergence of institutional conscientious objection represents a new frontier in the complex landscape of religious lawfare.

Institutional conscientious objection, or corporate conscience-based claims, both referred in this book as "the horizontal expansion," already exists across countries, which makes a compelling case for the need to delineate the confines and tools that different legal systems offer to regulate or limit as much as possible its impact on the enjoyment of rights in liberal democracies. In fact, institutions have been allowed to conscientiously object in countries across regions, like Chile, Turkey, Australia, Argentina, Colombia, Ghana, the U.S. and South Africa, among others.[89]

89 Bronwen Merner, et al., *Institutional objection to abortion: A mixed-methods narrative review*, 19 WOMEN'S HEALTH, 1–10 (2023).

Considering this recognition of institutional conscience rights across jurisdictions, the forthcoming discussion assumes that corporations and institutions' legal personhood allow them to exercise conscientious objection.[90]

Even so, the institutional exercise of conscience-based claims should be stringently regulated, not least because vesting conscience to institutions would arguably exacerbate or create additional problems like those already present in instances of political uses of individual conscientious objection. And, considering the different, larger, and often harmful role corporations play in society, regulations on the exercise of institutional conscientious objection should be substantially stricter than those dealing with individual conscience-based claims.

3.1 *Views on Institutional Conscientious Objection*

The debate, when it comes to the *horizontal* expansion, has mostly focused on whether institutions, by virtue of their legal personhood, can exercise conscientious objection. Arguments in response to this debate are typically framed in terms of institutions having or not having conscience.

There are those who argue that institutions do not have a conscience *per se*, but rather possess beliefs that are derivative from the actions of the individuals that compose the institution. That is to say, to the extent that it can be identified at all, institutional conscience is no more than the amalgamated conscience of the institution's members,[91] or, in Chief Justice Marshall's words, "a corporation will always be just a cover for the body of men."[92]

For instance, it has been argued that "a hospital is not a person; it is a physical structure within which providers give medical care. It does not perform procedures or counsel patients. It does not take lunch hours or vacations. And it does not have a conscience."[93] To a certain extent, this is consistent with Justice Stevens' dissent in *Citizens United*, where he explained that "corporations have no consciences, no beliefs, no feelings, no thoughts, no desires."[94] In

---

90 For a summary of the different theories of juridical personality, see Simon Chesterman, *Artificial Intelligence and the Limits of Legal Personality*, 69 INT'L & COMP. L. Q. 819–44 (2020).

91 Spencer L. Durland, *The Case against Institutional Conscience*, 86 NOTRE DAME L. REV. 1655 (2011).

92 Trustees of Dartmouth College v. Woodward, 17 U.S. 518, 636 (1819).

93 Spencer L. Durland, *The Case against Institutional Conscience*, 86 NOTRE DAME L. REV. 1655 (2011).

94 Citizens United v. Federal Elections Commission, 558 U.S. 310, 466 (2010). *See also* ELIZABET WOLGAST, ETHICS OF AN ARTIFICIAL PERSON: LOST RESPONSIBILITY IN PROFESSIONS AND ORGANIZATIONS 86 (1992).

essence, he defined personhood, and by extension the ability to enjoy fundamental rights, in terms of the natural attributes of human beings.

Even arguments focused on the *effects* of institutional conscience vis-à-vis individual conscience have been used to argue that these two manifestations of conscience are different: "the compulsion to act or not act arising from institutional conscience differs from the compulsion arising from individual conscience because the interaction between the conscience and the act is not self-contained—institutional conscience instead imposes obligations on others."[95] In other words, vesting conscience on institutions does not ensure equality, but instead elevates the institution's power by allowing it to impose its conscience on others. That is, institutional conscience imposes its values and commands on third-party individuals, and thus institutional conscience supersedes individual conscience in practice.

On the other hand, several arguments have been presented in favor of institutional conscientious objection. For instance, it could be argued that because both individuals and institutions make decisions based on values, principles, and deliberations grounded on their internal statutes and goals, they can be equated;[96] collective experiences occurring within a corporation or institution create a group conscience;[97]or because individuals within a corporation share similar moral values, so institutional conscientious objection can protect individuals employed by the same institution.[98]

In the same vein, some have argued that, based on the moral projection principle, "it is appropriate to describe organizations and their characteristics by analogy with individuals and it is appropriate normatively to look for and to foster moral attributes in organizations by analogy with those we look for in individuals."[99] Essentially, institutions are made up of individuals, individuals have conscience, and therefore institutions have a conscience. The required assumption here is that the characteristics of something's parts are characteristic of the entity as a whole, which evokes a common fallacy.

---

95 Spencer L. Durland, *The Case against Institutional Conscience*, 86 NOTRE DAME L. REV. 1655 (2011).

96 Glob. Doctors for Choice, *White Papers: Conscientious objection and refusal to provide reproductive healthcare: A White Paper examining prevalence, health consequences, and policy responses*, 123 INT'L J. OBSTETRICS & GYNECOLOGY 20 (2013). *See also* Luisa Cabal et al., *Striking a Balance: Conscientious Objection and Reproductive Health Care from the Colombian Perspective*, 16 HEALTH & HUM. RTS. J. 73 (2014).

97 *Id.*

98 *Id.*

99 Kenneth E. Goodpaster, *The Concept of Corporate Responsibility*, 2 J. OF BUS. ETHICS 1–22 (1983).

One of the more elaborate understandings of institutional consciousness argues that institutions are social phenomena, so it is not correct to approach the question of conscience through an individualist lens. In other words, the argument holds that human beings are social beings and, as such, are relational, including in the exercise of conscience. This perspective argues that institutional conscience exists and is necessary to set norms and values that inform the actions of individuals within the institution. Although a bit circular, the idea is that: (a) institutions can only realize their purpose or achieve their objectives through the actions of individuals; (b) these individuals must know how to act to achieve these objectives; and (c) the institution needs to inform individuals on how to act. The institution must have a conscience to set these standards.

3.2 *Institutional Conscientious Objection through Comparative Law Lens*

Notwithstanding these theoretical discussions on institutional personhood and the ability of institutions to exercise conscience rights, considering the *horizontal* expansion of conscience-based claims that society has witnessed in recent years,[100] several countries are struggling to find ways to deal with these questions at the legislative or judiciary level.

The Colombian Constitutional Court has stated that "legal persons," such as corporations, do not have a right to religious exemptions as they cannot experience "intimate and deeply-rooted convictions."[101] The Court expressly stated that institutional conscientious objection is forbidden: "The human right to respect for conscience is a right enjoyed by natural human beings, but not by institutions such as hospitals."[102]

The Spanish Bioethics Committee reached the same conclusion in a 2011 a report stating that "since we understand conscientious objection as a way of exercising individual freedom, it can only be accepted as a right of the individual, not as a collective right. Only individuals have conscience, not legal entities, or other collective bodies."[103]

---

100 *See* Chapter 2.

101 Constitutional Court of Colombia, Decision T-388/09 (May 28, 2009). *See also* A.A. Schvey & C. Kim. *Unconscionable: how the U.S. Supreme Court's jurisprudence lags behind the world when it comes to contraception and conscience.* 3 CONTRACEPTIVE REPRO. MED. (2018).

102 Luisa Cabal, et al., *Striking a Balance: Conscientious Objection and Reproductive Health Care from the Colombian Perspective,* 16 HEALTH & HUM. RTS. J. 73–83 (2014).

103 COMITÉ DE BIOÉTICA DE ESPAÑA, OPINION OF THE SPANISH BIOETHICS COMMITTEE ON CONSCIENTIOUS OBJECTION IN MEDICAL CARE (2011).

Regarding access to abortion in Argentina, the law is clear in that neither public nor private institutions possess an institutional right to conscientious objection.[104] And in individual conscientious objection cases, institutions must refer patients to non-objecting practitioners.[105]

Uruguay allows private health institutions to abstain from practicing an abortion under the notion of "ideology objection." A private institution must declare its objection before the National Health Junta within a maximum of 15 days after the law's issuance—the Ministry of Health oversees and determines whether the objection proceeds.[106]

As a federal country, Mexico defers abortion regulation to each state. Since 2007, Mexico City's regulations deny institutional conscientious objection to public institutions. Mexico City's Health Act states that public institutions must provide abortion services during the five days following a woman's request.[107] The 2021 Mexican Supreme Court of Justice decision clarified the role of conscientious objection in the Mexican legal system, its role vis-à-vis the protection of the right to health, and the role of regulation.[108] In particular, the Court noted that conscientious objection "can only be exercised in a personal capacity, and that health institutions cannot invoke it."[109]

Chile's National Congress passed a law in 2017 that legalized abortion under three specific circumstances, but the Constitutional Court modified the law to ensure it recognizes institutional conscience. The Court argued that if a private institution has an "ideology" in its founding principles that is not compatible with the practice of abortion, it should not be obligated to perform abortions as an institution.[110] In September 2023, the Constitutional Council of Chile,

---

104 *See* Law 27610, Dec. 30, 2020 (Arg.), https://www.boletinoficial.gob.ar/detalleAviso/primera/239807/20210115, art. 10 and 11 (last visited Nov 18, 2023); *see also* Ministerio de Salud – Dirección Nacional de Salud Sexual y Reproductiva, *Protocolo para la atención integral de las personas con derecho a la interrupción voluntaria y legal del embarazo,* Actualización 2021 (Ministerial Resolution 1531/2021), 35–38 (Arg.).

105 Luisa Cabal et al., *Striking a Balance: Conscientious Objection and Reproductive Health Care from the Colombian Perspective,* 16 HEALTH & HUM. RTS. J. 73–83 (2014).

106 *Id.*

107 *Id.*

108 Suprema Corte de Justicia de la Nación, acción de inconstitucionalidad 54/2018, 21 de septiembre de 2021, M.P., Luis María Aguilar Morales (Mex.).

109 *Id.* ¶ 423.

110 Amnesty Int'l, *Why the conscientious objection protocol should outrage everyone,* AMNESTY INT'L NEWS (Apr. 4, 2018), https://www.amnesty.org/en/latest/news/2018/04/por-que-el-protocolo-de-objecion-de-conciencia-debiera-indignar-a-todo-el-mundo/ (last visited Nov 18, 2023). According to the Constitutional Court ruling, the invocation of conscientious objection by institutions is based not only on recognition of the confessional tenets of religious institutions or legal entities protected under the freedom of conscience and

the organ in charge of discussing and approving the text of the country's new constitution, approved a new article that indicates that the right to freedom of thought, conscience and religion "includes individual *and institutional* conscientious objection" (emphasis added).[111]

The United States allows institutions to make conscience-based claims—46 states permit healthcare institutions to refuse the provision of abortion-related services.[112] How this will change in a post-*Roe* world is yet to be seen.

Additionally, the Ecuadorian Constitutional Court ordered the amendment of the country's legal framework to change a constitutional norm that previously restricted access to abortion services in cases of rape.[113] In its judgment,

---

religion clause (Art. 19 N°6 of the Constitution), but also on the freedom granted to educational establishments that hold those ideals (Art. 19 N°11), on the right to freedom of association (Art. 19 N°15), and on the protection of the autonomy of intermediate groups (Art. 1 N°3).

111 *Consejo aprobó la objeción de conciencia institucional y norma que beneficiaría de Punta Peuco*, CNN CHILE, (Sept. 9, 2023), https://www.cnnchile.com/pais/consejo-constitucional-objecion-conciencia-reos-punta-peuco_20230920/ (last visited Nov 18, 2023).

112 The United States is a paradigmatic case as healthcare institutions can actually claim an exemption to the provision of "objectionable services" under the 1973 Church Amendment, which allows institutions to refuse to provide services that conflict with their religious moral values. *See* Health Programs Extension Act of 1973 (the Church Amendment). Pub. L. No. 93–45, § 401, 487 Stat. 491, 495. According to the American Civil Liberties Union and MergerWatch, one in six hospital beds in the United States is in a Catholic hospital and, in some states, more than 40 percent of all hospital beds are in a Catholic facility. *See* Julia Kaye et al., *Health Care Denied: Patients and Physicians Speak Out About Catholic Hospitals and the Threat to Women's Health and Lives*, ACLU (2016), https://www.aclu.org/report/report-health-care-denied?redirect=report/health-care-denied (last visited Nov 18, 2023); *see also* J. R. Fuchs et al. *Patient Perspectives on Religiously Affiliated Care in Rural and Urban Colorado*. 12 J. PRIMARY CARE & COMM. HEALTH (2021); Susan Berke Fogel & Lourdes A. Rivera, *Religious Beliefs and Healthcare Necessities: Can They Coexist?*, AM. BAR ASS'N (Apr. 1, 2003), https://www.americanbar.org/groups/crsj/publications/human_rights_magazine_home/human_rights_vol30_2003/spring2003/hr_spring03_religiousbeliefs/ (last visited Nov 18, 2023). *See generally* S. E. Smith, *He needed a gender-affirming procedure. The hospital said no.*, VOX (Nov. 1, 2019), https://www.vox.com/the-highlight/2019/10/25/20929539/catholic-hospitals-religious-refusal-rural-health-care-evan-minton (on the problems that derive from this situation) (last visited Nov 18, 2023); Michelle Truong & Susan Y. Wood, UNCONSCIONABLE: WHEN PROVIDERS DENY ABORTION CARE, INTERNATIONAL WOMEN'S HEALTH COALITION (2018). *See also*, Guttmacher Institute, *Refusing to Provide Health Services* (Aug. 31, 2023), https://www.guttmacher.org/state-policy/explore/refusing-provide-health-services.

113 Ecuadorian Constitutional Court, Case No. 34–19 and others, Apr. 28, 2021, http://esacc.corteconstitucional.gob.ec/storage/api/v1/10_DWL_FL/e2NhcnBldGE6J3RyYW1pdGUnLCB1dWlkOidiZGE2NDE0YS1jNDI1LTQzMGMtYWViNi1jYjY0ODQ1YTQ2NWUucGRmJ30 (last visited Apr. 27, 2022).

the Court ordered the Legislative Assembly to enact a law to guarantee access to abortion in cases of rape for all women, without discrimination. In addition, it ordered the Public Defender's Office to submit a bill to the Legislative Assembly. Complying with this decision, the Public Defender's Office submitted a bill in mid-2021, which included provisions to regulate conscientious objection according to international legal standards. During the bill's legislative debate, a large portion of the discussion was devoted to the issue of conscientious objection. Eventually the bill was adopted with amendments, but, in general, provisions related to conscientious objection complied with international legal standards.[114] Nevertheless, a few days later the Ecuadorian President, Guillermo Lasso, vetoed the law. In its veto, the President included substantive changes to the conscientious objection provisions, including many which contravene current international legal standards.[115] In particular, the veto recognized that medical personnel asserting conscientious objection are not subject to any obligation to provide health care to patients. Additionally, it extended the exercise of conscientious objection to institutions in the private sector and regulated the referral process in a way that does not ensure access to abortion services in an adequate and timely matter, among other changes. This veto carries a great risk of restricting access to abortion services in Ecuador and will establish a legal framework that allows for the expansion of conscience-based claims.[116]

3.3 *Healthcare, Institutions and Role of the State*

In most countries, the provision of health services is considered a public service which the State has the duty to guarantee to the entire population without any type of discrimination.[117] Although the provision of health services can be delegated to private institutions, such delegation does not exempt the healthcare

114 Ecuadorian Legislative Assembly, Specialized Justice and State Structure Commission, *Final Text for vote of the "Organic Law that guarantee the Voluntary Interruption for Girls, Teenagers and Women in cases of rape,"* Feb. 11, 2022.

115 Ecuadorian Presidency, Partial Veto, Document T 180-SCJ-22-0050, Mar. 15, 2022, Objection 25, 43, 44, 45 and 46.

116 *See* Ángela Meléndez, *Abortion on the grounds of rape can be provided until the 12th week in Ecuador*, Bloomberg Linea (Apr. 15, 2022), https://www.bloomberglinea.com/2022/04/15/aborto-por-violacion-podra-practicarse-hasta-las-12-semanas-en-ecuador/ (last visited Nov 18, 2023); *A year in the frustrating labyrinth of the abortion law in rape cases*, La Prensa Latina, Ecuador, (Apr. 28, 2022), https://www.laprensalatina.com/ecuador-a-year-in-the-legal-labyrinth-for-abortion-due-to-rape/ (last visited Nov 18, 2023).

117 CEDAW Committee, Alyne da Silva Pimentel v. Brazil, Communication No. 17/2008, CEDAW/C/49/D/17/2008 (2011); Luisa Cabal et al., *Striking a Balance: Conscientious Objection and Reproductive Health Care from the Colombian Perspective*, 16 Health &

providers and the State from complying with the duty to guarantee the provision of a public service without discrimination.[118] In addition to this duty, the State must also comply with the obligation to monitor and guarantee access to health services at all times. In this sense, in cases where a legal person provides public services, the profit motive of the legal person or the private or public nature of the institution does not exempt the institution from its duty to guarantee the required medical service.[119]

States have a responsibility to ensure available, accessible, acceptable, and quality health care that does not solely comprise of individual health care providers or health institutions exercising a legitimate right to conscientious objection. This obligation is clear in regard to public hospitals. Since public sector providers are state employees, they have an obligation to serve the public for the greater good by providing the highest "standard of care." [120] Through them, the State acts, and for this reason it would be unacceptable to allow institutional conscientious objection of health services in public institutions. The State cannot object or disobey its own rules, and it would be preferable for the State to establish, as a condition for occupying a position in the public health system, a willingness to carry out all the services that the position or function requires.[121]

Regarding private hospitals, the partial or total privatization of services, does not exempt the State from its obligation to guarantee access without discrimination, nor does it give private actors total freedom of action. On the contrary, the State has an obligation to monitor and regulate these actors. According to the CESCR, the State's obligation to protect the right to health includes the duty to "ensure that the privatization of the health sector does not represent a threat to the availability, accessibility, acceptability, and quality of health care services."[122]

HUM. RTS. J. 73–83 (2014); ROGER B. DWORKIN, LIMITS: THE ROLE OF THE LAW IN BIOETHICAL DECISION MAKING (1 ed. 1996).

118 Luisa Cabal et al., *Striking a Balance: Conscientious Objection and Reproductive Health Care from the Colombian Perspective*, 16 HEALTH & HUM. RTS. J. 73–83 (2014); ROGER B. DWORKIN, LIMITS: THE ROLE OF THE LAW IN BIOETHICAL DECISION MAKING (1 ed. 1996).

119 Mark R. Wicclair, *Managing Conscientious Objection in Health Care Institutions*, 26 HEC FORUM 267–83 (2014).

120 Marcelo Alegre, *Conscious Oppression: Conscientious Objection in the Sphere of Sexual and Reproductive Health*, 65 SELA (SEMINARIO EN LATINOAMÉRICA DE TEORÍA CONSTITUCIONAL Y POLÍTICA) (2009).

121 *Id.*

122 U.N. Committee on Economic, Social and Cultural Rights, General Comment No. 14, U.N. Doc. E/C.12/2000/4 (Aug. 11, 2000), ¶ 35.

3.3.1 Institutional Conscientious Objection in Private Hospitals

Most countries do not consider institutions as having the capacity to exercise institutional conscientious objection. As noted, in fact, some countries, such as Spain, Colombia, and South Africa, have laws that explicitly state that refusal to perform abortions is always an individual decision, not an institutional one.

The case of France, however, is illustrative and relevant insofar as its regulation contemplates what happens to private institutions that have signed agreements with the State. France only allows institutional conscientious objection to private healthcare facilities. According to French regulations: "A private health facility can refuse to have abortions performed on its premises. However, this rejection can only be raised by a private health institution … as long as other institutions can respond to local needs."[123] In other words, it is required that there be an alternative institution that can respond in a timely manner (understood as an institution that is at a reasonable distance and that is not an objector). Furthermore, in France, if the establishment has a public interest and participates in a public service mission, or if it has signed a concession contract or an agreement with the State, its rejection is only valid if other establishments can satisfy local needs.

123 France. Ordonnance n°2017-31 du 12 janvier 2017—art. 1, Article L. 2212-8 : "Un médecin ou une sage-femme n'est jamais tenu de pratiquer une interruption volontaire de grossesse mais il doit informer, sans délai, l'intéressée de son refus et lui communiquer immédiatement le nom de praticiens ou de sages-femmes susceptibles de réaliser cette intervention selon les modalités prévues à l'article L. 2212-2. Aucune sage-femme, aucun infirmier ou infirmière, aucun auxiliaire médical, quel qu'il soit, n'est tenu de concourir à une interruption de grossesse. Un établissement de santé privé peut refuser que des interruptions volontaires de grossesse soient pratiquées dans ses locaux. Toutefois ce refus ne peut être opposé par un établissement de santé privé habilité à assurer le service public hospitalier que si d'autres établissements sont en mesure de répondre aux besoins locaux. Les catégories d'établissements publics qui sont tenus de disposer des moyens permettant la pratique des interruptions volontaires de la grossesse sont fixées par décret." ("A doctor or midwife is never required to carry out a voluntary termination of pregnancy but he must inform, without delay, the interested party of his refusal and immediately communicate to her the names of practitioners or midwives likely to carry out this intervention according to the terms provided for in article L. 2212–2. No midwife, nurse or medical assistant of any kind is required to assist in the termination of a pregnancy. A private health establishment may refuse to allow voluntary terminations of pregnancies to be carried out on its premises. However, this refusal can only be opposed by a private health establishment authorized to provide public hospital service if other establishments are able to meet local needs. The categories of public establishments which are required to have the means allowing the practice of voluntary terminations of pregnancy are fixed by decree.") (unofficial translation).

The fact that private hospitals often receive public funding and are the only providers of health services in certain areas requires reciprocal obligations to provide certain services. Since a license to operate as a private hospital grants certain rights and privileges to an institution, "when licensees accept and enjoy these rights and privileges, they incur reciprocal obligations, including obligations to protect patients from harm, promote their health, and respect their autonomy."[124]

3.3.2 How to Regulate Institutional Conscientious Objection

Corporations are a fundamental group in society, existing for more than two thousand years. They first emerged in the Roman Empire and eventually spread throughout the world.[125] The most important function that corporations fulfilled then and fulfill today is to provide goods and/or services to individuals in exchange for an economic benefit.

In the last two centuries, companies have increased their power exponentially. Such is the role they play in the global economy and market that even States depend on them to provide essential goods and/or services to their citizens. Consequently, States face a dilemma when it comes to finding a balance between, on the one hand, giving way to private interests and, on the other, protecting the interests of society through the regulation of the private sector.

In general terms, and to achieve a categorization that does not pretend to be exhaustive, but rather seeks to delineate the boundaries within which institutional conscientious objection is and has been exercised, this book proposes the adoption of a categorization for institutional conscientious objection practice that finds its essential and defining element in the relationship that the institution has with the State.

To that end, there are two subtypes of relationships between institutions and the State: (1) relationship of dependency; or (2) purely commercial. The first refers to those situations in which institutions have signed a contract or agreement with the State and that, within the terms of said arrangement, the former provides certain goods and/or services to the State, here referred to as "dependent companies." The second type of relationship refers to those companies that only carry out their commercial operations in the State in question,

124 Mark R. Wicclair, *Refusals by hospitals and emergency contraception*, 20 Cambridge Q. Healthcare Ethics 130–38 (2011). *See also* R. A. Charo, *American Constitution Society for Law and Policy, Health Care Provider Refusals to Treat, Prescribe, Refer or Inform: Professionalism and Conscience*, J. ACS Issue Grps. 119–35 (2007). Mark R. Wicclair, Conscientious Objection in Health Care (2011).

125 Samuel Williston, *History of the Law of Business Corporations Before 1800*, 2 Harv. L. Rev. 105, 106 (1888).

but that do not directly have an agreement with the government of the State where they do business and operate (beyond the obvious import or business permits, of course), here referred to as "purely commercial companies." Undoubtedly, the same company can relate in both ways with the State.

Notwithstanding the subtlety between the two categories, the distinction (and the decision to limit the focus of this book to these two subtypes) is relevant for this work insofar as the type of responsibility that could be awarded to and the obligations that could be required from a company for its actions could vary depending on the nature of the relationship that the company has with the State.

Regarding *dependent companies*, the businesses possess a more intimate relationship with the State than in the case of purely commercial companies, evidenced through their need to have permits (that, in some cases, exceed just the import or usual business permits), certifications, licenses or, ultimately, authorizations from the State to carry out its activities. In turn, the dependency component can also arise from privatization processes, through which the State delegates the provision of certain services and/or goods to companies. Privatization is a model increasingly used by States for the fulfillment of the progressive development of economic and social rights.[126] Outsourcing, public-private partnerships, and other approaches by which the private sector assumes responsibility for supporting the State in the provision of goods and services have advanced aggressively in recent years.[127]

The distinction between the two subtypes of state-institution relationships is extremely relevant in terms of obligations. *Purely commercial institutions* only have a general obligation not to do harm. But, in the case of *dependent institutions*, by virtue of their stronger link with the State, all the same obligations that were attributable to the State should be attributable to them.

The nature and conceptual foundations of a corporate right to conscientious objection for dependent institutions remain remarkably—and perhaps surprisingly—underexplored. Literature examining the exercise of conscientious objection in the corporate realm has focused mostly on marketplace conscience-based claims, in cases that involve institutions or corporations that fall under what is referred to here as a "purely commercial" categorization.

126 Aoife Nolan. *Privatization and Economic and Social Rights*. 40 HUM. RTS. Q. 815–58 (2018).

127 KOEN DE FEYER & FELIPE GÓMEZ ISA, PRIVATISATION AND HUMAN RIGHTS IN THE AGE OF GLOBALISATION (2005); MANFRED NOWAK, HUMAN RIGHTS OR GLOBAL CAPITALISM: THE LIMITS OF PRIVATIZATION (2016).

As such, most of the debates around corporate conscience-based claims operate within obscure and rudimentary boundaries that do not shed light on the distinctive nature and features of the conversation. Therefore, a more systematic and nuanced theorization is necessary as corporate conscience-based claims are starting to emerge as part of existing law and corporations are taking on a larger role in societies.[128]

What follows is a critique of various analyses in literature with regards to purely commercial institutions. Then, using healthcare institutions as a case study, an analysis and examination of dependent institutions in a way that better allows for the protection of rights is included.

3.3.2.1 *Purely Commercial Institutions*

Authors have tried to distinguish conscience-based claims in the marketplace, such as the objection of a florist or a baker, from objectors' claims to, for instance, military service. They have argued that if conscientious objectors are not prepared to abide by generally applicable laws because they conflict with the objectors' values, they should not enter the marketplace under such a profession in the first place. This language reflects the idea that entering a profession is an optional and conscious decision, unlike the compulsory military service against which gave rise to the first manifestations of conscientious objection. Another difference lies in the fact that conscientious objection in the marketplace can affect the rights of third parties directly. On the contrary, when an individual opposes compulsory military service, the risk of impact to third parties is speculative—a threat to national security at most—and, in any case, not comparable.

Some have argued that the main factor against granting a conscientious objection in the marketplace is the risk that by granting it, different forms of discrimination will follow.[129] There is a reason why people working in the commercial sphere generally cannot choose which patrons to serve, even when the service may conflict with their religious beliefs: it is the environment in which equality in civil society prevails. This imposition derives from the general

128 *See, e.g.*, Institut Montaigne, Religion au travail: croire au dialogue—Baromètre du Fait Religieux en Enterprise 2020–2021 (2021); Louise Couvelaire, *Le "paradoxe" du fait religieux en enterprise*, Le Monde (May 6, 2021), https://www.lemonde.fr/emploi/article/2021/05/06/le-paradoxe-du-fait-religieux-en-entreprise_6079297_1698637.html (last visited Nov 18, 2023).

129 Taylor Flynn, *Clarion Call or False Alarm: Why Proposed Exemptions to Equal Marriage Statutes Return Us to a Religious Understanding of the Public Marketplace*, 5 Nw. J. L. & Soc. Pol'y 236, 238–39 (2010). *See also* Ted Poston, *Religious Conscience and the Private Market, in* Kevin Vallier and Michael Weber, Religious Exemptions (2018).

determination of the common law that, in a conflict between the supplier's rights or beliefs and the provision of services to a buyer, the burden must fall on the supplier who has placed himself on the market to make a profit. If an exemption were granted from the obligation of not discriminating against religious people, other individuals would have to conform to their beliefs as a condition of obtaining equal market share.

To illustrate the problem of marketplace conscience-based claims, one can turn to the *Masterpiece Cakeshop* case in the United States. A Free Exercise Clause claim was the dispositive issue in this landmark case.[130] In the case, the petitioner was a cakemaker who refused to make a wedding cake for a same-sex couple because of his "religious opposition to same-sex marriages."[131] He claimed that making the cake would effectively force him to participate "through artistic expression in an event he regards as sacrilegious."[132] At the time, gay marriage was not legal in Colorado, but the couple would marry in Massachusetts and then celebrate in Colorado.[133] The couple filed a discrimination complaint with the Colorado Civil Rights Commission.[134] After an investigation and hearing, a state administrative law judge eventually ruled that the cakemaker's "actions constituted prohibited discrimination on the basis of sexual orientation."[135]

The U.S. Supreme Court ultimately held that the Colorado Civil Rights Commission was impermissibly hostile toward the cakemaker's religious beliefs in violation of the Free Exercise Clause.[136] This ruling was based on two main points. First, several Colorado Civil Rights Commission members made comments during the hearing process that the Court thought were overly hostile toward the petitioner's religious beliefs.[137] In one instance, a Commissioner said that when religious freedom is used to justify discrimination, that is "one of the most despicable pieces of rhetoric that people can use."[138] The Court found this statement and others like it to be overly hostile to the cakemaker's religious beliefs. It held that the Free Exercise Clause prohibits government officials from "pass[ing] judgment upon or presuppos[ing] the illegitimacy of

130 Masterpiece Cakeshop v. Colorado Civil Rights Commission, 138 S.Ct. 1719, 1732 (2018).
131 *Id.* at 1723.
132 Reply Brief for Petitioners at 25, Masterpiece Cakeshop v. Colorado Civil Rights Commission, No. 16–111 (Nov. 22, 2017).
133 Masterpiece Cakeshop v. Colorado Civil Rights Commission, 138 S.Ct. 1719, 1724 (2018).
134 *Id.* at 1725–26.
135 *Id.*
136 *Id.* at 1732.
137 *Id.* at 1729.
138 *Id.*

religious beliefs."[139] Second, the Court pointed out that the Commission had, on previous occasions, allowed cakemakers to refuse to bake cakes with messages *against* same-sex marriages.[140] This "disparate consideration" led the Court to rule that the Commission was not acting neutral toward the petitioner's religious beliefs but instead displayed a hostility in violation of the Free Exercise Clause.[141]

Masterpiece Cakeshop provides a classic example of a so-called complicity-based conscience claim made against the recognition of LGBTQ rights.[142] Conservative religious groups, mainly Catholics and Evangelicals, often resort to these kinds of claims to limit same-sex couples' rights.[143] In essence, the general structure of conscience-based claims is as follows: a religious person can legitimately refuse to provide a service or benefit to a same-sex couple, even when doing so is otherwise required by law, because forcing the religious person to provide the service or benefit would make them complicit in behavior that violates his or her constitutionally-protected religious beliefs.[144] Thus, in the *Masterpiece* case, the cakemaker refused to bake a cake for a same-sex couple because he did not want to be complicit in a same-sex marriage ceremony, as that would violate his religious beliefs.[145] To support this argument, the cakemaker even claimed that he *would* make other baked goods for gay couples but simply did not want to, directly or indirectly, participate in a same-sex marriage.[146]

The problem with allowing such conscience-based claims is that they can harm third parties, such as the same-sex couple in *Masterpiece*, and they contradict anti-discrimination provisions in public accommodations law.[147] For

---

139 *Id.* at 1731.

140 *Id.* at 1730.

141 *Id.* at 1732.

142 *See* Masterpiece Cakeshop v. Colorado Civil Rights Commission, 138 S. Ct. 1719 (2018); Reply Brief for Petitioners at 25, Masterpiece Cakeshop v. Colorado Civil Rights Commission, No. 16–111 (Nov. 22, 2017); *See generally* Douglas NeJaime & Reva B. Siegel, *Conscience Wars: Complicity-Based Conscience Claims in Religion and Politics*, 124 YALE L. J. 2516, 2518–19 (2015).

143 Douglas NeJaime & Reva B. Siegel, *Conscience Wars: Complicity-Based Conscience Claims in Religion and Politics*, 124 Yale L. J. 2516, 2545 (2015). *See* Chapter 2.

144 *See, e.g., id.*; James C. Nelson, *The Religion Clauses: A Sword with Two Edges*, ACS EXPERT FORUM (Feb. 25, 2014), https://www.acslaw.org/expertforum/the-religion-clauses-a-sword-with-two-edges/ (last visited Nov 18, 2023).

145 Reply Brief for Petitioners at 25, Masterpiece Cakeshop v. Colorado Civil Rights Commission, No. 16–111 (Nov. 22, 2017).

146 Masterpiece Cakeshop v. Colorado Civil Rights Commission, 138 S. Ct. 1719, 1723 (2018).

147 *See, e.g.*, Elizabeth Sepper, *Gays in the Moralized Marketplace*, 7 ALA. C.R. & C.L. L. REV. 129, 129–31 (2015); Douglas NeJaime & Reva B. Siegel, *Conscience Wars: Complicity-Based Conscience Claims in Religion and Politics*, 124 YALE L. J. 2516, 2519 (2015).

this very reason, the U.S. Supreme Court has historically rejected similar conscience-based claims regarding race issues.[148] For example, in the 1966 case of *Newman v. Piggie Park Enterprises*, the Court rejected a Free Exercise Clause claim that was remarkably similar to the cakemaker's claim in *Masterpiece*.[149] In *Newman*, a restaurant owner claimed that his religion did not allow him to serve people of other races in his restaurant.[150] The restaurant owner stated that his "religious beliefs compel him to oppose any integration of the races whatever."[151] He, therefore, claimed that the recently enacted Civil Rights Act of 1964, which prohibited racial discrimination in public accommodations, violated his constitutional right to the free exercise of religion.[152] In a *per curiam* decision, the Supreme Court rejected the restaurant owner's claim, calling it "patently frivolous."[153] Interestingly, in 2001, decades after losing the case, the restaurant owner wrote an autobiography in which he echoes right-wing populist rhetoric. He noted that "the civil rights movement is a Satanic attempt to make it easier for a global elite … working at an international level to eventually seize power in this country."[154]

There is one way to distinguish *Newman* from *Masterpiece*, which may explain their divergent rulings. In *Masterpiece*, the Court based its decision almost entirely on the Colorado Civil Rights Commission's perceived hostility toward the cakemaker's religious beliefs because of the Commissioners'

148 *See* Elizabeth Sepper, *Gays in the Moralized Marketplace*, 7 Ala. C.R. & C.L. L. Rev. 129, 129–31 (2015); *50 Years Ago vs. Today: Piggie Park & The High Stakes of the Masterpiece Cakeshop Case*, Movement Advancement Proj. (Mar. 2018), http://www.lgbtmap.org/file/Brief-OTA-Piggie-Park.pdf (last visited Nov 18, 2023).

149 *See* Elizabeth Sepper, *Gays in the Moralized Marketplace*, 7 Ala. C.R. & C.L. L. Rev. 129, 129–31 (2015); Newman v. Piggie Park Enterprises, 390 U.S. 400 (1968) (per curiam).

150 *See* Elizabeth Sepper, *Gays in the Moralized Marketplace*, 7 Ala. C.R. & C.L. L. Rev. 129, 129–31 (2015); Newman v. Piggie Park Enterprises, Inc., 256 F. Supp. 941, 944 (D.S.C. 1966).

151 Newman v. Piggie Park Enterprises, Inc., 256 F. Supp. 941, 944 (D.S.C. 1966); *50 Years Ago vs. Today: Piggie Park & The High Stakes of the Masterpiece Cakeshop Case*, Movement Advancement Proj. (Mar. 2018), http://www.lgbtmap.org/file/Brief-OTA-Piggie-Park.pdf (last visited Nov 18, 2023).

152 Newman v. Piggie Park Enterprises, Inc., 256 F. Supp. 941, 944 (D.S.C. 1966); *50 Years Ago vs. Today: Piggie Park & The High Stakes of the Masterpiece Cakeshop Case*, Movement Advancement Proj. (Mar. 2018), http://www.lgbtmap.org/file/Brief-OTA-Piggie-Park.pdf (last visited Nov 18, 2023).

153 Newman v. Piggie Park Enterprises, 390 U.S. 400, 402 (1968) (per curiam); Elizabeth Sepper, *Gays in the Moralized Marketplace*, 7 Ala. C.R. & C.L. L. Rev. 129, 129–31 (2015).

154 Christian Farias, *We've Already Litigated This*, Slate (Dec. 4, 2017), https://slate.com/news-and-politics/2017/12/the-key-principle-in-the-masterpiece-cakeshop-case-was-litigated-in-1968.html (last visited Nov 18, 2023).

disparaging comments.[155] In fact, the majority opinion cites *Newman* as still good law for the proposition that religious beliefs cannot supersede "neutral and generally applicable public accommodations law."[156] Thus, one can interpret *Masterpiece* as a relatively narrow holding based on the particular facts of that case, rather than a much broader holding that religious beliefs against same-sex marriage always supersede non-discrimination laws.[157] This narrow interpretation is bolstered because both Justices Kagan and Breyer joined the majority opinion in *Masterpiece*.[158] Their joint concurrence stresses that "state actors cannot show hostility to religious views; rather, they must give those views neutral and respectful consideration."[159]

Nevertheless, the combination of cases like *Masterpiece* and *Hobby Lobby* provide powerful precedent to conservative religious groups arguing against LGBTQ or reproductive rights.[160] In these and similar cases, the U.S. Supreme Court has at least opened the door to conscience-based exemptions in the marketplace to laws regarding issues such as LGBTQ rights and contraception.[161] The Court's precedent has even opened the door for such claims when state statutes expressly prohibit discrimination based on sexual orientation in public accommodations.[162] Thus, when it comes to issues of sexual orientation, conscience-based claims—in line with what has been explained when discussing political uses of conscience-based claims—could, in theory, allow religious persons, both natural and juridical, to "opt-out of any law" that is "incompatible with their religious beliefs," in the words of Justice Ginsburg.[163]

---

155 Masterpiece Cakeshop v. Colorado Civil Rights Commission, 138 S. Ct. 1719, 1732 (2018) ("The Commission's hostility was inconsistent with the First Amendment's guarantee that our laws be applied in a manner that is neutral toward religion.").

156 *Id.* at 1727.

157 *See* Leslie Kendrick & Micah Schwartzman, *The Etiquette of Animus*, 132 HARV. L. REV. 133, 133–34 (2018).

158 Masterpiece Cakeshop v. Colorado Civil Rights Commission, 138 S. Ct. 1719, 1732–33 (2018) (Kagan J., concurring).

159 *Id.*

160 *See generally* Vincent J. Samar, *The Potential Impact of Hobby Lobby on LGBT Civil Rights*, 16 GEO. J. GENDER & L. 547 (2015); *see also* Fulton v. City of Philadelphia, 922 F.3d 140, 153–54 (3d Cir. 2019) (religion adoption agency cites *Masterpiece* in their Free Exercise claim).

161 Elizabeth Sepper, *Gays in the Moralized Marketplace*, 7 ALA. C.R. & C.L. L. REV. 129, 129–31 (2015).

162 *See, e.g.*, Boy Scouts of America v. Dale, 530 U.S. 640, 659 (2000) (holding that the constitutional right of expressive association supersedes state law that explicitly prohibited discrimination on the basis of sexual orientation).

163 *Hobby Lobby*, 573 U.S. 682, 739–40 (Ginsburg, J., dissenting); *See also* Douglas NeJaime & Reva B. Siegel, *Conscience Wars: Complicity-Based Conscience Claims in Religion and Politics*, 124 YALE L. J. 2516, 2518–19 (2015).

3.3.2.2 *Dependent Institutions*

Dependent institutions, by virtue of the legal relationship derived from the contract between the company and the State, assume all or most of the obligations to protect, respect, and fulfill human rights. Thinking about these institutions in terms of dependency allows for a shift in focus from international human rights law as the source for the legal obligation to instead the agreement between both parties as the obligation's source. This obligation can be demonstrated in the healthcare setting: guaranteeing the right to health represents, in essence, an obligation to do something. That duty usually falls under the States' purview and is not possible to impose it upon a corporation knowledgeable in the healthcare space. To make that obligation to act in a certain manner applicable to a particular corporation there needs to be a juridical relationship like the ones seen in civil or commercial law, such as a contract. In those cases, the source of the obligation is the contract itself.[164] This conceptualization, of course, becomes relevant in efforts to limit and regulate institutional conscientious objection.

Additionally, considering the current power that corporations have over people's lives and its impact on the enjoyment of human rights, States should adopt measures to prevent these corporations from playing a leading role in the political and social spheres. Society should mitigate as much as possible opportunities for unequal influence, which in this case translates into limiting the power of institutions in making crucial decisions over individuals' lives.[165]

Under this proposed categorization, the debate around institutional conscientious objection no longer focuses on the legal personality and the public or private nature of those who own buildings, transport, infrastructure, information, communications, and services. As long as goods and services are open or offered to the public, they must be accessible to all, regardless of whether they are owned or provided by a public authority or a private company. The denial of access must be considered constitutive of a discriminatory act and a violation of human rights regardless of whether the perpetrator is a public or private entity.[166]

The power of the State to regulate non-state actors, particularly to protect public health, has been widely recognized under the doctrine of the State's

164 *See* Urbaser S.A. y Consorcio de Aguas Bilbao Bizkaia, Bilbao Bizkaia ur Partzuergoa v. Argentina, ¶ 1210.

165 Aditi Gowri, *Speech and Spending: Corporate Political Speech Rights under the First Amendment*, 17 J. Bus. Ethics 1850 (1988).

166 U.N. Committee on Economic, Social and Cultural Rights, General Comment No. 2, U.N. Doc. E/1990/23 (Feb. 2, 1990), ¶ 13.

police power.[167] As such, allowing the exercise of individual conscientious objection while excluding from said exercise private institutions under signed agreements with the State for the provision of healthcare services could be considered to be a valid exercise of a State's police power.

The ultimate goal of regulating the exercise of institutional conscientious objection is to protect public health by guaranteeing access to healthcare services and preventing conscientious objection from becoming a barrier that prevents such access. The police power doctrine has been applied in several cases to dismiss claims against regulatory measures specifically designed to protect public health.[168]

The provision of healthcare services should always be based on individual needs, not the interests of the service provider. States must establish mechanisms to supervise said providers, adopt measures to protect people, and create appropriate mechanisms to detect situations of violence exerted by third parties against said people.[169]

States must refrain from taking measures that obstruct the decisions of the people to achieve the effective enjoyment of their health.[170] Allowing the private sector to provide services does not in any way reduce the State's obligation to guarantee to all women within its jurisdiction the full recognition and fulfillment of their rights. Thus, States always retain the obligation to regulate private actors to ensure that the services they provide are accessible to all, appropriate, regularly evaluated to meet the changing needs of the public, and adapted to those needs.[171]

---

167 ICSID, Philip Morris Brands Sàrl et al v Oriental Republic of Uruguay, Case No ARB/10/7 https://www.italaw.com/cases/460 (last visited Oct. 4, 2021), ¶ 291. *See generally* LAWRENCE O. GOSTIN & L.F. WILEY, PUBLIC HEALTH LAW: POWER, DUTY, RESTRAINT (2016).

168 German-Venezuelan Commission, Bischoff case, Decision (1903), 10 U.N.R.I.A.A. (RLA-138). UNCITRAL, Methanex Corporation v. United States of America, (RLA-164), Part 4, Chapter. D, ¶ 7. UNCITRAL, Chemtura Corporation v. Government of Canada, (RLA-053), ¶ 266.

169 European Committee of Social Rights, International Planned Parenthood Federation European Network (IPPF-EN) v. Italy, No. 87/2012 (2014). European Committee of Social Rights, Confederazione Generale Italiana del Lavoro (CGIL) v. Italy, Nro. 91/2013, (2016).

170 U.N. Committee on the Elimination of Discrimination against Women, *General Recommendation* N° 24: *Article 12 of the Convention on the Elimination of all Forms of Discrimination Against Women—Women and Health* (1999), ¶14.

171 U.N. Committee on Economic, Social and Cultural Rights, *General Comment No. 24*, U.N. Doc. E/C.12/GC/24, ¶ 22 (2017).

4 Conclusion

A deeper analysis of the expansion of conscience-based claims in healthcare settings within the context of liberal democracies allows for a comprehensive assessment of the challenges posed to the enjoyment of other rights. The dynamic interplay between deeply-held moral or religious beliefs and the provision of healthcare services raises profound questions about the balance between respecting conscience-based claims and upholding the legal rights and needs of individuals.

This exploration has revealed that addressing the expansion of conscience-based claims necessitates a delicate equilibrium that respects both individual autonomy and societal obligations. On one hand, it is essential to recognize the rights of healthcare practitioners to conscientiously object to procedures they find morally or religiously objectionable, provided that alternative arrangements are made to ensure patients' access to care. On the other hand, the rise of new uses of conscience-based claims underscores the importance of extending regulatory frameworks to encompass uses that go beyond the traditional understandings of conscience, thereby safeguarding individuals' rights.

It has increasingly become clear that liberal democracies must grapple with the evolving landscape of conscience-based claims. Plausible solutions which not only consider the need for a balance between competing rights and interests, but also the broader societal impact and outcomes of these new conscience-based claims must be sought. This involves a reconsideration of the best normative frameworks to protect the interests of individuals while adhering to the fundamental principles of democracy.

CHAPTER 6

A Path Forward: Mitigating the Impact of Religious Lawfare

In addition to the responses that the universal and regional human rights systems have sketched to counter the effects of religious lawfare, attempts to find ways to deal with new uses of conscience-based claims have also emerged in academic literature.[1] Despite these efforts, no proposal has yet succeeded in establishing a robust normative framework to guide decisions on how to handle these conflicts while upholding democratic values in modern liberal democracies. While scholars' instincts and endeavors in proposing solutions seem promising, without a well-defined normative foundation, their ideas stand on shaky ground. Delineating the philosophical and normative foundations for the changes experienced by liberal democracies is imperative in charting the best course of action.

Political uses of conscience-based claims, as argued before, pose a direct threat to democracy by jeopardizing two elements of the democratic ideal: the equal influence element and the deliberative democracy element.[2] These conscience-based claims often clash with laws that protect other rights, such as reproductive rights—specifically, access to contraception and abortion—as well as the right to same-sex marriage. Some opponents to abortion and same-sex relationships, unable to prevent these rights from being legally recognized, now strategically invoke conscience-based objections to frustrate the enjoyment of these rights.[3] Nonetheless, the main arguments present in the literature addressing this issue largely overlook the antidemocratic deficit and the threat posed by the use of conscience-based claims as tool of religious lawfare. Most proposals fail to consider the complexity, particularities, and subjectivities at play when dealing with conscience-based claims.

Authors have framed solutions as efforts to avoid the conflicts between conscience and other rights either by limiting the exercise of conscience-based claims or by regulating it. For instance, in their book,[4] Mancini and Rosenfeld

1 *See* Chapter 4.

2 *See* Chapter 3.

3 The Conscience Wars: Rethinking the Balance between Religion, Identity, and Equality (Susanna Mancini & Michel Rosenfeld eds., 2018).

4 *Id.*

 | DOI:10.1163/9789004685406_008

called for a regulation of the exercise of the right to freedom of conscience so as not to encourage another dimension of discrimination, one which could be legally recognized under this right. They noted that although the claims of conscientious objectors are valid faith-based claims, their accommodation by the law may become a tool through which legal orders would be validly opposed, and/or rights of other persons may be limited. Essentially, the right to freedom of conscience, when unrestricted, may legitimize discrimination and hamper the enjoyment of rights.

Some authors have bluntly argued that conscience-based claims ought not to have a place in any reasonable democracy and should thus be banned.[5] The basic idea is that religious adherents must accept and coexist with multiple religions and beliefs which may contain positions contrary to theirs. They are more so urged to respect and tolerate these beliefs as well as the believers therein. The European Court of Human Rights in *Dogru*,[6] commenting on restrictions on religion-inspired dressings, noted that "in a democratic society, in which several religions coexist within one and the same population, it may be necessary to place restrictions on this freedom [of religious exercise] in order to reconcile the interests of the various groups and ensure that everyone's beliefs are respected."[7] In that case, a young girl had approached the court after being prevented from wearing her *hijab*. The court ruled against her.

Similarly, other authors have argued that States have a responsibility to protect democracy by promoting pluralism.[8] As such, the government's duties extend to compelling compliance and requiring the citizenry to fulfill duties that contribute to these values. When people, based on religious or other type of beliefs, decide not to provide certain services to others, they subvert pluralism, which is the very concept that protects their right to conscience from the majority's will. To safeguard pluralism and equality, these authors recommend that the freedom of conscience, thought, and religion be limited as soon as there exists a potential for harm and discrimination. In their words, they "urge that responses to requests for exemption from legal and social duties be based on the bedrock values of pluralism, equity, and non-discrimination."[9]

5 Christian Fiala & Joyce C. Arthur, *"Dishonourable disobedience"–Why refusal to treat in reproductive healthcare is not conscientious objection,* 1WOMAN-PSYCHOSOMATIC GYNECOLOGY & OBSTETRICS 12 (2014).

6 Dogru v. France, App. No. 27058/05, Eur. Ct. H. R. (2008).

7 INTERNATIONAL NETWORK OF CIVIL LIBERTIES ORGANIZATIONS, DRAWING THE LINE: TACKLING TENSIONS BETWEEN RELIGIOUS FREEDOM AND EQUALITY (2015).

8 Wendy Chavkin, et al., *Balancing freedom of conscience and equitable access*, 108 AM. J. PUB. HEALTH 1487 (2018).

9 *Id.*

This proposal considers that granting conscience-based exemptions will lead to less tolerance and less respect for everyone—a result that is contrary to the interests of both religious and secular people. While sincere religious views should not be ignored, they must not be allowed to cause damage to society.[10]

Instead of a blanket ban or rejecting the exercise of certain types of conscience-based claims in their entirety, some authors have proposed regulating elements of the exercise of conscientious objection.[11] For example, Ramón Michel et al. have suggested such approach in the context of the provision of healthcare services. They maintain that: (1) conscientious objection shall only be invoked by individuals—not institutions—and be limited to moral or religious reasons; (2) people who hold leadership positions within an institution shall never be objectors. Likewise, no objector may refuse to refer a patient to a professional who can perform the service; (3) for conscientious objection to be valid, it must be expressed in writing and shared with the health center authorities, disclosing the moral or religious reasons and motives behind the refusal. The request will be subject to approval and review by the health authorities; and (4) health institutions—especially people who hold leadership positions within them—and national and provincial agencies will be responsible for guaranteeing access to the healthcare services within existing legal regulations and, at the same time, respecting conscientious objection on moral or religious grounds.

Nevertheless, all of the proposed solutions fail to adequately consider and address the antidemocratic deficit of political uses of conscience-based claims and overlook the need for a robust normative basis in their proposals.

In fact, it has been argued that some of these proposals could run contrary to democracy by holding that freedom of conscience must yield to other values.[12] Arguably, this approach could end up completely disregarding the objector's dignity and, in some cases, it may inflict profound and tangible suffering on

10 Mark Strasser, *On Same-Sex Marriage and Matters of Conscience.* 17 WM. & MARY J. WOMEN & L. 1, 37 (2010).

11 Agustina Ramón Michel et al., *Regulating Conscientious Objection to Legal Abortion in Argentina: Taking into Consideration Its Uses and Consequences*, 22 HEALTH & HUM. RTS. J. 272 (2020). *See also* Morten Magelssen et al., *Secularity, abortion, assisted dying and the future of conscientious objection: Modelling the relationship between attitudes*, 20 BMC MED. ETHICS (2019).

12 *See* BRIAN BARRY, CULTURE AND EQUALITY: AN EGALITARIAN CRITIQUE OF MULTICULTURALISM 19–63 (2002); Richard J. Arneson, *Against Freedom of Conscience*, 47 SAN DIEGO L. REV. 1015 (2010).

them, under the veil of tolerance and pluralism.[13] Delineating the contours of when and to what extent a particular action substantially burdens (or will burden) one party would necessarily depend on the sincerity of their beliefs, which is entirely up to each person and is something that cannot be generalized but will instead need to be assessed on a case-by-case basis.[14] Additionally, proving the sincerity of a specific belief may prove impractical, if not impossible, in most cases.

Some of these solutions disregard the actual value of conscientious objection to democracy. As mentioned, conscientious objection is and has traditionally been—in most cases—healthy to democracy as a tool to communicate specific claims, inform public debate, and allow citizens to exercise their communicative power and freedom in a meaningful way.[15] Conscientious objection is both about the subjective right of the person to protect his or her conscience and intimate beliefs, and the collective right of the citizenry to benefit from a diversity of views that could serve to prevent the majority's abuses of power.

Along these lines, for instance, Professor Thomas Berg has highlighted the importance of remaining true to one's faith in the workplace.[16] Resorting to the example of same-sex marriage, he argued that just as it is unreasonable to tell LGBTQ people that they will only receive "tolerance" in their private "behavior," denying them the right to make a marital commitment to someone of their same-sex, it is unreasonable to ask religious people to keep their beliefs to themselves and to tell them that it is inappropriate for them to bring them up in their respective work environments. According to Professor Berg, anyone who takes the arguments for same-sex marriage seriously should also

---

13 *See generally* Kent Greenawalt, Religious Convictions and Political Choice (1988).

14 An argument against judicial review of the sincerity of a conscience claim contends that doing so would violate the conscientious objector's privacy. *See* Joseph Raz, The Authority of Law: Essays on Law and Morality 288 (2009) (noting that "freedom of conscience is compromised if it is guaranteed only through compromising other aspects of one's autonomy, and self-respect, i.e., one's privacy and one's dignity"). *But see* John Adenitire, A General Right to Conscientious Exemption: Beyond Religious Privilege 242 (2020) (arguing that "even the legal right to privacy entails individuals having to convince a court, with the consequent loss of some privacy, that their privacy interests are worth protecting through law" and that it is counterintuitive to think that individuals would not be willing to sacrifice an aspect of their well-being, such as their privacy, to receive a benefit they value more, like living according to their beliefs).

15 *See generally* Kimberley Brownlee, Conscience and Conviction: The Case for Civil Disobedience 28–30 (2012).

16 Thomas Berg, *What Same-Sex-Marriage and Religious-Liberty Claims Have in Common*, 5 Nw. J. L. & Soc. Pol'y 206 (2010).

give weight to the views of religious people. There is a risk that the same type of prejudice against LGBTQ people will be exercised in relation to religious people, in the sense that only conduct that they do not ostensibly practice in society is tolerated, forcing them to live aspects essential to their identity only in the private sphere. As a way of resolving the conflict, Professor Berg believes that the State should allow conscience-based claims in the workplace unless this exemption causes the same-sex couple to be unable to obtain the service or makes it very difficult for them to get it.

In healthcare contexts, some authors have argued that pursuing a career in medicine carries a consent to provide a health service even if its provision would create a conscience conflict for the healthcare provider.[17] However, it has also been argued that forcing an individual to choose between providing a service against his or her conscience and changing or pursuing a different profession may impose a hefty burden on the free exercise of his or her religion, as working towards a particular career usually involves prior investment of time, money, and personal effort, as well as a sense of personal fulfillment and happiness that can come from that activity, which contributes to the formation of the individual's identity. Giving it all up could be very costly.[18] Professor Berg does not deny that the act of refusing to provide services to LGBTQ people is an offense that causes suffering to them. However, he believes that the suffering caused to religious people is even greater and more concrete. The religious person is obliged to act contrary to a dogma of faith, risking excommunication from their Church and community, or abandon a profession. For Professor Berg, understanding that the "disturbance" felt by LGBTQ people who request a service for a same-sex wedding is enough to overcome the freedom to deny the provision of the service in question simply does not give due importance to the suffering that can be caused to those who are forced to collaborate with a ceremony that, in its conception, violates principles of their religion. However, not regulating or limiting specific conscience-based claims would significantly overestimate the marginalization that religious individuals are supposed to

---

17 *See generally*, Alberto Giubilini & Julian Savulescu, *Beyond Money: Conscientious Objection in Medicine as a Conflict of Interests*, 17(2) J. BIOETH. INQ., 229–243 (2020). *See also*, Joyce Arthur, et al., *The dishonourable disobedience of not providing abortion*, 22 EUR. J. CONTRACEPTION & REPROD. HEALTH CARE 1 (2017).

18 *See also* Richard John Lyus, *Response to: 'Why medical professionals have no moral claim to conscientious objection accommodation in liberal democracies' by Schuklenk and Smalling*, 43 J. MED. ETHICS 4, 250–252 (2017); *and* Stephen W. Smith, *Individualised claims of conscience, clinical judgement and best interests*, 26 HEALTH CARE ANAL. 1, 81–93 (2018) (noting that individual's conscience may change over time due to personal or professional experiences).

suffer and underestimate the damage they cause to other people while failing to consider the damage to their dignity and equality, a harm inherent in discrimination against a group that has historically been marginalized.[19]

In the ever-evolving landscape of liberal democracies, the clash between individual rights and societal interests has increasingly come to the forefront of legal and political debates in the form of conscience-based claims. These claims, rooted in deeply held beliefs and convictions, have come at odds with the principles of equality, and social harmony that underpin democratic societies. Naturally, the proposed solutions in academic literature have addressed these claims under the traditional framework of "freedom from interference," which seeks to protect individuals from state or societal intrusion into their beliefs and practices, placing great value on the autonomy of the individual. However, as societal values change and new uses of conscience-based claims emerge, the limitations of this paradigm have become increasingly evident. This leaves us at a crossroads on how to deal with political uses of conscience-based claims.

1 The Need for a New Normative Basis

The emergence of the phenomenon that this book refers to as "religious lawfare," where conservative religious groups strategically employ conscience-based objections to challenge laws that protect rights, such as reproductive freedom and LGBTQ rights, raises questions about whether the traditional approach of freedom from interference remains effective in safeguarding the democratic ideal, or whether a new normative basis is necessary to strengthen the foundations and merits of existing proposals aimed at dealing with political uses of conscience-based claims.

Any normative basis that seeks to solve the problems that political uses of conscience-based claims pose must avoid imposing on someone a directive that in essence becomes coercive on one of the parties involved. The goal should be to avoid situations of complete disregard or prioritization of one right over the other in any of its forms, whether it comes from the conscientious objector or from the State that seeks to reconcile the conflict of rights in search of some type of "middle ground."

19 Taylor Flynn, *Clarion Call or False Alarm: Why Proposed Exemptions to Equal Marriage Statutes Return Us to a Religious Understanding of the Public Marketplace*, 5 NW. J. L. & SOC. POL'Y 236, 247 (2010).

Most of the recent conflicts between freedom of conscience and other rights have been framed in terms of "culture wars" or, even at times, as "conscience wars." Liberal democracies that take rights seriously must move away from the idea of a mutual threat, which only leads to polarization and erodes democratic institutions while consolidating oppressive extremes that ultimately give rise to extremist movements, such as the ones described in earlier chapters of this book. The notion of threat and counter-threat only leads to more divergence and conflict instead of stability. Such a contentious environment enables the exercise of arbitrary power and influence, limits deliberation, produces a significant amount of litigation, which is not sustainable in the long term.[20] The goal should not be to strip people of their rights or win a fight over rights but rather to produce a climate in which different worldviews can coexist with less mutual hostility and threat.

Under the traditional paradigm of "freedom from interference," proposals on how to deal with these conflicts have aimed at striking a compromise or balance between rights, which in some cases end up nullifying one right in favor of the exercise of the other. Under the guise of technical tests to find a balance or determine what is proportional and what is not, one right ends up being discarded.[21] Instead of promoting mitigating instances of domination

---

20 Grégor Puppinck, *Conscientious Objection and Human Rights: a Systematic Analysis: A Systematic Analysis*, 1 Brill Rsch. Persp. L. & Rel. 1, 4 (2017).

21 It may be argued that proportionality/balancing is actually a fair tool that precisely takes into consideration arguments on both sides that leaves room for future cases where the opposing right could prevail. It is not my intention here to provide and exhaustive and detailed analysis of critiques to the proportionality/balancing test, but rather acknowledge its inherent flaws, which ultimately render it inadequate for addressing complex matters, such as the conflict that arises between the exercise of conscientious objection in healthcare settings and the provision of legal abortion services. For a general overview of critiques to the proportionality/balancing test, *see generally* Francisco J. Urbina, A Critique of Proportionality and Balancing (2017); *see also*, Stijn Smet, Resolving Conflicts between Human Rights. The judge's dilemma (2017); Janneke Gerards, *The Age of Balancing Revisited?* 6 Eur. Data Protection L. Rev. (2020). Such flaws include, among others, a misleading appearance of neutrality, the perpetuation of structural bias, and the incommensurability of moral considerations. While proportionality/balancing is often perceived as a versatile tool capable of meeting many expectations, it is not a neutral framework. It structurally favors one principle of another, perpetuating structural biases and failing to address the nuances of both rights adequately. This structural bias does not disappear simply because proportionality allows for different outcomes in different contexts; rather, it embeds a predisposition towards certain rights, perpetuating an imbalance. Moreover, the incommensurability of values present in the conscientious objection-right to legal abortion conflict often leads courts to face accusations of subjectivity and abuse of discretion. *See* Aharon Barack, Proportionality: Constitutional Rights and their Limitations (2012);

and arbitrary influence to promote deliberation and a tolerant life in society, these solutions have fueled the "war" narrative and have allowed rights to be used as swords.

Dealing with the issue of conscientious objection in healthcare in terms of positive vs negative liberty (with negative liberty being the absence of interference from others) disregards the complexity, particularities, and subjectivities at play when dealing with these claims, making it easier for critics to argue that proposals to regulate conscience-based claims lack legitimacy, validity, and coherence. This, in turn, has reinforced the mainstream general idea—which arguably has contributed to the polarization and the expansion and rise of political uses of conscience-based claims seen today—that a right is something that allows the right-holder to do as he or she pleases.

In what follows, this chapter embarks in an effort to strengthen the normative foundations of existing proposals by advocating for the adoption of a paradigm shift in how liberal democracies think about conscience-based claims—one that centers on the concept of "freedom as non-domination." Drawing from the works of political philosopher Philip Pettit, it will be shown how this paradigm shift can provide a more nuanced and stronger framework for resolving conflicts arising from conscience-based claims, particularly in the

---

see also, Mattias Kumm, *Constitutional Rights as Principles: On the Structure and Domain of Constitutional Justice* A review Essay on *Theory of Constitutional Rights by Robert Alexy*, 2 INT'L J. OF CON. L. 3, 581 (2004); Başak Çalı, *Balancing Human Rights? Methodological Problems with Weights, Scales and Proportions*, 29 HUM. RTS. Q. (2007); *and* KATHLEEN A. BRADY, THE DISTINCTIVENESS OF RELIGION IN AMERICAN LAW: RETHINKING RELIGION CLAUSE JURISPRUDENCE 195 (2015) (arguing that proportionality tests within the context of conscience-based claims lead to "manipulation, unprincipled or arbitrary decision making, and inconsistent and potentially discriminatory application"). Conscientious objection and the right to abortion represent deeply held beliefs and moral values that cannot be easily compared or measured against each other. The balancing test's attempt to do so inevitably leads to a reductionist approach that obscures the true nature of the conflict and the moral considerations involved. When each side perceives its right as fundamental and deserving protection, the courts' balancing act is criticized as being overly discretionary and subjective. The balancing approach shifts the focus from what is morally right or wrong to whether something is appropriate, adequate, or proportional. *See* Stavros Tsakyrakis, *Proportionality: An Assault on Human Rights?* 7 INT'L J. OF CON. L. 3 (2009). This shift can be particularly problematic in human rights adjudication, where moral considerations are paramount. *See* Martin Luterán, *The Lost Meaning of Proportionality*, *in* PROPORTIONALITY AND THE RULE OF LAW (Grant Huscroft et al., eds., 2014); Jochen Von Bernstorff, *Proportionality Without Balancing: Why Judicial Ad hoc Balancing is Unnecessary and Potentially Detrimental to the Realisation of Individual and Collective Self-determination*, in REASONING RIGHTS: COMPARATIVE JUDICIAL ENGAGEMENT (Liora Lazarus et al., eds., 2014).

reproductive health space. By examining the key principles and implications of this shift, this approach's potential to address contemporary challenges while upholding the core principles of human rights and democratic values will become evident.

The proposal for a paradigm shift from the traditional "freedom from interference" paradigm to the "freedom as non-domination" paradigm is important and highly relevant to the existing literature on conscience-based claims for several compelling reasons. The rise of political uses of conscience-based claims, often as part of religious lawfare strategies, presents a contemporary and pressing challenge to liberal democracies, one that affects key elements of the democratic ideal. Existing literature has often struggled to provide effective solutions to this challenge. The proposal acknowledges and aims to address the antidemocratic threat posed by political uses of conscience-based claims and goes beyond traditional discussions of individual rights and interference to consider the impact of these claims on the broader democratic ideals of equal influence and deliberative democracy.

The adoption of a freedom as non-domination framework recognizes the complexity and subjectivity inherent in these cases and seeks to harmonize individual autonomy with state authority, offering a framework that encourages public deliberation and equitable participation in decision-making. This compatibility enhances its relevance in the context of democratic theory.

In a world marked by ideological conflicts, this discussion explores a potential path for conflict resolution and the reduction of polarization—a path that promotes dialogue and mutual understanding, addressing a critical need in contemporary societies.[22]

1.1 *From Non-interference to Non-domination*

The concept of freedom as non-interference has its roots in classical liberalism, and posits that individuals are free to the extent that they are not subject to direct interference by others. John Locke, in his *Second Treatise of Government*, argued that the role of government is to protect individuals from the interference of others, ensuring that each person can pursue their own interests within the bounds of the law. Similarly, Isaiah Berlin, in his influential essay "Two Concepts of Liberty," distinguished between negative and positive liberty, with negative liberty being the absence of interference from others. In contrast, Philip Pettit's framework of freedom as non-domination offers a more nuanced understanding by emphasizing the importance of power dynamics

22 Philip Pettit, Republicanism: A Theory of Freedom and Government (1997).

and the potential for coercion even in the absence of direct interference. Pettit argues that true freedom requires the absence of domination, defined as the capacity of others to arbitrarily interfere in one's choices.

Pettit contends that traditional notions of freedom, whether positive or negative, fail to capture a crucial aspect of true freedom. He critiques the liberal framework for its focus on safeguarding against direct interference, while overlooking subtler or "potential" forms of interference. For Pettit, "being dominated involves occupying a position where another can interfere on an arbitrary basis in your life: specifically ... where another can interfere with greater or lesser ease on a more or less arbitrary basis across a smaller or larger range of choices."[23] For Pettit, the critical issue lies in adopting a broader, structural perspective that differentiates between mere interference and domination. To illustrate this distinction, he often refers to the example of a slave whose master is absent, highlighting that domination persists regardless of actual interference. To him, domination is

> exemplified by the relationship of master to slave or master to servant. Such a relationship means, at the limit, that the dominating party can interfere on an arbitrary basis with the choices of the dominated: can interfere, in particular, on the basis of an interest or an opinion that need not be shared by the person affected. The dominating party can practice interference, then, at will and with impunity: they do not have to seek anyone's leave and they do not have to incur any scrutiny or penalty.[24]

However, a slave might have a benevolent master who refrains from interfering. The dominant individual may never impose directives or control over the one who is structurally subordinate, and the "master" may never actively intrude upon the actions of the dominated. Nonetheless, this does not alter the fact that the slave remains in a state of servitude; their condition or position as a slave is determined by the inherent power imbalance, irrespective of whether

---

23 Philip Pettit, *Keeping Republican Freedom Simple: On a Difference with Quentin Skinner*, 30 Pol. Theory 3, 341 (2002). *See also*, Quentin Skinner, Liberty Before Liberalism 69–70 (1998).

24 Philip Pettit, Republicanism: A Theory of Freedom and Government 22 (1997).

the master chooses to exercise that power.[25] As we will see, this relational dynamic may be expanded to other relationships of inequality.

Pettit argues that the negative conception of freedom fails to account for subtle forms of interference, while the positive conception overlooks the importance of institutional mechanisms that prevent arbitrary exercises of power. Freedom as non-domination addresses these shortcomings by acknowledging when the state intervention is justified and ensuring that such intervention is not arbitrary.[26] According to Pettit, true freedom is not merely the absence of interference, but rather the absence of domination by others—being free from their arbitrary control and the unpredictability of their desires.[27] According to Pettit, we are free if we are not arbitrarily dominated by any other, and we are protected against arbitrary interference.[28] Freedom as non-domination means that one's actions are not constrained by the power of others.[29]

To identify instances of domination that warrant redress or government action, Pettit offers a definition and outlines several conditions under which domination occurs. Pettit considers that "one agent dominates another if and only if they have a certain power over that other, in particular a power of interference on an arbitrary basis".[30] First, an agent may experience domination if another agent possesses the actual capacity to interfere in their choices; the interference may be dormant, but the potentiality is present.[31] Therefore, Pettit considers not only the act of interference but also the power to interfere as crucial to understanding domination. Moreover, domination occurs when one agent interferes with another without their consent and in a manner contrary to their interests.[32] Pettit also acknowledges that domination may be confined to specific areas of life; for instance: "the husband may dominate the wife in the home, the employer dominates the employee in the workplace,

25 Philip Pettit, Republicanism: A Theory of Freedom and Government (1997).

26 Philip Pettit, Republicanism: A Theory of Freedom and Government 22 (1997).

27 Philip Pettit, *Freedom as Nondomination*, *in* What is Freedom? Conversations with Historians, Philosophers, and Activists (Toby Buckle ed., 2021).

28 David W. Lovell, *Review of Freedom as Non-domination by Philip Pettit*, 5 Agenda 2 (1998).

29 Philip Pettit, *Freedom as Nondomination*, *in* What is Freedom? Conversations with Historians, Philosophers, and Activists (Toby Buckle ed., 2021).

30 Philip Pettit, Republicanism: A Theory of Freedom and Government 2 (1997).

31 *Id*, 54.

32 *Id*, 55.

while that domination does not extend further".[33] Finally, the relationship of domination is often characterized by "common knowledge," where both the dominant and the dominated are aware of the control and vulnerability, and each is conscious of the other's awareness.[34]

The notion of freedom as non-domination is inclusive of much more subtle barriers to freedom than are most liberal accounts of freedom. This view of freedom extends beyond specific acts of arbitrary interference to include the potential for such actions. A person's freedom is not only compromised when she is directly threatened—such as being held at gunpoint and robbed—but also when the structural conditions allow someone to arbitrarily and with little consequence take her money. Similarly, under a legal system that fails to effectively prosecute and convict those who commit violence against women, the principle of non-domination is violated. The vulnerability of women to such attacks, due to their social position, exemplifies the potential for arbitrary interference. When institutions show a lack of commitment to punishing crimes against women, it leads to the implicit legitimization of such violence, resulting in a pervasive fear among women that undermines their freedom in subtle and internalized ways.

Moreover, non-domination differs fundamentally from the mere absence of coercion, particularly when considering the role of equality and consent within liberal social contract theories of freedom. Liberal conceptions assume a basic equality among individuals in the state of nature, where no one holds a higher status than another. Any inequalities that emerge after the formation of the social contract are seen as relatively minor and legitimate, on the basis that all parties would have consented to the contract's terms. In this framework, consent and coercion are treated as mutually exclusive: if an individual has freely consented to a situation, it is assumed that no coercion has occurred, and conversely, if coercion is present, it is believed to invalidate any consent given.[35] Naturally, the challenge arises when there is no clear evidence of active coercion. For example, in contexts of generalized violence against women, a woman may choose to stay home and refrain from taking a walk at night due to fear. In such case, it could be difficult to argue that coercion has taken place when no specific agent can be identified as the coercer. The liberal pairing of consent and coercion, which frames the issue as one of individual versus individual, fails to account for the broader institutional forces—both material

33 *Id*, 58.

34 *Id*, 60.

35 Robin West, *A comment on consent, sex, and rape*, 2 LEGAL THEORY 3, 247 (1996). *See also*, Robin West, *Consent, Legitimation and Dysphoria*, 83 THE MODERN LAW REV. 1 (2020).

and symbolic—that shape individual actions and choices in complex ways. This narrow focus overlooks how systemic and structural factors can influence behavior, even in the absence of direct coercion.

Pettit's non-domination framework aims precisely to address and duly consider the symbolic and structural dimensions of freedom, particularly in relation to institutional arrangements and social contexts. These structures of domination have aptly been defined by Iris Marion Young as "structural or systemic phenomena which exclude people from participating in determining their action or the conditions of their lives."[36]

Relationships of equality and inequality, domination and subjection, are formed and mediated both through and among institutions not usually considered to be political, such as the family, religion, the healthcare system, and economic institutions.[37] Pettit's framework of freedom as non-domination captures all of these concerns, and aligns with notions of relational autonomy and reproductive justice that have been advanced by feminist scholars and reproductive rights advocates over the years.[38] In fact, in line with Pettit's concerns, some feminists scholars have argued for the adoption of a relational approach to autonomy, which can help identify influences on 'autonomous' decisions by shedding light on people's relationships with others, their socio-political circumstances and environment.[39] As Nedelsky summarizes, "[a] relational approach always directs attention to context and consequences. In asking how a law structures relationships it directs attention to the difference context makes, to how the law affects different people in different circumstances."[40] As McLeod and Sherwin suggest, while oppression can present in forms of coercion, compulsion, and ignorance, most often it is displayed in "complex and often largely invisible ways, affecting social groups rather than simply disrupting isolated individuals; as a result, its effects tend to be ignored

36 Iris Marion Young, Justice and the Politics of Difference 31 (1990).

37 Consider "institution" as "not just formal rules, procedures or norms, but the symbol systems, cognitive scripts, and moral templates that provide the 'frames of meaning' guiding human action". *See* Peter A. Hall & Rosemary C. R. Taylor, *Political Science and the Three New Institutionalisms*, xliv Pol. Stud., 947 (1996).

38 *See* Himani Bhakuni, *Reproductive justice: Non-interference or non-domination?*, 23 Developing World Bioeth. 93–98 (2023) (arguing that the non-domination approach better fits the ideals of reproductive justice, as the non-interference framework fails to consider the numerous ways in which individuals make choices and how these choices are by-products of larger social contexts).

39 Carolyn Ells, et al., *Relational autonomy as an essential component of patient-centered care*, 4 Int'l J. Feminist Approaches to Bioeth. 2 (2011).

40 Jennifer Nedelsky, Law's Relations: A Relational Theory of Self, Autonomy, and Law 221 (2012).

within the traditional autonomy framework that focuses solely on individuals".[41] The non-interference framework tends to obscure the social factors and inequities that shape and constrain women's reproductive decisions. In medical settings, the unwillingness to acknowledge these inequities perpetuates stereotypes that disproportionately affect marginalized and racialized patients and promote medical paternalism.[42]

To illustrate the distinction between non-interference and non-domination we could examine the issue of laws allowing self-managed medication abortions (SMA) through medication abortion drugs, like mifepristone and misoprostol, to see how applying the non-domination framework would account for subtler forms of oppression. On its outset, one could argue that laws that allow SMA using medication abortion pills would be a good "middle ground" as they afford patients the care they seek while at the same time adequately respect health service providers' religious conscience.

The freedom as non-interference framework would suggest that women should have the ability to terminate their pregnancies without undue interference from the state or other individuals. Laws that facilitate access to SMA by allowing women to obtain the necessary medication could be seen as upholding this form of freedom. For example, South Africa's Choice in Termination of Pregnancy Act 1996, which allows non-physician healthcare providers such as midwives and nurse practitioners to perform early abortions, could be interpreted as a means of reducing interference by increasing access to abortion services.[43]

However, the non-interference framework has limitations when it comes to recognizing subtler forms of coercion, or instances of potential domination, that may arise even in the absence of overt interference. While women in South Africa may have formal access to termination of pregnancy, including through abortion medication, the requirement to obtain a prescription from a healthcare provider, which is arguably universal for mifepristone and misoprostol, or to undergo mandatory clinical assessments as a condition to access

41 Carolyn McLeod & Susan Sherwin, *Relational Autonomy, Self-Trust, and Health Care for Patients Who Are Oppressed*, IN RELATIONAL AUTONOMY: FEMINIST PERSPECTIVES ON AUTONOMY, AGENCY AND THE SOCIAL SELF (Catriona Mackenzie & Natalie Stoljar, eds., 2000), 259.

42 SUSAN SHERWIN, NO LONGER PATIENT: FEMINIST ETHICS & HEALTH CARE (1992).

43 Choice on Termination of Pregnancy Amendment Act (South Africa), Act No. 92, Art. 2(1)(a) (1996). *See also*, Choice on Termination of Pregnancy Amendment Act (South Africa), Act No. 1 of 2008, Art. 6(1)(a) (2008).

medication abortion pills, can enable opportunities for domination.[44] While these requirements are ostensibly designed to ensure the safety and well-being of the patient, they also create opportunities for domination.[45] The non-interference framework might regard these requirements as non-coercive, as they do not involve direct interference with a woman's decision to terminate her pregnancy. However, these requirements can still place women in a position of dependency on healthcare providers, who hold the power to grant or withhold access to abortion medication.

Philip Pettit's concept of freedom as non-domination, in contrast, would provide a more nuanced understanding of freedom by emphasizing the importance of power relations and the potential for coercion. According to Pettit, freedom as non-domination is the absence of arbitrary interference, where interference is considered arbitrary if it is not subject to the control and consent of the person affected. This framework shifts the focus from merely preventing interference to ensuring that individuals are not subject to the discretionary power of others.

In the context of SMA, the non-domination framework highlights the potential for domination in the doctor-patient relationship, even in the absence of direct interference. For instance, it acknowledges that the requirement for women to obtain a prescription for abortion medication places them in a position of dependency on healthcare providers. While the healthcare provider may not actively interfere with the woman's decision to terminate her pregnancy, the mere fact that they hold the power to grant or deny access to the medication introduces a form of domination. The woman is not free from the arbitrary power of the healthcare provider, as her ability to obtain an abortion is contingent on the provider's will and consent.

---

44 National Department of Health, Republic of South Africa, *National Clinical Guidelines for Implementation of the Choice on Termination of Pregnancy Act*, Ed. 1 (2019). *See also*, Department of Health (South Africa), *Medicines and Related Substances Act, 1965 (Act 101 of 1965): Consolidated Schedules 24 March 2023*, 130 (2023).

45 Note that these requirements are still present in most legislations and policies dealing with self-managed abortions, despite the fact that the combination regimen of mifepristone and misoprostol has been found to be safer than many non-prescription drugs. *See* Ferid Abubeker, et al., *Medical Termination for Pregnancy in Early First Trimester (≤ 63 Days) Using Combination of Mifepristone and Misoprostol or Misoprostol Alone: A Systematic Review*, 20 BMC WOMEN'S HEALTH 142 (2020). The World Health Organization recommends the use of these drugs, which have been part of the WHO List of Essential Medicines since 2005, for medication abortion, *See* World Health Organization, *Abortion Care Guideline*, 68 (2022). *See also*, WHO, *Safe Abortion: Technical and Policy Guidance for Health Systems*, 95 (2012).

In Great Britain, medication abortion up to 24 weeks is permitted.[46] However, additional requirements, such as the certification by two registered medical practitioners that one of the statutory exceptions applies; or the requirement to obtain a prescription still places women in a position of dependency on healthcare providers.[47] The involvement of healthcare providers introduces the potential for domination.

From a non-interference perspective, Great Britain's approach to SMA might be seen as largely successful, as it minimizes direct barriers to access. However, the non-domination framework highlights the subtle forms of coercion that persist, such as the dependency on healthcare providers.

The non-domination framework also draws attention to the broader social and political context in which SMA laws are enacted. In many countries, such as the United States, abortion access is a highly contentious issue, with conservative religious groups exerting significant influence over the legal and regulatory frameworks governing abortion. As previously explained, these groups often engage in religious lawfare tactics to restrict access to abortion services. Even in jurisdictions where SMA is legally permitted, the influence of these groups can result in the imposition of restrictive norms that incorporate additional requirements to access medication abortion, such as mandatory counseling or waiting periods, which only serve to limit reproductive autonomy and reinforce power imbalances.

Pettit's framework allows us to see that freedom is not just about the absence of direct interference, but also about the absence of power relations that enable arbitrary interference. In the case of medication abortion laws, requirements that increase the need to interact with healthcare providers, for instance, coupled with the broader societal pressures and influences surrounding abortion, could create conditions for domination that are not adequately captured by the non-interference framework.

This dynamic can be particularly problematic in countries where access to qualified healthcare providers is limited, such as in rural areas or regions where

---

46 Abortion Act 1967, as amended by the Health and Care Act 2022 (Great Britain), Section 1(1)(b)-(d) (2022). *See also*, National Health Service (Great Britain), What Happens: Abortion (2020), https://www.nhs.uk/conditions/abortion/what-happens/; Royal College of Obstetricians & Gynecologists (Great Britain), *Medical Abortion from 12 weeks of Pregnancy: Summary Sheet* (last accessed 13 Dec. 2024), https://www.rcog.org.uk/media/oz4adqix/4580-rcog-summary-sheet_med-abortion-from-12-wks-v6.pdf.

47 *See* The Prescription Only Medicines (Human Use) Order (Great Britain), Statute No. 1830 (1997); Abortion Act 1967, Sections 1(3), (3B)(a) (1967, amended as of 2022).

many doctors invoke conscientious objection to performing abortions.[48] For example, in Italy, where physicians frequently invoke conscientious objection, entire regions of the country are effectively devoid of legal abortion services, forcing women to seek out unsafe, clandestine methods of terminating their pregnancies.[49] This situation represents a clear example of how the exercise of conscientious objection can lead to domination, as women are left with no viable options for obtaining safe and legal abortion care. In these cases, women may find themselves with no choice but to seek out alternative, potentially unsafe, methods of terminating their pregnancies.[50] The non-interference framework might view the imposition of these requirements as a necessary safeguard, as they do not directly prevent women from obtaining an abortion. However, from a non-domination perspective, these requirements represent a form of coercion, as they place women in a position of dependency and limit their ability to make autonomous decisions.

Moreover, the involvement of healthcare providers in the abortion process can also give rise to other subtle forms of coercion through the exercise of discretionary power. For instance, a healthcare provider who holds personal or religious objections to abortion may subtly dissuade a patient from pursuing

---

48 *See* Tomasso Autorino, et al., *The impact of gynecologists' conscientious objection on abortion access*, 87 SOCIAL SCIENCE RESEARCH 102403 (2020); and Eileen K. Fry-Bowers, *A matter of conscience: Examining the law and policy of conscientious objection in health care*, 21 POLICY, POLIT. NURS. PRACT. 2 (2020) (showing that conscientious objection disproportionally impacts people of low socio-economic status, and those residing in rural or remote areas, leading them to either procure an illegal abortion or continue an unwanted pregnancy).

49 *See* Francesca Minerva, *Conscientious objection, complicity in wrongdoing, and a not-so-moderate approach*, 26 CAMBRIDGE Q. HEALTHCARE ETHICS 1 (2017); Wendy Chavkin, et al., *Regulation of conscientious objection to abortion: An international comparative multiple-case study*, 19 HEALTH & HUM. RTS. J. 1 (2017); and Tomasso Autorino, et al., *The impact of gynecologists' conscientious objection on abortion access*, 87 SOCIAL SCIENCE RESEARCH 102403 (2020). Similar cases have been reported elsewhere, for instance in Uruguay and Zambia. *See* Francisco Coppola, et al., *Conscientious objection as a barrier for implementing voluntary termination of pregnancy in Uruguay: Gynecologists' attitudes and behavior*, 134 INT'L J. GYNAECOLOGY & OBSTETRICS S1 (2016); and Marte E. S. Haaland, et al., *Silent politics and unknown numbers: Rural health bureaucrats and Zambian abortion policy*, 251 SOC. SCI. MED. (2020).

50 Jasmine Meredith Davis, et al., *A narrative literature review of the impact of conscientious objection by health professionals on women's access to abortion worldwide 2013–2021*, 17 GLOB. PUBLIC HEALTH 9 (2022) (noting that a shortage of non-objecting healthcare professionals may make the duty to refer ineffective, as those objecting may struggle to direct patients to providers located within a reasonable distance).

an abortion by emphasizing the risks or suggesting alternatives, such as adoption.[51] Even if the provider ultimately grants the prescription, the patient may feel pressured to reconsider her decision due to the influence of the provider's authority. The non-domination framework is particularly attuned to these dynamics, recognizing that the mere possibility of arbitrary interference can undermine an individual's autonomy.

Even in countries where abortion is legal, but still a highly stigmatized and politicized issue, women who seek abortions may face social ostracism, discrimination, or other repercussions. The fear of such consequences can lead women to self-censor or avoid seeking medical care altogether, opting instead for unsafe, clandestine methods of abortion. The non-interference framework may fail to account for these indirect forms of coercion, as they do not involve direct interference by the state or other individuals. However, the non-domination framework recognizes that these social, religious and cultural pressures can exert a significant influence on a woman's ability to make autonomous choices, effectively limiting her freedom.

For instance, the recent legal challenges to the governmental authorization of mifepristone in the United States, driven by conservative religious groups, have created a climate of legal uncertainty and fear among women seeking abortions.[52] In some states, access to self-managed medication abortion within the formal healthcare system faces several barriers, with mandatory counseling,

---

51 The mere act of objecting may be understood as a mechanism for passing moral judgement on other's actions. *See e.g.*, Angela Harden & Jane Ogden, *Young women's experiences of arranging and having abortions*, 21 SOC. HEALTH & ILLNESS 4 (1999); Sarah Finnie, et al., *The pathway to induced abortion: Women's experiences and general practitioner attitudes*, 32 BMJ SEXUAL & REPROD. HEALTH 1 (2006); and Frances M. Doran & Julie Hornibrook, *Barriers around access to abortion experienced by rural women in New South Wales, Australia*, 16 RURAL AND REMOTE HEALTH 1 (2016) (indicating that patients can experience moral judgement from objecting healthcare professionals, which can be traumatic for patients). *See also*, Sarah Raifman, et al., *Dualities between Tunisian provider beliefs and actions in abortion care*, 26 REPROD. HEALTH MATTERS 52 (2018); and Louise Anne Keogh, et al., *Conscientious objection to abortion, the law and its implementation in Victoria, Australia: Perspectives of abortion service providers*, 20 BMC MED. ETHICS 1 (2019) (showing that some healthcare professionals have imposed moral judgements on patients by trying to convince them not to abort).

52 While the U.S. Supreme Court unanimously rejected the anti-abortion groups' challenge to the availability of mifepristone nationwide, advocates have warned that the Court's ruling on the FDA's authority to regulate the pill was purely on procedural grounds, leaving the issue open for future challenges. *See*, Sheela Ranganathan, Sarah Wetter & Lawrence O. Gostin, *The Supreme Court Did Not Deliver 'Wins' for Reproductive Rights This Term*,

waiting periods, and physical examination requirements imposed on women seeking to terminate their pregnancies.[53] The requirement for women to interact with healthcare providers, coupled with the influence of conservative religious groups in these states, places women in a position of dependency and vulnerability.[54] Even in states with more liberal abortion laws, the fear of legal repercussions or social stigma can lead women to avoid seeking medical care, opting instead for unsafe methods of self-managed abortion.[55]

From a non-domination perspective, the legal and social pressures surrounding SMA in the United States represent a form of coercion that goes beyond direct interference, highlighting the importance of addressing power dynamics and domination in the regulation of abortion.

One key implication of adopting the non-domination framework in this context is the need to ensure that women have access to safe and legal abortion care without being subject to arbitrary interference or domination by healthcare providers, religious groups, or the state. In the case of self-managed medication abortions, this may require revisiting existing laws and policies to reduce or eliminate barriers to accessing medication abortion, such as prescription requirements, mandatory counseling, and waiting periods. Additionally, the non-domination framework suggests that the involvement of healthcare providers in the abortion process should be minimal to prevent the exercise of discretionary power in a way that undermines women's autonomy.

MEDPAGETODAY (July 17, 2024), https://www.medpagetoday.com/opinion/the-health-docket/111132.

53 *See* Cathryn Streifel, *A Patchwork of Access: Self-Managed Medication Abortion in Post-Roe America*, PRB (June 21, 2024), https://www.prb.org/articles/a-patchwork-of-access-self-managed-medication-abortion-in-post-roe-america/. *See also*, Amy Friedrich-Karnik, et al., *Medication Abortion Within and Outside the Formal US Health Care System: What You Need to Know*, Guttmacher (April 2, 2024), https://www.guttmacher.org/2024/02/medication-abortion-within-and-outside-formal-us-health-care-system-what-you-need-know (noting that over half of all US states have laws mandating medically unnecessary barriers that restrict access to medication abortion).

54 *See also*, Laura Florence Harris, et al., *Conscientious objection to abortion provision: Why context matters*, 13 GLOB. PUBLIC HEALTH 5 (2018) (noting that social factors, including stigma may also shape medical practitioners' decision on whether to claim objector status).

55 *See* Lauren Ralph, et al., *Self-Managed Abortion Attempts Before vs After Changes in Federal Abortion Protections in the US*, 7 JAMA NETW. OPEN 7 (2024). *See also*, Nisha Verma & Daniel Grossman, *Self-Managed Abortion in the United States*, 12 CURR. OBSTET. GYNECOL. REP. 2 (2023).

Another important implication is the need to address the broader social and cultural context in which SMA laws operate. Policymakers should recognize that legal and social pressures surrounding abortion can create conditions for domination, even in the absence of direct interference. This may require efforts to reduce the stigma associated with abortion, protect women from social ostracism and discrimination, and ensure that they have access to accurate information and support when making decisions about their reproductive health.

While the non-interference framework may be useful in identifying direct barriers to access, it may inadequately address the subtler forms of coercion that can arise in the doctor-patient relationship and the broader societal context surrounding abortion care. Adopting the non-domination framework as a guiding principle for, in this example, the regulation of SMA, would allow policymakers to better protect reproductive autonomy and ensure that people are free to make decisions about their reproductive health without fear of coercion or domination.

1.2 *Freedom as Non-domination and New Uses of Conscience-Based Claims*

The conventional approach to addressing conscientious objection conflicts has primarily revolved around the concept of freedom from interference. Under this paradigm, the focus has been on ensuring that individuals are not subject to unwanted external constraints that impede their pursuit of personal beliefs and values. However, as the complexities of modern society have given rise to a multitude of conscience-based claims, it has become increasingly evident that the non-interference normative framework falls short in providing effective solutions that balance individual freedoms with the needs of a democratic society. Shifting our perspective towards a freedom as non-domination approach offers a promising alternative that can better account for the complexities inherent to conscientious objection conflicts while preserving the core principles of a democratic society.

While the freedom from interference perspective aims to safeguard personal autonomy, it often leads to a zero-sum game where one individual's rights are pitted against another's, resulting in an arbitrary prioritization of one right over another. The prevailing approach seeks to strike a delicate balance, but it can inadvertently sideline or disregard the broader structural dynamics that come into play to affect agency.

For example, imagine a small rural community where a pharmacist objects to providing contraception based on their conscience. Under the "freedom from interference" paradigm, the pharmacist's refusal may be upheld as an exercise of personal autonomy. However, if this refusal results in the community being unable to access contraception due to the absence of alternative providers, the pharmacist's position could be considered to be one where he has the *power* to interfere with his community's reproductive choices. An individual is regarded as having the *capacity* to interfere with another person when they can limit the dominated party's freedom to choose among a set of options. This can occur through actions such as removing an option from consideration, substituting one option for another, imposing penalties on certain options, providing misleading information about the nature or consequences of the options, or manipulating the dominated party to influence their choice.[56] In this case, the pharmacist has the capacity to remove an option from the dominated party (access contraceptives).

The non-interference paradigm is also subject to additional concerns when used to deal with conscience-based claims. Its reliance on subjective judgments can turn assessing the sincerity of an individual's conscience-based objection a particularly challenging task. This subjectivity can result in inconsistent application and potential abuse. What is worse, conscientious objectors may exploit this subjectivity by invoking their beliefs to justify actions or refusals that may not genuinely align with their convictions, but rather disguise other reasons that should not be tolerated in liberal democracies, such as blunt discrimination or hate speech.

Shifting the normative foundations to a freedom as non-domination approach offers a more robust way for addressing conscientious objection conflicts in liberal democracies, as the non-domination paradigm acknowledges that domination can occur without interference and that interference can take place without domination. As mentioned, domination does not necessarily involve active interference but pertains to the power and capacity to interfere arbitrarily, without obstacles or deterrent costs.[57] It signifies the absence of conditions that subject one individual to the arbitrary will of another. Domination occurs when one party has unchecked, arbitrary authority over another. Domination does not require an actual exercise of interference, but it does necessitate the power to do so in an arbitrary way with no obstacles or deterrent costs. Unlike the traditional paradigm, this approach seeks to

56 *See* Philip Pettit, On the People's Terms 50 (2012); and Philip Pettit, Just Freedom: A Moral Compass for a Complex World 53 (2014).

57 Philip Pettit, Republicanism: A Theory of Freedom and Government (1997).

balance individual autonomy with legitimate authority.[58] It recognizes that the exercise of authority is essential for social order and can coexist with individual autonomy when done in a non-arbitrary manner.[59] The paradigm

58 At its core, the need for the exercise of conscientious objection arises primarily in the context of the tension between norms dictated by the authority vis-à-vis the autonomy of the person who wants to live under the precepts of his or her conscience. Under the non-interference paradigm, these conflicts are framed as a paradox between the notion of authority and its relationship with autonomy. By contrast, when conceptualizing "autonomy" in light of the "freedom as non-domination" paradigm that Pettit proposes, authority and the enjoyment of individual autonomy can indeed coexist. Under this framework, an "autonomous person" is understood as a deliberating person. That is, a person who examines every aspect of his or her moral life, who is responsible for his or her actions, and who takes responsibility for them, while understanding said responsibility as acting in accordance with personal moral decision-making. An autonomous person has a duty to act on the basis of his or her own moral conception of good and evil, reflecting on what is right and what is wrong in each particular course of action. Such a person would be violating the duty to act autonomously if he or she complies with the directives of the authority solely by virtue of their authoritative status. *See* Robert Paul Wolff, In Defense of Anarchism (1970). *See generally Authority*, *in* The Oxford Handbook of Jurisprudence and Philosophy of Law (Jules Coleman & Scott Shapiro eds., 2002); Robert Paul Wolff, *The Conflict between Authority and Autonomy*, *in* Authority (Joseph Raz ed., 1990).

59 Conceptualizing "conscience-based claims" in light of the notion of freedom as non-domination, it could be argued that, as long as the directives of the authority are not arbitrary, nor do they mean or reflect the exercise of domination by the authority, they will not negatively impact people's freedom of conscience. Even if the person considers that the State directive or guideline is wrong, since the authority is legitimate, the guideline must be followed. If the legitimacy of the authority that issued the guideline is assumed, the person who considers the erroneous guideline must obey it. If the person who disagrees with the guideline wants to modify it, they must follow the other regulations in force in the legal system that govern the processes to modify and/or repeal that guideline. In this way, the alleged paradox in the authority–autonomy relationship in regard to conscientious objection is solved, since there is no loss of autonomy as long as the authority is legitimate, and the norm is not arbitrary. And if a citizen or a group of citizens still considers it to be erroneous, they have a series of legal institutions through which they can try to modify the norm. Of course, an objector could counterargue by saying that the authority in these cases is not legitimate and thereby circumvent this solution. In principle, however, a State action should be considered legitimate as long as the people enjoy equal control over the government (equal influence) and as long as the authority manages to impose a social order. *See* Philip Pettit, On the People's Terms 130–86 (2012). "Equal control over the government" is understood as citizens who have: (1) equally accessible influence; (2) unconditional (robust over changes) and effective influence (in the sense of being intuitively sufficient to protect citizens from state domination); and (3) equal ability to influence the government to act according to the will of the citizenry and not according to the interests of an outsider. *See* Philip Pettit, On the People's Terms 166–79 (2012). In this way, under the idea of freedom as non-domination, an

aligns with principles of deliberative democracy, emphasizing the importance of equal participation and reasoned discourse in decision-making. Freedom as non-domination could fundamentally be helpful in reconceptualizing the relationship between individuals and authorities when faced with exercises of conscience-based claims.

Under the freedom as non-domination paradigm, the assessment of conscience-based claims shifts from a binary consideration of interference to a more nuanced evaluation of arbitrary power. It acknowledges that the exercise of conscience-based claims, even when sincere, can become a form of domination if unchecked. This paradigm shift allows for a broader understanding of freedom than the conventional freedom from interference approach. While the latter simply requires the absence of direct coercion or interference, freedom as non-domination recognizes that genuine freedom encompasses more than that. It considers the absence of arbitrary influence or power that can be exerted over an individual's life and choices. In the context conscience-based claims in healthcare, particularly concerning abortion services, the non-domination approach shifts the focus away from simply questioning why healthcare professionals object, and instead emphasizes the context and outcomes of such objections. One primary concern under this framework is the impact these objections have on patients and prospective patients.

Additionally, the non-domination approach duly considers and accounts for the fact that the religious and sociocultural environment significantly shapes the experiences of those seeking abortions, as well as the availability of such services. In some countries, this context is intimately intertwined with abortion stigma, often resulting in a high prevalence of conscientious objectors. For example, research in Croatia revealed how the religious sociocultural context fostered a discourse that controls access to abortion services and

authority is legitimate even if it intervenes in the life and the choices of its citizens, so long as that interference is done in a non-arbitrary way. *See* José Luis Martí, La república deliberativa 42 (2006). *See generally* Amy Gutmann & Dennis Thompson, Democracy and Disagreement (1996); Thomas Christiano, The Rule of the Many 53–55 (1996); Debating Deliberative Democracy 2 (James Fishkin & Peter Laslett, eds., 2003); Joshua Cohen, *Deliberation and Democratic Legitimacy*, *in* The Good Polity: Normative Analysis of the State 17–21 (Alan Hamlin & Philip Pettit, eds., 1989); Bernard Manin, *On Legitimacy and Political Deliberation*, 15 Pol. Theory 352–53 (1987); David Estlund, *"Who's Afraid of Deliberative Democracy? On the Strategic/Deliberative Dichotomy in Recent Constitutional Jurisprudence,"* 71 Texas L. Rev., 1437–77 (1993). Balancing autonomy with non-domination allows for a more nuanced evaluation of these situations.

information, by legitimizing and normalizing conscientious objection.[60] The non-domination framework also acknowledges that the mere act of a healthcare professional objecting to provide an abortion could influence a patient's decision, potentially due to the inherent power imbalance, the specialized knowledge of healthcare providers, and the societal authority vested in them.[61]

As such, the non-domination approach calls attention to the gendered nature of conscientious objection, highlighting how it reflects and reinforces the unequal power dynamics faced by women and pregnant individuals in patriarchal societies. This perspective recognizes conscientious objection as a mechanism of control that perpetuates the marginalization of those who can become pregnant, often excluding them from critical decision-making processes and stripping them of power and influence.[62]

In essence, the non-domination paradigm not only broadens our understanding of freedom but also provides a critical lens to examine how conscience-based objections, particularly in healthcare, can perpetuate systemic inequalities and control, thereby impacting the autonomy and well-being of those seeking services like abortion.

The freedom as non-domination paradigm proves to be superior to the traditional freedom from interference paradigm when addressing new uses of conscience-based claims, particularly in cases where these claims are employed as part of a religious lawfare strategy by conservative religious groups. While the freedom from interference paradigm tends to view rights as absolute, often leading to a clash of rights with little room for compromise, the freedom as non-domination paradigm recognizes that rights must be balanced with other legitimate interests, such as preventing harm or discrimination.[63] This balance is crucial in cases where conscience-based claims intersect with other rights, such as reproductive rights or LGBTQ rights. This framework acknowledges that the unrestricted exercise of conscience-based claims can lead to harm or discrimination against certain groups. Balancing these claims with the prevention of harm becomes essential in situations where conservative religious

---

60 Dubravka Håkansson, et al., *Navigating the minefield: Women's experiences of abortion in a Country with a conscience clause—The case of Croatia*, 22 J. Int'l Women's Studies 1 (2021).

61 *See* Arianne Shahvisi, *Conscientious objection: A morally insupportable misuse of authority*, 13 Clinical Ethics 2 (2018).

62 *See generally*, Bernard M. Dickens, *The right to conscience*, *in* Abortion Law in Transnational Perspective (Rebecca J. Cook, Joanna N. Erdman & Bernard M. Dickens, eds., 2014), 210–238.

63 *See* Jonathan A. Hughes, *Conscientious objection in healthcare: Why tribunals might be the answer*, 43 J. Med. Ethics 4 (2017).

groups rely on conscience-based claims as lawfare tactics to advance their agendas.

Unlike the freedom from interference paradigm, which often results in a winner-takes-all approach, the freedom as non-domination paradigm encourages deliberation and dialogue. In cases involving conscience-based claims, this allows for a more nuanced understanding of differing perspectives and fosters a spirit of cooperation rather than confrontation. In the context of religious lawfare, where opposing sides may be deeply entrenched, fostering dialogue through deliberation can lead to cooperative solutions that respect the dignity and autonomy of all parties involved. One of the primary goals of the freedom as non-domination paradigm is to move away from the adversarial notion of rights' warfare. Instead of viewing rights as weapons to be wielded against others, this paradigm encourages a climate where diverse worldviews can coexist with reduced hostility and threat.

In pluralistic societies characterized by diversity in beliefs and values, the freedom as non-domination paradigm promotes pluralism. It allows for the coexistence of various worldviews and beliefs without one group imposing its values on others, which is essential for maintaining social harmony.

Moreover, shifting to the freedom as non-domination paradigm prompts a fundamental reevaluation of conscience-based claims. Rather than treating them as absolute exercises of personal autonomy, this framework calls for a balanced assessment of the potential for domination and harm to others. In healthcare settings, conscientious objection to providing certain medical procedures, such as abortion, is evaluated not solely on the basis of personal beliefs but on the potential for harm or domination over patients seeking care and over prospective patients. This paradigm shift would encourage a consideration of the broader societal impacts and outcomes of these objections.

Furthermore, the freedom as non-domination paradigm aligns closely with democratic values, particularly the principles of equal influence and the prevention of arbitrary power. It safeguards democratic institutions from being manipulated or dominated by powerful interest groups through religious lawfare tactics. As mentioned before, conservative religious groups engaging in religious lawfare strategies often wield significant influence and power. The freedom as non-domination paradigm provides a safeguard against the domination of minoritarian (quantitively speaking), but powerful, voices and ensures that the rights and interests of marginalized communities are not ignored or trampled upon, thus balancing power dynamics.

This framework also aligns with principles of legitimacy and democracy. It views the legitimacy of authority as a matter of degree, depending on the extent to which citizens have equal control over the government and the degree of arbitrariness in government actions. In this sense, it acknowledges that no government can fully eliminate domination, but the goal is to minimize it. As such, deliberative democracy—a theory that seeks to involve all members of society in decision-making—aligns with this perspective. It assumes the equality of conditions and non-self-interested preferences, promoting reasoned discourse as a means to make political decisions. The deliberative approach complements freedom as non-domination by ensuring that power is exercised non-arbitrarily, contributing to the prevention of domination.

By emphasizing the prevention of domination and the promotion of tolerance and cooperation, the freedom as non-domination paradigm contributes to long-term stability within societies. It mitigates the risk of prolonged legal battles and social conflicts. It facilitates the prevention or resolution of conscience-based conflicts in a manner that respects the rights and dignity of all parties involved, leading to more sustainable and just outcomes. The freedom as non-domination paradigm recognizes that achieving a society entirely free from domination is an ideal, and such an ideal may be challenging to fully realize. However, it acknowledges that the legitimacy of authority and the control citizens have over it are matters of degree. In practice, this means that conscientious objections may, in fact, be considered legitimate in situations where the authority's actions are deemed less legitimate or non-arbitrary. While not an all-encompassing solution, it provides a framework for evaluating objections within a broader context that is able to capture subtler forms of coercion.

In the end, the non-domination paradigm helps liberal democracies avoid extreme positions. While respecting individual conscience-based claims, it also ensures that these claims do not lead to extreme outcomes, such as the denial of essential healthcare, discrimination, or undue harm to vulnerable groups. This balanced approach contributes to the overall stability of a democratic society. The paradigm emphasizes the need to balance competing rights and interests within a democratic framework. It acknowledges that individuals may have sincerely held beliefs but also requires those beliefs not to dominate or harm others' rights. This encourages a more nuanced approach to resolving conflicts between conscience-based claims and other human rights, fostering a sense of equilibrium among competing values. By adopting this paradigm, liberal democracies would actively promote pluralism and inclusivity. It sends a message that diverse beliefs and values can coexist within society as long as they do not dominate or harm others. This can help create a more harmonious and inclusive social environment. Liberal democracies often face evolving societal values and norms. The freedom as non-domination paradigm allows for adaptation to these changes while maintaining a commitment to protecting human rights. It acknowledges that what may have been acceptable as a conscientious objection in the past may need reassessment in light of evolving values.

The freedom as non-domination paradigm offers a more robust normative basis to proposals that strive to deal with new uses of conscience-based claims in healthcare settings, particularly when it comes to reproductive health. Its emphasis on preventing arbitrary authority, fostering deliberation, and respecting individual autonomy makes it better equipped to address the complex and contentious issues that arise in such cases. Allowing unrestricted and unchecked exercise of conscience-based claims in healthcare settings exacerbates scenarios of systemic domination, where rules operate to favor some participants, like conservative religious actors, over others. This situation may be further compounded by additional forms of domination, such as those grounded in the uneven distribution of power in society, where some individuals have more influence over norms and can more effectively challenge them. Shifting to a freedom as non-domination paradigm helps identify these subtler forms of compounded domination. In countries where legal and political frameworks are not overtly exclusionary but where social norms and culture prevent women, for instance, from enjoying reproductive autonomy and being viewed as equal members of society instances of domination are still present.

2 A Path Forward for Conscience-Based Claims and for Liberal Democracies

This shift to the freedom as non-domination paradigm offers a novel approach to addressing conscience-based claims that avoids the pitfalls of the freedom from interference paradigm. Under this normative framework, judges, policymakers, and society at large have a clearer and more solid new path to navigate tensions and conflicts more effectively while preserving the core tenets of a democratic society. By recognizing that autonomy and authority can coexist when exercised in a non-arbitrary manner, society moves away from the zero-sum approach that often pits one right against another. Instead, a nuanced understanding of freedom and legitimacy is fostered, one that promotes tolerance, pluralism, and a cooperative coexistence of diverse worldviews. This paradigm shift provides a promising avenue for fostering dialogue and consensus in today's complex, pluralistic societies, in the hopes of ultimately leading to more just, solidary, and compassionate communities.

To be sure, a more robust normative basis to deal with conscience-based claims in liberal democracies is a necessary, but not a sufficient condition for achieving the goal of strengthening democracies. While shifting from the freedom from interference paradigm to the freedom as non-domination paradigm holds promise in strengthening the foundations of proposals to address conscientious objection conflicts in liberal democracies, it is only fair to acknowledge that its practical implementation within legal frameworks worldwide presents feasibility challenges.

At its core, this paradigm hinges on the nuanced evaluation of what qualifies as an "arbitrary" intervention, a judgment often steeped in subjectivity and contextual nuances. Determining what is non-arbitrary can be an intricate and contentious process, demanding careful consideration of individual cases. Moreover, ensuring the consistent application of this paradigm across diverse cases and jurisdictions poses its own set of challenges. Legal systems worldwide strive to provide clear guidelines and establish precedents to maintain predictability in outcomes, but achieving this harmony in the context of the freedom as non-domination paradigm may be demanding.

In addition to these practical challenges, the transition to this new normative framework and understanding may encounter resistance from established legal frameworks and deeply ingrained cultural norms. Various stakeholders, including religious groups themselves, could resist such a fundamental shift in the understanding of conscientious objection. Resistance may emerge due to concerns about the impact on religious freedom or fear of destabilizing a prevailing status quo that is favorable to powerful groups.

One of the most significant challenges to implementing Pettit's framework is precisely the likelihood that religious activists will resist yielding or compromising on political uses of conscience-based claims, particularly when they perceive these claims as essential to their religious identity and community standing. The fear of excommunication or ostracism can drive activists to pursue aggressive strategies that have been effective over the past few years, even when these strategies lead to broader social conflict. In fact, the success of religious lawfare strategies has, in many cases, reinforced and invigorated the power and influence of religious groups, allowing them to continue to impose their moral and ethical standards on society at large. However, these victories have not come without costs. The aggressive pursuit of legal exemptions, as argued before, has led to the erosion of democratic principles and undermined the rule of law. Moreover, these religious lawfare strategies have exacerbated societal divisions, pitting religious groups against secular institutions and other religious or non-religious groups with differing beliefs.

To answer to this, Pettit's model offers some insights that could be translated into how religious activists might be incentivized to adopt less aggressive strategies. First of all, adopting Pettit's approach would require a redefinition of religious freedom as a right that must be balanced against the potential for domination, incorporating due consideration for the broader context, putting a greater emphasis on mutual accountability, and highlighting subtler forms of coercion. Furthermore, Pettit's emphasis on institutional arrangements that facilitate contestation and compromise could foster dialogue and encourage conflicting parties to find common ground. Naturally, the state has a big role to play as a mediator and protector of freedom as non-domination, preventing religious groups from using legal strategies that impose their will on others arbitrarily. In dealing with religious lawfare, the state would need to consider not only the specific legal cases brought by religious activists but also the underlying social, economic, and political structures that enable these cases to arise. This might involve reforms to the legal system, changes to public policy, and efforts to address the social inequalities that often underpin conflicts over religious freedom.

The practical application of Philip Pettit's concept of freedom as non-domination in courts and legislatures would necessarily demand a rethinking of how conscience-based claims, particularly those rooted in religious beliefs, are addressed. In some cases, implementing this approach would require changes in legal reasoning, legislative frameworks, and the broader culture of rights and freedoms.

Courts would adopt a more rigorous standard of review to determine whether conscience-based claims are being used to exercise arbitrary power. This would involve examining the power dynamics at play, the potential for harm, and the extent to which the claimed right might undermine the freedom of others. Courts would increasingly frame religious freedom within the context of the public interest, emphasizing that individual or group rights must be reconciled with the broader public interest. This might involve a more nuanced analysis of how religious claims intersect with issues of public welfare, equality, and social cohesion.

In fact, the 2021 Mexican Supreme Court's decision, described in Chapter 5, urging the Congress of the Union to "regulate it urgently and as a priority" and outlining the different limits the legislation could or should have, reflects a nuanced approach to the issue of conscience-based claims that seem to incorporate some of the concerns that a non-domination approach aims to address.[64]

In addition to the principles the Court outlined throughout its judgment as necessary limits to conscientious objection and in line with current legal standards at the regional and international human rights level, the Mexican

64 Supreme Court of Justice, acción de inconstitucionalidad 54/2018, Sept. 21, 2021 (Mex.), M.P., Luis María Aguilar Morales, ¶ 504.

Supreme Court considered that the legislation *could* or *should* clearly specify "the medical or nursing staff that will be empowered to exercise the right to conscientious objection in the institutions of the National Health System, taking into account that this right should be limited to the staff that directly participate in the required health procedure," in order to avoid unjustified expansion of this right;[65] "establish a short term to assert conscientious objection" to avoid abusive or opportunistic uses of conscience-based claims;[66] "consider that the person or authority who is responsible for deciding on the admissibility of the conscientious objection must do so within a short period of time, on the understanding that, if they do not rule on their admissibility, it will be understood that the denial of service is operating" to prevent unduly delays;[67] "consider that conscientious objection cannot be invoked by medical and nursing staff when its exercise puts the life of the patient at risk, when it is a medical emergency or when its exercise implies a disproportionate burden on patients."[68]

In this sense, the Mexican Supreme Court considered that the regulation could include the impossibility of exercising conscientious objection when:[69] (i) the denial or postponement of the service involves a risk to health or an aggravation of this risk; (ii) the denial or postponement of the service may cause damage, aggravate damage, or produce consequences or disabilities; (iii) the refusal of the service results in prolonging the suffering of the patient by the delay in the provision of medical care, or results in a disproportionate burden on the patient; and (iv) when there is no viable and accessible alternative to provide the required health service to the patient in conditions of quality and timeliness (for reasons of distance, lack of availability of non-objecting personnel, or some other inconvenience).

While not explicitly mentioning it, a freedom as non-domination approach seems to lie beneath the Court's reasoning, ensuring that patients are not left vulnerable to delays, establishing mechanisms aimed at protecting individuals from being subject to arbitrary decisions that could undermine their well-being, and addressing potential abuses to ultimately mitigate instances or opportunities for domination. Naturally, explicit references to the freedom as non-domination framework could have strengthened the court's decision and provided a more robust justification for the proposed regulations. But this case

65 *Id.*, ¶ 507.
66 *Id.*, ¶ 508.
67 *Id.*, ¶ 509.
68 *Id.*, ¶ 510.
69 *Id.*, ¶ 512–15.

illustrates that the paradigmatic shift advocated in this chapter has already started to permeate some of the discussions surrounding conscience-based claims in healthcare.

Legislatures, for its part, would be tasked with revising existing laws that grant broad leeway to conscience-based claims to ensure they align with the principle of non-domination. For instance, legislatures could amend laws to narrow the scope of exemptions, add sunset clauses that require periodic review, or ensure that any exemptions granted are accompanied by safeguards that prevent their abuse. Legislators might also introduce new laws that explicitly incorporate the concept of non-domination, providing a clear legal standard for courts to apply in conscience-based claims cases. When drafting new legislation, lawmakers would need to consider the potential for laws to either prevent or perpetuate domination. In some cases, this could involve impact assessments that evaluate how proposed laws might affect different groups differently, particularly those at risk of being dominated. Legislatures might establish or strengthen committees tasked with evaluating conscience-based matters, ensuring that a wide range of perspectives are considered. These bodies could include representatives from religious groups, secular organizations, and marginalized communities, fostering dialogue and encouraging compromise. The goal would be to create a more inclusive legislative process that mitigates potential domination. States could also create mechanisms to hold religious groups accountable for the broader social impact of their legal claims. This could involve requiring periodic reporting on the effects of conscience-based exemptions, conducting audits of how exemptions are being applied in specific matters or regions, and facilitating public challenges to laws or policies that appear to disproportionately favor certain religious groups at the expense of others.

Despite these challenges, the benefits of transitioning from the freedom from interference paradigm to the freedom as non-domination paradigm in addressing conscience-based claims in liberal democracies appear to outweigh the hurdles posed by practical implementation within legal frameworks around the world.

The benefits of embracing the freedom as non-domination paradigm for evaluating conscientious objection conflicts are substantial. Its philosophical foundation, firmly rooted in theories of freedom and democratic legitimacy, offers a principled and coherent framework for guiding legal deliberations in a manner that respects individual conscience while upholding societal values and interests. In striving for this paradigm shift, liberal democracies may ultimately strike a balance that fosters a more inclusive, equitable, and just society for all.

This paradigm aligns seamlessly with the fundamental principles of democratic societies, chief among them being the notion of equal control over government and the prevention of arbitrary exercise of power. As such, it not only respects but actively promotes the core tenets of democratic governance and pluralism. In democratic systems, the emphasis on citizens' shared authority and the protection against arbitrary power imposition is paramount. By adopting the freedom as non-domination paradigm, societies can manifest their commitment to these principles and demonstrate their dedication to safeguarding the rights and freedoms of all citizens, irrespective of their beliefs or values.

Moreover, the attractiveness of this framework lies in its adaptability and flexibility. It possesses the capacity to accommodate a wide spectrum of conscientious objection scenarios, spanning various domains, from the contentious realms of healthcare to the intricate landscape of education and a wide array of other industries. Its applicability extends beyond religious or moral disputes, encompassing all conscientious objections that may arise within a diverse and pluralistic society. This adaptability ensures that the paradigm can serve as a robust tool for addressing contemporary challenges and evolving societal needs, making it an invaluable addition to the arsenal of legal frameworks.

It becomes self-evident, then, that any effort to transition to this paradigm would require a thoughtful and nuanced process. To successfully embark on this transition, societies must consider a series of strategic steps for its adoption. Any serious effort to adopt this new paradigm would require a deliberate and gradual shift away from the established freedom from interference paradigm to the freedom as non-domination paradigm within legal systems. A gradual transition would permit a methodical, step-by-step adaptation of existing laws and regulations. In doing so, it would ensure a smooth integration of the new framework into the legal landscape, minimizing disruptions and facilitating a harmonious coexistence of both paradigms. Developing comprehensive legal guidance and precedents that interpret the freedom as non-domination framework in practical terms would be another crucial step. This action would enhance the much-needed consistency and predictability in legal decision-making. It would provide clear directives to judges, lawyers, and other stakeholders, facilitating a shared understanding of how the new paradigm should be applied in various conscientious objection scenarios. Furthermore, public education campaigns and meaningful engagement with stakeholders would play a pivotal role in this transition. These initiatives would serve to build acceptance and understanding of the freedom as non-domination paradigm among the general public. Additionally, engaging in a constructive dialogue with relevant groups would be of utmost importance. This dialogue would allow for the identification and addressing of concerns that may arise during the transition, ultimately fostering cooperation and mutual respect between all parties involved. To ensure the effective application of the freedom as non-domination paradigm in legal proceedings, training judges, lawyers, and legal scholars in its nuances would be crucial. This would ensure that those responsible for interpreting and applying the framework possess the requisite knowledge and skills to do so effectively and fairly. Lastly, regular monitoring and evaluation of the paradigm's implementation would be essential components of a successful transition. This ongoing assessment would help identify challenges and areas for improvement within the legal frameworks, leading to necessary refinements and adaptations.

While the practical implementation of the freedom as non-domination paradigm within legal frameworks may pose substantial challenges, its alignment with democratic principles, adaptability across diverse domains, and promotion of tolerance and cooperative coexistence underscore its potential as a transformative force. Embracing this paradigm in conscientious objection conflicts offers the promise of achieving a harmonious balance between individual rights and societal interests, embodying the very essence of democratic societies. In doing so, liberal democracies can take a significant stride toward fostering a more inclusive, equitable, and just society for all their citizens. Overcoming the challenges will require careful legal drafting, public engagement, and cooperation among stakeholders to ensure a smoother transition and the realization of its potential benefits in fostering tolerance and pluralism within societies.

3 Conclusion

In conclusion, the paradigm shift from "freedom from interference" to "freedom as non-domination" offers a promising path forward for liberal democracies grappling with the complexities of conscience-based claims and strengthening the normative foundations of existing proposals on how to deal with new uses of conscience-based claims. While challenges will lie ahead, the potential benefits of this shift—enhanced pluralism, reduced conflicts, and a more inclusive democratic discourse—underscore its significance.

Reconceptualizing the evaluation of conscience-based claims in terms of arbitrary exercises of power offer liberal democracies tools to better balance individual rights with societal interests. This paradigm shift aligns with the principles of deliberative democracy and promotes a culture of reasoned discourse, fostering social cohesion and mutual respect, while addressing the root causes of rights conflicts and offering a framework for resolution that reduces the prevalence of rights warfare. Thus, minimizing the use of rights as weapons in ideological battles.

In embracing the freedom as non-domination paradigm, liberal democracies can navigate the complex terrain of conscience-based claims with greater sensitivity, fairness, and respect for the principles of human rights, dignity and autonomy. This paradigm shift holds the potential to strengthen the foundations of democracy itself, ensuring that the protection of conscience-based claims aligns with the broader values of liberal societies.

This chapter embarked on a comprehensive exploration of a paradigmatic shift in the way societies conceptualize and address conscience-based claims, particularly in the context of contemporary challenges posed by political uses of these claims, often associated with religious lawfare strategies. The transition from a "freedom from interference" paradigm to a "freedom as non-domination" paradigm represents a profound reimagining of fundamental principles that underpin democratic societies, individual rights, and the role of the state. As this discussion concludes, it becomes evident that this shift carries far-reaching implications for legal frameworks, human rights, and the future of liberal democracies.

Certainly, it has become clear that for the transition to the "freedom as non-domination" paradigm to break the walls of a mere theoretical exercise would demand a profound reevaluation of the legal systems in liberal democracies. While the path forward is loaded with challenges, it is also illuminated by the promise of a more just and inclusive society. Embracing this paradigm shift requires a commitment to democratic values, ongoing dialogue, and a willingness to evolve legal, political, and social systems to better protect autonomy, societal interests and prevent domination. In the face of the antidemocratic threat posed by religious lawfare and political uses of conscience-based claims, the "freedom as non-domination" paradigm offers a beacon of hope for the future of liberal democracies and the preservation of human rights in an ever-evolving world.

Conclusion

In the journey through the intricate intersections of religion, politics, and law, this book has examined the phenomenon of religious lawfare, with a focus on the use of conscience-based claims to shape public policy and law within liberal democracies. The book traced the historical, sociological, and legal dimensions of this issue, delving into the rise of conservative religious groups, their strategies to challenge secularism, and the resulting threats to democracy and human rights. Moreover, the book critically analyzed existing legal responses and proposed solutions to mitigate the impact of religious lawfare.

The book identifies, categorizes, and clarifies different conscience-based claims, including political uses of conscience-based claims. By categorizing cases across vertical, horizontal, and depth axes, the book not only contributed to ongoing research but also unveiled the complexities brought about by this deliberate expansion, orchestrated by conservative religious groups seeking to reclaim lost power. In turn, the shift in perspective advocated throughout the book moves from exploring this expansion as an independent and siloed issue to viewing it as part of a larger context.

The expansion of conscience-based claims represents not just a legal challenge, but a profound contestation of the foundational values that underpin the modern democratic state. The demise of cosmopolitanism and the ascent of conservative religious groups have brought to the fore a clash between competing visions of society and governance. The backdrop of right-wing populism and the rise of assertive multiculturalism has set the stage for religious lawfare to flourish. The book has explored how these groups exploit the very tools meant to protect minority rights to advance their own conservative agendas, effectively utilizing conscience-based claims as a means to theocratize secular societies.

The analysis that permeates throughout the chapters has dissected the intricate web of how conscience-based claims serve as potent tools for theocratization. These claims, originally intended to protect individual religious liberties and minority rights, have been weaponized to suppress the rights of others and to reassert values that align with the agendas of conservative religious groups. This transformation has profound implications for the delicate balance between freedom of conscience, religion and beliefs, and the preservation of democracy, as it results in an erosion of the wall between church and state.

The exercise of political uses of conscience-based claims, those used to obstruct the recognition and enjoyment of rights, undermines the democratic process. Instead of functioning as a shield for minorities, these claims serve as

 | DOI:10.1163/9789004685406_009

a veto power that permits a select group to stifle the collective choices made by a democratic society. As such, they challenge the legitimacy of democratic decision-making and endanger the very principles that democracy seeks to uphold.

The first half of the book painted a somber picture of the future of democracies and fundamental rights. The second half pivots to a legal claim, examining the limitations imposed by regional and international human rights standards to counter this expansion of conscience-based claims. The pivotal "can" question drives the exploration of whether existing legal standards can effectively prevent, mitigate, and control the harmful impacts of political uses of conscience-based claims.

While international human rights frameworks and regional systems have attempted to offer safeguards against the abuse of conscience-based claims, the effectiveness of these efforts has been limited. Similarly, various scholarly proposals that aimed to address the issue have often failed to adequately consider the complexity and nuance surrounding conscience-based claims and their potential implications. The expansion's harmful and largely undemocratic consequences call for strict regulation. However, while relying on existing legal standards seems to offer a solution, the book argues for a more foundational and paradigmatic change to align this expansion with ongoing secularization processes.

A novel normative framework for addressing the challenges posed by religious lawfare could help mitigate this threat. Shifting from a perspective of freedom from interference to one of freedom as non-domination, the book proposes a nuanced approach that seeks to balance competing rights and values. This framework encourages dialogue, promotes an inclusive understanding of the human good, and mitigates the risk of excessive judicialization. By adopting this approach, liberal democracies can steer away from the hostile terrain marked by religious lawfare and towards a more harmonious coexistence of diverse perspectives.

Central to this proposed paradigm shift is the reframing of conscience-based claims from a perspective of freedom from interference to one of freedom as non-domination. Traditional interpretations of conscience rights often center on the idea of shielding individuals or groups from external coercion or interference. However, the expansion of these claims to obstruct the rights of others challenges this conception.

By reimagining conscience-based claims under a freedom from domination framework, the book emphasizes the importance of ensuring that the exercise of one person's rights does not infringe upon the dignity of others. This shift places a premium on mutual respect, dialogue, and the equitable balancing of competing interests. Rather than treating conscience-based claims as absolute and unassailable, this approach invites a broader conversation about the limits of rights and the responsibilities that accompany their exercise.

At the heart of the proposed paradigm shift is the recognition that a healthy democracy thrives on the exchange of ideas, respectful discourse, and deliberative processes. Adopting a framework that prioritizes freedom as non-domination can encourage conversations that bridge ideological divides.

The phenomenon of religious lawfare and the expansion of conscience-based claims challenge the very foundations of liberal democracies. This book illuminated the complex interplay between religious beliefs, political agendas, and legal rights, urging us to reassess our approaches and responses. The struggle between competing visions of society will persist, but the knowledge and insights presented here can serve as a guiding light for policymakers, scholars, activists, and citizens alike. It is imperative that liberal democracies continue to evolve, adapting their frameworks to address the evolving nature of religious lawfare while safeguarding the principles that uphold the democratic project.

As the world navigates uncertain and changing waters, the hope is that the challenges and lessons discussed in this book will continue to resonate and shape the ongoing dialogue about the role of religion, and conscience in our societies.

In the end, this is a tale of tension, transformation, and possibility. It is a call to action, a reminder that the choices we make today will shape the future of our shared world. Moving forward, the principles of democracy, human rights, and a sincere respect for the diverse tapestry of beliefs that enrich societies should be a guiding beacon. Only through such a collective commitment can the complexities of religious lawfare be addressed, laying the foundation for a future that upholds these cherished fundamental values.

The insights gained from the exploration into the intricate dynamics of religious lawfare and its implications for liberal democracies open the door to a multitude of future research directions and intellectual inquiries. The journey through the pages of this book has unearthed important questions, challenged established notions, and highlighted the need for further investigation.

While this book has provided a thorough examination of the use of conscience-based claims in religious lawfare, further research could delve into the ways in which courts, legal scholars, and policymakers grapple with the challenges of accommodating the proposed paradigm shift into evolving legal doctrines. The proposed paradigm shift has implications beyond the legal realm, extending to the shaping of public policy and legislation. As policymakers confront the complexities of religious lawfare, they can draw on the principles of freedom as non-domination to inform their decision-making processes.

This approach encourages policy formulation that takes into account the potential impact on all citizens, without granting unchecked power to any particular group.

Future research can explore ways in which democratic institutions adapt their mechanisms for public consultation, debate, and decision-making to align with the values of freedom as non-domination, contributing to a deeper understanding of how this normative approach translates into practical governance.

Contemplating the potential of the proposed paradigm shift requires recognizing that its realization will demand a collective effort from scholars, policymakers, activists, and citizens. Implementing a framework that prioritizes freedom as non-domination represents a departure from established norms and systems, and its success hinges on a commitment to democratic principles, inclusivity, and the recognition of the inherent dignity of all individuals.

The journey towards mitigating the impact of religious lawfare through this paradigm shift is undoubtedly a complex and challenging one. Yet, it is a journey that holds the promise of fostering a more equitable and just society—one in which the exercise of rights is guided by a spirit of mutual respect and a commitment to democratic ideals.

Table of Cases

International Tribunals and Bodies

German-Venezuelan Commission, *Bischoff* case, Decision (1903), 10 U.N.R.I.A.A. (RLA-138).

Philip Morris Brands Sàrl et al v Oriental Republic of Uruguay, ICSID Case No ARB/10/7 (2016).

UNCITRAL, *Chemtura Corporation v. Government of Canada*, (RLA-053).

UNCITRAL, *Methanex Corporation v. United States of America*, (RLA-164).

Urbaser S.A. and Consorcio de Aguas Bilbao Bizkaia, Bilbao Bizkaia ur Partzuergoa v. Argentina, ICSID Case No. ARB/07/26 (2016).

United Nations Human Rights Treaty Bodies

Human Rights Committee

U.N. Human Rights Committee, Communication No. 1608/2007 (*L.M.R. v. Argentina*), U.N. Doc. CCPR/C/101/D/1608/2007 (Apr. 28, 2011).

Committee on the Elimination of Discrimination against Women

Alyne da Silva Pimentel v. Brazil (CEDAW Committee) (2011), Communication No. 17/2008, CEDAW/C/49/D/17/2008.

Regional Human Rights Courts and Bodies

Inter-American System

Inter-American Commission of Human Rights

Inter.-Am. Comm'n. H.R., Report No. 21/07, *Petition 161–02: Friendly Settlement*, Paulina del Carmen Ramírez Jacinto v. Mexico (Mar. 9, 2007).

Inter.-Am. Comm'n. H.R., Report No. 43/05, *Case 12.219, Merits*, Cristián Daniel Sahli Vera et al. v. Chile (Mar. 10, 2005).

Inter.-Am. Comm'n. H.R., Report No. 97/05, *Petition 14/04, Friendly Settlement*, Alfredo Díaz Bustos v. Bolivia (Oct. 27, 2005).

Inter-American Court of Human Rights

Albán Cornejo et al v. Ecuador, Merits, Reparations and Costs, Inter-Am. Ct. H.R. (Ser. C) No. 171 (Nov. 22, 2007).

Artavia Murillo v. Costa Rica, Preliminary Objections, Merits, Reparations, and Costs, Inter-Am. Ct. H.R. (Ser. C) No. 85/10 (Nov. 28, 2012).

Cuscul Pivaral and Others v. Guatemala, Preliminary Objections, Merits, Reparations and Costs, Inter-Am. Ct. H.R. (ser. C) No. 359 (Aug. 23, 2018).

Lagos del Campos v. Peru, Preliminary Objections, Merits, Reparations, and Costs, Inter-Am. Ct. H.R. (ser. C) No. 340 (Aug. 31, 2017).

Poblete Vilches et al. v. Chile, Merits, Reparations and Costs, Inter-Am. Ct. H.R. (ser. C) No. 349 (March 8, 2018).

Manuela et al. v. El Salvador, Preliminary Objections, Merits, Reparations, and Costs, Inter-Am. Ct. H. R. (ser. C) No. 441 (Nov. 2, 2021).

European System

European Committee of Social Rights

European Committee of Social Rights [ECSR], Complaint No. 140/2016, *Confederazione Generale Italiana del Lavoro (CGIL) v. Italy* (2016).

European Committee of Social Rights [ECSR], Complaint No. 87/2012 *International Planned Parenthood Federation European Network (IPPF-EN) v. Italy* (2014).

European Committee of Social Rights [ECSR], Complaint No. 99/2013, *Federation of Catholic Families of Europe (FAFCE) v. Sweden* (2015).

European Court of Human Rights

A. B. and C. v. Ireland, App. No. 25579/05, Eur. Ct. H. R. (2010).

Bayatyan v. Armenia, App. No. 23459/03, Eur. Ct. H. R. (2011).

D.H. v. Czech Republic, App. No. 57325/00, Eur. Ct. H. R. (2007).

Dogru v. France, App. No. 27058/05, Eur. Ct. H. R. (2008).

Dudgeon v. UK, App. No. 7525/76, Eur. Ct. H. R. (1981).

Evans v. United Kingdom, App. No. 6339/05, Eur. Ct. H. R. (2007).

Eweida v. United Kingdom, App. Nos. 48420/10, 59842/10, 51671/10 and 36516/10 Eur. Ct. H.R. (2013).

Grimmark v. Sweden, App. No. 43726/17, Eur. Ct. H. R. (2020).

Jehovah's Witnesses of Moscow and Others v. Russia, App. No. 302/02, Eur. Ct. H. R. (2010).

Lautsi and Others v. Italy, App. No. 30814/06, Eur. Ct. H.R. (2011).

P. and S. v. Poland, App. No. 57375/08, Eur. Ct. H.R. (2013).

Pichon and Sajous v. France, App. No. 49853/99, Eur. Ct. H.R. (2001).

Pretty v. UK, App. No. 2346/02, Eur. Ct. H.R. (2002).

R.R. v. Poland, App. No. 27617/04, Eur. Ct. H.R. (2011).

Savda v. Turkey, App. No. 42730/05, Eur. Ct. H.R. (2012).

Steen v. Sweden, App. No. 62309/17, Eur. Ct. H. R. (2020).

Sunday Times v. UK, App. No. 6538/74, Eur. Ct. H.R. (1979).

Domestic Court Judgments

Australia

Christian Youth Camps (CYC) v. Cobaw Community Health Services, [2014] VSCA 75.

Canada

Eadie v. Riverbend Bed and Breakfast 2012 BCHRT 247.
Christian Med. & Dental Soc'y of Canada v. Coll. of Physicians and Surgeons of Ontario (2019), 147 O.R. 3d 393 (Can. Ont. C.A.).
Syndicat Northcrest v. Amselem 2 SCR 551 [50] (2004).

Chile

Constitutional Court, *decision No. 3725*, Aug. 28, 2017.

Colombia

Constitutional Court, *Decision SU108-16*, March 3, 2016.
Constitutional Court, *Decision T-388/09*, May 28, 2009.
Constitutional Court, *Judgment SU096/18*, Oct. 17, 2018.

Ecuador

Constitutional Court, *Decision No. 34–19*, April 28, 2021.

France

Conseil constitutionnel [CC] [Constitutional Council] *decision no. 2013-353 QPC*, Oct. 18, 2013, Rec. 1000.

Hungary

Alkotmánybíróság [AB] [Constitutional Court] Mar. 25, 2010, No. 32/2010.

India

Laxmi Mandal v. Deen Dayal Harinagar Hospital, WP(C) No. 8853/2008 (Del. H.C.) (2010).

Israel

Jerusalem Magistrate Court 2012, Tal Ya'akovovich v. Yad Hashmona Guest House, CS 5901/09.

Italy

Court of Cassation, *decision no. 12929* (4 June 2007) (Ct. of Cass. III).

Mexico

Supreme Court of Justice, *acción de inconstitucionalidad 54/2018* (2021).

Norway

Sauherad municipality v. A, Norges Kristelige Legeforening; A, Norges Kristelige Legeforening (Counsel Håkon H. Bleken) v. Sauherad municipality (HR-2018-1958- A (case no. 2018/199), Oct. 11, 2018 (Supreme Court of Norway).

Scotland

St. Margaret's Children and Family Care Society v. Office of the Scottish Charity Regulator, [2014] SCAP 02/13.

South Africa

Soobramoney v. Minister of Health, (1) SA 765 (CC) (1998).

Spain

Tribunal Constitucional (Constitutional Court), *Sentencia S.T.C. 145/2015,* 25 de junio de 2015, 2015–182 BOE 66654.

United States of America

Arlene's Flowers, Inc., dba Arlene's Flowers and Gifts, et al., v. Washington, et al., No. 91615-2 (Wash. Sup. Ct. 2019 *appeal dismissed* June 6, 2019), *petition for cert. filed,* No. 19-333 (U.S. Sept. 11, 2019).

Bostock v. Clayton County, 590 U.S. 644 (2020).

Boy Scouts of America v. Dale 530 U.S. 640 (2000).

Brownfield v. Daniel Freeman Marina Hospital, 208 Cal. App. 3d 405, 256 Cal. Rptr. 240 (1989) (California Second District, Court of Appeal).

Brush & Nib Studio v. City of Phoenix, No. CV-18-0176-PR (Ariz. Sup. Ct. Sept. 16. 2019).

Burwell v. Hobby Lobby Stores, Inc., 573 U.S. 682 (2014).

Citizens United v. Federal Election Commission, 558 U.S. 310 (2010).

City of Boerne v. Flores, 521 U.S. 507 (1997).

Elane Photography v. Willock, 309 P.3d 53 (N.M. 2013), *cert. denied,* 134 S. Ct. 1787 (2014).

Employment Division v. Smith, 485 U.S. 660 (1990).

First Nat'l Bank of Boston v. Bellotti, 435 U.S. 765 (1978).

Fulton v. City of Philadelphia, 922 F.3d 140, 153–54 (3d Cir. 2019).

Gonzales v. O Centro Espírita Beneficente União do Vegetal, 546 U.S. 418 (2006).

Hale v. Henkel, 201 U.S. 43 (1906).

Lexington-Fayette Urban County Human Rights Commission v. Hands On Originals, No. 2017-SC-000278-DG (Ky. Sup. Ct. R. Oct. 31, 2019).

Masterpiece Cakeshop, Ltd. v. Colorado Civil Rights Comm'n, 138 S. Ct. 1719 (2018).

Minneapolis & St. Louis Ry. Co. v. Beckwith, 129 U.S. 26 (1888).
New York et al. v. U.S. Department of Health and Human Services et al., U.S. District Court, Southern District of New York, No. 19-04676 (Nov. 6, 2019).
Newman v. Piggie Park Enterprises, 390 U.S. 400 (1968) (per curiam).
Rodriguez v. City of Chicago, 156 F.3d 771 (1998).
Santa Clara Cnty. v. S. Pac. R. Co., 118 U.S. 394 (1886).
Telescope Media Group v. Lucero, No. 17-3352 (8th Cir. R. Aug. 23, 2019).
Thomas v. Review Board of Indiana Employment Security Division, 450 U.S. 707 (1981).
Trustees of Darmouth College v. Woodward, 17 U.S. 518 (1819).
Wisconsin v. Yoder, 406 U.S. 205 (1972).

United Kingdom

Barr v. Matthews (2000) 52 B. M. L. R. 217 (Queen's Bench Division).
Bull v. Hall [2013] UKSC 73.
Greater Glasgow Health Board v. Doogan and another [2014] UKSC 68.
Janaway v. Salford Health Authority (1989) A.C. 537 (House of Lords).
Ladele v. London Borough of Islington (2009) EWCA Civ 1357.
Preddy v. Bull, [2013] UKSC 73, [2014] 3 OJLR II-262.
R. (on the application of Smeaton) v. Secretary of State for Health, [2002] E.W.H.C. 610 (Admin) (High Court of England and Wales).

Table of Instruments

International Instruments

Convention on the Elimination of All Forms of Discrimination Against Women (CEDAW) (Dec. 18, 1979).
Convention on the Rights of the Child (Nov. 20, 1989).
International Covenant on Civil and Political Rights (ICCPR) (Dec. 16, 1966).
International Covenant on Economic, Social and Cultural Rights (ICESCR) (Dec. 16, 1966).
International Labor Organization (ILO), Convention No. 111 concerning Discrimination in Respect of Employment and Occupation (1958).

Regional Instruments

African System

African Charter on Human and Peoples' Rights (June 27, 1981).
African Commission on Human and Peoples' Rights, *General Comment No. 2 on Article 14.1 (a), (b), (c) and (f) and Article 14. 2 (a) and (c) of the Protocol to the African Charter on Human and Peoples' Rights on the Rights of Women in Africa.*
Protocol to the African Charter on Human and Peoples Rights on the Rights of Women in Africa (July 11, 2003).

European System

European Convention on Human Rights, E.T.S. No. 5 (Nov. 4, 1950).
European Social Charter, E.T.S. No. 163 (May 3, 1996).

Inter-American System

Access to Information on Reproductive Health from a Human Rights Perspective, Inter-Am. Comm'n H.R., OEA/Ser.L/V/II. doc. 61 (2011).
Access to Maternal Health Services from a Human Rights Perspective, Inter-Am. Comm'n H.R., OEA/Ser.L/V/II. Doc. 69 (2010).
Inter-Am. Comm'n H.R, 1997 Annual Report of the Inter-American Commission on Human Rights, OEA/Ser.L/V/II.98, Doc.6 (Feb. 17, 1998).
Inter-Am. Comm'n H.R, 1998 Annual Report of the Inter-American Commission on Human Rights, OEA/Ser.L/V/II.102 Doc 6. Rev (April 16, 1999).

Organization of American States, Additional Protocol to the American Convention on Human Rights in the Area of Economic, Social, and Cultural Rights, "Protocol of San Salvador", O.A.S.T.S. No. A-52 (Nov. 16, 1999).

Organization of American States, American Convention on Human Rights, O.A.S.T.S. No. 36, 1144 U.N.T.S. 123 (Nov. 22, 1969).

Other Materials

United Nations

Committee on Economic, Social, and Cultural Rights

Committee on Economic, Social and Cultural Rights, Concluding Observations on the Sixth Periodic Report of Poland, U.N. Doc. E/C.12/POL/CO/6 (Oct. 26, 2016).

Committee on Economic, Social and Cultural Rights, Concluding Observations on the Combined Third to Fifth Periodic Reports on Romania, U.N. Doc. E/C.12/ROU/CO/3-5 (Dec. 9, 2014).

Committee on Economic, Social and Cultural Rights, Concluding Observations on the Sixth Periodic Report on Canada, U.N. Doc. E/C.12/CAN/CO/6 (March 23, 2016).

Committee on Economic, Social and Cultural Rights, General Comment No. 14, U.N. Doc. E/C.12/2000/4 (Aug. 11, 2000).

Committee on Economic, Social and Cultural Rights, General Comment No. 22, U.N. Doc. E/C.12/GC/22 (May 2, 2016).

Committee on Economic, Social and Cultural Rights, General Comment No. 2, U.N. Doc. E/1990/23 (Feb. 2, 1990).

Committee on Economic, Social and Cultural Rights, General Comment No. 24, U.N. Doc. E/C.12/GC/24 (2017).

Committee for the Elimination of All Forms of Discrimination against Women

Committee for the Elimination of All Forms of Discrimination Against Women, Inquiry concerning Poland conducted under article 8 of the Optional Protocol to the Convention, U.N. Doc. CEDAW/C/POL/IR/1 (Aug. 21, 2024).

Committee for the Elimination of All Forms of Discrimination Against Women, Concluding Observations on the Combined Seventh and Eighth Periodic Reports of Poland, U.N. Doc. CEDAW/C/POL/7-8 (Nov. 7, 2014).

Committee for the Elimination of All Forms of Discrimination Against Women, Concluding Observations on the Combined Seventh and Eighth Periodic Reports of Hungary, U.N. Doc. CEDAW/C/HUN/CO/7-8 (March 26, 2013).

Committee for the Elimination of All Forms of Discrimination Against Women, Concluding Observations on the Seventh Periodic Report of Italy, U.N. Doc. CEDAW/C/ITA/CO/7 (July 21, 2017).

Committee on the Elimination of All Forms of Discrimination Against Women, General Recommendation No. 24, U.N. Doc. A/54/38/Rev.1, chap. I (1999).

Committee on the Elimination of All Forms of Discrimination Against Women, Concluding Observations on the Combined Seventh and Eighth Periodic Reports of Romania, U.N. Doc. CEDAW/C/ROU/7-8 (July 21, 2017).

Committee on the Elimination of All Forms of Discrimination Against Women, Concluding Observations on the Combined Eighth and Ninth Periodic Reports of Canada, U.N. Doc. CEDAW/C/CAN/CO/8-9 (Nov. 18, 2016).

Committee on the Elimination of Discrimination against Women, Concluding Observations on Croatia, U.N. Doc. A/53/38 (1998).

Committee on the Elimination of Discrimination against Women, Concluding Observations on Italy, U.N. Doc. A/52/38 Rev.1, Part II (1997).

Committee on the Elimination of Discrimination against Women, Concluding Observations on South Africa, U.N. Doc. A/53/38/Rev.1 (1998).

Committee on the Elimination of Discrimination against Women, Concluding Observations on Romania, U.N. Doc. CEDAW/C/ROU/CO/7-8 (July 24, 2017).

Committee on the Elimination of Discrimination against Women, Concluding Observations on Argentina, U.N. Doc. CEDAW/C/ARG/CO/7 (Nov. 25, 2016).

Committee on the Rights of the Child

Committee on the Rights of the Child, Concluding Observations on the Combined Third to Fifth Periodic Reports of Slovakia, U.N. Doc. CRC/C/SVKCO/3-5 (July 20, 2016).

Economic and Social Council

Economic and Social Council (Commission on Human Rights), U.N. Doc. E/CN.4/AC.1/SR.8 (June 20, 1947).

Economic and Social Council (Commission on Human Rights), U.N. Doc. E/CN.4/SR.161 (April 28, 1950).

Sub-Commission on the Promotion and Protection of Human Rights, *Globalization and its Impact on the Full Enjoyment of Human Rights, Final Report*, U.N. Doc. E/CN.4/Sub.2/2003/14 (June 25, 2003).

General Assembly

General Assembly, *Draft International Covenants on Human Rights (Annotation)*, U.N. Doc. A/2929 (July 1, 1955).

General Assembly, Res. 217 A (III), Universal Declaration of Human Rights (UDHR) (Dec. 10, 1948).

Human Rights Committee

Human Rights Committee, CCPR General Comment No. 22, U.N. Doc.CCPR/C/21/Rev.1/Add.4 (July 30, 1993).

Human Rights Committee, CCPR General Comment No. 36, U.N. Doc.CCPR/C/GC/36 (Sept. 3, 2019).

Human Rights Committee, Concluding observations on the fifth periodic report of Romania, U.N. Doc. CCPR/C/ROU/CO/5 (Dec. 11, 2017).

Human Rights Committee, Concluding Observations on the Seventh Periodic Report of Colombia, U.N. Doc. CCPR/C/COL/CO/7 (Nov. 17, 2016).

Human Rights Committee, Concluding Observations on the Seventh Periodic Report of Poland, U.N. Doc. CCPR/C/POL/CO/7 (Nov. 23, 2016).

Human Rights Committee, Concluding Observations on the Sixth Periodic Report of Italy (May 1, 2017).

Human Rights Committee, Concluding observations on the sixth periodic report of Mexico, U.N. Doc. CCPT/C/MEX/CO/6 (Dec. 4, 2019).

Human Rights Committee, Concluding observations on the third periodic report of Lebanon, U.N. Doc. CCPR/C/LBN/CO/3 (May 9, 2018).

Human Rights Committee, General Comment No. 22: Article 18 (Freedom of Thought, Conscience or Religion), U.N. Doc. CCPR/C/21/Rev.1/Add.4 (July 30, 1993).

Human Rights Council

Human Rights Council, *Promoting Human Rights and Fundamental Freedoms through a Better Understanding of Traditional Values of Humankind: Best Practices*, U.N. Doc. A/HRC/RES/ 21/3 (Oct. 9, 2012).

Human Rights Council, *Protection of the Family: Contribution of the Family to the Realization of the Right to an Adequate Standard of Living for Its Members, particularly through Its Role in Poverty Eradication and Achieving Sustainable Development*, U.N. Doc. A/HRC/RES/29/22 (July 22, 2015).

Office of the High Commissioner for Human Rights

Office of the High Commissioner for Human Rights, *Conscientious Objection to Military Service*, U.N. Doc. HR/PUB/12/1 (2012).

Office of the High Commissioner for Human Rights, *Joint Statement by UN human rights experts on the occasion of the 25th anniversary of the adoption of the Programme of Action of the International Conference on Population and Development* (ICPD).

Special Procedures

Ahmed Shaheed, *Report of the Special Rapporteur on freedom of religion or belief*, U.N. Doc. A/HRC/43/48 (Feb. 27, 2020).

Anand Grover, *Report of the Special Rapporteur on the right of everyone to the enjoyment of the highest attainable standard of physical and mental health, Mission to Poland,* U.N. Doc. A/HRC/14/20/Add.3 (May 20, 2010).

Anand Grover, *Report of the U.N. Special Rapporteur on the Right to the Highest Attainable Standard of Physical and Mental Health,* U.N. Doc. A/64/272 (Aug. 10, 2009).

Anand Grover, *Report of the U.N. Special Rapporteur on the right of everyone to the enjoyment of the highest attainable standard of physical and mental health,* U.N. Doc. A/66/254 (Aug. 3, 2011).

Dainius Pūras, *Report of the U.N. Special Rapporteur on the Right to the Highest Attainable Standard of Physical and Mental Health, Visit to Ecuador,* U.N. Doc. A/HRC/44/48/Add. 1 (May 6, 2020).

Heiner Beilefeldt, *Report of the Special Rapporteur on Freedom of Religion or Belief,* U.N. Doc. A/HRC/31/18 (Dec. 23, 2015).

Juan E. Méndez, *Report of the U.N. Special Rapporteur on torture and other cruel, inhuman or degrading treatment or punishment,* U.N. Doc. A/HRC/31/57 (Jan. 5, 2016).

Philip Alston, *Report of the Special Rapporteur on Extreme poverty and human rights,* U.N. Doc. A/73/396 (Sept. 26, 2018).

Radhika Coomaraswamy, *Report of the U.N. Special Rapporteur on violence against women, its causes and consequences, in accordance with Commission on Human Rights resolution 1997/44, policies and practices that impact women's reproductive rights and contribute to, cause or constitute violence against women,* U.N. Doc. E/CN.4/1999/68/Add.4 (Jan. 21, 1999).

Bibliography

ABORTION LAW IN TRANSNATIONAL PERSPECTIVE (Rebecca J. Cook, Joanna N. Erdman & Bernard M. Dickens, eds., 2014).

ABORTO EN AMÉRICA LATINA: ABOGACÍA, TRABAJO EN RED Y ESTÁNDARES DE PROTECCIÓN (Viviana Bohórquez Monsalve ed., 2021).

Abubeker, Ferid, et al., *Medical Termination for Pregnancy in Early First Trimester (≤ 63 Days) Using Combination of Mifepristone and Misoprostol or Misoprostol Alone: A Systematic Review*, 20 BMC WOMEN'S HEALTH 142 (2020).

ADENITIRE, JOHN, A GENERAL RIGHT TO CONSCIENTIOUS EXEMPTION: BEYOND RELIGIOUS PRIVILEGE (2020).

Ahdar, Rex, *Is Secularism Neutral?* 26 RATIO JURIS 404 (2013).

Ahmed, Sameer, *The Religious Right to Refuse Service: Accommodating Muslims in a "Christian" America*, 7 ALB. GOV. L. REV. 379 (2014).

ALEGRE, MARCELO & ROBERTO GARGARELLA, EL DERECHO A LA IGUALDAD. APORTES PARA UN CONSTITUCIONALISMO IGUALITARIO (2007).

ALKIVIADOU, NATALIE, THE FAR-RIGHT IN INTERNATIONAL AND EUROPEAN LAW (2019).

Alston, Philip, *Conjuring up New Human Rights: A Proposal for Quality Control*, 78 AM. J. INT'L L. 607 (1984).

Alston, Philip, *The Populist Challenge to Human Rights*, 9 J. HUM. RTS. PRAC. 1 (2017).

Amuchastegui, Ana, et al., *Politics, religion and gender equality in contemporary Mexico: women's sexuality and reproductive rights in a contested secular state*, 31 THIRD WORLD Q. 6 (2010).

ANDERSON, BENEDICT, IMAGINED COMMUNITIES (1983).

Anderson, Elisabeth, *The Epistemology of Democracy*, 3 EPISTEME 8 (2006).

APPIAH, ANTHONY, COSMOPOLITANISM: ETHICS IN A WORLD OF STRANGERS (2007).

ARCHIBUGI, DANIELE, THE GLOBAL COMMONWEALTH OF CITIZENS: TOWARD COSMOPOLITAN DEMOCRACY (2008).

ARISTOTLE, NICOMACHEAN ETHICS (Ingram Bywater ed., 1894).

ARISTOTLE, POLITICS (Benjamin Jowett trans., 1905).

Ariza Navarrete, Sonia & Agustina Ramón Michel, *Usos imprevistos y respuestas a la objeción de conciencia en el aborto legal*, 10 SERIE DOCUMENTOS REDAAS (2019).

Arneson, Richard J., *Against Freedom of Conscience*, 47 SAN DIEGO L. REV. (2010).

Arthur, Joyce, et al., *The dishonourable disobedience of not providing abortion*, 22 EUR. J. CONTRACEPTION & REPROD. HEALTH CARE 1 (2017).

ASAD, TALAL, FORMATIONS OF THE SECULAR: CHRISTIANITY, ISLAM, MODERNITY (2003).

Augustine's City of God: A Critical Guide (James Wetzel ed., 2013).

Authority (Joseph Raz ed., 1990).

Autorino, Tomasso, et al., *The impact of gynecologists' conscientious objection on abortion access*, 87 Social Science Research 102403 (2020).

Awoonor-Williams, John Koku, et al., *Exploring conscientious objection to abortion among health providers in Ghana*, 46 Int'l Perspectives on Sexual and Reprod. Health 1 (2020).

Barack, Aharon, Proportionality: Constitutional Rights and their Limitations (2012).

Barbalet, Jack, *Globalisation and Cosmopolitanism: Continuity and Disjuncture, Contemporary and Historical*, 50 J. Soc. 199 (2014).

Barnes May, Isaac, American Quaker Resistance to War, 1917–1973: Law, Politics, and Conscience (2022).

Barry, Brian, Culture and Equality: An Egalitarian Critique of Multiculturalism (2002).

Beauchamp, Tom L. & J. F. Childress, Principles of biomedical ethics (2001).

Beauchamp, Tom L. & James F. Childress, Principles of Biomedical Ethics (2009).

Benn, Stanley I. & Richard S. Peters, Social Principles and the Democratic States 88–107 (2010).

Berg, Thomas, *What Same-Sex-Marriage and Religious-Liberty Claims Have in Common*, 5 Nw. J. L. & Soc. Pol'y 206 (2010).

Bertoni, Eduardo Andrés, *The Inter-American Court of Human Rights and the European Court of Human Rights: A Dialogue on Freedom of Expression Standards*, 3 Eur. Hum. Rts. L. R. 332 (2009).

Betti, Emilio, Teoría General de las Obligaciones (1969).

Bhakuni, Himani, *Reproductive justice: Non-interference or non-domination?*, 23 Developing World Bioeth. (2023).

Blichner, Lars C. & Anders Molander, What is juridification? (2005).

Blofield, M., The Politics of Moral Sin: Abortion and divorce in Spain, Chile and Argentina (2006).

Bob, Clifford, Rights as Weapons: Instruments of Conflict, Tools of Power (2019).

Bob, Clifford, The Global Right Wing and the Clash of World Politics (2012).

Bocchiaro, Piero & Philip Zimbardo, *On the dynamics of disobedience: experimental investigations of defying unjust authority*, 10 Psychology Research and Behavior Management 219 (2017).

Boffi Boggero, Luis María, Tratado de las Obligaciones, Tomo iv (1979).

Borges, Jorge Luis & Osvaldo Ferrari, En diálogo i (1998).

Borja Soriano, Manuel, Teoría de las Obligaciones (1994).

Brack, Chelsey E., et al., *"It's a race against the clock": A qualitative analysis of barriers to legal abortion in Bogotá, Colombia,* 43 Int'l Perspectives on Sexual and Reprod. Health 4 (2017).

Brady, Kathleen A., The Distinctiveness of Religion in American Law: Rethinking Religion Clause Jurisprudence (2015).

Brock, Dan W., *Conscientious refusal by physicians and pharmacists: Who is obligated to do what, and why?* 29 Theoretical Med. & Bioeth. 3 (2008).

Brock, Peter, *'A Light Shining in Darkness': Tolstoi and the Imprisonment of Conscientious Objectors in Imperial Russia,* 81 The Slavonic & East Eur. Rev. 683 (2003).

Brown, Grattan T., *Institutional Conscience and Catholic Health Care,* 16 Life & Learning (2006).

Brownlee, Kimberley, Conscience and Conviction: The Case for Civil Disobedience (2012).

Brysk, Alison & Michael Stohl, Contracting Human Rights: Crisis, Accountability and Opportunity (2018).

Brysk, Alison, *Speaking Rights to Power,* Am. Pol. Sci. Ass'n (2017).

Bush, Randall K., *Remembering Rosa Parks: Recognizing a Contemporary Prophetic Act,* 65 Theological Studies 838 (2004).

Butler, Jennifer S., Born Again: The Christian Right Globalized (2006).

Cabal, Luisa, et al., *Striking a Balance: Conscientious Objection and Reproductive Health Care from the Colombian Perspective,* 16 Health & Hum. Rts. J. 73 (2014).

Çalı, Başak, *Balancing Human Rights? Methodological Problems with Weights, Scales and Proportions,* 29 Hum. Rts. Q. (2007).

Campbell, David E., *The Perils of Politicized Religion,* 149 Dædalus, the J. of the Am. Academy of Arts & Sciences 87 (2020).

Carrillo-Santarelli, Nicolás, *The Autonomous Justiciability of the Right to Health and Supervision of Immediate Obligations of States in the Inter-American Human Rights System,* 4 dpce Online 1207 (2018).

Castañeda, Jorge Eugenio, Instituciones de Derecho Civil, Tomo iii (1957).

Cazeaux, Pedro N. & Félix A. Trigo Represas, Compendio de Derecho de las Obligaciones, Tomo ii (1986).

Ceva, Emanuela, *Political Justification through Democratic Participation: The Case for Conscientious Objection,* 41 Social Theory & Practice 26 (2015).

Chandler, Matthew, *Moral Mandate or Personal Preference? Possible Avenues for Accommodation of Civil Servants Morally Opposed to Facilitating Same-Sex Marriage,* 2011 byu L. Rev. 1625 (2011).

Chappell, Louise, *Contesting women's rights: Charting the emergence of a transnational conservative counter-network*, 20 GLOBAL SOC. 4 (2006).

Charo, Robin A., *The Celestial Fire of Conscience—Refusing to Deliver Medical Care*, N. ENGL. J. MED. 2471 (2005).

Charo, Robin. A., *American Constitution Society for Law and Policy, Health Care Provider Refusals to Treat, Prescribe, Refer or Inform: Professionalism and Conscience*, THE JOURNAL OF THE ACS ISSUE GROUPS (2007).

Chavkin, Wendy, et al., *Balancing freedom of conscience and equitable access*, 108 AMERICAN J. OF PUBLIC HEALTH 1487 (2018).

Chavkin, Wendy, et al., *Conscientious objection and refusal to provide reproductive healthcare*, 123 INTERNATIONAL J. OF GYNECOLOGY AND OBSTETRICS 41–56 (2013).

Chavkin, Wendy, et al., *Regulation of conscientious objection to abortion: An international comparative multiple-case study*, 19 HEALTH & HUM. RTS. J. 1 (2017).

Chervenak, Frank A. & McCullough, Laurence B., *The ethics of direct and indirect referral for termination of pregnancy*, 199 AM. J. OBSTETRICS & GYNECOLOGY 3 (2008).

Chesterman, Simon, *Artificial Intelligence and the Limits of Legal Personality*, 69 INT'L & COMP. L. Q. (2020).

CHRISTIANO, THOMAS, THE CONSTITUTION OF EQUALITY: DEMOCRATIC AUTHORITY AND ITS LIMITS (2008).

CHRISTIANO, THOMAS, THE RULE OF THE MANY (1996).

COLIVER, SANDRA, THE RIGHT TO KNOW: HUMAN RIGHTS AND ACCESS TO REPRODUCTIVE HEALTH INFORMATION (1995).

COMPARATIVE CONSTITUTIONAL LAW (Tom Ginsburg & Rosalind Dixon eds., 2011).

CONSTITUTIONAL DEMOCRACY IN CRISIS? (Mark A. Graber, Sanford Levinson, & Mark Tushnet eds., 2018).

CONTROVERSIES IN LATIN AMERICAN BIOETHICS (Eduardo Rivera-López & Martin Hevia eds., 2019).

Cook, Rebecca J. & Bernard M. Dickens, *The Growing Abuse of Conscientious Objection*, 8 VIRTUAL MENTOR 337 (2006).

Coppola, Francisco, et al., *Conscientious objection as a barrier for implementing voluntary termination of pregnancy in Uruguay: Gynecologists' attitudes and behavior*, 134 INT'L J. GYNAECOLOGY & OBSTETRICS S1 (2016).

Cover, Robert M., *The Supreme Court 1982 Term. Foreword: Nomos and Narrative*, 97 HARV. L. REV. 4, 4–68 (1984).

Cowley, Christopher, *Conscientious objection in healthcare and the duty to refer*, 43 J. MED. ETHICS 4 (2017).

Craddock, Joshua J., *The Case for Complicity-Based Religious Accommodations*, 12 TENN. J.L. & POL'Y 233, 233–85 (2018).

Craske, N. & M. Molyneux, Gender and the politics of rights and democracy in Latin America (2002).

Critical Theory and Authoritarian Populism (Jeremiah Morelock ed., 2018).

Dalton, Dennis, Mahatma Gandhi: Nonviolent Power in Action (1993).

Daly, Tom G., *Understanding Multi-directional Democratic Decay: Lessons from the Rise of Bolsonaro in Brazil*, 14 The Law & Ethics of Hum. Rts. J. 2 (2019).

Darzé, Omar Ismail & Júnior Ubirajara Barroso, *Prevalence, attitudes, and factors motivating conscientious objection toward reproductive health among medical students*, 40 Rev. Bras. Ginecol. Obstet. 10 (2018).

Davis, Jasmine Meredith, et al., *A narrative literature review of the impact of conscientious objection by health professionals on women's access to abortion worldwide 2013–2021*, 17 Glob. Public Health 9 (2022).

De Feyer, Koen & Felipe Gómez Isa, Privatisation and Human Rights in the Age of Globalisation (2005).

De la Torre, Carlos, *Populism and Democracy: Lessons from Latin America*, 18 Seton Hall J. Dipl. & Int'l Rel. 33 (2017).

De la Torre, Carlos, *Trump's Populism: Lessons from Latin America*, 20 Postcolonial Stud. 187 (2017).

de Londras, Fiona, et al., *The impact of 'conscientious objection' on abortion-related outcomes: A synthesis of legal and health evidence*, 129 Health Pol'y (2023).

de Souza Levenhagen, Antonio José, Comentarios didacticos, direito das obrigaçoes (1978).

Debating Deliberative Democracy (James Fishkin & Peter Laslett, eds., 2003).

Deliberative Systems: Deliberative Democracy at the Large Scale, (John Parkinson & Jane Mansbridge eds., 2012).

Derecho de obligaciones y contratos (Valpuesta Fernández ed., 1994).

Derecho de Obligaciones, (Martínez de Aguirre ed., 2000).

Dickens, Bernard M. & Rebecca J. Cook, *Conscientious commitment to women's health*, 113 Int'l J. of Gynecology and Obstetrics (2011).

Dickens, Bernard, *Conscientious Objection and the Duty to Refer*, 115 Intl J. of Gynecology and Obstetrics (2021).

Dillon, Michele, *Asynchrony in Attitudes Toward Abortion and Gay Rights: The Challenge to Values Alignment*, 53 J. for the Scientific Study of Religion 1 (2014).

Doran, Frances M. & Julie Hornibrook, *Barriers around access to abortion experienced by rural women in New South Wales, Australia*, 16 Rural and Remote Health 1 (2016).

Down Hall, Jacquelyn, *The long civil rights movement and the political uses of the past*, 91 J. of American History 1233 (2005).

Dubow, Sara, *"A Constitutional Right Rendered Utterly Meaningless": Religious Exemptions and Reproductive Politics, 1973–2014*, 27 J. of Pol'y Hist. 1 (2015).

Dupichot, Jacques, Derecho de las obligaciones (1984).

Durland, Spencer L., *The Case against Institutional Conscience*, 86 Notre Dame L. Rev. 1655 (2011).

Dworkin, Roger B., Limits: The Role of the Law in Bioethical Decision Making (1996).

Dworkin, Ronald, A Matter of Principle (1985).

Dworkin, Ronald, *Equality, Democracy, and Constitution: We The People in Court*, xxviii Alberta L. R. 324 (1990).

Dworkin, Ronald, Taking Rights Seriously (1977).

Eisgruber, Christopher L. & Lawrence G. Sager, Religious Freedom and the Constitution (2010).

Ells, Carolyn, et al., *Relational autonomy as an essential component of patient-centered care*, 4 Int'l J. Feminist Approaches to Bioeth. 2 (2011).

Encyclopedia of Modern Political Thought (Gregory Claeys ed., 2013).

Estlund, David, *Who's Afraid of Deliberative Democracy? On the Strategic/Deliberative Dichotomy in Recent Constitutional Jurisprudence*, 71 Texas L. Rev. (1993).

Ewig, C., Second-wave neoliberalism: Gender, race, and health sector reform in Peru (2010).

Favier, Mary, et al., *Safe abortion in South Africa: "We have wonderful laws but we don't have people to implement those laws"*, 143 Int'l J. of Gynecology & Obstetrics S4 (2018).

Feinberg, Joel, Harm to Self: The Moral Limits of the Criminal Law (1986).

Feldman, Noah, Divided by God: America's Church-State Problem and What We Should Do About It (2006).

Feminist perspectives on health care law (S. Sheldon ed., 1998).

Fiala, Christian & Joice Arthur, *"Dishonourable disobedience" – Why refusal to treat in reproductive health care is not conscientious objection*, 1 Psychosomatic Gynecology and Obstetrics (2014).

Fiala, Christian & Joice Arthur, *Refusal to Treat Patients Does Not Work in Any Country— Even If Misleadingly Labeled "Conscientious Objection,"* 19 Health & Hum. Rts. J. 299 (2017).

Finegan, Thomas, *Conscientious objection to referrals*, 45 J. Med. Ethics 4(2019).

Fink, Lauren, et al., *"The fetus is my patient, too": Attitudes toward abortion and referral among physician conscientious objectors in Bogota, Colombia*, 42 Int'l Perspectives on Sexual and Reproductive Health 2 (2016).

Finnie, Sarah, et al., *The pathway to induced abortion: Women's experiences and general practitioner attitudes*, 32 bmj Sexual & Reprod. Health 1 (2006).

First Do no Harm: Law Ethics, and Healthcare (Sheila A.M. McClean ed., 2006).

FITZGERALD, FRANCIS, THE EVANGELICALS: THE STRUGGLE TO SHAPE AMERICA (2017).

Flynn, Taylor, *Clarion Call or False Alarm: Why Proposed Exemptions to Equal Marriage Statutes Return Us to a Religious Understanding of the Public Marketplace*, 5 NORTHWESTERN J. OF L. AND SOCIAL POLICY 236 (2010).

Fontana, David, *Unbundling Populism*, 65 UCLA L. REV. 1482 (2018).

Fraser, Barbara, *Tide Begins to Turn on Abortion Access in South Africa*, 383 THE LANCET 2113 (2014).

FREEDOM OF ASSOCIATION (Amy Gutmann ed., 1998).

Freeman, Emily & Coast, Ernestina, *Conscientious objection to abortion: Zambian healthcare practitioners' beliefs and practices*, 221 SOC. SCI. MED. (2019).

FROM BIRTH TO DEATH AND BENCH TO CLINIC: THE HASTINGS CENTER BIOETHICS BRIEFING BOOK FOR JOURNALISTS, POLICYMAKERS, AND CAMPAIGNS (Mary Crowley ed., 2008).

Fry-Bowers, Eileen K., *A matter of conscience: Examining the law and policy of conscientious objection in health care*, 21 POLICY, POLIT. NURS. PRACT. 2 (2020).

Fuchs, Joseph R., et al., *Patient Perspectives on Religiously Affiliated Care in Rural and Urban Colorado*, 12 J. OF PRIMARY CARE & COMMUNITY HEALTH (2021).

Fung, Archong, *Deliberation before the Revolution: Toward an Ethics of Deliberative Democracy in an Unjust World*, 33 POLITICAL THEORY 397 (2005).

Galston, William A., *The Populist Challenge to Liberal Democracy*, 29 J. DEMOCRACY 5 (2018).

Gargarella, Roberto, *La última carta. El derecho de resistencia en situaciones de alienación legal*, 80 LECCIONES Y ENSAYOS (2004).

Gargarella, Roberto, *Latin American Constitutionalism: Social Rights and the "Engine Room" of the Constitution*, 4 NOTRE DAME J. INT'L & COMP. L. 9 (2014).

Genius, Stephen J. & Chris Lipp, *Ethical Diversity and the Role of Conscience in Clinical Medicine*, 1 INT'L J. OF FAM. MED (2013).

Gerards, Janneke, *The Age of Balancing Revisited?* 6 EUR. DATA PROTECTION L. REV. (2020).

Girardi Fachin, Melina & Bruna Nowak, The Joint Declaration to the Inter-American System of Human Rights: Backlash or Contestation? INT'L J. CONST. L. BLOG (Dec. 12, 2019).

Giubilini, Alberto & Julian Savulescu, *Beyond Money: Conscientious Objection in Medicine as a Conflict of Interests*, 17(2) J. BIOETH. INQ., 229–243 (2020).

Goodpaster, Kenneth E, *The Concept of Corporate Responsibility*, 2 J. OF BUSINESS ETHICS 1 (1983).

Gostin, Lawrence, *The "Conscience" Rule: How Will It Affect Patients' Access to Health Services?* JAMA F. (May 15, 2019).

Gowri, Aditi, *Speech and Spending: Corporate Political Speech Rights under the First Amendment*, 17 J. of Business Ethics (1988).

Gozdecka, Dorota A., et al., *From Multiculturalism to Post-Multiculturalism: Trends and Paradoxes*, 50 J. Soc. 51, 51–64 (2014).

Greenawalt, Kent, Religious Convictions and Political Choice (1988).

Gutmann, Amy & Dennis Thompson, Democracy and Disagreement (1996).

Haaland, Marte E. S., et al., *Silent politics and unknown numbers: Rural health bureaucrats and Zambian abortion policy*, 251 Soc. Sci. Med. (2020).

Håkansson, Dubravka, et al., *Navigating the minefield: Women's experiences of abortion in a Country with a conscience clause—The case of Croatia*, 22 J. Int'l Women's Studies 1 (2021).

Hall, Peter A. & Rosemary C. R. Taylor, *Political Science and the Three New Institutionalisms*, xliv Pol. Stud. (1996).

Halmai, Gábor, *Populism, Authoritarianism and Constitutionalism*, 20 German L.J. 296, 296–313 (2019).

Harden, Angela & Jane Ogden, *Young women's experiences of arranging and having abortions*, 21 Soc. Health & Illness 4 (1999).

Harper Ho, Virginia E., *Theories of Corporate Groups: Corporate Identity Reconceived*, 42 Seton Hall L. Rev., 880–952 (2012).

Harries, Jane, et al., *An Exploratory Study of What Happens to Women Who Are Denied Abortions in Cape Town, South Africa*, 12 Reproductive Health 1 (2015).

Harries, Jane, et al., *Conscientious objection and its impact on abortion service provision in South Africa: A qualitative study*, 11 Reprod. Health 1 (2014).

Harris, Laura Florence, et al., *Conscientious objection to abortion provision: Why context matters*, 13 Glob. Public Health 5 (2018).

Harris, Lisa H., *Recognizing Conscience in Abortion Provision*, 367 N. Engl. J. Med. (2012).

Hart Ely, John, Democracy and Distrust: A Theory of Judicial Review (1980).

Healthcare as a Human Rights Issue: Normative Profile, Conflicts and Implementation (Sabine Klotz, et al., eds., 2017).

Held, David, et al., *Globalization*, 5 Global Governance 483 (1999).

Helfand, Michael, *Religious Arbitration and the New Multiculturalism – Negotiating Conflicting Legal Orders*, 86 N.Y U. L. Rev. 1231(2011).

Hevia, Martin & Andrés Constantin, *Gendered Power Relations and Informed Consent: The I.V.v. Bolivia Case*, 20 Health & Human Rts. J. (2018).

Hirschl, Ran, *"Negative" Rights vs. "Positive" Entitlements: A Comparative Study of Judicial Interpretations of Rights in an Emerging Neo-Liberal Economic Order*, 22 Hum. Rts. Q. 1060 (Nov. 2000).

HOMER, THE ILIAD (Richmond Lattimore trans., 1951).

HOMER, THE ODYSSEY (Robert Fitzgerald trans., 1990).

HTUN, MALA, SEX AND THE STATE: ABORTION, DIVORCE, AND THE FAMILY UNDER LATIN AMERICAN DICTATORSHIPS AND DEMOCRACIES (2003).

Huber and Schimpf, *On the Distinct Effects of Left-wing and Right-wing Populism*, 5 POL. & GOV. 146 (2017).

Huckerby, Jayne, Sarah Knuckey & Meg Satterthwaite, *Trump's "Unalienable Rights" Commission Likely to Promote Anti-Rights Agenda*, JUST SECURITY (July 9, 2019).

Hughes, Jonathan A., *Conscientious objection in healthcare: Why tribunals might be the answer*, 43 J. MED. ETHICS 4 (2017).

Hussein, Julia, et al., *Abortion in Poland: Politics, Progression and Regression*, 26 REPROD. HEALTH MATTERS 52 (2018).

Hutler, Brian, *Against the Political Use of Religious Exemptions*, 47 PHILOSOPHY & PUBLIC AFFAIRS (2019).

IYER, RAGHAVAN, THE MORAL AND POLITICAL THOUGHT OF MAHATMA GANDHI.

Johnson, Kevin, *The Struggle for Civil Rights: The Need for, and Impediments to, Political Coalitions among and within Minority Groups*, 63 LOUISIANA LAW REVIEW (1995).

Johnson, Lyman, *Law and Legal Theory in the History of Corporate Responsibility: Corporate Personhood*, 35 SEATTLE U. L. REV. (2012).

Kaba, R. & P. Sooriakumaran, *The evolution of the doctor-patient relationship*, INTERNATIONAL JOURNAL OF SURGERY 57–65 (2007).

Kallis, Aristotle, *Populism, Sovereigntism, and the Unlikely Re-Emergence of the Territorial Nation-State*, 11 FUDAN J. HUM. SOC. SCI. 285 (2018).

Keith, Katie, *Provider Conscience Rule Delayed Due to Lawsuits*, HEALTH AFF. BLOG (Jul. 2, 2019).

KELSEN, HANS, GENERAL THEORY OF LAW AND STATE (1945).

Kendrick, Leslie & Micah Schwartzman, *The Etiquette of Animus*, 132 HARV. L. REV. 133 (2018).

Kennedy, David W., *The International Human Rights Regime: Still Part of the Problem?*, 15 HARV. HUM. RTS. J. 101 (2002).

Keogh, Louise Anne, et al., *Conscientious objection to abortion, the law and its implementation in Victoria, Australia: Perspectives of abortion service providers*, 20 BMC MED. ETHICS 1 (2019).

Kessler, Jeremy K., *The Invention of a Human Right: Conscientious Objection at the United Nations, 1947–2011*, 44 COLUM. HUM. RTS. L. R. 753 (2013).

Kessler, Michael, *Conflicted Ideas of Conscience*, BERKLEY CENTER (Apr. 29, 2016).

Killian, Lewis M., *What or Who is a 'Minority'?* 10 MICHIGAN SOCIOLOGICAL REV. 18–31 (1996).

KINNAMAN, DAVID & GABE LYONS, UNCHRISTIAN: WHAT A NEW GENERATION REALLY THINKS ABOUT CHRISTIANITY... AND WHY IT MATTERS (2012).

Kolodny, Niko, *Rule Over None II: Social Equality and the Justification of Democracy*. 42 PHILOSOPHY & PUBLIC AFFAIRS 287 (2014).

KORSGAARD, CHRISTINE M., KANT: GROUNDWORK OF THE METAPHYSICS OF MORALS (Mary Gregor & Jens Timmermann, trans., 2d ed. 2012).

Kumm, Mattias, *Constitutional Rights as Principles: On the Structure and Domain of Constitutional Justice - A review Essay on Theory of Constitutional Rights by Robert Alexy*, 2 INT'L J. CON. L. 3 (2004).

Kuru, Ahmet, *Passive and Assertive Secularism: Historical Conditions, Ideological Struggles, and State Policies toward Religion*, 59 WORLD POLITICS 568 (July 2007).

KYMLICKA, WILL, MULTICULTURAL ODYSSEYS: NAVIGATING THE NEW INTERNATIONAL POLITICS OF DIVERSITY (2007).

Kymlicka, Will, *The rise and fall of multiculturalism? New debates on inclusion and accommodation in diverse societies*, 68 INT'L SOCIAL SCIENCE J. 133 (2018).

LABORDE, CÉCILE, LIBERALISM'S RELIGION (2017).

Landau, David, *Abusive Constitutionalism*, 47 UC DAVIS L. REV. 189 (2013).

Laurie, Timothy & Rimi Khan, *The Concept of Minority for the Study of Culture*, 31 CONTINUUM: J. OF MEDIA & CULTURAL STUDIES 1 (2017).

LAW, RELIGION AND HEALTH IN THE UNITED STATES (Holly Fernandez Lynch, I. Glenn Cohen & Elizabeth Sepper eds., 2017).

Lawrence, Ryan & Curlin, Farr, *Clash of definitions: Controversies about conscience in medicine*, 7 AM. J. BIOETH. 12 (2007).

Lemieux, Pierre, *Populism and Protectionism*, 40 REG. 6 (2017).

LESNICK, HOWARD, RELIGION IN LEGAL THOUGHT AND PRACTICE (2010).

Lienesch, Michael, *Right-Wing Religion: Christian Conservatism as a Political Movement*, 97 POL. SCI. Q. 403 (1982).

Lippman, Matthew, *The Recognition of Conscientious Objection to Military Service as an International Human Right*, 21:1 CALIF. W. INT'L L. J. 31, 32 (Oct. 1990).

LLAMBÍAS, JORGE JOAQUÍN, TRATADO DE DERECHO CIVIL, TOMO III (1983).

Lovell, David W., *Review of Freedom as Non-domination by Philip Pettit*, 5 AGENDA 2 (1998).

Luhmann, Niklas, *Differentiation of Society*, 2 THE CANADIAN J. OF SOCIOLOGY 29 (1977).

Lyus, Richard John, *Response to: 'Why medical professionals have no moral claim to conscientious objection accommodation in liberal democracies' by Schuklenk and Smalling*, 43 J. MED. ETHICS 4 (2017).

MACLURE, JOCELYN & CHARLES TAYLOR, SECULARISM AND FREEDOM OF CONSCIENCE (Jane Marie Todd trans., 2011).

Magelssen, Morten, Nhat Quang Le and Magne Supphellen, *Secularity, abortion, assisted dying and the future of conscientious objection: Modelling the relationship between attitudes*, 20 BMC MEDICAL ETHICS (2019).

Malaurie, Philippe & Laurent Aynes, Cours de Droit Civil. Les obligations (1992).

Manin, Bernard, *On Legitimacy and Political Deliberation*, 15 Pol. Theory 3 (1987).

Marblestone, Claire, *A Matter of Conscience:* United States v. Seeger *and the Supreme Court's Historical Failure to Define Conscientious Objector Status Under the First Amendment*, 38 Hastings Const. L. Q. 201 (2010).

Markovits, Daniel, *Democratic Disobedience*, 114 Yale L. J. 1897 (2005).

Marshall, Claire, *The Spread of Conscience Clause Legislation*, 39 Hum. Rts. 15 (2013).

Martí, José Luis, La república deliberativa (2006).

Martin, William C., With God on Our Side: The Rise of the Religious Right in America (2005).

Marzouki, Nadia, Duncan McDonnell & Olivier Roy. Saving the People: How Populists Hijack Religion (2016).

Mayo, Marjorie, Cultures, Communities, Identities (2000).

Mazeaud, Leon Henri, Lecciones de Derecho Civil, Volumen ii (1974).

McGoldrick, Dominic, *Multiculturalism and its Discontents*, 5 Hum. Rts. L. Rev. 27 (2005).

Melling, Louise, *The Religious Freedom Restoration Act is Used to Discriminate. Let's Fix It*, Religious News Service (May 19, 2016).

Merner, Bronwen, et al., *Institutional objection to abortion: A mixed-methods narrative review*, 19 Women's Health (2023).

Methods of Comparative Law (P. G. Monateri ed., 2006).

Millward, Megan, *Should pregnant doctors work in termination of pregnancy clinics?*, BMJ 340 (2010).

Minerva, Francesca, *Conscientious objection, complicity in wrongdoing, and a not-so-moderate approach*, 26 Cambridge Q. Healthcare Ethics 1 (2017).

Mishtal, Joanna Z, *Matters of "Conscience": The Politics of Reproductive Healthcare in Poland*, 23 Med. Anthropology Q. 161 (2009).

Movsesian, Mark L., *Masterpiece Cakeshop and the Future of Religious Freedom*, 42 Harv. J. L. & Pub. Pol'y 711 (2019).

Moya, Federico Arnau, Lecciones de Derecho Civil ii (2009).

Moyers, Bill, *9/11 and God's Sport*, 55 Cross Currents 442 (2006).

Moyn, Samuel, Not Enough: Human Rights in an Unequal World (2018).

Nedelsky, Jennifer, Law's Relations: A Relational Theory of Self, Autonomy, and Law (2012).

Nehushtan, Yossi, Intolerant Religion in a Tolerant-Liberal Democracy (2015).

NeJaime, Douglas & Reva B. Siegel, *Conscience Wars: Complicity-Based Conscience Claims in Religion and Politics*, 124 Yale L. J. 2516 (2015).

Neuman, Gerald L., *Import, Export, and Regional Consent in the Inter-American Court of Human Rights*, 19 EUR. J. INT'L L. 101, (2008).

Nolan, Aoife, *Privatization and Economic and Social Rights*, 40 HUM. RTS. Q. 815 (2018).

NOMOS XXXV: DEMOCRATIC COMMUNITY (J. W. Chapman and I. Shapiro eds., 1993).

NOMOS XXXVIII: POLITICAL ORDER (Ian Shapiro & Russel Hardin, eds., 1996).

Nordstrand, Sven, et al., *Medical students' attitudes towards conscientious objection: A survey*, 40 J. MED. ETHICS 9 (2014).

NOWAK, MANFRED, HUMAN RIGHTS OR GLOBAL CAPITALISM: THE LIMITS OF PRIVATIZATION (2016).

NUSSBAUM, MARTHA & AMARTYA SEN, THE QUALITY OF LIFE (1993).

O'DALY, GERARD J. P., AUGUSTINE'S CITY OF GOD: A READER'S GUIDE (1999).

Oleske, James M., *The Evolution of Accommodation: Comparing the Unequal Treatment of Religious Objections to Interracial and Same-Sex Marriages*, 50 HARVARD CIVIL RIGHTS-CIVIL LIBERTIES L. REV. 111 (2015).

Oliver, Daniel, *The Right Way to Talk About Rights*, FIRST THINGS (Nov. 5, 2019).

Palaver, Wolfgang, *Populism and Religion: On the Politics of Fear*, 58 DIALOG 1 (2019).

PALLY, MARCIA, THE NEW EVANGELICALS: EXPANDING THE VISION OF THE COMMON GOOD (2011).

Parkinson, Patrick, *Accommodating religious belief in a secular age: the issue of conscientious objection in the workplace*, 34 U. NEW SOUTH WALES L. J. 281 (2011).

PEKKANEN, ROBERT, ET AL., THE GLOBAL IMPLICATIONS OF POPULISM ON DEMOCRACY (2018).

PETTIT, PHILIP, JUST FREEDOM: A MORAL COMPASS FOR A COMPLEX WORLD (2014).

Pettit, Philip, *Keeping Republican Freedom Simple: On a Difference with Quentin Skinner*, 30 POL. THEORY 3 (2002).

Pettit, Philip, *Legitimacy and Justice in Republican Perspective*, 65 CURRENT LEGAL PROBLEMS (2012).

PETTIT, PHILIP, ON THE PEOPLE'S TERMS (2012).

PETTIT, PHILIP, REPUBLICANISM: A THEORY OF FREEDOM AND GOVERNMENT (1997).

Pettit, Philip, *The Democratic Riddle*, 1 ARGUMENTS 2 (2016).

PHILOSOPHY, SCIENCE, AND METHOD (Sidney Morgenbesser, Patrick Suppes & Morton White, eds. 1969).

PLANIOL, MARCEL & GEORGES RIPERT, TRATADO PRÁCTICO DE DERECHO CIVIL FRANCÉS, LAS OBLIGACIONES (1994).

PLATO, FIVE DIALOGUES: EUTHYPHRO, APOLOGY, CRITO, MENO, PHAEDO (John M. Cooper ed., George M. A. Grube trans., 2002).

PLATO, GORGIAS (Donald J. Zeyl trans., 1987).

PLATO, THE REPUBLIC (Benjamin Jowett trans., 1943).

Polletta, Francesca, *Legacies and liabilities of an insurgent past: Remembering Martin Luther King Jr., on the House and Senate Floor*, 22 SOCIAL SCIENCE HISTORY 479 (1998).

POST, ROBERT, CONSTITUTIONAL DOMAINS: DEMOCRACY, COMMUNITY, MANAGEMENT (1995).

POTHIER, ROBERT JOSEPH, TRATADO DE LAS OBLIGACIONES (1979).

PRIVATISATION AND HUMAN RIGHTS IN THE AGE OF GLOBALISATION (Koen De Feyter & Felipe Gómez Isa eds., 2005).

PROPORTIONALITY AND THE RULE OF LAW (Grant Huscroft et al., eds., 2014).

Puppinck, Grégor, *Conscientious Objection and Human Rights: A Systematic Analysis*, 1 BRILL RESEARCH PERSPECTIVES IN LAW AND RELIGION 1 (2017).

RACE, ETHNICITY, GENDER, & CLASS: THE SOCIOLOGY OF GROUP CONFLICT AND CHANGE (Joseph F. Healey, Andi Stepnick, Eileen O'Brien, eds. 2019).

Raifman, Sarah, et al., *Dualities between Tunisian provider beliefs and actions in abortion care*, 26 REPROD. HEALTH MATTERS 52 (2018).

Ralph, Lauren, et al., *Self-Managed Abortion Attempts Before vs After Changes in Federal Abortion Protections in the US*, 7 JAMA NETW. OPEN 7 (2024).

Ramón Michel, Agustina, Stephanie Kung, Alyse López-Salm & Sonia Ariza Navarrete, *Regulating Conscientious Objection to Legal Abortion in Argentina: Taking into Consideration Its Uses and Consequences*, 22 HEALTH & HUMAN RTS. J. 272 (2020).

RAWLS, JOHN, A THEORY OF JUSTICE (1971).

RAZ, JOSEPH, THE AUTHORITY OF LAW: ESSAYS ON LAW AND MORALITY (2009).

REASONING RIGHTS: COMPARATIVE JUDICIAL ENGAGEMENT (Liora Lazarus et al., eds., 2014).

REIMAGINING GLOBAL ABORTION POLITICS: A SOCIAL JUSTICE PERSPECTIVE (2018).

RELATIONAL AUTONOMY: FEMINIST PERSPECTIVES ON AUTONOMY, AGENCY AND THE SOCIAL SELF (Catriona Mackenzie & Natalie Stoljar, eds., 2000).

RELIGION AND INTERNATIONAL LAW (Mark W. Janis and Carolyn Evans eds., 2004).

RELIGION, LAW AND THE POLITICS OF ETHICAL DIVERSITY: CONSCIENTIOUS OBJECTION AND CONTESTATION OF CIVIL NORMS (Claude Proeschel, David Koussens & Francesco Piraino eds., 2021).

RELIGIOUS BELIEFS AND CONSCIENTIOUS EXEMPTIONS IN A LIBERAL STATE (John Adenitire ed., 2019).

RELIGIOUS EXEMPTIONS (Kevin Vallier and Michael Weber eds., 2018).

RELIGIOUS FREEDOM AND GAY RIGHTS: EMERGING CONFLICTS IN NORTH AMERICA AND EUROPE (Timothy Shah, Thomas Farr & Jack Friedman eds., 2016).

RENO, RUSSELL R., RESURRECTING THE IDEA OF A CHRISTIAN SOCIETY (2016).

Ripken, Susanna Kim, *Corporations Are People Too: A Multi-Dimensional Approach to the Corporate Personhood Puzzle*, 15 FORDHAM J. CORP. & FIN. L. 1 (2009).

Roy, Olivier, *A Kitsch Christianity: Populists Gather Support while Traditional Religiosity Declines*, LSE RELIGION & GLOBAL SOC'Y BLOG (Oct. 22, 2018).

SADURSKI, WOJCIECH, POLAND'S CONSTITUTIONAL BREAKDOWN (2019).

SAINT AUGUSTINE OF HIPPO, CITY OF GOD (CONCERNING THE CITY OF GOD AGAINST THE PAGANS) (Henry Bettenson trans., 1980).

SALVAT, RAYMUNDO M., TRATADO DE DERECHO CIVIL ARGENTINO: OBLIGACIONES EN GENERAL (1952).

Samar, Vincent J., *The Potential Impact of Hobby Lobby on LGBT Civil Rights*, 16 GEO. J. GENDER & L. 547 (2015).

Savulescu, Julian & Udo Schuklenk, *Doctors Have No Right To Refuse Medical Assistance in Dying, Abortion or Contraception*, 31 BIOETHICS (2017).

Scheinin, Martin, *Freedom of Thought, Conscience and Religion*, 54 STUDIA THEOLOGICA – NORDIC J. THEOLOGY 5 (2000).

Schragger, Richard & Micah Schwartzman, *Religious Antiliberalism and the First Amendment*, 104 MINN. L. REV. 1341 (2019).

Schuklenk, Udo & Ricardo Smalling, *Why Medical Professionals Have No Moral Claim to Conscientious Objection Accommodation in Liberal Democracies*, 43 J. OF MEDICAL ETHICS (2016).

Schuklenk, Udo, *Conscience-Based Refusal of Patient Care in Medicine: A Consequentialist Analysis* 40 THEORETICAL MEDICINE AND BIOETHICS (2019).

Schuklenk, Udo, *Conscientious Objection in Medicine: Accommodation Versus Professionalism and the Public Good*, 126 BRITISH MEDICAL BULLETIN 48 (2018).

Schvey, Aram A., & Claire Kim, *Unconscionable: how the U.S. Supreme Court's jurisprudence lags behind the world when it comes to contraception and conscience*, 20 CONTRACEPT. REPROD. MED. 3 (2018).

Sepinwall, Amy J., *Conscience and Complicity: Assessing Pleas of Religious Exemptions in* Hobby Lobby*'s Wake*, 82 U CHICAGO L. REVIEW 1897–1980 (2015).

Sepper, Elizabeth, *Gays in the Moralized Marketplace*, 7 ALA. C.R. & C.L. L. REV. 129, 129–31 (2015).

Sepper, Elizabeth, *Taking Conscience Seriously*, 98 VA. L. REV. 1501, 1501–75 (2012).

Severino, Roger, *Or for poorer? How same-sex marriage threatens religious liberty*, 30 HARVARD J. OF L. & PUBLIC POL'Y 975 (2007).

SEXO, DELITOS Y PECADOS. INTERSECCIONES ENTRE RELIGIÓN, GÉNERO, SEXUALIDAD Y EL DERECHO EN AMÉRICA LATINA (Macarena Sáez & José Manuel Morán Faúndes eds., 2016).

SHACHAR, AYELET, MULTICULTURAL JURISDICTIONS: CULTURAL DIFFERENCES AND WOMEN'S RIGHTS (2001).

Shahvisi, Arianne, *Conscientious objection: A morally insupportable misuse of authority*, 13 CLINICAL ETHICS 2 (2018).

Shanawani, Hasan, *The Challenges of Conscientious Objection in Health Care*, 55 J RELIG. HEALTH (2016).

Sherwin, Susan, No Longer Patient: Feminist Ethics & Health Care (1992).

Skinner, Quentin, Liberty Before Liberalism (1998).

Smet, Stijn, Resolving Conflicts between Human Rights. The judge's dilemma (2017).

Smith, Stephen W., *Individualised claims of conscience, clinical judgement and best interests,* 26 Health Care Anal. 1 (2018).

Smith, Steven D., Pagans and Christians in the City: Culture Wars from the Tiber to the Potomac (2018).

Smith, William, *Democracy, Deliberation and Disobedience,* 10 Res Publica 353 (2004).

Sonfield, Adam, *Trump Administration Rules Prioritize Refusal of Care and Conservative Ideology Over Protecting Patients Against Discrimination,* 22 Guttmacher Pol'y Rev. 49 (2019).

Sophocles, Antigone (Elizabet Wyckoff trans., 1954).

Spector, Horacio, *Constitutional Tranplants and the Mutation Effect,* 83 Chicago-Kent L. Rev. (2017).

Spector, Horacio, *La filosofía de los derechos humanos,* 15 Isonomia (2001).

Speeches and trials of the militant suffragettes: The Women's Social and Political Union, 1903–1918 (Cheryl R. Jorgensen-Earp, ed., 1999).

Stępkowki, Aleksander, Contemporary Challenges to Conscience: Legal and Ethical Frameworks for Professional Conduct (2019).

Stiglitz, Joseph E., Globalization and Its Discontents (2002).

Strasser, Mark, *On Same-Sex Marriage and Matters of Conscience.* 17 Wm. & Mary J. Women & L. 1 (2010).

Swartz, Martha S., *"Conscience Clauses" or "Unconscionable Clauses": Personal Beliefs Versus Professional Responsibilities,* 6 Yale J. of Health Pol'y, L., and Ethics 269 (2006).

Swartz, Martha S., *"Conscience Clauses" or "Unconscionable Clauses": Personal Beliefs Versus Professional Responsibilities,* 6 Yale J. of Health Pol'y, L., and Ethics 269 (2006).

Taylor, Charles, Multiculturalism and the Politics of Recognition (1992).

Teles, Steven M., The Rise of the Conservative Legal Movement: The Battle for Control of the Law (2008).

Teubner, Gunther, Constitutional fragments: Societal constitutionalism and globalization (2012).

Tew, Yvonne, *Stealth Theocracy,* 58 Va. J. Int'l L. 31 (2018).

The Conscience Wars: Rethinking the Balance between Religion, Identity, and Equality (Susana Mancini & Michel Rosenfeld eds., 2018).

The European Mainstream and the Populist Radical Right (Pontus Odmalm & Eve Hepburn eds., 2017).

The Good Polity: Normative Analysis of the State (Alan Hamlin & Philip Pettit, eds., 1989).

The Oxford Handbook of Comparative Law (M. Reimann & R. Zimmermann eds., 2006).

The Oxford Handbook of Global lgbt and Sexual Diversity Politics (Michael J. Bosia, Sandra M. McEvoy and Momin Rahman eds., 2020).

The Oxford Handbook of Jurisprudence and Philosophy of Law (Jules Coleman & Scott Shapiro eds., 2002).

The Oxford Handbook of Political Philosophy (David Estlund ed., 2012).

The Resilience of the Latin American Right (J. P. Luna & C. Rovira Kaltwasser eds., 2014).

The Rise Of Corporate Religious Liberty (Z. Robinson, C. Flanders & M. Schwartzman eds., 2015).

The Routledge Companion to the Philosophy of Law (Andrei Marmor, ed., 2012).

The Science of Man in the World Crisis (Ralph Linton ed., 1945).

The Stanford Encyclopedia of Philosophy (Edward N. Zalta ed., 2014).

Tilly, Charles & Sidney Tarrow, Contentious Politics (2015).

Topidi, Kyriaki, *Religious Freedom, National Identity, and the Polish Catholic Church: Converging Visions of Nation and God*, 10 Religions 5 (2019).

Toro-Flores, Rafael, et al., *Opinions of nurses regarding conscientious objection*, 26 Nursing Ethics 4 (2019).

Toward Assimilation and Citizenship: Immigrants in Liberal Nation-States (Christian Joppke & Ewa Morawska eds., 2003).

Tsakyrakis, Stavros, *Proportionality: An Assault on Human Rights?* 7 Int'l J. Con. L. 3 (2009).

Turner, Bryan S., *Cosmopolitan Virtue, Globalization and Patriotism*, 19 Theory, Culture & Soc'y. 45 (2002).

Tushnet, Mark, *Varieties of Populism*, 20 German L.J. 382 (2019).

Undurraga, Verónica & Michelle Sadler, *The Misrepresentation of Conscientious Objection as a New Strategy of Resistance to Abortion Decriminalization*, 27 Sexual & Reproductive Health Matters 17 (2019).

Urbina, Francisco J., A Critique of Proportionality and Balancing (2017).

Van Geest, Fred, *Changing Patterns of Denominational Political Activity in North America: The Case of Homosexuality*, 49 Rev. of Religious Research 199 (2007).

Varol, Ozan O., *Stealth Authoritarianism*, 100 Iowa L. Rev. 1673 (2015).

Vasilopoulou, Sofia, *Continuity and Change in the Study of Euroscepticism: Plus* ça *change?*, 51 J. Common Market Stud. 153 (2013).

Verma, Nisha & Daniel Grossman, *Self-Managed Abortion in the United States*, 12 CURR. OBSTET. GYNECOL. REP. 2 (2023).

Vermeule, Adrian, *Liturgy of liberalism*, FIRST THINGS (Jan. 1, 2017).

Vertovec, Steven, *Toward Post-Multiculturalism? Changing communities, conditions and contexts of diversity*, 61 INT'L SOCIAL SCIENCE J. 83 (2010).

VILAJOSANA, JOSEP, IDENTIFICACIÓN Y JUSTIFICACIÓN DEL DERECHO (2007).

VIRGIL, THE AENEID (Robert Fitzgerald trans., 1983).

VOICING DISSENT: THE ETHICS AND EPISTEMOLOGY OF MAKING DISAGREEMENT PUBLIC (Casey Rebecca Johnson ed., 2018).

VON THUR, ANDREAS, TRATADO DE LAS OBLIGACIONES, TOMO II (1934).

WALDRON, JEREMY, LAW AND DISAGREEMENT (1999).

Weitz, T.A. & S. Berke Fogel, *The denial of abortion care information, referrals, and services undermines quality care for U.S. women*, 20 WOMEN'S HEALTH ISSUES (2010).

West, Robin, *A comment on consent, sex, and rape*, 2 LEGAL THEORY 3 (1996).

West, Robin, *A Tale of Two Rights*, 94 B.U.L. REV. (2014).

West, Robin, *Consent, Legitimation and Dysphoria*, 83 THE MODERN LAW REV. 1 (2020).

WHAT IS FREEDOM? CONVERSATIONS WITH HISTORIANS, PHILOSOPHERS, AND ACTIVISTS (Toby Buckle ed., 2021).

White-Domain, Rachel, *Making Rules and Unmaking Choice: Federal Conscience Clauses, Provider Conscience Regulation, and the War on Reproductive Freedom*, 59 DEPAUL L. REV. 1249 (2010).

WICCLAIR, MARK R., CONSCIENTIOUS OBJECTION IN HEALTH CARE: AN ETHICAL ANALYSIS (2012).

Wicclair, Mark R., *Managing Conscientious Objection in Health Care Institutions*, 26 HEC FORUM (2014).

Wicclair, Mark R., *Preventing Conscientious Objection in Medicine from Running Amok: A Defense of Reasonable Accommodation*, 40 THEORETICAL MED. AND BIOETHICS (2019).

Wicclair, Mark R., *Refusals by hospitals and emergency contraception*, 20 CAMBRIDGE Q. OF HEALTHCARE ETHICS 1 (2011).

Wildes, Kevin W., *Institutional Identity, Integrity, and Conscience*, 7 KENNEDY INST. ETHICS J. 4 (1997).

Wilkinson, Doris, *Rethinking the Concept of "Minority": A Task for Social Scientists and Practitioners*, 27 J. OF SOCIOLOGY AND SOCIAL WELFARE (2000).

Williston, Samuel, History of the Law of Business Corporations Before 1800, 2 HARV. L. REV. 105 (1888).

WOLFF, ROBERT PAUL, IN DEFENSE OF ANARCHISM (1970).

WOLGAST, ELIZABET, ETHICS OF AN ARTIFICIAL PERSON: LOST RESPONSIBILITY IN PROFESSIONS AND ORGANIZATION (1992).

Wuerth, Ingrid, *International Law in the Age of Trump: A Post-Human Rights Agenda*, LAWFARE (Nov. 14, 2016).

Yamin, Alicia E. & Andrés Constantin, *A Long and Winding Road: The Evolution of Applying Human Rights Frameworks to Health*, 49 GEO. J. INT'L L. 191 (2018).

Yamin, Alicia E., *Will we take suffering seriously? Reflections on what applying a human rights framework to health means and why we should care*, 10(1) HEALTH & HUM. RTS., 45–63 (2008).

YOUNG, IRIS MARION, JUSTICE AND THE POLITICS OF DIFFERENCE (1990).

Zaiden Benvindo, Juliano, *Brazil's Increasingly Politicized Supreme Court*, INT'L J. CONST. L. BLOG (Feb. 16, 2017).

Zaręba, Kornelia, et al., *Moral Dilemmas of Women Undergoing Pregnancy Termination for Medical Reasons in Poland*, 22 EUR. J. OF CONTRACEPTION & REPROD. HEALTH CARE 4 (2017).

Index

www.ingramcontent.com/pod-product-compliance
Lightning Source LLC
Chambersburg PA
CBHW051401240926
51852CB00002B/83
9789004685390